S0-AAH-871

IMMIGRANTS IN INDUSTRY

The Institute of Race Relations is an unofficial and non-political body, founded in England in 1958 to encourage and facilitate the study of the relations between races everywhere. The Institute is precluded by the Memorandum and Articles of its incorporation from expressing a corporate view. The opinions expressed in this work are those of the author.

IMMIGRANTS IN INDUSTRY

SHEILA PATTERSON

Published for
the Institute of Race Relations, London
OXFORD UNIVERSITY PRESS
LONDON NEW YORK
1968

Oxford University Press, Ely House, London W.1
GLASGOW NEW YORK TORONTO MELBOURNE WELLINGTON
CAPE TOWN SALISBURY IBADAN NAIROBI LUSAKA ADDIS ABABA
BOMBAY CALCUTTA MADRAS KARACHI LAHORE DACCA
KUALA LUMPUR HONG KONG TOKYO

Printed in Great Britain by
Richard Clay (The Chaucer Press) Ltd, Bungay, Suffolk

CONTENTS

LIST OF MAPS AND CHARTS

MAPS

CHARTS

LIST OF TABLES

ACKNOWLEDGEMENTS

Now it remains only to express my appreciation and gratitude to all those who made this study possible and who contributed their information and counsel so generously. My thanks are due first to the Director of the Institute, Mr. Philip Mason, for commissioning the study, and being so patient over delays, and to the Nuffield Foundation for the grant which made it possible to carry out the project—and thereafter to various members of the staff of the Institute who helped to produce the final study. I also owe a debt of gratitude to Mr. Harold Pollins, who read the whole and proposed some major surgery, to Professor Maurice Freedman for valuable comments and criticism at an earlier stage, to Dr. Peter Wilson for lending me some notes of earlier interviews with local firms, and to Professor Ferdynand Zweig, Mr. Dennis Brooks, and Dr. Peter Wright for enlightening contributions on particular aspects of industrial absorption.

It would be impossible to name here all the firms, organizations, and individuals connected with Croydon industry and society who over the years have given so much of their time to this inquiry. They include the many management informants who agreed to be interviewed, and particularly the personnel managers and officers and other members of the three Croydon firms, called here Telelux, Chocolac, and Polplastics, which gave me facilities to carry out the more detailed studies reported in Part IV. Particular acknowledgements are also due to: the staff and successive managers of the Croydon Employment Exchange, the Town Clerk, Chief Librarian, and all the departments of the Croydon Borough Council, particularly the Education Department; the Youth Employment Officer; the editors of the *Croydon Advertiser* and the *Croydon Times*.

My sincere thanks also go to the following individuals who were especially helpful at different stages of this inquiry: the late Mr. F. A. Moxley, secretary of the Croydon Chamber of Commerce; Mr. Charles Hodge, J.P., Croydon branch of the National Union of General and Municipal Workers; Dr. Terence Morris (mainly in his capacity as a Croydonian); Mr. Bruce Reid; Mr. E. F. Neccles; Father W. Gajewski, Mr. S. Bien, and other leaders of the Polish community in Croydon; Father J. McKenna of the Parish of Our Lady of the Assumption, Addiscombe; the Rev. David Curwen, now Industrial Chaplain in Croydon; Mr. Terence Driscoll of the International Language Club; Councillor J. G. Southgate; Mrs. D. M. S. Morton and Mrs. W. O. Austin of the Croydon Guild of Social Service; and to many more citizens, residents, and workers in the Croydon area who helped to make the time spent there pleasant as well as profitable for this inquiry.

PREFACE

The major field-work for this study was begun in 1958 and finished some two years later. Final publication was delayed by several factors, notably the decision to undertake a major re-organization of the material. There was an obvious temptation to use hindsight and inject current thinking on immigration and race relations into the text but this was resisted, and the rather different climate of those years has been preserved. (For instance, controls were rarely discussed, anti-discrimination legislation never.) Developments and changes in social fact and social climate have nevertheless occurred both at national level and in Croydon itself in the interval, and they have obviously had an effect at shop-floor level, though perhaps less than is generally assumed. It may thus be useful to recall briefly here the most important of these changes in national and civic life and in immigrant–host relations and attitudes.

Late summer 1958 brought the shock of the Notting Hill disturbances, which left a widespread sense of disquiet. At this time some voluntary associations were beginning to tackle certain aspects of integration, and there was a small but growing anti-immigration lobby in Parliament. Nevertheless, the issue of immigration was politically peripheral and the climate of opinion remained basically *laissez-faire*, voluntaristic, and non-discriminatory (not only in the sense of rejecting immigration controls or planning but in such matters as refusing to make special provisions for newcomers and refusing to keep separate statistics). This formal allegiance to non-discrimination was maintained not only by the British, at all levels, but was also insisted upon by the West Indians, who were the Commonwealth peoples most involved. With the exception of the Barbadian Government, any talk of planned migration, selection, phasing, reception, or dispersal was rejected as contrary to the somewhat euphoric conceptions of an egalitarian, multi-racial Commonwealth and of a common Commonwealth citizenship which, during this transition period between an imperial past and an uncertain future, were shared by many opinion-formers on the Right as well as the Left.

A major reason for the continued existence of this climate of opinion through the 1950s was that the size of the problem, particularly as viewed from the metropolis, was not large enough to warrant official action at a time when it might have been less drastic in content and less odious in manner. At the end of 1958 there were, according to a Home Office estimate, about 210,000 coloured Commonwealth residents of the U.K., of whom 115,000 were West Indians (total population of the British Caribbean about three-and-a-half million), and only 55,000 from India and Pakistan (total population about 550 million). In 1959 another 16,400 West Indians entered and in 1960 this jumped to nearly 50,000. Meanwhile, there was increasing concern over the possibility of rising entry figures from India and Pakistan, whose Governments had until 1959 effectively maintained voluntary controls. By 1961, however, the net inward movement was rising steeply (66,300 West Indians, 23,750 Indians, 25,100 Pakistanis). Whether or not this rise was stimulated by fears of controls or was one of the factors that led to their introduction, *laissez-faire* attitudes began to give way to the increasingly restrictive and negative climate of opinion that has since characterized British reactions to Commonwealth immigration.

Immigration controls were announced in September 1961 and came into force in mid-1962, after a further beat-the-ban net increase in the first six months of 75,930 (including over 44,000 Indians and Pakistanis). Thereafter arrivals dropped, but soon picked up to reach over 41,000 in 1963 and 1964 and more thereafter (mostly dependants of the beat-the-ban immigrants). At the present time, therefore, less than a decade after this study was carried out, the overall number of coloured Commonwealth immigrants, including their British-born children, has trebled or quadrupled, and its national and socio-cultural make-up has been radically diversified by the large post-1960 inflow of Asians.

Over the same period, there has also been increasing disillusionment within the Commonwealth; an intensified preoccupation with the problems, as opposed to the possibilities, of multi-racial societies everywhere, focused increasingly on the deteriorating American situation; a growing self-consciousness among immigrants and hosts alike about colour and race, and a growing tendency to view situations everywhere on terms of simple black–white confrontations (trends stimulated or supported by sensationalism in the mass media and increasingly virulent activity at both extremes). The concentration of immigrants in decaying areas of large industrial cities has exacerbated existing shortages and problems, in such fields as housing, education, and welfare, thereby gravely impeding the work of positive integration. At national level, support for positive policies of integration has been meagre, tardy, and half-hearted. Anti-discrimination measures, which are preventive rather than positive, have been introduced, but only after years of opposition, as a counterbalance to increasingly rigid controls. For the time being, the general climate of opinion is over-charged, negative, legalistic, and 'discriminatory' in a number of senses, including the underlying assumption that the problems of coloured people everywhere are not only identical but unique.

In areas of economic expansion and self-limiting secondary immigrant settlement such as Croydon, a *laissez-faire*, tolerant climate of opinion was particularly strong in the late 1950s and early 1960s. Fortunately, recent inquiries suggest that the swing towards the opposite pole of negative restrictiveness has not been so strong as at the national level. It is hoped that the field-material in this study may suggest some reasons for this development.

In the years since the field-work for this study was carried out, there have in fact been far greater changes in Croydon itself than could have been predicted at the time. Apart from the formal incorporation into Greater London in 1965 of an enlarged Croydon (including the neighbouring urban district of Coulsdon and Purley, to give a total population of some 330,000 in 1967), the most striking changes are the visible ones. The bold, large-scale transformation of the town centre, whose beginnings are noted on page 12, has now made parts of the town virtually unrecognizable to its older residents, and has created a gleaming, multi-storeyed urban skyline visible for miles around.

The outward changes do however reflect profound changes in the borough's economy, employment patterns, and general socio-economic orientations. The industrial expansion of the inter-war years and the 1950s has been overtaken by extensive commercial development over the last decade. During this period Croydon has become the fifth largest commercial centre in Britain,[1] while the twin pillar of the borough's economic redevelopment, office blocks,

[1] In February 1968, Croydon was named as one of London's 'sector centres' in the first approved draft of the written statement on the Greater London Development Plan.

has also gone ahead. Between 1958 and 1967, nearly five million square feet of extra office and shop accommodation have come into use, with another three million under construction or approved, and an increasing number of residents have been able to find professional, managerial, and white-collar work locally instead of having to commute into London.[1]

On the other hand, the industrial climate is no longer so expansionist as it was some years ago. A tendency has developed for firms to move out because space was lacking for expansion. The reduction of Government defence contracts has adversely affected several firms manufacturing sophisticated instruments. Since September 1967 two or three firms have closed their Croydon factories, either because they could not get a Government Development Grant and have therefore moved the work elsewhere, or because rationalization has led them to concentrate the work in another part of their Group. Moreover, several of the successful small firms have been swallowed up or are threatened by mergers and takeovers. The Chamber of Commerce has expressed disquiet about this move towards 'administration' and the drop in the town's 'export potential', and there were notes of gloom over unemployment[2] and future prospects from the Trades and Labour Council in March 1968. The *Croydon Advertiser* wrote on 5 April:

> It cannot be emphasised too strongly that Croydon cannot afford to lose these firms or their staffs, for if the process continues we shall be brought to a dangerous state of imbalance. The commercial centre cannot continue to flourish as it should if a sizeable part of its custom is removed. And, as we have indicated, the prosperity of the whole town is bound up with it. Can we not now divert some of the drive that has created the new Croydon to consolidating its industrial foundation?

A comparison between the industrial situation in 1962 and 1967 showed an overall increase in the numbers employed of 21,160 (38 per cent) to a record total of 146,000. More specifically, major increases occurred in construction, and brick and cast concrete products. (The large increases in gas and electricity, and food

[1] See Appendix 2 for changing employment patterns between 1955 and 1965. See also an analysis of employment patterns in 1962 and 1967 made by Croydon's Youth Employment Sub-Committee (dated 30 January 1968).

[2] In February and March it reached about 2,400, the third highest total in over twenty years (previous 'highs' were 2,870 in February 1963, and 2,491 in March 1947).

manufacture, were mainly attributable to the fact that the South Eastern Gas Board and Nestlé's had moved their head offices into the borough.) There were sizeable increases in all the distributive services (except retail employment), insurance, banking and finance, and educational and other professional services. Overall numbers fell in engineering, but there was a large increase in the radio and electronics industry and smaller ones in metal goods and the paper industry.

How have these very radical changes and reorientations affected the newcomers, particularly the West Indian and other coloured immigrants, about whose long-term prospects of outward and upward dispersal in industry it was possible to be reasonably optimistic some years ago? To answer that question adequately another survey would be required, although some evidence is available from more recent inquiries. First, however, one should outline briefly the changes that have taken place in the immigrant settlements, and in host–immigrant relations within the town. For at the time of this study many more coloured Commonwealth immigrants worked in Croydon than lived there.

This is certainly no longer true. Croydon has become an area of mainly second-stage settlement for West Indians who have moved south from Brixton and elsewhere in South London. There are no certain statistics, but estimates of up to 15,000 coloured immigrant residents were being given in March 1968. The West Indians are still the major group, but in the 1960s there has been a growing influx of Indians[1] (including Asians from Kenya) and, more recently, of Pakistanis. A rough indication of numbers and distribution of immigrant families is provided by successive annual counts of immigrant children in Croydon schools taken by the County Borough and then the G.L.C. In 1964 there were 1,381 immigrant children in the schools, including 502 West Indians, 380 Indians, and fifty-two Pakistanis. In 1965 the total was up to

[1] Other indications of the arrival of Asians came from the borough health visitors' department, which in early 1968 arranged, in conjunction with the Croydon International Association, to run a special evening clinic to give courses in infant welfare and the English language for Asian mothers and advertised this by means of leaflets in four Asian languages.

The 1966 Sample Census showed that Croydon had an overall immigrant population of 20,160, of whom 13,070 were Commonwealth-born. Of this latter total 4,290 were born in the West Indies, 4,210 in India, and 730 in Pakistan. There was no indication how many in the latter groups were U.K. citizens, either British or Anglo-Indian.

2,099, including 887 West Indians, 444 Indians, and eighty-five Pakistanis. By 1967 the total had jumped to 2,748 (1,380 West Indians, 597 Indians, and 140 Pakistanis), and the figures for January 1968 showed a total of 3,625 immigrant children, or 8·6 per cent of all children in Croydon schools. Of these 1,817 were West Indians, 718 Indians, 215 Pakistanis, and there were 252 Africans. It is not clear how many of the 'Indians' were in fact Anglo-Indians and how many from Kenya. The other immigrant groups studied were represented by far fewer children: there were sixty-five Polish pupils in 1966 and thirty-one in 1968; and in 1968 seventy-four out of the 124 European children were Italian (Irish were not counted). The problem of children in need of special language tuition had arisen only since about 1965 when extra teachers were requested. An initial reception centre to receive newly-arrived immigrant children for their first half-term was being planned in 1968.

The settlement patterns of the coloured Commonwealth immigrants have apparently not changed greatly from those given on the map on p. 393. This shows what a local observer recently described as a horseshoe formation running north and east from Thornton Heath Station to South Norwood Station, and east and south again to East Croydon Station. There are also some indications of a southward movement, mainly into working-class areas. Clearly the settlements have become considerably more concentrated, but the 1968 school count showed that only five primary schools and two secondary schools had between 30 and 35 per cent of 'immigrant' children.

Relationships between newcomers and Croydonians do not seem to have changed very radically in the years since this study was made. The local press has continued to give a tolerant and objective coverage to issues of immigration and race. The left-wing Labour M.P. for Croydon South, Mr. David Winnick, has been one of the main supporters of anti-discrimination legislation and voted against the Labour Government's additional controls in early 1968 (on the other hand, the prospective Conservative candidate and former M.P., Sir Richard Thompson, has said that immigration should be suspended for seven years and all overseas aid ended). The Conservative M.P. for Croydon N.W., Mr. Fred Harris, who has interests in Kenya, voiced objections to the Government's lack of foresight and disregard of undertakings to holders of British passports and abstained from voting for the Bill. Mr. Bernard Weatherill, Conservative M.P. for Croydon N.E., voted for the measure, on the grounds that the inflow of Asians must be regulated so as to ease the sort of housing and school problems that had already been caused by immigrants congregating in parts of Croydon.

Despite the activities of the anti-immigrant National Front in such areas as Thornton Heath, no major tensions or conflicts were reported. One Thornton Heath youth club, indeed, was reported to be functioning successfully as a multi-racial club for 15 and 16-year-olds. A voluntary liaison committee, the International Association of Croydon, was increasingly active in the work of integration, although it had not yet succeeded in persuading the Council to provide office accommodation and help for a paid immigrant liaison officer. Its chairman, Councillor B. C. Sparrowe, became Mayor of Croydon in May 1968, which seemed a good augury for community relations.

The changes in the 'coloured' immigrant settlement just outlined were perhaps more in line with what might have been predicted in the early 1960s, except for the considerable increases in the Asian population. The radical socio-economic and other changes in Croydon itself have, however, obviously introduced important new factors into the continuing processes of industrial and overall absorption of first- and second-generation immigrants, of whom there are now an increasing number.

The shift away from engineering and industry generally towards commerce and specialized services means a shift away from the sectors and occupations in which most immigrants were equipped to work and were in fact working into the 'white-collar and professional' sector in which, with the exception of the hospitals, few immigrants were found. It was also the sector which, apart from the hospital service, many immigrants were likely to find most difficult to enter, because of such factors as their own lack of qualifications, the status-consciousness and insecurity characteristic of many clerical and retail workers, and widespread notions about public resistance to being served by dark-skinned immigrants.

My survey showed small-scale beginnings of accommodation in retail and clerical work, at a time when there were very few qualified applicants. Now there are many more clerical and higher jobs available,[1] there may be more qualified applicants among first-generation immigrants, and there are also an increasing number of coloured school leavers, some of whom must have been right through the school system and be as well- or ill-qualified as their fellow school leavers for such work. An unexplored factor here is the range of attitudes of management and supervisors in the many 'new' firms that have come to Croydon from many parts of London and provide most of the new opportunities.

Some detailed evidence from twelve Croydon private employment agencies in late 1966[2] suggests that, while first-generation immigrants were more frequently applying for white-collar jobs (even then few school leavers were applying), it was still extremely hard to place them (one agency suggested that it was more difficult than in the early 1960s). According to the largest agency, only three out of 1,000 firms on the books would take coloured applicants; two agencies with the largest proportion of coloured job-seekers estimated that 3 and 10 per cent respectively of firms on their books would accept them. Two agencies knew of no Croydon firms which would accept coloured applicants, but could place them in a number of firms in London. The 1966 credit squeeze and the introduction of S.E.T. had caused a drop in vacancies and therefore made placing more difficult. Low quotas were also accepted as normal policy. In publicly controlled organizations, however (e.g. local government, the civil service, the post office), the prospects for coloured school leavers seemed to be much more even, given adequate qualifications.

In industry, according to several local informants, employers are willing to consider immigrants for the rather small number of apprenticeships, though not necessarily to the same extent as other applicants. Altogether, industry is easier to enter, and one may speculate whether the shift in job opportunities which has put industry in third place behind offices and shops for young workers may still further improve the chances of immigrants in the considerable range of industries that remain in Croydon. A point here is that the number of immigrants on course at the local Government Training Centre is said to be relatively high.

In early April 1968, an informant wrote, commenting on this study:

[1] In 1967 nearly two-thirds of girl school-leavers in Croydon went into offices compared with one-third ten years before.

[2] Gaitskell, J., *Employment in Croydon*, Institute of Race Relations, Special Series, forthcoming, 1968.

There is in Croydon a mood of uncertainty about what the future holds (but) . . . no serious unemployment, and there is work available. . . . There have been no massive redundancies, though some firms have had to lay off some workers this winter. . . . (In one with) a high percentage of immigrant workers, I recently asked . . . whether they were experiencing any interracial tension or friction because of the laying-off. He reckoned that there had been none, though I understand that the laying-off had been achieved more by cutting out overtime than by deliberate selection.

I would think that the major 'pull' factor of chronic labour shortage is not as great as it was. My superficial impression is that the process of absorption has been uneven. It would seem to have continued in the hospital service fairly rapidly, though very little in the stores.

. . . I don't think there have been any developments towards pluralistic integration—i.e. ethnic work-gangs.[1] Generally speaking, the relationship between races remains good. I was impressed recently by the way one work-group accepted a Kenyan Asian, even though his punctuality and performance were poor. This was caused largely by the choice of his family circumstances at the time.

Despite all the changes, Croydon is still recognizably the same borough—with a continuity buttressed by approximately the same core-society, traditions, habits, and ethos, together with an increasingly settled immigrant community. The processes of absorption have continued, albeit unevenly and with certain checks or setbacks: socio-economic and cultural factors have assumed an ever greater importance in the wider society as well as in industry. Most studies of immigrants made in recent years have tended to be policy-oriented and to focus rather on the checks and failures than on the unobtrusive and long-term movement towards absorption, as I have tried to do here. This process may be too slow in particular national and international circumstances, but the fact that it is taking place in many areas like Croydon should not be overlooked by the policy-makers. For, whereas national and other initiatives to promote fair employment policies and opportunities and to prevent discrimination in such vital fields as employment now seem clearly indicated, they have far better prospects of success if they are geared to the complex absorptive processes that have long been at work in the British industrial scene, and to the expertise acquired by the firms and industrial agencies that have successfully pioneered in this field.

[1] This would suggest that many of the incoming Indians and Pakistanis may be either second-stage migrants (see p. 36, p. 173 n., and p. 184), Kenyan Asians or Anglo-Indians.

PART I

THE BACKGROUND

CHAPTER I

INTRODUCTION

(1) *Aims of the Study*

In the years 1956–8, during the course of an earlier study of immigrants in Britain, I visited some thirty industrial establishments in South London to inquire into the absorption of West Indians into industry.[1] As this inquiry proceeded, it became increasingly clear to me that such a study could not be carried out, particularly in the work situation, in terms of a simple white–coloured analysis. For, in addition to the West Indian workers, I found many other newcomers from the Commonwealth and from Europe who, though differing from each other and from their hosts in many ways—for instance, in economic qualifications, in social and cultural background, in motivation and intentions, as well as in ethnic or racial traits—all seemed to be experiencing, or to have experienced, similar processes and problems during their absorption into British industry.

In this earlier inquiry I was also struck by the similarity between the generally unfavourable views expressed, particularly by British workers and organized labour, about West Indians in 1955–8, and the reactions to Italians at the same period,[2] and to Poles and European Voluntary Workers (E.V.W.s) a decade earlier.[3] Indeed, similar views were recorded about earlier coloured migrants,[4] and about the 120,000 or more Jewish immigrants from East Europe

[1] *Dark Strangers*, London, Tavistock Publications, 1963, Chapters 5 and 6 *passim*.

[2] See J. Chadwick-Jones on Welsh workers' attitudes to Italian immigrants in a research note on 'Inter-Group Attitudes: A Stage in Attitude Formation', *British Journal of Sociology*, Vol. XIII, No. 1, March 1962.

[3] J. Zubrzycki, *Polish Immigrants in Britain*, The Hague, Martinus Nijhoff, 1956, pp. 81–88.

[4] K. L. Little, *Negroes in Britain*, London, Kegan Paul, Chapters 7–9, and A. H. Richmond, *Colour Prejudice in Britain*, London, Routledge and Kegan Paul, 1954, pp. 20, 59, 97.

who arrived in Britain between 1870 and 1914.[1] Of these, Ben Tillet, himself the son of Irish immigrant parents, wrote:

> The influx of continental pauperism aggravates and multiplies the number of ills which press so heavily upon us. . . . Foreigners come to London in large numbers, herd together in habitations unfit for beasts, the sweating system allowing the more grasping and shrewd a life of comparative ease in superintending the work.[2]

Earlier in the nineteenth century[3] it was the turn of Tillet's forebears, the Irish migrants, whose numbers, mobility (they were not tied by parish relief), low living standards, and alleged undercutting of local wages caused bitterness and rioting in the 1830s and 1840s. In the words of a Chartist:

> But work grew scarce, while bread grew dear,
> And wages lessened too;
> For Irish hordes were bidders here,
> Our half-paid work to do.[4]

These examples, which could easily be multiplied many times, illustrate the familiar point that there is, in Britain, something which might conveniently be called a 'stranger-bar' or barrier, industrial and otherwise. Even if the stranger comes not from overseas but from another part of Britain there is plenty of evidence of such barriers and antipathies. But it is the barriers that are set up against newcomers from overseas that attract more attention.

Whatever the reasons for these barriers—and their strength has undoubtedly fluctuated according to numerous and varied circumstances—we can be certain of one thing: they exist and they can exert a powerful influence in the work situation and social life generally.

The recent large-scale immigration of 'coloured' Commonwealth citizens has attracted the most research and public atten-

[1] See L. P. Gartner, *The Jewish Immigrant in England*, 1870–1914, London, Allen and Unwin, 1960, p. 161; and M. Freedman (ed.), *A Minority in Britain*, London, Vallentine Mitchell, 1955.

[2] B. Tillet, *The Dock Labourer's Bitter Cry*, London, 1898, p. 8, cited by J. A. Jackson, *The Irish in Britain*, London, Routledge and Kegan Paul, 1963, p. 179, note 21.

[3] There are also recorded complaints about Poles and Lithuanians being brought into the Lanarkshire mines as strike-breakers in 1894, and Poles, Hungarians, and Germans undercutting and strike-breaking in the Cheshire salt-mines and refineries at about the same period (Zubrzycki, op. cit., pp. 40–42).

[4] J. L. and B. Hammond, *The Age of the Chartists*, 1832–54, London, 1930, p. 25.

tion of all. It has become common to talk of a 'colour bar' in Britain, but there are many difficulties in the use of this term. It recalls but cannot be identified with the institutionalized colour bars in South Africa or parts of the Deep South. Indeed, we may fairly ask whether the so-called colour bar in Britain is in fact different in kind from the barriers erected against other strangers; or whether an immigrant's dark pigmentation, with its immediate notification of strangeness, its colonial associations with low status and simple culture, and the self-consciousness that it engenders in many who possess it,[1] is merely one of the factors that influence the processes of absorption in the British receiving society.

The history of earlier immigrations and my own fieldwork investigations of two post-war immigrant groups in Britain ('coloured' West Indians and 'white' Poles) inclined me very strongly to answer the first question in the negative and the second in the affirmative. Fortunately the opportunity soon came to take the inquiry farther, in an industrial area in which a number of different immigrant groups were employed. This area was Croydon, then a county borough on the southern outskirts of London.

The main purpose of this inquiry was to find out in what industries and what kinds of work the newcomers were to be found; what were their aptitudes, qualifications, and aspirations; what sort of relationships they were establishing with local employers and workers; how far the processes of absorption had gone for various groups; and what were the major factors which had influenced these processes.

It may be asked why this inquiry was restricted to an industrial situation and a working society. First and foremost, it is because in a complex urban industrialized society the work situation is the most important universal area of social interaction. It is the area in which the vast majority of newcomers have to make their first major effort to adapt to and win acceptance from the receiving society. This is particularly true of economically motivated immigrants, whose initial 'rank order of endeavour' would put well-paid jobs ahead of good housing and still more of participation in public and private social life. The work situation is also a highly institutionalized area of enforced proximity, interaction, and sometimes of competition, in which the processes of absorption can be

[1] For a more detailed discussion of these associations, see *Dark Strangers*, pp. 6–9, 23–24 *et al.*

seen at their most rapid,[1] but in which they can also meet with the sharpest set-backs in the event of an economic recession.

In the modern urban setting, moreover, the work situation, the system of industrial statuses and roles, is increasingly distinct, in both a geographical and a psychological sense, from the life of the wider society. It is true that the individual's job status tends to determine or influence his social status in the outside world while the values, norms, and experiences of the wider world naturally exert strong indirect influences on life and relationships within the factory. But in large cities social life seems to fall into more or less self-contained compartments or situations: for instance, a man who lives at a distance from his job rarely carries his contacts with fellow-workers over into his home life, or vice versa. What is more, he usually lives part of his life in several other compartments: he has his public-house circle, his racing cronies, his sports club associates, and so on, who are rarely or never invited to his home. This atomization of roles and relationships seems very characteristic of British urban life, in contrast to the situation described in smaller, more integrated communities such as 'Yankee City'.[2]

All these considerations make the work situation and the industrial community a relatively compact and self-contained field for study. There is also the practical aspect—relationships at work occur within certain temporal and geographical limits. Thus they can be studied more thoroughly and effectively over a given period than can relationships in other areas of association in a modern urban society.

(2) *The Processes and Phases of Absorption*

The terms which I shall be using in this study to denote the various phases of the processes of immigrant–host adaptation and

[1] This point was made by various speakers at the UNESCO Conference in Havana, 1956. For instance, J. Spengler wrote in his report of this conference: 'Economic absorption can proceed more rapidly than cultural integration because fewer changes in roles and institutions are involved in the former than in the latter. Cultural integration therefore takes longer than does economic integration and, being slower, limits in greater measure than does economic absorption the number of immigrants who can be accommodated per year.' W. D. Borrie, *The Cultural Integration of Immigrants*, UNESCO (Population and Culture series), 1959, Chapter V, pp. 101–2, 114.

[2] Cf. Geoffrey Gorer, *Exploring English Character*, London, Cresset Press, 1955, and W. L. Warner, and J. O. Low, *The Social System of the Modern Factory*, Yale University Press, 1947, p. 35, note 4, and Michael Banton, *White and Coloured*, London, Jonathan Cape, 1959, pp. 104 f.

acceptance or absorption have been defined at greater length in an earlier study.[1] At this point, however, it may be useful to go over them briefly, with particular reference to the industrial situation.

There is still no general agreement on the definition of the term *assimilation*.[2] Here it is used to denote complete adaptation by the incoming individual or group and complete acceptance by the receiving society. The process is a reciprocal one, in that the receiving society may move some way towards the newcomers, but the main effort of adaptation falls on the latter, particularly in such a relatively homogeneous and stable society as Britain.

Assimilation can apply both to individuals and to groups. There is, however, a phase that either falls short of complete assimilation or, in plural societies, can itself be the final phase and end-product. This is *pluralistic integration*,[3] a term that applies only to groups. In the phase of pluralistic integration the immigrant or minority group adapts itself to permanent membership of the receiving society and is accepted by the latter in such universal areas of association as economic and civic life; meanwhile it retains different patterns in some other spheres, such as family, religious, and cultural life, provided that these patterns do not conflict with the basic values and norms of the receiving society. British Jewry has long been an instance of an integrating group. Such a group may even retain a second language and secondary loyalties to a country of origin, as do many ethnic minorities in the United States. The fact that a minority group is, through its internal associations, moving towards integration does not, of course, prevent individual members from aiming at assimilation in the majority society.

In the early years of industrial absorption, however, we are less concerned with assimilation or even pluralistic integration than

[1] See *Dark Strangers*, Chapter 1. I have adopted Eisenstadt's term 'absorption' to cover the whole range of the reciprocal processes of 'adaptation and acceptance'. Both the general term and those indicating different phases denote both the processes leading to an end-product and the end-product itself.

[2] See discussions in *The Cultural Assimilation of Immigrants*, International Union for the Scientific Study of Population, Cambridge, Cambridge University Press, 1950, pp. 3, 115.

[3] For a discussion of this phase, see B. Berry, *Race and Ethnic Relations*, Boston, Houghton Mifflin, 1958, pp. 337 f., and Borrie, op. cit., pp. 93–98. Where the unqualified term 'integration' is used later in this study it refers to this phase, and is not used to cover everything from 'adjustment' to 'absorption', as is the current popular usage in Britain.

with what may be called *accommodation*. This means the attainment of a minimum *modus vivendi* between the newcomers and the receiving society. The immigrants establish themselves tolerably in the spheres of work and housing and begin to conform, at least outwardly, to the new society's behaviour patterns. For its part the receiving society accords the newcomers a limited acceptance, particularly in such universal and institutionalized spheres as employment, the public services, education, and civic rights. Considerable social distance remains, however, in less formal and more intimate relationships.

The indices of increasing accommodation in the industrial sphere are modest, and the degree of adaptation and acceptance limited on both sides.[1] We may look for the newcomers to settle in one job; to perform it to the reasonable satisfaction of fellow-workers and employers; to conform to local behaviour patterns on the job and in the canteen (for instance, eating and hygienic habits, comportment, relations between the sexes, knowledge and choice of language); to join the union where this is customary; not automatically to attribute set-backs and reprimands to the operation of a 'colour bar'. From fellow-workers and organized labour we may look for acceptance of the newcomers as fellow-workers and fellow-unionists, if not yet as supervisors. The most influential interest-group in this process, management, may be expected to begin regarding the newcomers as part of the permanent local labour force; not to discriminate against them as a group in the event of redundancy; to evolve certain techniques for training them or handling their specific difficulties or problems; and finally to begin advancing them to more responsible jobs. There will also be an increasing tendency for both employers and organized labour to disregard discriminatory agreements and quotas (whether formal or informal) or to interpret them more liberally.

After some years, migrant–host accommodation may begin to pass over into the further phases of pluralistic integration or assimilation, as both the host society and the newcomers gradually accept the fact that the latter are here to stay. It should not, however, be imagined that these phases follow each other in a tidy and regular sequence or without tensions and conflicts. Nor are they reached simultaneously in all areas of association; as we shall see, more or

[1] For a detailed presentation of the indices of industrial absorption, see Table 3, p. 206.

less complete assimilation or acceptance can be attained by immigrant individuals or groups in the working community long before such a phase is reached in the wider society. An example of this would be the Polish charge-hand or shop-steward who speaks fluent English, has an anglicized nickname and is very much 'one of us' at the works; on the other hand, this same man goes home to eat a Polish meal cooked by his Polish wife, sends his children to the nearest Polish 'Saturday school', attends a Polish Mass, and is an active member of a Polish Ex-Combatants' Association.

(3) *Preliminary Note on the Choice of Area and the Procedure*

Croydon was chosen for this study firstly because it is one of the expanding industrial areas which have attracted most immigrant workers, and secondly because the immigrant working population contains members of several ethnic groups, notably the Southern Irish, the Poles, and the West Indians, which were known to differ in certain important characteristics likely to exert a profound influence on their absorption in industry.

Apart from visible biological differences, these included social class and occupational background; such cultural traits as language; national status (British or alien); motivations for coming to Britain (ideological or economic); and length of settlement (the Irish have been coming to work in Britain for over a century, while the Poles entered British industry some five to ten years before the West Indians).

Another reason for the choice of this area was that Croydon contained several large, modern firms whose managements expressed interest and willingness to co-operate in the inquiry. Finally, the fact that the town prided itself on a 'cosmopolitan' and tolerant approach seemed to augur well for the inquiry's prospects.

The period allotted for the study was eighteen months, (although this proved over-optimistic, the fieldwork alone taking rather more than that) and the inquiry was planned in two stages. First an overall survey was made of the situation in every sector of local industry; this was followed up by more detailed and intensive investigation of migrant–host relationships in three contrasting establishments where the situation seemed to be of particular interest. A more detailed account of the procedures adopted is given at the beginning of Part II. It may, however, be said here that the main field-work technique used was the interview (augmented by some participant observation), and that because of the limited time available most interviews in the first stage were conducted with high-level representatives of management, so that the material collected had to be evaluated with an eye to possible bias, distortion, and omissions.[1]

Statistics relating to migrant workers were rarely available and so could not be used as a check.[2] A wider range of viewpoints was, however, assembled before the industrial investigation proper began, in interviews with local government officers, officials of the employment exchange and National Assistance Board, the editors of the two local weeklies, some prominent local politicians, trade-union leaders, ministers of religion, welfare workers, and other civic personalities. These contacts proved useful not only for the general information that they afforded but also because the same individuals were encountered in a variety of civic and industrial roles and a number of industrial doors were opened as a result of these initial meetings.

[1] See pp. 41–7, for further discussion of the possible drawbacks of this procedure.

[2] In most countries of immigration considerable statistical material is available on immigrants and ethnic groups, whether from official or private sources. In Britain the official material on Commonwealth and Irish immigrants is very sparse; in Croydon itself the various official agencies concerned had no means of keeping complete records of immigrant placings, unemployment rates, etc.; nor did most of the firms surveyed keep separate figures about migrant labour turnover, productivity, and such matters. The paucity of private statistical material may in itself be of some interest, as an indication of the assimilationist ethos found in much of Croydon's industry, and also, perhaps, of the reasonably satisfactory adaptation being made by the immigrants. On the other hand, it may simply reflect the paucity of all statistics kept by many firms.

CHAPTER 2

CROYDON

(1) *The Terrain and the People*

To the casual visitor Croydon might indeed appear little more than a characteristic southern municipal product of the Industrial Revolution and a greener, cleaner, airier extension of London's suburban sprawl south of the Thames. Following its administrative incorporation into Greater London, in early 1965, indeed, this may well come about, but Croydon is in fact an ancient town which celebrated its millenary in 1960 and which can trace its history back still further to Saxon and even Roman times.[1]

The nineteenth century brought a surge of industrial development, which caused the population to rise steeply from some 5,000 in 1801 to 20,000 in 1851, 78,000 in 1881, and over 130,000 in 1901. This rapid increase meant, particularly in the last half of the century and in the twentieth century, that a large proportion of Croydon residents were 'foreigners' in the sense of being newcomers born outside the town.

The Victorian tide of progress virtually engulfed the wood, brick, and stucco of the Tudor, William and Mary, and Georgian eras with a tide of neo-Gothic, neoclassical, and semi-functional building fanning out from the original centre in Old Town. Cobbles, coach-yards, inns, and even markets vanished, the picturesque and the shoddy alike being swept away. The town evolved from an insanitary and fever-ridden place, overhung when the wind was in the north by a pall of smoke from the charcoal-burners' kilns at

[1] 'If the stranger, trusting the evidence of his eyes alone, insists that we are really only an offshoot of London, he is as mistaken in this as in believing that we are merely a mushroom growth of the 19th and 20th centuries. For 1,000 years, and more, Croydon has been a separate entity, a community, a town of character and importance, living its own life and making its own history, as distinct and personal as if the Metropolis were 1,000 miles away' (*Croydon 1000*, Croydon, *Croydon Advertiser*, 1960, p. 1).

Thornton Heath, to 'one of the most healthy towns in the country'; it was recommended to prosperous commuters for its pure water supply, efficient sanitary arrangements, low death rate, good roads and communications with London, and lovely surroundings.[1]

Apart from the general industrial development of the Victorian era and the town's proximity to London, the main reason for this great leap forward was the opening up of road, water, and rail communications,[2] in which Irish navvies (many of whom were to settle in Croydon), played a considerable part. By 1887 fourteen railways had been built to serve commuters, and in 1888 the town became a County Borough after six years of incorporation as a municipal borough. By 1914 Metropolitan London had expanded so far southward as to meet Croydon, thus blurring the latter's urban identity and individuality.

The two decades between the World Wars saw a further expansionary phase, with the development of Coulsdon, Purley, Sanderstead, and Caterham as Croydon's own suburbs, although they were outside her administrative boundaries. In the Second World War the processes of residential deterioration and socio-economic change were accelerated by the effects of five years of enforced neglect and the bombings which destroyed or damaged some 54,000 houses. After the war came the further development of the new light industrial area along Purley Way and of the bulk of the remaining building land in the borough, most of this lying to the south-east in Addington Ward. Concurrently with the fieldwork for this study the town centre began to undergo a large-scale and radical 'Swedish-modern' style face-lift, which has diversified and enlivened its somewhat pedestrian Victorianism with new stores, office blocks, and public buildings. By 1961 the town's population was to rise to a total of over 250,000.[3]

[1] See George Sternman, *A History of Croydon*, 1883; *Croydon 1000*, Croydon, *Croydon Advertiser*, 1960, pp. 9, 11; J. Corbett Anderson, *A Descriptive and Historical Guide to Croydon*, 1887.

[2] 1801–46—Surrey Iron Railway; 1808—opening of the new main road to Brighton; 1809—Croydon Canal connecting with the Grand Surrey Canal at New Cross; 1839—London and Croydon Railway (the Canal was drained and the track laid along its bed); 1841—London–Brighton Railway. See also H. J. Dyos, 'The Suburban Development of Greater London South of the Thames, 1836–1914' (unpublished Ph.D. thesis, University of London, 1952), pp. 122 f., pp. 275–6 (here is noted an 1861 advertisement for land sites in Addiscombe, which mentions that the journey to the City or West End last only twenty minutes—the same as today!).

[3] 1961 Census figure: 252,387 (118,815 males, 133,572 females).

In terms of socio-economic stratification, Croydon seems always to have been a predominantly middle-class town.[1] This is supported by the fact that the town has only twice (in the routs of 1945 and 1966) returned a Labour Member of Parliament for any of its three divisions, and that—again except for a brief post-war period and in 1962–3—the Labour group on the Borough Council has always been outnumbered by anti-Labour Ratepayer[2] and Conservative groupings and coalitions.[3]

An impression of the socio-economic structure of Croydon not long before the period of this study is given in the map at the end of the present volume. This breakdown by wards is, however, not entirely straightforward, as there were considerable socio-economic differences within most wards, and even within council estates or between neighbouring streets.[4] For instance, a large new council

[1] A picture of the gradually declining middle-class Addiscombe district of Croydon before and during the Second World War is given in two novels by R. F. Delderfield: *Dreaming Suburb*, London, Hodder and Stoughton, 1958, and *The Avenue Goes to War*, London, Hodder and Stoughton, 1958. An earlier impression of middle-class Croydon is afforded in Malcolm Muggeridge's reminiscent contribution to the series 'John Bull's Schooldays' (*Spectator*, 13 May 1960). But see also n. 4, below.

[2] The Ratepayers' Association stood to the right of the national policy of the Conservative Party (T. Morris, *The Criminal Area*, London, Routledge and Kegan Paul, 1957, p. 118).

[3] For a more detailed analysis of Croydon's socio-economic structure in 1951, based on the Jurors' Index, on room density, and overcrowding, on types of land use, rateable value, and period of development, see Morris, op. cit., pp. 112–18, and particularly the table on p. 117, from which the socio-economic ward divisions on the map on p. 393, are taken, with sincere acknowledgements.

[4] See Morris, op. cit., pp. 115–16, 124–30. He pointed out that only East and Shirley Wards constitute 'natural areas' in a cultural sense, whereas Broad Green and Whitehorse Manor, which might appear working-class to the casual observer, in fact contained groups of costermongers, whose income-levels and political orientations diverged widely from those of the labourers among whom they lived.

In an analysis of 'The Structure of Greater London', using detailed 1951 Census and other data, John Westergaard maintains that none of the ninety-five local authority areas in the Greater London conurbation could be called 'solidly middle class' since none in 1951 had more than 45 per cent. of its occupied and retired male population in social classes I and II. Croydon fell within his 'Southern Intermediate Zone' with an overall 22 per cent. in social classes I and II; most of its neighbours, with the exceptions of Lambeth (inner working class) and Wandsworth, Penge and Mitcham (southern intermediate) fall into the category of southern suburban zones of high social status with 34 per cent. in classes I and II.

As regards housing conditions, Croydon in 1951 was classified in Group 3 (1 being the worst, 4th best) in terms of two indices, (*a*) the proportion living in dwellings which they had to share with one or more households, and (*b*) the pro-

estate has in recent years been developed in upper-class Addington to the south-west. Most of its dwellers are Croydonians of long residence who have been moved out of central slum areas or badly deteriorated housing.

The political, communal, and cultural life of the town still seems to be dominated by a middle-class core-society. The heyday of local cultural and communal activity was probably reached in the last two decades of the nineteenth century and the first four decades of the twentieth. There has, however, in recent decades been an increasing tendency for wealthier Croydonians to follow the example of earlier commuters to London by moving south or south-west to greener pastures beyond the borough boundaries.

Croydon, which has for decades been regarded as a dormitory suburb for London white-collar and professional workers,[1] now provides employment for a growing number of workers of this type; many of them, however, live farther south and commute into and out of Croydon.

This reversed trend is likely to become more marked as the development of the new business centre attracts more and more firms from the City and West End. As early as mid-1959 it induced the Editor of the *Croydon Advertiser* to publish some melancholy reflections on the possible effects on Croydon communal life of this trend in combination with the concurrent disappearance of so many central places of entertainment following the spread of television.[2] Despite the diminished attraction of the town centre as a place of entertainment for residents, however, Croydon still has an impressive number of cultural associations.

The town also has a large and active network of voluntary social associations grouped in the Croydon Guild of Social Service; this was formed in 1907 and has one of the longest histories of continuous social work in the country.[3] The town also possesses two flou-

portion of households in separate dwellings but without exclusive use of one or more main facilities (piped water, a W.C., a kitchen sink, a cooking stove, or a fixed bath). Group 3 classifications ranged between 14 to 30 per cent. for index (*a*) and 9 to 32 per cent. for index (*b*). (*London, Aspects of Change*, Centre for Urban Studies, Report No. 3, London, MacGibbon and Kee, 1964.)

[1] See ibid, p. 102 for 1951 figures.

[2] 'Croydon—a Live Town or Dead City', *Croydon Advertiser*, 14 August 1959.

[3] In October 1964 a local liaison committee to assist immigrant integration was set up in Croydon, sponsored by the Guild of Social Service. It is called the International Association of Croydon, and has Borough Council representatives, elected representatives of organizations, and other individual elected members on its executive committee.

rishing and lively weeklies, although this does not rival the situation in the 'boom town' days of the late Victorian era, when no fewer than ten dailies and weeklies were published in the town.

Community feeling is an elusive thing to pin down in contemporary urban England. Croydon probably has more sense of community than the majority of London boroughs, arising to some extent out of resistance to the lures and encroachments of the many-tentacled metropolis to the north,[1] but also out of a genuine and active individuality.

The low local political polls and the apparent apathy with which the majority of Croydon residents greeted the millenary celebrations which took place in 1960, just after the fieldwork for this study was finished, caused some local leaders to conclude that most Croydonians had no civic pride and took little interest in local affairs.[2] Others pointed out, probably with more justice, that it was too much to hope for a close-knit village-style community in a modern urban setting and that there was plenty of evidence of a continuing interest and pride in the town, of a sense of close association with a particular part of the town, and of a vast variety of community activities.[3]

Less superficially evident but at least of equal importance for this study are the sub-community ties which still prevail in certain streets and districts in the older, more centrally sited, working-class areas and council estates, although these have been weakened to some extent since the war by slum-clearance and rehousing on outlying housing estates.

These local sub-community links do, however, still play a considerable part in the industrial scene, since many, if not most, factories are either dependent on, or are trying to build up, an established nucleus of long-term local workers, charge-hands, foremen, and supervisors; in such cases management are usually

[1] This resistance flared up sharply in 1960 when the Report of the Royal Commission on Local Government in the greater London Area recommended the regrouping of the Greater London area into thirty-four new boroughs under a new Greater London authority; in this Croydon, instead of achieving the city status which it had long sought, was destined to lose even its county borough status.

[2] *Croydon Advertiser*, 23 December 1960.

[3] See *Observer*, 26 October 1958 (article entitled 'Archbishops' Retreat'); *Croydon Advertiser*, 7 November 1958, 23 January 1959, 19 August 1960 (speech by Mr. T. E. Callander, the borough's Chief Librarian); and the *Croydon Advertiser's* Millenary Croydon series in 1960.

prepared to make considerable concessions to such a group in order to retain goodwill, whether they are activated by expediency or by local sentiment.

(2) *The Croydon Industrial Area*

The industrial area which is served by the Croydon Employment Exchange, and which was the location of this inquiry, is somewhat larger than that contained within the pre-1965 County Borough of Croydon: it takes in Beddington and Wallington, Coulsdon and Purley, and part of Mitcham. This Croydon industrial area is thus much more than a dormitory area for city workers. It provides a considerable and increasing amount of professional and white-collar employment in the various public services and in the flourishing shopping and business centre.[1] In addition the post-war development of light engineering and other industries, particularly in the Purley Way area, made Croydon an increasing magnet for local industrial workers and work-seekers living outside the area.

At the outset, industrial Croydon seemed likely to provide a favourable terrain for the industrial absorption of newcomers. Since 1950 there has, despite mild fluctuations, been an expanding economy[2] and a chronic labour shortage, marked by an unemployment rate even lower than the Greater London average and considerably below the national average[3] and a larger number of

[1] Since this inquiry was carried out many more openings of these kinds have been made available as the extensive redevelopment of the city centre proceeds and London offices move south, attracted by lower rates, good communications, and cheaper services.

[2] The expansion was not, of course, an overall one: between 1955 and 1960 it was most conspicuous in building and construction; light engineering (radio and electronics); paper and printing; the distributive services (retail); catering and hotels; insurance, banking, and finance; and educational services. (Youth Employment Service Report, 1955–60, County Borough of Croydon Education Committee, Appendix II.)

[3] For instance, in October 1958, following the 1956–7 credit squeeze, the unemployed register was nearly double that for the preceding year, but the Croydon Employment Exchange Manager, Mr. G. G. Palmer, stated that this was only 0·9 per cent. of the local working population, as compared with the national average of 2·2 per cent. The increase was also said to be spread over all industries and trades and not to have fallen particularly heavily on a few (*Croydon Advertiser*, 10 October 1958). By March 1959 the Croydon and national figures were 1 per cent. and 2·5 per cent. respectively (*Croydon Advertiser*, 20 March 1959).

vacancies than unemployed. There are no local memories of industrial strife or misery comparable to those engrained in the thinking of generations of workers in the North, Scotland, and Wales, and the settled industrial community has had no unpleasant experiences of immigrant labour in the past which would stimulate fears and hostility today. For the most part local union branches have not taken a very restrictive line, preferring to maintain wages and standards by enrolling the immigrants as members.

As for the local working population, there are considerable pockets of clannishness left in the older central residential working-class areas[1] but rehousing and redevelopment have somewhat weakened these, as large numbers of Croydonians have been transferred from the centre to peripheral housing estates where community feeling is still weak and where many are some distance from their work-place and consequently feel less directly identified with it. The serious housing shortage (4,000 families were on the waiting list in early 1958) might, of course, have caused Croydonians to resent any large-scale influx of newcomers, but in fact there was little or no feeling of the kind at this time. The Poles settled inconspicuously in converted middle-class property, while West Indian settlement was not as yet particularly noticeable. It should also be pointed out that the tolerant and cosmopolitan approach on which many middle-class Croydonians pride themselves is matched among lower-class Croydonians by a 'live-and-let-live' attitude similar to that found among many metropolitan Londoners to the north.

The character of Croydon industry also favours the absorption of immigrant workers; this applies particularly to the larger, more recently established firms in which most immigrants have found work. Most of these have been characterized by a chronic labour shortage, a fairly high labour turnover and the incentive and facilities to experiment with the selection and training of new types of labour. They have also tended to be firms with country-wide and overseas links and less exclusive associations with Croydon society than the smaller local firms.

[1] The lower-class residential areas are approximately indicated by ward on the map on p. 393. A more detailed description can be found in Terence Morris's doctoral thesis, 'The Concept of Social Ecology in Criminological Research', University of London, 1955, Chapter VIII. It should, however, be remembered that the situation had probably changed somewhat even by 1958, as a consequence of steady slum-clearance and rehousing outside the central areas.

At the time of this investigation some 3,000 firms were listed in the files of the Croydon Employment Exchange.[1] The majority of these were situated within the Croydon municipal boundary, being concentrated in the western peripheral industrial areas along Thornton Road and Purley Way and in smaller pockets near East and West Croydon Stations, in Selhurst, Woodside, South Norwood, Thornton Heath, and elsewhere.[2] A minority of these firms were, however, situated in the less industrialized unofficial 'suburbs' of Croydon, Beddington, and Wallington to the west, and Coulsdon and Purley to the south; in particular, industrial clusters were found on Mitcham Common, at Hackbridge, and in Beddington.

Of these 3,000 firms the great majority were very small. Only 167 firms employed more than fifty workers. Of these, sixty-nine were listed as employing 50–100 workers, forty-seven as employing 101–250 workers, twenty-seven 251–500 workers, and twenty-four over 500. It was with the ninety-eight firms employing 101 workers or more (or '100-plus' firms) that this investigation was to be mainly concerned, or, more precisely, with the eighty-eight such firms on which adequate information could be obtained.

Of the 115,000 insured workers in the Croydon industrial area in 1958 (68,186 men, 46,773 women), over one-quarter were employed in the light engineering sector.[3] Twenty of the eighty-eight '100-plus' firms actually surveyed were engaged in light engineering. Seven of them employed over 500 workers, and they included the two largest firms in the Croydon industrial area, each employing several thousand men and women.

Next to light engineering came the distributive trades with over 16,000 workers, represented in this study by four large department stores, and building and contracting, with over 9,000 workers, many of them employed in twelve firms with over 100 workers.

[1] This list covered the great majority of all working establishments in Croydon, given as just over 1,000 factories and workshops and 3,500 shops and warehouses. (Youth Employment Service report, 1955–60, (op. cit.) p. 2. See also p. 40, n. 1.)

[2] The map on p. 392 indicates the main industrial areas involved. The *Croydon Official Guide* (eighth edition, 1959), p. 87, gave a full list of areas scheduled for industrial development under the 1947 Croydon Development Plan.

[3] These figures are taken from estimates supplied by the Croydon Employment Exchange and based partly on the number of N.H.I. cards exchanged and partly on returns rendered by employers of five or more workpeople showing the number of N.H.I. cards held by them.

The remaining '100-plus' firms surveyed were concerned with the following manufacturing or service industries: heavy engineering (2); other heavy industry (4); public transport and utilities (4); light industries (9); laundries and dry cleaners (3); garments (4); food and drink production (9); automobile service and distribution (3); clerical and office (3); local government councils (3); printing and bookbinding (5); and hospitals (3). From these figures and the occupational breakdown of the local insured population given in Appendix I it emerged that Croydon had few of the heavy, chronically undermanned industries into which foreign workers were directed after the war and compelled to remain for some years. Thus the fact that such foreign workers were found in Croydon industry in considerable numbers in itself indicated that their industrial absorption in Britain had proceeded some way.[1]

[1] See *Tannahill*, op. cit., p. 78, for this process in Northern England. In the case of non-British immigrants more data were available than for Commonwealth workers and it was quite possible to trace the drift into lighter, better-paid work in more attractive urban areas.

CHAPTER 3
THE NEWCOMERS

(1) *Post-War Immigration to Britain*

Britain is not usually regarded as a country of immigration, yet it has received successive and appreciable waves of immigrants and refugees over the centuries. Two large groups which may still be called minorities are the Irish and the Jews. The Irish are the oldest and most persistent immigrants, having begun to migrate in appreciable numbers at the end of the eighteenth century.[1] The largest group of Jews arrived in Britain between 1881 and 1905, after which date the operation of the Aliens Act made entry more difficult. This immigration was subsequently brought to a close by the outbreak of war in 1914, but British Jewry received appreciable new accessions of refugees in the 1920s and 1930s.[2]

After the 1939–45 war came the largest wave of immigration in British history. Hundreds of thousands of refugees from various countries and régimes were given asylum and the British Government began to tap every available labour source to meet the country's chronic labour shortage, which was simultaneously being aggravated by the emigration of many Britons to the Commonwealth. A further wave of Irish migration began, with a high rate of in-and-out movement and a balance in the early post-war years of several thousands, accruing annually to the population of the United Kingdom. This annual balance is estimated to have increased

[1] For the general historical background to Irish immigration in England, see J. A. Jackson, 'The Irish in London', M.A. thesis, University of London, 1958, and his book: *The Irish in Britain*, London, Routledge and Kegan Paul, 1963.

[2] Between 1914 and 1930 the group received an accession of Jewish refugees from Russia (nearly 20,000) (Freedman (ed.), *A Minority in Britain*, London, Vallentine, Mitchell, 1955). About 40,000 Jewish refugees from Germany, Austria, and the Sudetenland were also estimated to have come to Britain by May 1939 (Jacques Vernant, *The Refugee in the Post-War World*, London, George Allen and Unwin, 1953 p. 60).

considerably after 1950.[1] Most of these migrants were unskilled or semi-skilled and still continued to enter the traditional 'Irish' jobs of building, the docks, certain other types of heavy industry, and personal service. Others, however, followed the example of the children and grandchildren of earlier Irish settlers and sought employment in a wider range of occupations, including light industry, clerical work, and the professions.[2]

In addition to the Irish, however, Britain drew some 457,000 migrants (many of them permanent) from the European mainland in the years 1946–50. These included the following main groups (in broad figures): former members of the Polish armed forces under British command (115,000); certain categories of prisoner of-war (Ukrainians (8,000), Germans (15,000), Italians (1,000)); European Voluntary Workers (drawn mainly from the allied or other East European deportees or from prisoners released from German labour or concentration camps (90,000); distressed relatives (4,000); persons entering to marry residents (18,000); students (1,500); Ministry of Labour permit-holders (100,000); and other residual aliens (105,000, including some 36,300 Polish military families and civilian *emigrés*).[3]

The largest single post-war European ethnic minority was the Polish one, consisting mainly of 91,000 former members of the Polish armed forces who remained in this country, 33,000 wives and dependants, 14,000 E.V.W.s, and several thousand exiled

[1] The Economist Intelligence Unit report on Commonwealth immigration to Britain (No. 1) showed an estimated net immigration from the Republic of Ireland in the years 1946–59 inclusive of 352,900 or nearly half the grand Commonwealth total 685,500. This report also estimated that net annual emigration from Ireland to the United Kingdom had since 1951 fluctuated between 30,000 and 45,000, largely according to the state of the United Kingdom economy. According to the 1951 Census 527,700 residents of England and Wales were born in Southern Ireland. The 1961 Census showed a total of 644,398, or an increase of 116,698, which suggests that the E.I.U. estimates may have been too high. This would also apply to Jackson's estimate (op. cit., p. 15) of a net annual average of 30,000 immigrants (even though some of these would have gone to Scotland).

[2] In 1951 Irish doctors formed 12 per cent. of the total medical profession in England and Wales; Irish nurses and midwives represented 11 per cent. of the total; and 26 per cent. of all Roman Catholic priests were Irish-born (1951 Census of England and Wales, Occupational Tables). (Such a breakdown is not at present available for 1961.)

[3] J. Isaac, *British Post-War Migration*, National Institute of Economic and Social Research, Occasional Papers XVII, Cambridge, University Press 1954, p. 191.

civil servants. Today this Polish minority group may number about 130,000, including later arrivals from refugee camps or Poland, naturalized Poles, and children born of all-Polish parentage or with one Polish parent. This estimate does not include most Polish-born Ukrainians or Jews, the majority of whom have gravitated to their own ethnic communities in this country.

The educational and occupational background of this Polish exile group differed considerably from that of the Irish and other classic economic migrant groups, containing as it did a proportion of professionals, technicians, civil servants, and regular officers and N.C.O.s. Thus, although the great majority were compelled, as a result of official restrictions and labour policy, ignorance of the language, and the inapplicability of their qualifications to the new environment, to accept economic down-grading and enter the British economy as unskilled or semi-skilled workers, all but the elderly and disabled were potentially equipped to move farther up the economic hierarchy. In addition the very generous educational provisions made by the British Government ensured that many of the second generation have since then been able to revert to their parents' former professional status.[1]

Smaller refugee or exile groups of a similar type but drawn less from ex-combatants and more from former 'displaced persons' include Czechs, Slovaks, Yugoslavs, Rumanians, Ukrainians, nationals of the three Soviet-occupied Baltic States, Latvia, Lithuania and Estonia,[2] and Hungarians. The latter received a reinforcement of some 23,000 after the Hungarian Rising of 1956 and were the only group apart from the Poles to be represented in any numbers in Croydon, where one of the reception centres was situated. In socio-economic background most of these newcomers resembled the Polish exile group; they ranged from professionals to technicians, artisans, and young men and women who had not yet entered the labour market. The average age of the group was probably lower and it was not so occupationally and educationally top-heavy as the Polish community. Among the Hungarians there

[1] For further details, see S. Patterson, *The Polish Exile Community in Britain*, a paper read to the Annual Meeting of the British Association for the Advancement of Science (Section N) on 1 September 1961. The 1961 Census gave 119,503 Polish-born residents (of whom 82,468 were men). Of the overall total 25,817 were naturalized. (*Polish Review*, Vol. VI, no. 3, 1961.)

[2] According to Vernant (op. cit.), p. 365, the Baltic refugees in Britain totalled some 25,000 in 1951. They are not listed separately in the 1951 Census.

was also a small group of non-political criminals who had escaped from prison during the Rising, some adventurers and several hundred gipsies, most of whom proved relatively unadaptable and attracted unfavourable publicity on to the whole group. Within three years of their arrival, however, only 537 out of the 16,000 who were still in Britain remained unplaced in industry.[1]

Another large post-war immigrant contingent consisted of various economically motivated migrant groups. These included on the one hand selected aliens, mainly from Germany, Austria, Italy, and other West European countries, who entered on labour permits to fill jobs in the undermanned industries or to undertake specialized skilled work;[2] and on the other hand an increasing number of unselected economic migrants not only from Ireland but from underdeveloped Commonwealth or colonial territories. The latter, like the Irish, were, until the Commonwealth Immigrants Act came into operation in July 1962, entitled to enter Britain unconditionally and to settle and work wherever they pleased or could find lodging and a job. These newcomers came mainly from the West Indies, India and Pakistan, West Africa, Aden, and what was until 1961 British Somaliland.[3] No movement

[1] Of the remaining 7,000 about 1,500 had returned to Hungary and 5,500 had emigrated, the bulk of them to join the large Hungarian ethnic group established in Canada (*Daily Telegraph*, 19 December 1959). For an account of the efficient reception and resettlement of this group, see the annual reports (1956–61) of the British Council for Aid to Refugees, the voluntary organization which carried out the major part of this operation in co-operation with other voluntary associations and various ministries. See also W.V.S. reports on work for Hungarian refugees over the period 1956–9. The 1961 Census showed 17,938 Hungarian residents (11,052 men, 6,886 women) in England and Wales.

[2] In 1958 and 1959, the two years during which most of the fieldwork for this study was carried out, the largest groups of Ministry of Labour permit-holders were: German (11,021 and 10,844); Italians (6, 843 and 6,944); Swiss (4,602 and 4,950); Spanish (3,654 and 4,110); and French (2,957 and 3,193). The totals were 42,840 and 43, 371 respectively. In all there were something over 388,000 registered foreign-born aliens in the United Kingdom and another 200,000 foreign-born persons who were British by naturalization, registration or marriage (*Annual Abstract of Statistics*, 1958). This was a little less than the total of foreign-born residents shown in the 1951 Census. The 1961 Census gave the following totals of residents born in various European countries: Germany—120,951 (40,379 men, 80,572 women); Italy—81,327 (36,017 men, 45,310 women); Austria—30,414 (8,653 men, 21,761 women); Switzerland—12,784; Spain—20,829; France—30,392. In all national groups women very much outnumbered men.

[3] There were also smaller groups of immigrants from British Mediterranean territories. The 1951 Census enumerated 10,208 Cypriots, 14,503 Maltese, and 6,996 Gibraltese. The two first groups have increased considerably since then.

control or selectivity in regard to educational background or industrial qualifications was or could then be exercised by the British Government; so the great majority of the new arrivals, being ill-equipped in terms of the needs of Britain's complex urban and industrial society, followed the Irish into the lower level of the economic hierarchy.

By the end of 1958, when the fieldwork for this study was begun, the Home Office estimated that there were about 210,000 coloured Commonwealth residents of the United Kingdom: this total included 115,000 West Indians, 25,000 West Africans, and 55,000 Indians and Pakistanis.[1] Thereafter the overall numbers continued to rise. According to the 1961 Census of England and Wales, there were then some 172,000 residents born in British Caribbean territories, nearly 160,000 born in India, nearly 31,000 born in Pakistan and about 20,000 born in West Africa. These totals were generally regarded as under-estimates, particularly in the case of Indian and Pakistani immigrants who were not U.K.-born.[2] The Economist Intelligence Unit offered a minimum estimate of some 500,000 immigrants of West Indian, Indian, and Pakistani origins in 1963.[3] By 1967 the total was about one million.

Other smaller groups of newcomers from the Commonwealth consisted of several thousand 'post-colonial settlers', mainly Anglo-Indians, but including Anglo-Pakistanis, Anglo-Burmese, and Cape Coloured, who found their marginal status in newly independent Commonwealth or ex-Commonwealth countries increasingly unattractive and took advantage of their possession of British

The 1961 Census showed a total of 41,898 Cyprus-born residents (23,468 men, 18,430 women); and for Malta a total of 24,679 (12,629 men and 12,050 women). Migration to the United Kingdom from Australia, Canada, Rhodesia, New Zealand, and South Africa has been fairly low and relatively steady; it has also presented no particular problems since the majority of these newcomers seem to fit into British society with little or no more difficulty than a Briton moving from one part of the country to another. According to the 1961 Census England and Wales had some 49,000 Canadian-born residents, 36,700 born in Australia, and 13,500 in New Zealand. There were also 37,500 residents born in South Africa.

[1] Estimate given by the Under-Secretary, Home Office, in the House of Commons on 6 December 1958.

[2] The Indian total included over 100,000 citizens of the United Kingdom and colonies (the vast majority of these must have been children of British civil servants, servicemen, and others) born in India; in the Pakistan total the corresponding figure for this group was nearly 8,000.

[3] *Commonwealth Immigration: No.* 8, Supplement, August 1964.

passports to start a new life in this country. Their motivations were thus partly economic, partly escapist, but in this study they are grouped with the other Commonwealth economic immigrants. Unlike the European refugees, however, most members of these marginal immigrant groups aimed at rapid assimilation and formed no strong minority organizations or community bonds. The majority had held clerical or minor administrative posts at home and they seemed to have experienced relatively little difficulty in entering 'white-collar' jobs in Britain.

(2) *Newcomers to Croydon*

From the viewpoint of the British economy and its needs, the main immigrant groups that have entered Britain over the last two or three decades fall into three main categories: there are the strictly controlled and selected Western and Southern European economic immigrants; the East and Central European exiles and refugees, less selectively admitted but nevertheless representing a wide variety of talents, professions, and trades (a good part of which became available to the British economy as a result of the newcomers' own initiative and adaptability or of the resettlement and retraining and programmes carried out by the British Government and voluntary associations); and the uncontrolled and usually unselected mass movement of migrants from Southern Ireland and the underdeveloped areas of the Commonwealth and colonies,[1] the great majority of whom were equipped to enter only unskilled and semi-skilled work in Britain's undermanned industries.

As an expanding industrial area Croydon has drawn contingents mainly from ethnic groups within the last two categories, with a smaller number from the European economic migrant category. In the exile–refugee class Poles were most numerous, with Hungarians in second place. The third 'Commonwealth economic migrant' class was represented by Southern Irish and West Indians, and smaller numbers of Anglo-Indians and others.[2]

As the fieldwork for this study proceeded it became clear that considerably more immigrants worked in the Croydon industrial area than as yet lived in Croydon proper. Many still lived in South

[1] Controls and some measure of selection were of course imposed on all but the quasi-Commonwealth Southern Irish by the Commonwealth Immigrants Act, 1 July 1962.

[2] For totals of immigrants employed in Croydon industry, see Table 2.

London districts a few miles to the north: Clapham, Sydenham, Balham, Chiswick (Poles); Brixton, Peckham, Wandsworth, Battersea (West Indians). The Irish were even more widely dispersed residentially, although a considerable number lodged with settled families of Irish extraction in Croydon.

It seemed useful to collect some information about immigrant residential settlements and organizations in the borough, since there was considerable evidence to show that settled workers tended ultimately to move into Croydon, for convenience in getting to work and sometimes also because of its better amenities. These settled immigrant workers were usually those who were most likely to act as pioneers and to enter the settled labour-core that in so many working communities exerts a strong influence on the culture of the factory and the absorption of all newcomers.[1] The extent of residential settlement and intra-group social organization also afforded an indication of the extent and manner of the various immigrants' adaptation to local society as a whole.

In the county borough of Croydon only the Irish, the Poles, the Hungarians, the Anglo-Indians, and the West Indians could be located residentially in any appreciable numbers or clusters in 1958–9.[2] The bulk of the Irish, both old-established and migrant,[3] were still concentrated mainly in the older and deteriorating working-class residential sectors of Central, Waddon, and Broad Green Wards, in which the original navvies had settled after 1834, but the existence of Roman Catholic churches in Addiscombe, East Croydon, and South Croydon suggested that a fair amount of dispersal and upward social mobility had taken place since the original settlement by the immigrant navvies who helped build the railways from 1839 onwards.[4] Most local middle-class and professional inform-

[1] See pp. 243–50 and p. 271 f.

[2] See Map at end of book for an indication of the main areas of settlement of the different immigrant groups.

[3] The 1951 Census showed the presence in Croydon County Borough of 1,368 men and 1,919 women born in the Irish Republic. In 1961 the respective totals were 2,020 and 2,633.

[4] It is not, of course, suggested that all Roman Catholics in the area have Irish antecedents or origins, but people in this category appear to have constituted a large proportion of the pre-1939 Catholic minority. The first Roman Catholic chapel in Croydon is mentioned in the 1851 Directory; it was situated in Broad Green and was superseded in 1860 by St. Mary's Roman Catholic church in Wellesley Road. The parish of Our Lady of the Assumption in Addiscombe was founded in 1925 to provide for a settled resident Catholic population, which was largely though by no means entirely of Irish origin. This parish church now

ants, however, still tended to regard the Irish as labourers, to talk of their low living standards and to attribute to them traits such as 'roughness', belligerence, superstition, and drunkenness. It seems likely, however, that this local picture was based largely on superficial observation or press-reporting of the behaviour of a conspicuous but small minority of recent arrivals, usually young single men.

Whereas the Irish have been in Croydon for over a century, the Polish and West Indian settlements there are very recent. In both cases the great majority seem to have come to live in Croydon only after they found work in the area.[1]

Some Polish airmen from nearby Biggin Hill aerodrome were billeted in Croydon during the 1939–45 War.[2] Few of them, however, seem to have returned to settle there as there is no local branch of the generally active and flourishing Polish Air Force Association. Poles began to move into Croydon in the late 1940s, and the settlement received a substantial reinforcement in 1954, when a Polish-owned plastics factory, whose staff and labour core was and has continued to be Polish, moved to the Purley Way industrial area from Brixton. Apart from some scatter, mainly in West Croydon, the main area of Polish settlement was and has remained the precariously middle-class eastern section of Addiscombe, whose capacious pre-1914 houses have undergone some structural deterioration since 1940.[3] The principal reasons for this choice of area appear to have been: the relative cheapness of the houses, particularly compared with London property values; their size (which

serves as a centre for the Polish ethnic parish and has a fair number of parishioners from other immigrant groups, notably Anglo-Indians.

[1] In 1961 (1951 figures are given in brackets) there were 634 (587) Polish-born residents (420 (367) men, 214 (220) women) in the town, of whom a few may have been earlier Jewish immigrants not connected with the Polish exile community. This was the second largest European national group in the borough, the largest consisting of Germans, mainly women (531 out of a total of 727 (1951 Census figures were 422 women out of a total group of 597)), many of them presumably being employed in domestic service.

[2] I am indebted to Dr. Terence Morris, himself Croydon-born and bred, for this and much other local information. See also Delderfield, *The Avenue Goes to War*. This novel includes a Polish airman among the minor characters.

[3] Information as to the whereabouts of the main areas of Polish settlement was obtained from the Polish priest and officers of various Polish voluntary associations, from the parish priest of the Addiscombe Catholic church in which ethnic parish services and functions are held, from addresses in newspaper reports, and from some local informants, including branch librarians who are called upon to provide a supply of Polish-language books.

permitted conversion into flats or the taking of one or two lodgers to help mortgage payments); the healthiness and attractiveness of the area (it has quiet, wide streets and well-wooded gardens) and its proximity to the more definitely middle- and upper-middle class residential areas of East Croydon and Shirley and to the magnificent heathland and woods of the Addington Hills.

The Poles who came to Croydon to live were already fairly well-established in civilian life and this move often represented a step up from the poorer housing in Brixton, Peckham or Battersea which was all the majority had been able to afford in the first years of settlement. It also illustrated the upward mobility (economic if not occupational) that is characteristic of this particular exile group and its members' tendency to follow the southward or south-westward movement of upwardly mobile Londoners.

By 1950 the Polish settlement was large enough to justify the establishment of an ethnic 'parish' and the appointment of a Polish parish priest, who holds a Polish-language Mass at the church of Our Lady of the Annunciation in Addiscombe. By 1958–9 local Polish informants who were active in community life estimated that, including the British-born second generation, there was a potential Polish community (*Polonia*) of well over 500 in Croydon alone.[1]

It is of some interest that most Croydonian informants, whether from the employment exchange, the Assistance Board, local government, the local Press, or the voluntary services, expressed surprise when they were told of the presence of so large and cohesive a settlement. This may be attributed to the fact that the bulk of the Polish group in Croydon consists of settled, middle-class families whose initial adjustment to civilian life and a strange environment is long since over. No local informant could remember any trouble or expressions of hostility in relation to Poles in earlier years and one borough official said to me: 'After all, they're one of us now—good workers and ratepayers. They don't have any problems or make any trouble.'

Another reason for this relative 'invisibility' of the Poles may be

[1] The Croydon 'parish' covers the Crystal Palace area as well so that it is difficult to determine precisely what proportion of its members, actual or potential, live in Croydon. A representative of the joint Parish Committee gave the number of Polish or Anglo-Polish (British wives, children of mixed marriages) residents within the parish area as about 950 (250 married couples, 50 unattached males, 400 children). Of these well over half were believed to live in Croydon.

that they are an integrating rather than an assimilating group, conforming to local norms in major areas of association such as employment and housing and also in outward behaviour, but not attracting attention by seeking full acceptance by the receiving society in the social and cultural spheres.[1] On the other hand, the Poles have accommodated themselves sufficiently to local life to establish their own 'locals'. One pub with a particularly 'European' exile flavour, even including a European musical accompaniment, is on the main Brighton road south of the city centre. This the Poles share with their former neighbours and traditional friends, the Hungarians, and pre-war European café customs are retained to the extent that most of the regulars are men, rarely accompanied by their womenfolk. Just opposite this public house is an Irish 'local', which has its own atmosphere.

In past and present socio-economic affiliations the Polish settlement in Croydon is predominantly middle-middle or lower-middle class. As one Pole said: 'There are no aristocrats and few former members of the liberal professions here. The Poles here keep together because there are no real class differences.' Leadership is provided by the priest and a few laymen drawn from a small group of former regular officers and members of the pre-war intelligentsia; they work through the parish organizations and the active local branch of the Polish Ex-Combatants' Association.

The majority of older Poles in Croydon have been and will probably remain economically 'down-graded' ('de-classed' is the common Polish expression), doing unskilled or semi-skilled work, but most of them are moderately well-to-do. Many own their own houses and some their own cars. An index of this relative prosperity is that for the last few years very few Polish women have gone out to work. Instead, they look after the house and the lodgers, while some may take in home dressmaking or do other 'cottage industry' work. An even more prosperous minority are the scientists, engineers, and skilled artisans with pre-war or British qualifications, who are now accepted in most local factories and who, unlike many others in the Polish group, are usually better off than they were before the war.

[1] At this time most leaders of the Polish exile community had not taken British nationality and had to report any changes of address to the local C.I.D. One index of this group's exile orientations and avoidance of assimilation is the fact that only 33 per cent. of Polish-born men and 40 per cent. of women had taken British nationality by 1961 (Croydon Census).

So far as could be ascertained the age structure and sex ratio of the Polish community in Croydon seem fairly typical of the Polish exile group in Britain as a whole. The majority are in the 30–49 age group and there is a higher proportion of old people than in the British population. The two decennial groups covering the 10–29 age group are proportionately smaller, as a result of such factors as the long separation of marital partners and the high mortality rate of children in occupied Poland or Russian labour camps, but there is a relatively larger group of children in the lowest decennial group. The sex ratio for the Polish group in Britain as a whole is about three women to eight men. In Croydon, as elsewhere, this has led to a fair number of mixed marriages with English or Irish women and usually to the speedier assimilation of the children of such marriages into the local community.

Unlike the Poles, the Hungarians arrived in Croydon, as elsewhere in Britain, with a blare of publicity and on the crest of a wave of popular sympathy. This even extended into many left-wing recesses of the craft unions, where a number of Communists broke with the Party over the Soviet intervention in Budapest; thus most Hungarian artisans experienced much less difficulty in getting skilled work in British industry than the Poles and other earlier refugees from Communism had done.

During the autumn and winter of 1956–7 a considerable number of Hungarians passed through Croydon; they were accommodated in houses specially bought for the purpose and the employment exchange was able to place many of them locally. The field-material shows, however, that relatively few Hungarians remained in their first placings and many seem to have moved out of the area altogether. The honeymoon period of Hungarian–British relations was followed by a period of disillusionment and friction on both sides, but by the end of 1959 the *Croydon Advertiser* found that the majority of the fifty or so Hungarian families who had stayed in Croydon had settled down happily, despite considerable economic down-grading and the difficulty of learning English.[1]

Unlike other ethnic groups in Croydon, housing was found for

[1] 13 November 1959. The 1961 Census registered 256 Hungarian-born residents (138 men, 118 women). As only a few of them were naturalized British subjects, and there were too few Hungarian-born residents in Croydon in 1951 for a separate enumeration, it seems likely that the bulk of the 256 arrived after 1956.

most of the Hungarians and their settlement pattern was therefore somewhat artificial. In fact, most were housed in converted flats in large old houses bought for the purpose out of a special fund[1] and situated in areas in Addiscombe or South Croydon similar to those in which most Poles live. Understandably enough, the Hungarian group that was least settled and provoked most local friction and hostility consisted of single youths and young men who had been brought up under two extremes of totalitarian régimes, in which poor workmanship, theft of tools and materials, minor hooliganism, and drunkenness were, in the absence of freedom of political expression, covert ways of expressing disapproval of the authorities. Reports of such anti-social actions by individuals appeared from time to time in the Croydon Press but were not unduly emphasized.

The other major group of immigrants with whom this study is concerned—the West Indians—began to settle in Croydon in noticeable numbers about 1957–8.[2] Thereafter the inflow was quite rapid. Whereas in 1951 the Census report showed a total of only 317 men and 262 women born in the colonies and protectorates (not broken down by area), there were by 1961 1,669 Croydon residents (891 men, 778 women) born in British Caribbean territories alone. By mid-1962 a figure, possibly exaggerated, of some 5,000 to 6,000 was mentioned.[3] Although this movement was in part a residential overspill from earlier settlements in Lambeth, Lewisham, and Wandsworth, the majority of newcomers appear to have moved south in order to be nearer their work in Croydon. For the most part they had found this work themselves or through south London employment exchanges and only a handful were registering at the Croydon exchange.

Most of the newcomers went into cheap, old, dilapidated, middle- or lower-middle-class property in areas in North and West Croydon which had undergone considerable social down-grading. The main nuclei were the streets round South Norwood Station,[4] but

[1] See *Croydon Advertiser*, 4 September 1959, for a statement about the Croydon Guild of Social Service's activities in this connexion.

[2] In 1958, indeed, even the active Migrant Services Division of the High Commission for the West Indies Federation had no definite information about West Indian settlement in Croydon, nor names of individual contacts.

[3] *Croydon Times*, 29 June 1962.

[4] This may have been the earliest area of settlement. An item in the *Croydon Advertiser* of 17 August 1956 records a brawl in a West Indian-tenanted house in Oliver Grove.

there was also some infiltration into the upper-middle-class Park Hill area of Addiscombe, where local residents had for twenty years campaigned against the presence of the International Language Club, with its conspicuous proportion of coloured student residents. In some cases the West Indians moved into accommodation where earlier immigrants such as the Irish had been tenants, but there was not much evidence of the sort of immigrant residential succession that seems to have occurred in many North American cities.

At the time of this study there was little or no social cohesion or organization among West Indians in Croydon and it is therefore extremely difficult to give any definite picture of the settlement. Time did not permit a thorough first-hand investigation to be carried out except in the industrial sphere, and information had to be drawn from local informants, from a few coloured residents, and from the local Press.

The general view of local officials, welfare officers, and other informants was that the Croydon West Indians were 'a cut above the Brixton type, quieter and more respectable'. This impression was probably accurate, since the earlier arrivals were often settled families who had moved away from the poorest parts of Brixton. The relatively even sex-ratio (seven women to eight men) also suggests that most members of the group were relatively established. They were, in fact, following the example of the Poles a few years earlier, although at a lower socio-economic level. And, while the one-room household remained the norm, a few families were found to be renting two or more rooms, or reserving more than one room for themselves in their own houses. Nevertheless, in terms of the local class structure and of the requirements of local industry the great majority of the West Indian newcomers were lower-class, unskilled or semi-skilled, ill-qualified, poorly educated, and unused to the pace or discipline of large-scale urban industry. As such they were to find themselves competing for unskilled or manual work with the long-familiar Irish immigrant group rather than with their immediate predecessors, the Poles. The small minority of West Indian students, nurses, and professional or salaried workers attracted little notice; indeed, most seemed to keep themselves aloof from the mass of the migrants for fear of being identified with them.

Throughout the period of this study, West Indian residents

continued to make little impact on Croydon public opinion. The two local weeklies, the *Croydon Advertiser* and the *Croydon Times*, have on the whole reported all matters concerned with immigrants and immigration objectively and temperately, usually omitting such terms as 'coloured', 'West Indian', or 'Jamaican' from the headlines, and using them sparingly in the text. A survey of their coverage of these matters from 1958 to 1961 may therefore give some indication of the development of the settlement and of the newcomers' relations with the local population, although allowance must be made for a certain tendency in newspaper reporting to select 'newsworthy' (for instance, exceptional or anti-social) items.

In 1958, when this inquiry began, only a handful of reports were published in either paper. Most significant perhaps for this 'middle-class borough' was a Lands Tribunal appeal in December; this was brought by the local valuation officer against a local valuation court's decision to cut the assessment of a first-floor flat in a road near Oliver Grove in South Norwood on the grounds that the proximity of coloured residents lowered values. Other recorded items were the setting up of the racialist British National Party with headquarters in Thornton Heath; a resolution by the Croydon Trades Council opposing curbs on immigration from the Commonwealth as 'tantamount to support for the colour bar'; a statement by the Mayor deprecating special legislation to enable local authorities to make loans for house purchase to West Indians on the principle of 'no discrimination, no privileges'; and a call for a Royal Commission on immigration problems and controls, issued by the Conservative Member of Parliament for Croydon North-East (the area most affected).

Reports in 1958 also included an account of an evangelical service held for Croydon, Brixton, and Kilburn West Indian congregations and of a *fracas* in Surrey Street Market during which a stallholder had part of his ear bitten off by a coloured man following an argument over a pound of tomatoes.

In 1959 there were reports of: a successful attempt by South Norwood Methodist Church to bring coloured families into the congregation; an inter-racial outing to Southend by customers and friends of an off-licence in Clifford Road, South Norwood; a Jamaican couple's marriage at Croydon Parish Church followed by a honeymoon in Paris; a warning by the vicar of St. Saviour's to

English girls considering marriage to Muslims; several court cases;[1] a few cases of assault and minor theft; some participation by coloured boys in local school sporting events; the coming-of-age of the International Language Club, through which 18,000 students from 127 different countries were reported to have passed in twenty-one years; increased activity by local groups concerned with promoting friendly contacts between local people and overseas students, culminating in a 'People to People Week' in November.

In 1960 little change was noted, but in 1961 and later years there was a moderate increase in reports concerning noisy parties, assaults, housing shortages, rent tribunal cases, unmarried mothers, and the like—reports already so familiar in the pages of South London local papers farther to the north. Some correspondence in the summer months of 1961 was evoked by reports of a demand by local busmen for restriction of immigration[2] and there was also a report that West Indian immigrants were causing unemployment (this was a period of recession). In July 1961 the Standing Conference of Women's Organizations of Croydon issued a call for some form of restriction on the flow of migrants 'before it is too late'; at this meeting some delegates expressed strong views about the coloured newcomers' standards of behaviour and cleanliness.[3] Towards the end of this year the *Croydon Advertiser* for the first time published a fairly comprehensive feature on the degree to which coloured people had been integrated into the community and the way in which Croydonians regarded them. The reporter came to the fairly optimistic conclusion that there was little tension, that the immigrants presented few problems for the local

[1] During one case in which a coloured building worker was accused of using abusive language to a bus conductress it seemed that the plaintiff and the bench were under the impression that English was not the mother-tongue of Jamaicans. The conductress said that the West Indian had 'mumbled a few Jamaican words' and then called her a 'thieving ——'. She had asked him to speak English as 'it is the only language I understand'. The West Indian said that he had learned the word 'on the buildings' and did not know it was abusive. Summing up, the presiding magistrate said: 'There is no doubt about whether you used the word. You may not be sure of what it meant, having regard to the fact that you do not speak English as well as some' (*Croydon Advertiser*, 29 May 1959).

[2] See pp. 95–7.

[3] *Croydon Advertiser*, 26 May 1961. One of the speakers (on 'Coloured People in the Community') was Croydon's Industrial Chaplain of that time, who said that coloured people very often lowered local standards and that he personally had some colour prejudice to a small extent; like many other people he looked upon a coloured man as a brother but would not wish to have him as a brother-in-law.

authorities, and that in the schools at least the children were mingling without barriers.[1]

In the years 1958 to 1961 the local Press afforded a picture of a predominantly middle-class community reacting to the early stages of a working-class immigrant settlement—first with kindly toleration or aloofness, later with a certain disquiet and resistance. All through this period, the Press continued to report instances of liberal and benevolent local attitudes and initiatives among an active minority of middle-class Croydonians in relation to such matters as World Refugee Year, *apartheid* in South Africa, missionary work, and assistance to underdeveloped countries. Such attitudes and initiatives tend, however, to be second-hand and long-range, their objects rarely being near at hand. It remained to be seen how adequate they would be in face of the arrival of a large, predominantly lower-class coloured settlement in the immediate neighbourhood.[2]

At the time of this inquiry, the attitudes and behaviour of local workers towards coloured workers were hardly affected by contacts off the job or by housing or social frictions. But, as in earlier areas of coloured settlement, one could expect this interaction between the industrial society and the wider society to increase.

Of the other immigrant groups to Britain only the Jews and the Anglo-Indian community seemed to reside in Croydon in any noticeable numbers.

The Jewish community in Croydon is small, inconspicuous, and of fairly recent origin. The congregation was established in 1900 and the present Jewish population is estimated at about 400 families, of which 300 are members of the synagogue. The overwhelming

[1] *Croydon Advertiser*, 6 October 1961.

[2] As one local upper middle-class informant told me: 'Until recently the Croydonian's first-hand stereotype of a coloured person was that of a student or professional. Since Driscoll started up his International Language Club just before the War they've been used to seeing a certain amount of coloured faces about the street but they were all of that type.' Attitudes to coloured people with such a background seem to have been reasonably tolerant and kindly in the 1950s, if we may judge by the testimony of Ruth Khama, who lived in Addiscombe for two years with her husband and two children before they returned to Bechuanaland: contrasting it with Chelsea and Chipstead, where they had lived earlier, Mrs. Khama wrote: 'I think the two years we have spent in Addiscombe have been the happiest of our six years in exile. People have seemed more friendly to us. Whenever I go shopping in the market with Seretse, people chat with us, and seem pleased to see us. Already with the news of our return to Bechuanaland only a few days old, we have received many messages of regret from neighbours.'

majority of these are said to be first-generation immigrants to Croydon, mainly from London, only 5 per cent. being second-generation residents. They have not settled in any particular area but are scattered all over the borough. Most are engaged in business, trade, or the professions, so that few were located in the industrial survey and then mainly on the technical or administrative staff.

The self-effacing and 'assimilating' Anglo-Indians were not at first easy to trace, but a fair number of Roman Catholic Anglo-Indians were finally located living in more or less the same lower-middle-class Addiscombe area as the Poles.[1] This residential association was not particularly surprising, since the majority of Anglo-Indians are probably closer in socio-economic level and cultural patterns to the Poles and other European immigrants than they are to the bulk of the West Indian working-class migrants. Their relatively low 'visibility' would also make it easier for them than for other, darker-coloured newcomers to find accommodation in a lower-middle-class area.

A few Indians and Pakistanis[2] were also found, living in the poorer, working-class districts settled by the Irish and West Indians. There were also some Asian students or professionals in the large, Victorian flatlet-houses and rooming-houses which have become a feature of some streets in such districts as the once-exclusive Park Hill area, south-east of East Croydon station.

[1] Two informants who had special ties with the Anglo-Indian community in India confirmed that Croydon had attracted a considerable settlement of Anglo-Indians ('a little Anglo-India'—as one called it). The other commented: 'Very often Anglo-Indians do not like to admit that they are anything but English. When they come to the United Kingdom they regard it as returning home in the same way as an ordinary Englishman does. I would strongly advise you to go cautiously about talking of immigration as they do not usually regard themselves as immigrants.'

Whereas in 1951 there was no separate Census enumeration of persons born in the Asian Commonwealth, the 1961 Croydon report showed 2,973 Indian-born residents (1,523 men; 1,450 women). In view of the balanced sex-ratio and the fact that 2,135 of this total were U.K. citizens, it seems probable that the majority of these Indian-born residents were British or Anglo-Indian, not Indian immigrants proper; for members of the two former groups who have settled in Britain constitute a considerable proportion of the total; most Indian students and recent Indian migrant workers have been men, and so far only a minority have brought their wives over to join them.

[2] See previous note on the numbers of Indian-born in 1961. The 1961 Census gave a total of 204 persons born in Pakistan (114 men, 90 women). Of these, 142 were United Kingdom citizens.

PART II
FIELDWORK REPORT

CHAPTER 4

FIELDWORK PROCEDURE

The main objects of this investigation were, first, to ascertain the distribution and general situation of the principal immigrant groups in Croydon industry, and then to consider how far each had moved towards industrial absorption and to identify the major factors which appeared to be speeding or slowing the absorptive processes in each case.

The inquiry had to be restricted in some way since it was clearly impossible to make a thorough survey of the 3,000 firms listed at the local employment exchange.[1] As the great majority employed only a handful of workers, however, it seemed improbable that many immigrants would be found among them, except in a self-employed capacity or in a family business (there were quite a number of these, particularly in catering).

(1) *The Preliminary Questionnaire*

On the basis of past fieldwork and the experience of the local employment exchange it at first seemed unlikely that many immigrants would be found in the sixty-nine firms employing between fifty and a hundred workers. In addition, previous experience in South London had shown that firms of this size had little time for or interest in such inquiries. A brief questionnaire was, however, sent out to all of them; this was designed to ascertain whether

[1] Initially this seemed the most comprehensive source, as compared with the 675 industrial properties and 940 warehouses, stores, and workshops known to the Borough of Croydon on 1 April 1958 (the number of employees in each being unknown). The Employment Exchange lists could not be absolutely accurate or up to date, but on the whole the information afforded by them proved adequate. Not every firm in Croydon was listed with the Exchange, but the lists covered almost all establishments with labour requirements which they could not meet from their own resources, a feature which emerged as one of particular importance for this study. The principal exception was in the hotel and catering industry—the handful of larger hotels and clubs, which certainly employed a number of immigrants, were not listed with the Exchange.

members of any of the main immigrant groups were or had been employed by the firm.

Thirty-seven or just over one-half of the sixty-nine firms returned a completed questionnaire. Four others were subsequently returned by the Post Office marked 'gone away'. It seemed reasonable, from past experience, to assume that the remaining twenty-eight non-respondents employed few or no immigrants.

The thirty-seven responding firms represented a wide range of industries, and between them they employed a total of some 3,400 workers. This figure included, or in some cases had included, a total of some 170 coloured workers from the Commonwealth, the majority being West Indian men. Also included were eighteen Poles, six Hungarians, six Germans, six Europeans of other nationalities, and over thirty Southern Irish migrants. It was not always possible to determine whether all these workers were still in the firm's employment but the majority certainly were. Thus, somewhat contrary to my expectations, it emerged that up to 5 per cent. of the labour force in these thirty-seven smallish firms could be 'coloured', up to 1·5 per cent. European and up to 1 per cent. Irish. In sum, up to 6·5 per cent. of this labour force could be composed of immigrant workers, excluding the Irish, although the actual percentage at that particular time was probably somewhat lower.

These immigrants were not, however, evenly distributed through the thirty-seven firms. Ten firms, most of them small or highly specialized, employed no immigrants at all. Another nine employed between 5 and 10 per cent. of immigrant labour of all origins. The overall average was brought up by one firm of whose labour force over 25 per cent. were West Indians. Three other firms (a store and two firms manufacturing precision instruments) employed Europeans but no coloured workers, while five firms employed no Europeans but only coloured workers. These included not only establishments offering heavy, low-paid work, but also, less predictably, a lithographic printer, and a firm manufacturing hospital equipment. The remaining nine firms employed a sprinkling of European and Commonwealth immigrants.

This preliminary questionnaire was useful not only because it indicated that, contrary to expectations, over half of these small firms in Croydon had already been willing to try out immigrant workers in an effort to solve the labour shortage, and that a somewhat higher proportion of immigrant workers was employed than had been expected from experience in nearby industrial areas.[1] In addition, the fact that thirty-two of the thirty-seven responding firms indicated their willingness to co-operate further in the inquiry, if called upon, seemed a happy augury for the main inquiry.

(2) *The Main Survey—Questionnaire and Interviews*

For the main investigation it was decided to interview management representatives of the ninety-eight firms employing 101 or more workers, wherever the number of immigrant workers employed seemed to merit this and wherever the management was willing to co-operate. It was realized that, while this approach would undoubtedly give a reasonably accurate picture of the numbers and distribution of immigrants and of employers' views of their qualities and abilities, working relationships and industrial adaptation would be seen through a more or less biased managerial lens.

On the other hand, the bias of management (including supervising) is in itself an essential element in such situations. For in most cases it is the management that has the final say as to whether immigrants (like all other workers) are hired, retained, trained, or fired, and the views and reactions of workers and unions are usually taken into account by management only in so far as they are sufficiently strong to affect production or labour relations within the firm. It was, therefore, as important to learn to what extent different managements were familiar with these views and took them into account as to interview shop-stewards and working-groups, even if time had permitted and all the management representatives been willing to arrange for such interviews.

Allowance had, however, to be made for the possibility that some employers might seek to shift the responsibility for their own reluctance to employ immigrants on to their labour force or the unions. Wherever possible, therefore, workers' and union reactions and information acquired from other informants on other occasions were used to fill in the picture outlined by management

[1] It was interesting to note that although in the initial approach and questionnaires I referred to immigrants in general, and European, Southern Irish, and Commonwealth immigrants in particular, most respondents assumed that I was referring to coloured immigrants only.

representatives. In the final stage of the inquiry, moreover, a more detailed study was made of three firms which exemplified diverse aspects of immigrant employment and the development of immigrant–host relations in the industrial situation, and it was possible to obtain a more rounded picture of the informal as well as the formal organization of the working societies through more systematic interviewing of union officials, shop-stewards, and some workers.[1]

The managements of the ninety-eight firms listed as employing 101 or more workers were approached by letter with a request for an interview to discuss their experience of employing European and Commonwealth immigrant workers. The letters were sent off in batches over a nine-month period, usually to firms in the same or related industrial categories.[2] This ensured that most interviews could be carried out fairly soon after the firm had replied and also that attention could be focused on one industry or type of work instead of switching from one to another and possibly missing certain clues and characteristics common to a particular industry which might be of significance in the processes of absorption.

The letters elicited an immediate response of approximately 60 per cent. This was subsequently increased to just 90 per cent. when a short questionnaire was sent to those firms which had not replied to the first request for an interview. The information given in these responses confirmed the supposition that most non-respondents were fairly small firms[3] with a low labour turnover, engaged for the most part on skilled or highly specialized work, and that they employed few or no immigrants. Of the remaining ten firms, three were connected with aircraft manufacture and repairs or with air transport and had moved or were moving out of the area because of the closing of Croydon Airport. Another six were small precision engineering firms. Of these, four refused an interview without giving any information, and two others did not reply at all. A small laundry firm also failed to reply.

The survey and analysis that follow in this section and the next are, therefore, based on information about eighty-eight establishments, representing a wide range of industries, trades, and occupa-

[1] See Part IV for these three studies carried out in late 1959 and early 1960.

[2] This nine-month period coincided with the ending of the moderate recession of 1956–8 and some allowance had to be made for the resulting changes in labour needs.

[3] i.e. employing 101–250 workers.

tions, and employing an approximate total of nearly 48,000 wage- and salary-earners, or two-fifths of the total of 115,000 registered workers in Croydon at this time.

The Interviews

Before turning to the main survey I should perhaps say more about the procedure adopted for the sixty interviews which were actually carried out with management representatives. The purpose of the interview was to obtain two kinds of information. First of all it was necessary to get a factual picture of the nature of the production or work and the skills involved; wages and conditions of work; the overall number of employees in various types of work and of immigrants in each category, now and earlier; the labour situation since the 1939–45 War and the labour turnover; the degree of joint consultation and unionization and the unions involved; the date of and reason for first employing various groups of immigrants; methods of selection and induction; and policy and practice over redundancy and promotion of local workers and immigrants.

Rather more impressionistic but equally necessary to round out the picture was the second kind of information, concerning: the informant's view of the working capacity and general characteristics of various immigrant individuals and groups; their observed behaviour and relationships with fellow-workers and supervisors on the bench, in the canteen and elsewhere; the extent to which they had been accepted and absorbed in the working community; general management–labour relations; the attitudes and behaviour of the old-established nucleus or core of local workers; the past and present status of the industry and the firm and the latter's ties with the local community; and the activities of any 'sponsors' or actively prejudiced persons in management or the labour force, and of leaders or cliques among the newcomers.

To sum up, it was hoped at the interview to get as complete a picture as possible not only of the formal but of the informal organization and also of the 'culture' of each establishment[1] viewed not so much as a unit of production (central as that aspect clearly is), but as a working community—in the words of Gordon Rattray Taylor, 'not so much a place where things are produced

[1] Jaques, Elliot, *The Changing Culture of a Factory*, London, Tavistock Publications, 1951, p. 251.

as a place in which people spend their lives: as an environment for living'.[1]

Accordingly a questionnaire was drawn up incorporating the various points listed above[2] and endeavouring to take into account all the factors that seemed likely to promote or impede the absorption of outsiders. This questionnaire was not, however, rigorously administered or even displayed prominently during interviews. After a few factual questions the interview tended, and was allowed, to develop freely and only from time to time was it guided back to particular points which had been omitted. Notes were taken in so far as this did not hinder the discussion but much of the most interesting information and comment emerged when the pencil was not in motion or with the proviso: 'Don't put this down.' Sometimes interesting and significant points emerged during a tour of the works, over coffee or lunch, or in a group discussion in a staff common room.

This rather informal approach produced a rather uneven body of information about different firms and any gaps had to be filled in later wherever this was possible. On the other hand, rigid adherence to a questionnaire would certainly have inhibited discussions which sometimes led to the emergence of situations and factors unconsidered in the original questionnaire.[3]

The interviews varied considerably in length, form, and atmosphere. None lasted less than one hour and over half ran to two or even three hours. Some informants were brief and businesslike, while others felt so enthusiastic about their establishment or the subject under discussion that it was difficult to terminate the interview. At eleven of the interviews one or more other informants lower in the managerial hierarchy were called in after a while to give more detailed information on particular departments, welfare, or other aspects of the work situation. Two interviews were joint sessions from the start; in one case with the personnel manager and several male and female personnel officers of a large mass-production firm, in the other with six working directors who headed the various craft sections of a family firm of building contractors. Some

[1] *Are Workers Human?*, London, Falcon Press, 1950, p. 20.

[2] See Appendix I for this questionnaire, slightly revised and expanded for the detailed studies of three establishments in Part IV.

[3] During interviews I was also concerned to gauge whether a particular firm would be suitable for a more detailed case-study and how much co-operation could be counted on for this purpose from the management.

interviews took place in the elegant remoteness of top management offices, others in small noisy offices sectioned off from the works, or in first-aid rooms; the latter were punctuated by the entry of employees with cut fingers, headaches, and the like. Despite such distractions these interviews afforded a glimpse of everyday working relationships and whenever possible the more formal interviews were augmented by a tour round the factory floor and canteen.

(3) *A Note on Management Informants*

Management informants fell into three main groups and their information tended to vary accordingly. These groups were: personnel officers, works managers, and managing directors. Almost all of the large and some of the medium-sized establishments had specialized executives or administrative staff to deal with personnel matters, although in some more conservative firms the individual or department was nominally concerned not with 'personnel' but with 'staff', 'labour', or 'welfare'. About one-third of the interviews included discussions with informants of this type and it was among them that most women informants were found.

On the whole, the 'personnel' informants tended to be more open-minded and human in approach to immigrant and labour problems in general than informants from the other two groups. There were, however, considerable differences of approach and also of status among personnel informants and these seemed to be roughly correlated with the character and policy of their firms.[1] In large, progressive firms the personnel staff were usually specially qualified, held high status in the managerial hierarchy, and exerted a considerable influence on employment policy. In smaller firms 'personnel' and welfare informants might be either harassed trouble-shooters coping with a series of human problems created by management, or efficient, cheerful, sympathetic individuals reflecting or perhaps influencing their particular industrial environment. One 'labour officer' at a large heavy engineering plant

[1] At a conference organized early in 1964 by the Birmingham College of Advanced Technology, for teachers of personnel management, Joan Woodward distinguished two strands in contemporary personnel work: first, that which differs little from the (mainly routine administrative) work done by the original welfare officers or labour managers, and secondly, the emergent tendency for the personnel managers to 'be involved in' the actual process of management (*New Society*, 6 February 1964, pp. 19–20).

exemplified the latter type. He had been with the firm since he left school, described himself as 'self-made', and had a pleasant, tolerant, quietly authoritative personality. The following passage illustrates both this approach to his work and the social climate of the firm for which he worked.

This is a traditional sort of place and not too large. Just the right size so that I can handle all comers personally and know everyone. One-third of our labour force belong to the 'Quarter-Century Club' and many have worked here much longer than that. Labour relations are good and there's never been a strike in the firm. We have suffered from a certain degree of labour shortage but not to the extent that we would take on just anybody. We look for normally fit men who want a settled job with good working and welfare conditions. We've tried various groups of immigrants to combat the shortage, after consultation with the unions, but only those who can make the grade and fit in socially have lasted.[1]

In a handful of firms a rather specific type of personnel officer was encountered. This was the ex-officer, often appointed not for his training in personnel management but for his ability to 'handle men'. In a few cases these informants proved to have strongly hostile views about coloured workers—an attitude which I have elsewhere called the 'wog complex'.[2] It was not surprising to learn that the experiment of employing coloured workers in these firms had not been particularly successful.[3] One such informant said: 'We've no dark-coloured workers. I'll take British nationals from Hong Kong. We've had applications from Anglo-Indians but I'd be the last to take them on after years of experience of them in the R.A.F. in India and Egypt.'

Some medium-sized (251–500 labour force) establishments, particularly those concerned with a male labour force, did not have a specific 'personnel' staff and interviews were conducted with works managers or managing directors. Sometimes a supervisor or nurse would be called in to give details of working relations or welfare and health problems. In almost all interviews with smaller firms (101–250 employees) the informant was the managing director.

Most of the works managers interviewed had risen from the

[1] See pp. 74–81.
[2] See *Dark Strangers* (Tavistock), pp. 233–4.
[3] See pp. 112–13.

factory floor and their approach to the work situation, while it might be authoritarian or democratic in manner, tended to be more directly concerned with production and less with human problems than that of the 'personnel' informant. In relation to newcomers, however, these informants often seemed to reflect and share the general viewpoint of their firm's lower supervisory staff, and also of the long-term labour-core.

Some managing directors were similar in background and attitudes to the 'works manager' type. Others, however, conformed to no particular type but made up a wide range of gifted, forceful, individualistic, even eccentric people whose personalities appeared to be strongly stamped on the small industrial communities at whose head they stood.[1]

These, then, were the variously focused eyes through which I viewed the absorption of immigrant workers in Croydon industry —those of qualified personnel managers, semi-amateur personnel officers, welfare officers, nurses, works managers, supervisors, departmental heads, directors, and idiosyncratic owner-managers. Some omissions, inaccuracies, and slanted presentations were inevitable, but as far as possible these were remedied or counteracted by follow-up calls and by cross-checking with other informants and sources.

[1] See, for instance, the interview with the Managing Director of Firm B in the Light Industrial sector (pp. 109–10).

CHAPTER 5

THE GENERAL SURVEY

METHOD OF CLASSIFICATION

The 100-plus firms were originally grouped according to the Ministry of Labour's standard industrial classification. For the purposes of this survey the industrial groupings were arranged (with some minor readjustments and subdivisions) into four main industrial sectors: (1) 'light' engineering; (2) 'heavy' industry, including heavy engineering, other heavy industries, building and contracting, and public transport and utilities; (3) the 'consumer' sector, covering various light industries, the garment trade, laundry and dry cleaning, and food production and distribution; (4) the white-collar and professional sector, covering mainly service industries and comprising the retail trade, including automobile sales and repairs, clerical work, printing, local government service, and the hospital service.

The main initial criteria for this classification were: the type of manufacture or service, the nature and status of the work done (light, heavy, skilled, semi-skilled, unskilled, regular, seasonal, etc.), and the sex of the majority of the labour force.

These, along with other differences, seemed to confer a distinctive character and culture on each sector;[1] and as the fieldwork progressed it became increasingly clear that such distinctions were important for the analysis of the processes of immigrant absorption in industry.

FIELDWORK REPORT

It may be asked why the reports should have been been published in such detail. One reason is that in a pioneer inquiry of this kind later researchers often find it useful to have available a number of straightforward accounts of actual situations, which they may then

[1] See pp. 264f.

be able to subject to further analysis. More important, however, I wished, by describing each individual firm, to emphasize once again not only the similarities but also the differences produced by the combination and weighting of different factors or variables in apparently similar situations. These differences emerge even more strongly in the three firms studied in detail; here immigrant–host relationships and degrees of immigrant absorption were found to differ between one department and another, between sections and primary working groups within a department and between differing occupational status groups.

(1) *The Light Engineering Sector*

As the most important factor that induces employers to try a new and strange source of labour appears to be a chronic, large-scale labour shortage, we may begin the field reports with a survey of the situation within the largest, fastest-expanding, and most labour-hungry industrial sector in Croydon, that concerned with light engineering. This sector had a total labour force of over 18,000. It was found to employ nearly two-fifths of all the immigrants employed in Croydon's 100-plus firms; within the sector immigrants constituted nearly 5 per cent. of the works labour force and 4·5 per cent. of the total.

All but two of the '100-plus' engineering firms in Croydon fell into this class. The situation in the two fairly large firms engaged in heavy engineering was found to be very different and is described in the second section.

As the investigation proceeded in the light engineering sector, it was found that the situation was considerably affected by the degree of skill required and the degree of mechanization and automation reached in individual firms. Accordingly the twenty light engineering firms surveyed were subdivided into three sub-sectors: (*a*) those firms which were engaged on highly skilled work (and which usually employed a majority of men); (*b*) those firms where the production process involved various skills and degrees of skill (usually with a mixed labour force); and (*c*) the large, mass-production firms where the production processes had been broken down into a large number of operations requiring little or no skill and only a short training. Such firms usually had a large female labour force.

(a) *The 'Skilled' Firms*

Information was collected about twelve '100-plus' firms in this group, most of them engaged in the manufacture of specialized precision instruments. They employed an estimated total of over 6,000 wage- and salary-earners, mostly men.[1] Two of them employed between 1,000 and 1,500 workers, two had over 500, while three fell into the 251–500 group, and the remaining five employed between 100 and 250 workers.

Firm A employed over 900 men and about 550 women on the works side.[2] It produced and repaired watches as well as other scientific instruments. Most men required watchmaking or other skills, while the women's work was very delicate and required excellent eyesight and great dexterity. The firm was old-established but moved to Croydon only after the Second World War. As a consequence the entire labour force had to be built up from scratch. The work was, however, agreeable and well enough paid to attract many work-seekers; labour turnover is low and the firm's labour situation has not been particularly difficult in recent years.

Firm A's main labour problem had been a shortage of trained watchmakers. This was one of the trades taught in the Polish Resettlement Corps and in 1947–8 the firm took on a considerable number of Poles, together with other European exiles and refugees. A fair proportion of these were still with the firm at this time. Most departments were well unionized (A.E.U., E.T.U., Woodworkers' and Transport and General Workers' Union); but although the unions were not officially consulted before taking on European or coloured workers there had been no objections from the unions or workers to their employment nor demands for redundancy priorities, even in a recent case where a fair number of workers had to be laid off.

Nearly 4 per cent. of Firm A's labour force consisted of European or Commonwealth immigrants: about half of these immigrants were coloured. The two largest contingents consisted of fourteen Polish men, twelve of them watchmakers, and sixteen West Indians,

[1] The total number employed in '100-plus' firms in this skilled group at this time would in fact have been somewhat larger, since it included six of the ten firms, most of them small, which refused co-operation, failed to answer, gave completely inadequate information, or were moving out of the area.

[2] It also employed a large sales staff operating from an office in Central London; there were no immigrants among the salesmen.

of whom thirteen were women. There were also Ukrainians, Latvians, Czechs, Germans, Spaniards, Italians, Swiss (including one charge-hand), Anglo-Indians, Indians, and a West African costing clerk. All the Anglo-Indian, Indian, and West Indian men had acquired some jewellers' skills before migrating ('though not as much as they think'—according to my informant) and were engaged on skilled work. In this cosmopolitan assembly only Irish migrants were lacking. The personnel officer informed me that most departmental managers regarded them as 'ham-handed' and would not accept them.

The European immigrants were widely distributed through the various departments, but some managers still refused to take coloured workers. It was, however, interesting to note that in this firm the traditionally exclusive and insular A.E.U. preserve, the machine-shop, contained two Poles, two Swiss, a German, and an Anglo-Indian.

Firm A had been able to apply a very selective employment policy and informant expressed satisfaction with the performance of the various immigrant workers. Nor had it experienced to any great extent the frictions that arise between immigrants and local workers in some firms over behavioural, political, and other differences; this was perhaps because most of the newcomers were skilled workers, some even coming from a middle-class background, and they mixed easily with the local workers in the activities of the social club.

Firm B manufactured scientific instruments and employed some 500 on the works side. It was a pre-1939 firm whose production and labour force soared dramatically during the War. After the War there were drastic cut-backs, the most recent having occurred in 1956. Half of the present labour force had been there for ten years or more and the supervisors and foremen had twenty or thirty years' service. The latest cut-back had hardly affected the skilled workers, immigrant or other, of whom there was still a shortage.[1]

The skills required were similar to those needed by Firm A and my informant at Firm B suspected that many immigrant skilled workers formerly employed here had moved to Firm A, because it paid a higher hourly rate.

After the War Firm B took on a number of Poles, mainly watch-

[1] The cut-back did, however, coincide with the arrival and placing of Hungarian refugees and this firm was, therefore, unable to accept any of them.

makers trained by the P.R.C., of these only three remained. The others probably did leave for the reason given—that they could get better-paid work elsewhere—but the fact that this firm until recently had a German supervisor (a former prisoner-of-war) may not have been without influence.

Firm B was one of the earliest in Croydon to start employing West Indians. In 1948 its advertisements for skilled workers brought a number of replies from West Indians who had served in the R.A.F. and were more or less skilled. Only one of these early applicants still remained, but about fifty West Indian men and women had passed through the firm since then. The personnel officer commented:

> About 50 per cent. of the women have been satisfactory workers but they're all rather slow. Two foremen wouldn't have them at all because they didn't think them sufficiently skilled. Recently applicants have been no good—unskilled and truculent when we tell them there's nothing for them. The West Indians we've had mixed in fairly well and we never had any complaints about cleanliness, eating habits or aggressiveness. The Anglo-Indians, of whom we've got four now, including two staff trainees, want to be accepted and they are. The firm prefers them to any other group. As for the Irish, we have some in less skilled work but I personally regard them as aliens and would treat them as such.

The other large firm in this sub-sector, Firm C, presented a very different picture. It was one of the oldest firms in Croydon and had a large nucleus of stable local labour. About 50 per cent. of its male workers were skilled and most of the remainder semi-skilled. Firm C had some Indian industrial links and had employed Indians, though not in great numbers, since before the 1939–45 War. This was, however, a special case and other immigrants had been tried only because of the post-war labour shortage. At this time the firm employed about 1·5 per cent. of immigrants, consisting of one Polish and two Indian skilled workers and one Polish, one Indian, and eight 'Jamaican' labourers. Two Hungarians had been taken on in 1956, but they did not stay long. 'Both had a chip on their shoulder and it wasn't a success.' The personnel manager's name suggested that he is of Irish extraction, but he did not take on many Irish migrants:

> They are rather a curse and I'd rather have a Jamaican any day. Their turnover's much lower. We made some mistakes with West Indians in

the early days but now we're careful over selection. Those that we have work as well as anybody else and they're treated the same as everybody else in the shop. They live locally and don't leave readily—we pay London rates and individual bonuses.

Labour relations between management and workers and between local workers and immigrants were said to be generally good. I was told:

The unions' attitude is favourable so long as we pay the rate for the job, although one of the A.E.U. men was a bit suspicious about the Pole on political grounds. There have been no requests for special redundancy agreements to provide for foreigners or coloured workers being put off first. In any case we wouldn't agree to any such conditions, but I must admit to the fact that I would employ white labour whenever possible. I have that amount of prejudice. As for skills, the management decides who is skilled and the men make no difficulty about upgrading so long as the man's capacity is checked by the union. In fact, I was surprised not to get a reaction from the tool-makers when we took on two dusky Indians from another firm. But these two are good workers and the foremen and most of the men are only interested in the job and there's no shop-steward. I don't know how they'd feel about working under an Indian but there are so many long-service workers that the question of promotion is unlikely to arise. As for personal habits, I've had no particular complaints.

Firm D had also been established in the Croydon area for a long time and had a considerable nucleus of workers who had been with the firm for thirty or forty years. It was engaged on vehicle manufacturing and general light engineering. In recent years it had been compelled to reduce its semi-skilled and unskilled labour force almost by half, and was employing some 400 workers and 100 staff when I visited it. Most of the work was highly skilled and there was still a shortage of skilled men.

Despite the redundancy Firm D employed about thirty immigrants, i.e. 7 per cent. of its total labour force. These included a score of Poles, most of them skilled, and some Indians and Anglo-Indians, of whom one was a records clerk on the staff, while three others were apprentices. In past years it had also employed Czechs and Hungarians and a large contingent of Indians. Of the dozen or so labourers in the firm nearly half were West Indians.

Within limits Firm D was a 'good' firm for Europeans and Anglo-Indians; but less so, it seemed, for most coloured workers. The personnel manager had formed very definite views on the working qualities of the different groups:

> Most of the European workers are skilled, particularly the Hungarians. On the other hand, most coloured workers[1] are unskilled or semi-skilled at best and no skilled West Indian has ever applied. Most of them can't even drive a car. The Europeans generally settle down but coloured workers don't, with one or two shining exceptions. For example, we had one labourer who's now a semi-skilled machinist. But most of the darkies are youngish and they have itchy feet. In British industry all labourers must expect to be ordered about by every Tom, Dick, and Harry and not just by the chargehand, but the coloured boys often resent that. Also, labouring in the engineering industry is poorly paid compared with road work and building. The result is that they never stay long—not more than two years at the most. This has made me chary of taking them on, though the darkies are suited to engineering. They might be good at packing, like women, but there's very little of that here.

Firm D was an open shop but there were some shop-stewards and the majority of employees were said to belong to a union (A.E.U. or Sheet Metal Workers). No objections had ever been raised by unions or workers in general against the employment of any immigrant groups. No special redundancy agreements existed, but if there were to be further redundancy in practice it was thought that some trouble might arise. My informant said: 'I just don't want to think about it—but the firm certainly wouldn't dismiss men just because of their colour.'

The local workers in this firm seemed to have accepted coloured workers without particular friction:

> We've never had any bother sufficiently large to reach management level over personal habits. There's no voluntary segregation in the canteen and some of the Nigerians in particular are very endearing. But off the job the darkies don't seem to participate much in social or sporting events, of which there are quite a lot here.

The personnel manager's own views could have been one of the important factors conditioning the acceptance of immigrants, particularly coloured workers in Firm D. He was more expansive on the subject than most informants and his remarks illustrated

[1] This informant appeared to be roughly equating 'coloured' worker with 'West Indian' and 'African'.

his own rather benevolent and paternalistic version of the 'wog complex':

> I had a lot of experience of coloured people during the war in the Army. Fundamentally they are all children compared with our centuries of civilization. If they could accept that situation all would be well but some don't. We freed the colonial territories too soon and they're like self-confident 'L' drivers.

In answer to a question about the possible promotion of immigrant workers this informant was one of the few to make it clear that he was ascribing his own bias to others rather than explaining his own behaviour in terms of other people's bias:

> It hasn't been considered because of the existence of a nucleus of long-service workers. In theory, promotion would be open to those who are qualified but I would be against promoting any immigrants unless they were quite outstanding. I myself would feel an instinctive resentment against such promotion over my head and I expect the men would too.

Firm E, with about 420 employees in all, was the local subsidiary of a very large vehicle manufacturers. Most of the work was highly skilled and highly paid and thus attracted the cream of skilled male applicants. A few skilled Polish workers were employed and one was a shop-steward. Hungarians were accepted at the end of 1956, but their ignorance of the English language apparently constituted a problem and none were left at the time of the interview. Nor were there any coloured workers, although a few West Indians had been employed in unskilled jobs there in the past. The firm was said to be 'sympathetic to the problem of coloured workers', but in practice there seemed to be a covert ban on taking on any more of them for the time being.

The situation in most of the seven remaining medium and smaller firms in the 'skilled' section was fairly uniform. Most of the work was skilled, there was a low labour turnover and a large nucleus of local long-service workers. Such firms are not large enough nor in sufficiently dire need of labour to experiment with or train outsiders on a long-term basis. Instead, remedies tend to be sought in improved techniques and machinery. For instance, one of these firms has increased its production of precision instruments fourfold over ten years without greatly increasing its labour force.

The percentage of all immigrant workers employed in six of these firms ranged from nil to about 3 per cent. Firm F had tried European and Commonwealth workers in the past, but no longer did so. The reason given was:

We are engaged in the manufacture of very fine instruments which calls for highly skilled and specialized technicians, and our experiences have been that these immigrants have not had that type of experience.

Firm G was engaged in a similar type of manufacture. The management was not anxious to grant an interview but wrote guardedly to say that, while a 'fair percentage' of such workers were employed, past experience showed that these groups did not provide the 'type of labour in which we are interested'. Firm H had never employed more than one or two immigrants of any group and clearly regarded them as unskilled. Firm I, which was a closed shop and employed only skilled men and apprentices, claimed to follow a non-discriminatory policy. It had in fact never employed Poles, Hungarians, or West Indians, but did have a number of Indians and had in recent years also employed some African graduate scientists on its staff.

The small firms J and K differed somewhat from the other precision engineering firms in that part of their manufacturing process involved the rare and specialized skill of glass-blowing, whose practitioners were said to be in exceptionally short supply. Firm J was efficient, progressive, and well-established in the area. It prided itself on good labour relations: 'We try to get a happy atmosphere and we try to get people to enjoy their work here.' Its labour force of 170 included two Poles, one German, and two Indians, who were regarded as part of the permanent labour force. They were treated as individuals and no differences of working performance or general behaviour had been noted. The firm was still recruiting workers from any source, 'provided they meet the job specification'.

Firm K differed from Firm J in that it moved into the area only after the War and was, therefore, compelled to build up a new labour force locally. It was sited on the periphery of the Croydon area and drew most of its workers from a large housing estate in the neighbourhood:

[1] See *The British Glass Industry*, The Times Publishing Co., 1966.

Labour turnover is fairly low and we're gradually building up a stable nucleus, although we haven't yet had time to become a family affair. We're never held up for labour but I'd rather go without than take the wrong type. It's a small firm and we need jolly types here.

Like most small establishments, Firm K had a rather individual atmosphere, considerably influenced by the personality of its managing director. It was run on lines of paternalistic efficiency, and there was no recognized union, but management–labour relations appeared to be informal and good. Coloured workers had been an accepted part of the less skilled labour force for the last ten years. Like many employers, however, my informant had developed a preference for one particular group, in this case West Africans (mostly Nigerians). Five were with the firm at this time and there was also an Indian part-time student. This represented over 3 per cent. of the whole staff. My informant did not remember employing or even seeing European applicants. Of the West Africans he said:

I prefer them to West Indians, whose turnover is too high. Most of them come here from the Employment Exchange, which knows our requirements and does a good job of preliminary sorting out. Then they have to walk up the path to the office. It's a long walk and I can tell whether they'll do or not before they get to the door.

I'm satisfied with the way they do their work and they're very popular with the other workers. This is probably because we had a dear old West African boy here for years as a night-watchman. He was a jolly black nigger type and everybody liked him. This left a good flavour and made it easier for the rest to fit in. Another reason is that we never have more than four or five on the labour strength at a time. I would expect trouble if the percentage rose to 15 or 29 per cent. If there were ever to be redundancy the rule would be 'first in, last out' and the coloured workers would be treated like anyone else.

Firm L provided an even more notable example of a small firm with a highly individual character. Like Firm K, it had only moved to the area since the War and had been compelled to build up and expand its labour force more or less from scratch: 'We were new in the area and consequently suspect. But we made our connexions and got local recommendations as a good firm to work in.' The work was skilled and specialized, but there was no union and no formal apprenticeship.

This firm was situated in the Purley Way industrial area and was more easily accessible than Firm K. It had therefore been able to tap larger sources of skilled labour.

In 1947 we timidly engaged a few Poles from the Resettlement Corps. This went down with no difficulty and indeed there was a time about 1948–9 when it seemed as if we might have too many P.R.C. chaps. A little later we took on some E.V.W.s and latter several German wives of local English workers, some Anglo-Indians and West Indians. We're always prepared to take on coloured workers who are skilled but not labourers. Black labourers have proved a poor proposition and impermanent. We want men who will stay, though we make an exception for Irish migrants who come for in labouring jobs in the winter, when the building trade's slack.

Our employment policy is a pretty liberal one. There's no staff department—the half-dozen foremen engage their own labour and there is a woman on the staff side who acts as an unofficial personnel officer and filter for all applicants. We have only one limiting principle. We wouldn't want to employ too many of one race or group in the same shop for fear of their forming their own little cliques.

At this time immigrants formed about 9 per cent. of Firm L's total staff. They included half a dozen Poles and one Hungarian from the Polish Resettlement Corps and E.V.W. periods. All were now on the staff or in fairly senior technical positions. There were also quite a number of more recently joined East European refugees, German women, Anglo-Indians, and West Indians, one of the latter being a shorthand-typist in the office.

The interview at Firm L lasted nearly two hours and gradually became a discussion group, with several supervisors giving their views and experience. As time went on an increasing number of immigrants were identified, usually with the qualification: 'Oh yes, I suppose so-and-so's a Pole [or Anglo-Indian] but we don't think of him [or her] in that way.' This bore out the managing director's earlier statement:

We like to judge each individual on his merits and not to generalize on the grounds of origin or race. On and off the job there's a pleasant, intimate atmosphere. Everyone fits in together and all of them seem to go to the social club. The Poles always talk to each other in English and don't seem to cling together. One of the West Indians is so anglicized that we hardly think of him as West Indian. And then there's old N——; he's really an Anglo-Indian but we inherited him with the building and he's an institution. As for promotion, you've heard how the Poles are accepted. They've been here a long time—but so far as coloured workers are concerned I think that at present it might cause a bit of friction if one were to put them over others.

At Firm L the traditionally isolationist engineering department differed from the others in displaying a certain resistance to outsiders. This resistance was fully shared and probably influenced by its foreman:

> Recently I took on a dusky welder. He's a good worker but I've put him on an individual job in an isolated part of the shop. I wouldn't put another man with him for fear of trouble. He keeps himself to himself. We've just lost a Ukrainian. He was what I'd call artful and very unpopular. I don't want any men of his race [*sic*]. We've had Poles in the shop but I don't think a Pole could hold a position of authority in it.

It would have been interesting to carry out a detailed case study of this firm but my informant felt that this would be undesirable, for reasons which were given by several other smaller firms which felt that they were absorbing their immigrant workers satisfactorily: 'We have such an easy, unselfconscious atmosphere here that I would not like it disturbed. It's all right to carry out that sort of inquiry in the larger firms but here we're so small that everyone would be talking about it and it might upset the *status quo*.'

The twelve firms in this 'skilled' section of light engineering employed a fairly large number of immigrants, about 152 in all, mostly men. Of this total ten held various staff jobs, about a hundred were doing skilled work and only about forty were in the smaller semi-skilled and unskilled class. Two-thirds of the skilled immigrants were from Europe; about half of them being Poles. Twenty-five of the thirty-four skilled workers from the Commonwealth were Indian or Anglo-Indian while only eight were West Indian. The reason given for this by most informants was the West Indian applicants' lack of the necessary skills and qualifications. The overall skilled total may appear modest, but it was probably in the neighbourhood of 3 to 4 per cent. of the total number of skilled male workers employed in these twelve firms, that is to say of what was probably the best-paid, most skilled, and highest status group of skilled workers in the area. This finding runs counter to the general supposition that immigrants must always be content with the least attractive, lowest paid, least skilled jobs.

In this mainly skilled sub-sector of light engineering the craft unions were strong in most firms. It was noted that only in a firm in which there was little or no union organization (Firm L) was there much suggestion of hostility to outsiders (and there only in the engineering department). Otherwise, relatively little resistance from skilled workers or unions to the entry of outsiders could be definitely established in this section, whether or not they were officially consulted by management about the employment of various immigrant groups. Such hostility could have existed in the medium-sized firms F, G, and H, about which information was scanty; but if so one might have expected management informants to have mentioned it rather than to attribute their rather unfavourable policy to their own views and to the immigrants' lack of skills.

In this section the chronic shortage of skilled labour had, it seemed, not only driven many managements to try out new sources of labour but also reduced skilled labour's resistance to the entry of newcomers. Highly paid, working in good conditions, and enjoying a high status both in industry and in the local community, most local skilled workers were sufficiently protected by the high standards and scarcity value of their craft to tolerate the entry of a few score qualified outsiders without undue apprehension. It would, however, be true to say that most skilled immigrants were found in open shops and in rather unusual skilled jobs such as watchmaking and glass-blowing.

In this group of firms management attitudes and the working capacity or potentiality of particular immigrant groups appeared, in fact, to have had the greatest influence on the situation. All three firms (A, K, and L) which moved into the area after the War and were compelled to build up a stable nucleus of workers from scratch had shown particular willingness to try out immigrant labour. Firm L was indeed, the firm in which the absorption of immigrants had proceeded farthest and most successfully.

Size was another factor which seemed to be of some importance. The firms with satisfactory experience of immigrant workers were firms A, B, D, and perhaps E of the five '500-plus' firms, and K and L of the small firms. The views and experience of the two medium-sized firms, F and G, were unfavourable. The explanation for this might be that the larger firms had greater absorptive capacity and facilities for experimenting with the employment of groups of newcomers, while the small firms could absorb them individually or in twos and threes on a more individual and informal basis.

Yet another factor that had influenced the situation was the fairly obvious one of length of settlement. It was not surprising to find that, other considerations apart, there were more Poles and other refugees in skilled work than there were representatives of the more recently arrived Asians and West Indians. Ten years ago, on the other hand, even Poles with perfectly acceptable skills were knocking their heads in vain against the closed doors of the craft unions. The element of duration is usually accompanied by that of permanency of intention. Recently arrived immigrants who intend to return home after a year or so tend to seek high-paid work and overtime rather than to embark on the more arduous process of acquiring or improving their formal skills. In Croydon this still applied to most West Indians as much as it had for decades applied to the majority of Irish migrants.

Attention should also be drawn to the way in which particular firms appeared to favour particular immigrant groups and to dislike or avoid others. This 'favoured nation' policy was often something more than a mere pragmatic assessment of qualifications and suitability. Probably the main principle behind such differentiation was that of 'like attracts like'. If a newcomer proved a good worker and workmate, employers and fellow-workers would look all the more favourably upon others from the same group. And when jobs were vacant the immigrant himself was likely to 'sponsor' suitable applicants from among his relations or friends, a process that was welcomed by some managements as a preliminary selection device.

The survey of the 'skilled' engineering firms showed how the numerically larger immigrant groups tend to cluster in particular establishments. When such 'clustering' and such 'favoured nations' were found in a firm there could also be a corresponding tendency to avoid employing immigrants from other groups who were or were thought to be incompatible with the favoured group. For instance, Poles were rarely found together in the same work-group or shop with Germans, or West Indians with West Africans. The emergence of the favoured nation in a firm could, of course, be accidental and arbitrary, depending as it did on personal relationships and the calibre and performance of a few pioneering individuals. The arrangement had, however, its objective aspect, in that the preferred group or groups usually met the particular requirements of the work and the firm.[1] In this 'skilled' sector firms looked not only for skilled workers but for those who were likely to stay for a considerable time. Recent migrants from Southern Ireland were therefore regarded with disfavour even if they had the required skills, while for labouring jobs West Indians or West Africans were generally preferred because of their reputedly lower turnover.

Another reason for 'sponsoring' and 'favoured nation' arrangements was found where firms had industrial or organizational links overseas. For instance, Firm A, a considerable employer of European skilled workers, was largely concerned with watchmaking, a traditionally European craft, and had European trade affiliations. And even in the conservative and insular establishment, Firm C, which was an old-established local institution, an exception was made for Indian workers because the firm had industrial links with India.

(b) *The 'Intermediate' Firms*

There were six firms in this 'intermediate' section, which employed fewer skilled workers and a majority of semi-skilled workers, male and female. Nearly two-thirds of the total of almost 4,000 workers and staff employed in this section worked in one large firm which was part of an immense Commonwealth-wide organization. The other five firms were far smaller, two falling within the medium-sized 251–500 category and three in the 101–250 group.

The large establishment, Firm A, suffered from the prevailing shortage of skilled labour. Until there was a cut-back in 1957 it also had difficulty in finding suitable semi-skilled operators and experimented with a number of different immigrant groups. The firm was 80 per cent. unionized; there was formal consultation with the unions before these experiments began and the unions were said to have taken a 'very fair-minded attitude', although there was some trouble from the A.E.U. concerning the Poles, on political grounds. The relative failure to absorb most newcomers appeared to be attributable to a certain rigidity of training methods

[1] Firm A, for instance, was aware that watchmaking was one of the trades taught to members of the Polish Resettlement Corps. It had employed Poles since 1947–8 and whenever watchmakers were needed, would insert a Polish-language advertisement in the *Polish Daily*.

and perhaps to rather unfavourable attitudes in the personnel department:

> We give everyone instruction before they go on to the shop floor but once there they are on their own and just get the odd hint from the supervisors. With the Poles and other East Europeans there was the language difficulty. This presented an acute problem of instruction. Six months ago we still had three Poles, but now they've drifted away like the rest. With the West Indians—both men and women—the problem was their extreme slowness. We've none of either group now and we don't encourage the Ministry of Labour to send them, though we'd consider a good coloured engineer if one turned up. As for the East Europeans, the firm does a lot of confidential government work and I wonder whether there isn't a risk of their being infiltrated by the Commies?

Firm A had, however, its 'favoured nation' group, consisting of seven Indians (the 'lighter-coloured ones') and Anglo-Indians, three in skilled jobs and one an apprentice. This seemed to be attributable to the fact that the organization had another plant in India.

Firm A's spokesman had not himself been long with the firm but had formed his views on coloured workers during his army service and in a factory in his Midlands home town. He expanded his theme well beyond the industrial situation:

> Up there we tried a dozen but only one was any good. The rest kept mooching about and congregating together. They were never where they should be and didn't do a great deal of work. I once found one of them asleep behind a shed and another crowned the supervisor with a brush. If the Government must let them come in why doesn't it train them in R.E.M.E. factories for six months after their arrival and house them in old army camps? I don't think they're quite ready for us yet. Not up to our ways of living. They're bringing whole streets down to their level in the Midlands—putting seven or eight in a room and charging £2 a head. They live on a bowl of rice and aren't particular how or where they sleep. Why not stop them coming in and making passes at Englishmen's daughters?

Of the two medium-sized firms one, Firm B, employed no immigrants at all and had never done so, with the exception of one Pole who stayed four months and two Anglo-Indian girl clerks. One of these had stayed with the firm for three years and was described as 'a very efficient worker and well conducted'.

Firm C presented a very different picture. This firm had been nearly forty years in Croydon and was described by its welfare officer as 'a thoroughly nice firm to work for'. It began as a small local firm, amalgamated with a larger group before the War and has since expanded steadily. There was a fair-sized nucleus of long-term labour, including the foremen. Most workers lived locally in Thornton Heath and turnover was low. There was no active union in the firm although it was thought that a few employees belonged to local branches of the Transport and General Workers' Union. Wages were above union rates and there was a bonus system for groups; this ensured good performance because the groups 'soon get rid of a passenger on their own'. Despite the pleasant atmosphere there was little social life within the works community and the social club had been disbanded several years before for lack of support.

Since the War this firm had employed Poles, Germans, Italians, Maltese, Dutch, and many Irish, who were not here regarded as outsiders, apparently because one of the supervisors was Irish and did the recruiting and selecting from settled local residents. At this time fifteen out of its 150 male employees were immigrants;[1] they consisted of two Maltese, three Poles, three Anglo-Indians, one Anglo-Coloured,[2] and six West Indians.[3] The Poles had been longest with the firm and it was said: 'They're part of the firm; any one of the foremen would take on more like them immediately.'

All but one of the West Indians had been with the firm for eighteen months or more; they were all working as labourers. A management informant commented:

They have the natural darkie slowness. Half of them don't even seem to know the name of the place where they worked before this, nor why

[1] Only two of the 150 female workers were, however, non-British (Italians).

[2] This man was one of the few British-born coloured adults (i.e. the offspring of earlier coloured immigrants and local mothers) located during the survey.

[3] This breakdown was given by the works manager (who added that his secretary was 'probably a Eurasian'), but a certain vagueness over precise ethnic origins prevailed in the firm. The welfare officer, who subsequently joined the discussion, mentioned a Pakistani and two Tunisians, while one of the foremen spoke of the Poles as Germans. It transpired that they were, in fact, Poles from Western Poland who had been conscripted into the German Army, and after deserting or being captured had been re-enrolled in the Polish Army. There were also six women (two Italians, four West Indians).

they left. The women were the slowest and we've only men left now. None of the foremen want to take on any more full-blooded coloured any more. It's not that they're prejudiced but the result of years of experience. I've never had any objection from the local workers, nor friction serious enough to reach management level. I don't think there will be as long as we keep the numbers low.

The sixth West Indian had just been taken on as a qualified paint-sprayer. Of him the Scots foreman said cautiously:

He's a real Cherry-Blossom type. It's too early to tell what sort of worker he is. He's only been in the country three weeks and must settle in. He knows how to handle a spray-gun but he's slow. I'm reserving my judgement.

Of the three smaller establishments, Firm D employed one Anglo-Indian out of a labour force of 150 and had employed only two other immigrants since the War. The major reasons for this situation seemed to be associated with the fact that the firm was mainly concerned with confidential government contract work and that the unions were strong and opposed to the entry of foreigners. Firms E and F, on the other hand, employed about 10 per cent. and 3 per cent. of immigrants respectively and were excellent examples of the small firm of character and individuality.

Firm E had been operating for thirty years in an old-established central industrial area and drew on a solid nucleus of long-term local labour. About 140 of its 200 operatives were women. The firm was described by my informant, the managing director, as 'rather a hilarious set-up'. A tour round the factory suggested that working relationships were unusually informal and intimate, probably as a result of the brisk, cheerful, and liberal personality of the young managing director himself.

This firm employed four Poles, one Hungarian, four Germans (two men, two women), one Indian, eight Anglo-Indians, and six West Indians. The Poles (all men) had been employed since 1948 and all had skilled or responsible jobs: one was a floor-inspector,[1] one a charge-hand, and the other two were in the tool-room. One of the latter was described as 'a mechanical genius but otherwise lacking. He was in a concentration camp and hasn't a word of English.' The Poles were said to be 'much more amenable to discipline than

[1] It was stressed that this one was 'not an ex-officer' but had the appropriate technical qualifications.

the locals or the West Indians'. The Hungarian was the best draughtsman in the firm, although some young Hungarians employed after 1956, reportedly proved less satisfactory. Of the Indian it was said, somewhat revealingly: 'He's an excellent worker. Would he be classed as an immigrant?' The Anglo-Indians were also said to be in responsible jobs. Most of the West Indians were, however, regarded as 'of poor working quality, slow and only suitable for labouring'. The youngish works manager, who joined in the interview later, expressed himself with greater directness on the subject of what he termed 'my black cherubs' and asked quizzically: 'Do they really have tails, as some of our girls think, or do they cut them off before they come?'

There were many union members in this firm but there was no shop-steward or convenor. The local labour force had never objected to the presence of coloured or other immigrant workers and in recent redundancies there was no call for them to go first. On the other hand, certain reservations clearly remained. My informant said:

> Last July we put off a lot and in August we got some unexpectedly early orders. This presented a tricky situation as we couldn't get all our local people back. Someone suggested taking on coloured workers but it was obvious we would have a riot on our hands.[1] Finally we compromised and took a few *after* we'd taken on some whites.

In this close-knit working community the managing director was fully aware of the informal social network within his labour force:

> The Anglo-Indians look upon themselves as English and white and join the cliques as individuals. The Poles join in too and don't form a Polish clique. The coloured girls, on the other hand, aren't yet included in the cliques though there's absolutely no bar against them. Of course we've only been taking them on for three or four years.

Only in the office has Firm E experienced any staff resistance to the employment of outsiders:

> We've never had any coloured applications for clerical work but some time ago we did try to fit an Indian who used to manage a large business in Karachi into the sales office. The manager there wouldn't buy it,

[1] Such an action would presumably have laid the management open to suspicions of taking on immigrants with a view to undermining the cohesion of the local labour-force and perhaps even using them to undercut established wages.

however, because of staff objections and possible difficulties with the public. Finally we found him a responsible job on the works side.

Firm F was old-established in the Norbury district and is best described not as 'hilarious' but as 'select'. It employed some 125 men and the same number of women, mostly semi-skilled, on the manufacture of scientific instruments. My informant, a woman welfare officer, said:

> Most of our labour is local and the turnover is low. The girls are all very smart and it isn't by any means an ordinary industrial set-up. We have no labour shortage and if we have to put off nice people we always write and notify them as soon as we can take them back again. Only the tool-room is an A.E.U. closed shop, but some of the other workers belong to the T. and G.W.U. Industrial relations are good and we never have any trouble. Even in the 1957 strike only a few came out.[1]

When visited, this firm employed three Anglo-Indian men (one skilled fitter, one store-keeper, and one labourer), one Malay, and a West Indian. On the female side there were three; a German clerical worker, a Maltese, and an Irishwoman. In earlier years the firm had also employed Poles, a Hungarian, and some Irishmen. Speaking about the working performance and behaviour of its immigrant workers my informant commented:

> Those that we have now all conform to our specific requirements. We like them to take an interest in the work and try to educate themselves. The Hungarian, for instance, was an exceptionally good worker and after learning English he went on to technical college. The Malay is all right and he's married to an English girl. And with us appearance is very important, even in the works. The one West Indian we have is very nice-looking—not at all negroid. He dresses well without being flashy, comes to the socials and mixes in well. We get a lot of West Indian applicants but most of them just won't do. They're Teddy-boy types and would create trouble. Besides we've found from experience that in a small firm like this we can't manage more than one West Indian at a time—otherwise they gang up and their work slows down. A single one takes his time from the rest.

Relations between immigrants and other workers were said to be good and no friction, objections to the employment of immigrants or demands for them to be laid off first had been reported in this

[1] The reference here is to the national strike called by the Amalgamated Engineering Union from 23 March to 3 April 1957 (see Ministry of Labour *Gazette*, May 1958).

firm, despite fairly frequent though temporary and minor lay-offs. The management did, however, exercise considerable caution when taking on immigrants among the new workers hired after such a redundancy. My informant also felt that local workers might resent the promotion of immigrants to supervisory posts: 'An Anglo-Indian might be acceptable but I just can't imagine it with a West Indian. The women might take a more easy-going view of it than the men. Of course, the West Indians we have are only labourers.'

As in many firms, the A.E.U. tool-shop in Firm F presented a different picture from the rest of the factory, according to the welfare officer:

> It's virtually a factory on its own and we have to be careful. In the past one or two Poles worked there but the supervisor was rather against them. He doesn't seem too keen on West Indians either, though the management insists that he interviews any sent to us by the labour exchange who claim to be skilled. Recently there was a minor incident—a West Indian who was being questioned about his skills got aggressive and walked out. The shop-steward there is more understanding and if the decision depended on him would probably accept them.

Looking back over the six firms in this predominantly semi-skilled' sub-sector of light engineering one could note that there were relatively fewer immigrant workers here than in the 'skilled' sub-sector or in the 'mass-production' sub-sector. This could be due to the fact that there had not since the 1956–7 recession been so desperate a shortage of semi-skilled labour, while skilled labour remained in chronically short supply. Out of nearly 3,000 employees on the works side and 1,000 or more staff sixty (or 1·5 per cent.) were immigrants, most of them being men from the Commonwealth. The largest contingents were Anglo-Indians (18), West Indians (13), and Poles (7). The Irish, who are not included in the count, were found in considerable strength only in one firm (C). There were proportionately more immigrants in the small group of skilled workers than in the large semi-skilled group. Of these thirteen, eight were European, five Anglo-Indian. Despite the overall shortage, there were no West Indians in skilled work, and the majority of the latter group were labourers.

There was evidence that most firms had employed larger numbers of semi-skilled immigrants in past years than they did at this time. Several reasons could be advanced for this: notably the minor recession of 1956–7, which caused redundancies; the drift of better-qualified immigrants like the Poles into more skilled or better-paid work; and employers' dissatisfaction with the working or temperamental traits displayed by particular immigrant groups. This last factor had operated mainly in relation to the two most recently arrived and least acclimatized groups, the West Indians and the Hungarians, though not on the same grounds.

In none of the four firms which employed immigrants did there seem to have been any very strong resistance by local workers, whether organized or not, to their entry. As in the 'skilled' sub-sector, the main exception was again found in some A.E.U. strongholds in machine-shops or tool-shops. Resistance was not, however, total, but rather took the form of unwillingness to accept outside qualifications or of political suspicions about anti-Communist refugees. In most other departments the tone seemed, as in the skilled section of light industry (see p. 111–12), to have been set by management or supervisors, and the success of the experiment appeared to have depended in a large measure on the working ability and adaptability of the newcomers themselves.

In this sub-sector the absorption of immigrants had proceeded further and more successfully in one medium-sized and two small firms (C, E, and F). Unlike most large establishments, Firm A had not persevered with the experiment, except in the case of its 'favoured nation' group, the Anglo-Indians. Reasons for this included the nature of its training and manufacturing processes and also, after 1957, the fact that it could meet its semi-skilled labour needs locally. Firms C, E, and F appeared to be alike in their informal, close-knit, rather democratic organization and it was here that we found newcomers accepted as individuals, becoming part of the permanent labour force ('our own people') and gradually moving into more skilled and responsible jobs, on to the staff, and even into direct supervisory positions.

In this sub-sector, too, 'clustering' and the 'favoured nation' principle were in operation. The Anglo-Indians were greatly esteemed in all four firms, while there are old established nuclei of Poles in two firms (C and E). West Indians were, however, not really accepted in any firm except E, and then only as labourers or semi-skilled female operatives. The other most recently arrived group, the Hungarians, were also not favoured in five out of the six firms, because of language and temperamental difficulties.

In general, this group of firms seemed to constitute a 'transit camp' for the younger, more able, and ambitious immigrants, who passed on to the 'skilled' firms or to the greater rewards of the 'mass-production' group. There was some evidence that such a drift of Anglo-Indians and West Indians had already begun.

(c) *The 'Mass-Production' Firms*

This sub-sector consisted of two giant mass-production firms engaged in manufacturing similar types of electrical components. Between them they employed nearly 6,000 hourly paid workers (half of them women) and some 2,500 managerial, technical, and clerical staff. Some 7·4 per cent. of the total were immigrants from Europe or the Commonwealth, not counting the Irish, whom neither firm regarded as significantly different from the more transient and mobile local worker. This was, indeed, the only industrial class (apart from the hospital service) in which so large a number of immigrants were found in professional, white-collar, and salaried employment generally; two-thirds of the immigrants on the staff were, however, European, while four-fifths of the immigrants on the works side were coloured workers from the Commonwealth. Precise numbers were difficult to establish since no exact counts were kept; informants in these vast establishments tended to speak in terms of 'a few', 'a dozen or so', 'a lot', and so on, and no precise records of ethnic origin were available.

Firm A later became the subject of a more detailed case study, the results of which are given in Part IV (see Chapter 9 on Telelux). Firms A and B were similar in most important aspects; in being part of a young, dynamic industry with few traditions, rituals or taboos; in the breakdown of most of the production processes into simple operations which could be learned by most people after a brief training; in the high turnover of a large proportion of the labour force and the degree of reliance on full- and part-time women workers; in the provision of good pay and working conditions, recreational facilities, and so on; in management's policy of enlightened self-interest with regard to labour relations, union recognition, and joint consultation; and in the elaboration by specialized departments of techniques for the selection, induction, training, and integration of new workers. Most of these features seemed likely to further the absorption of immigrants.

One difference between the two firms was that Firm B had recently moved to new premises some miles away from the old factory and had also expanded its labour force by one thousand or more just over a year before the survey. This had the effect of reducing the informal authority and influence of the old-established nucleus of workers and also of setting up temporary tensions between the workers who moved from the old premises and those who lived locally and who were already installed in the new premises when the others arrived. This dislocation and the subsequent deliberate 'scrambling' of the original in-group could be expected to ease the entry and reception of other newcomers by weakening in-group solidarity and spreading any potential hostility to newcomers over a very wide range. Another difference was that Firm A had close links with West European industry, and in consequence employed a certain number of high-level Dutch staff and also of Indonesian technical staff.

Both of these firms had a high labour turnover and a steadily expanding labour force. They had, therefore, experimented with every new labour source as it became available, in all cases after consultation and agreement with the unions over placing and numbers.[1] Poles and other European refugees had been recruited for the technical staff and works side for over a decade and were now regarded as more or less absorbed. At this time between sixty and seventy Poles, almost all men, were employed in the two firms. About two-thirds of this total consisted of salaried technicians and other staff members; only a score or so were left in the manual labour force, where most were doing responsible jobs. In one firm a personnel officer recalled friction on the shop floor in earlier years and a refusal by the A.E.U. to accept Poles in skilled work. In the other, informants could not recall any such troubles, though it was conceded that they could have happened.

Both firms took on appreciable contingents of Hungarians in 1956–7. Despite the sympathetic welcome which they received from most workers and unions, with the exception of the A.E.U. in one firm,[2] both firms found the majority of Hungarians unsatis-

[1] No special redundancy agreements had, however, been negotiated for any group.

[2] Like the earlier objections to the Poles, this hostility was basically political and was inspired by the Communists and left-wing sympathizers who are most active in some branches of this union. In the other firm, however, a leading A.E.U. Communist broke with the party over the Hungarian Rising and in consequence the union did not oppose the entry of Hungarians.

factory employees; reasons given were language difficulties and the instability and restlessness characteristic of the early phase of exile. Nevertheless, about two dozen Hungarian men and women were still with these two firms and they had now settled down satisfactorily. It may be noted that whereas ten Hungarian women were working in the two firms there was only one Polish women left out of the group whose presence was reported in earlier years.[1]

Coloured workers had been employed since the end of the War by both firms, but in large numbers only since about 1955. In 1958–9 the great majority were West Indians (about 115 men and 220 women), but there were smaller contingents of Anglo-Indians (about thirteen men, five women), Indians (about twenty men), and West Africans (about fifteen men). After 1955 a quota of some 3 to 4 per cent. for coloured workers was requested by the unions; this was accepted by both managements. More recently this quota had been somewhat exceeded, particularly as regards women workers, without evoking any protest from unions or other workers. This development was an indication that accommodation was proceeding fairly satisfactorily on both sides.

Much of the credit for this satisfactory progress should be given to the personnel staffs in both firms. Through a process of trial and error they had evolved increasingly satisfactory techniques for the selection, induction, training, and industrial integration of West Indians and other coloured workers. The process in one firm was outlined by an informant:

> At first we lumped them all together by the colour of their skin, but we soon learned our lesson and stopped mixing West Indians with West Africans. We also learned not to mix West Indians from the various islands—Jamaicans and British Guianians in particular. Then we tried the experiment of having one coloured team and one white team but this didn't work out—in fact it aroused extra antagonism. Now we spread them out over the departments although there are still some that won't take them at all. Nor are there any in the smaller women's working-groups, which are very closely integrated.
>
> We have a large number of coloured applicants as we're known to take them. We never have a 'No Vacancies' notice up at the gate; we interview them all even if they obviously lack the good eyesight and manual dexterity required and allow them to go through the whole

[1] See p. 29 above for this drift out of industry, indicative of increasing economic stability and prosperity within the Polish exile community.

selection procedure, including the eye-test and dexterity test. We can't always take on those who are suitable so we explain to them about the quota system by saying that this is intended as a reasonable reflection of the proportion of West Indians in the community as a whole (in fact it's far above!), and put their names on a waiting list. Almost all respond to this in a most heartening way, but some weep and one pulled a knife. As vacancies arise we notify those on the list.[1]

At the beginning we lost quite a few trainees and operators before we realized that their learning curve is longer. Those who are any good get to the same point ultimately though they usually continue to *appear* slower. The rejection rate for coloured women trainees is relatively high but those who get through have a lower than average turnover.

The work situation in Firm A and the face-to-face relations between immigrants and local workers on the job, in the canteen, cloakrooms, and recreational clubs are described at greater length in Part IV. So far as could be ascertained during the course of a three-hour visit to the personnel department of Firm B, the position there was not significantly different. With the exception of the recently arrived Hungarian contingent, the Poles and other European immigrants were nearing the stage of industrial assimilation at the professional and semi-skilled levels, although promotions were modest and there was still a tendency for them to be upgraded to posts of greater responsibility rather than to direct supervisory posts. At the skilled level, however, union resistance and hostility in the strongly organized or closed tool-rooms and shops had caused most East European craftsmen and indeed others to seek work in other industries.

Anglo-Indians, other Anglo-Asians, and Asians were also beginning to be absorbed in the same way as the Europeans. The Irish were fully accepted at all levels, on the basis of their individual skills and qualifications. The West Indians and other 'negroid' immigrants were moving through the first phase of absorption, having established themselves and been accepted in most departments as a permanent component of the semi-skilled and unskilled labour force. The acceptance was, however, qualified by reservations as to numbers, skills, status, and the like.

These large, efficient, rapidly expanding mass-production plants were less individualistic and showed less evidence of a 'favoured

[1] The other firm also explained the quota system in a similar way, but did not have a waiting list, on the grounds that this was administratively impracticable.

nation' policy at factory level than did the smaller firms in the two previous groups. The presence of Dutch and Indonesians, noted at one of the firms, was attributable to the firm's Dutch links, but otherwise variations and individuality were to be found at departmental, sectional, and working unit levels.

(2) *The 'Heavy' Industries*

This sector covers a set of industries which have two important and related features in common: much of the work is heavy and requires considerable physical strength, and the bulk of the labour force is male. Most establishments also resemble one another in being more traditional in management–labour relations and also less dynamic and rapidly expanding than those in the light engineering sector. On the other hand, there are appreciable differences between individual industries and establishments in such criteria as skills, organization of work, wage and status levels, labour shortage, job security, and unionization; all these are elements which could have a considerable influence upon the entry and reception of immigrant workers in each industry.

Between them the 100-plus establishments in Croydon's four 'heavy' industrial groups employed over 8,000 wage-earners and nearly 1,700 staff. Of these over half worked in the building industry; next came transport and public utilities with 3,000, heavy engineering with 1,400, and other 'heavy' industries with approximately 1,000. About 340 immigrants (of whom only eleven were staff employees) worked in the 'heavy' sector as a whole, but they were very unevenly distributed between the four industrial groups. The highest percentage (about 7 per cent.) was found in the small heavy industrial group; transport and public utilities employed 3·7 per cent. of immigrants, and heavy engineering 1·3 per cent.; building employed 2·3 per cent., not counting the Irish who are this trade's traditional source of immigrant labour. There were also very considerable differences in the numbers and ethnic origins of the immigrants employed in different establishments within the various industries.

(a) *Heavy Engineering*

There were two firms in this category, one employing over 1,100 people, the other about 250. The larger of the two, Firm A, was rather different from most large Croydon firms and nearer in type and atmosphere to the large traditional firms found in the north of England. It did, however, resemble the 'skilled' class of light engineering firms in that much of the work required considerable skill (whether union-recognized or not), in its good rates of pay and fringe benefits, its high status, and its high degree of unionization. Situated on the extreme periphery of the Croydon industrial area, it drew much of its stable labour force from a neighbouring and rather 'select' housing estate which was within easy cycling distance. It had been established for nearly forty years and was part of a specialized and rather closed industry in which a worker could acquire skills which were not always formally recognized and which were useful only within that industry. The basic wage was nationally set and was not very high, but the firm provided many additional benefits in the form of differentials, bonus and profit-sharing schemes, extra pay for shift-work, pensions for all with more than one year's service, and so on. Most of the work was done by gangs working on a bonus basis, so that individual performance did affect other workers' earnings.

Labour relations were good in the industry as a whole—there had been no strike action over the last half-century. They seemed particularly good in Firm A, in which one-third of the labour force belonged to the 'Quarter-Century Club', which meant that they had worked there for at least twenty-five years: 'A lot have worked here much longer than that. The works manager is a member of the Club but some still regard him as a new boy. He worked his way up from the ranks and so have all the foremen and supervisors. A lot of the 250 full- and part-time women are wives or relatives of the chaps.'

Firm A was pervaded by a strong team spirit and the general climate of opinion was dictated by old-timers both on the floor and the management side. It was well-unionized, with a fair minority of A.E.U. and E.T.U. members; but the bulk belonged to the N.U.G.M.W., which my informant characterized as 'the respectable union'.

The firm suffered from a certain labour shortage, but 'not to the degree that we would take on just anybody. Those who think that they have helped to build the firm—and they have—resent outsiders and all who don't pull their weight.'

Despite its traditional clannish character, Firm A had from the early post-war period experimented with immigrant workers, after full consultation with the unions involved, which neither then nor later made any special conditions or raised any serious objections. At this time the firm employed about ten immigrants, mainly Poles and Hungarians, and a couple of West Indians. In the past, however, it had employed larger numbers of immigrants than at present because 'only those who can make the grade on the job and fit in socially have lasted'. The earliest post-war group were the Poles. Those still with the firm included a 60-year-old labourer ('a peasant type—he can just about make himself understood but he gets on all right. Recently he was very pleased when we helped him with the formalities to get his daughter over here on a visit from Poland. He hadn't seen her for nearly twenty years'). Another of the Poles was a trade-union leader in Poland before the War; a third was a young man who had been educated in Britain and had just worked his way up on to the technical staff: 'Everyone calls him Mr. Stan—his other name's too complicated—and he's thoroughly accepted.'

The Hungarian refugees of 1956 found a sponsor in this firm. One of the chief designers was a Hungarian who had worked there since 1937.

He's universally liked and respected in spite—or perhaps because—of the fact that he still remains a typical Hungarian. After the Rising he asked us to give the Hungarians a chance and we took on eight or so, most of them good types. We only have three left now because most of them, while they definitely weren't work-shy, really weren't suited to this kind of work and were just marking time till they could find something more suitable. For instance, one was a violinist and I could see him worrying about ruining his hands with this heavy work.

The established labour force had greeted the Hungarians with rather mixed feelings:

We have a terrible housing problem in the immediate area—some workers even have to leave because they can't get permanent accommodation. The men felt bitter when some local people and organizations offered houses to Hungarian refugees. One of the trade union chaps voiced this resentment but then the same man organized a collection for Hungarian relief. There's no objection to them as people.

Of the three Hungarian newcomers who remained with Firm A one was said to be doing particularly well:

He's young with no family or roots but he's settled down well. He plays for the works football team, which probably helps to make him accepted.

Firm A's experience with coloured workers had been rather less satisfactory and only two remained out of the large numbers that had passed through the firm. The firm's experience of Anglo-Indians and Pakistanis had been that they lacked the necessary physical stamina for this particular kind of work. One unspecified coloured male clerk ('an Egyptian, I think') was also no longer working for the firm because he was 'too fond of the young girls and they objected'.

The firm's experience of West Indian workers began when there was a shortage of women applicants for one particular job. This was broken down into a number of simple processes which could be learned in a couple of days. The firm then took on a batch of about thirty West Indian women from the Brixton employment exchange. This 'block' experiment was not successful from the angle either of working performance or of relations with fellow-workers:

They took a long time to learn and were always slow. But the worst trouble was over their personal habits. There are a lot of very motherly types among the local women and I don't think any of them were particularly prejudiced. But there were complaints over their smell and above all toilet habits. We had to point out what toilets were for. The worst incident came when a white girl and a black girl were sharing the same wash-basin. The white girl chose to wash there so presumably she wasn't prejudiced. She said to the other girl, joking: 'It [i.e. the dirt] doesn't show up on you like it does on me.' The black girl spat in her face. We nearly had a strike and if she'd been a white girl I'd have sacked her for such behaviour. I didn't want to sack a black girl so I smoothed it over but the others took it as a sign of weakness and got uppish. When we had some redundancy soon after I thought it best to clear the lot out. I've interviewed a few coloured girls for clerical jobs but I found them useless—below the ordinary factory level.

This firm later took on a few West Indian men and scattered them through the labour force. On the whole, the experience was discouraging:

Most of them were bone lazy. Are they used to the whip at home or what? The foreman actually had to wake two of them up. I wish they would try to work like white men and not like niggers. One chap *was* quite able and we intended to give him a job in the lab—but he went round the bend and started brandishing a knife, so he had to go.

Two West Indian skilled workers had, however, survived the course at Firm A and were well accepted as individuals:

One has been here for seven years. He's a running champion and very popular. Another worked for years with another firm in the same industry. He's a very nice chap and captain of the cricket team. He talks, laughs and jokes like an Englishman. In fact he's so English that everyone forgets he's coloured. But he's not entirely sure of himself yet. He's a skilled man and should be training others but he said he was sure whites wouldn't agree to train under him. He himself suggested that we might put coloured men under him to train and we've done so quite successfully.

This firm's labour organization was, as has been stressed already, based on stability, long service, and a great sense of working community. It was, therefore, not surprising to find that migrant Southern Irish labour was viewed with disfavour. The personnel manager said:

They're worse than any other immigrants. We've had a fair number, possibly because this is a strong Catholic area, but their turnover is very high and few even stay as long as two years. A handful do settle in low category jobs but they never get to the point where they can be given responsibility. They're slow and want driving. They're also unintelligent but have a certain cunning and they certainly stick together. We nearly had trouble with them once. A ringleader got hold of them and they were 'going to show the English something'. We haven't got any of them here at present.

To sum up, Firm A was a stable, clannish, well-integrated working community into which few outsiders could fit unless they were efficient and adaptable. Those immigrants who had survived the somewhat arduous period of initiation did, however, seem to be increasingly well on the way to absorption in the working community, both on the shop floor and on the technical staff. Only in the matter of promotion to direct supervisory positions in the works hierarchy was there some resistance to the idea of putting newcomers, particularly coloured workers, in authority over local workers. These posts were, however, held by employees with very long service and it seemed likely that such resistance would have disappeared well before the newcomers qualified for the Quarter-Century Club.

Firm B was less than a quarter the size of Firm A, but employed a considerably larger percentage of immigrants. It was in one of the main industrial areas and differed from Firm A in that much of the work was 'de-skilled' and broken down into simpler and lighter operations during the War for more efficient production by the unskilled female labour that had to be used. Only thirty women were still employed, but the work remained lighter and less skilled than in Firm A and very little of it was organized on a team basis. Firm B was also less unionized than Firm A, but three unions were represented and there was a shop-steward in the tool-room. The two firms resembled each other in having a low overall labour turnover, so that they were not 'desperate for labour', and in the presence of a hard core of older local employees. In Firm B one group had been there since before the 1939–45 War, another for ten years or more. The prevailing atmosphere was easy-going and pleasant.

The firm expanded greatly during the War, but afterwards had to cut down its labour force considerably. This was during the years when the Poles and European Voluntary Workers were entering the labour market and the firm therefore gained little experience of these groups. A few Poles had, however, been employed and on the whole they were regarded as good workers. The managing director told me:

> We had one a couple of years ago—young, keen and highly thought of. Unfortunately we had to make him redundant on a 'first in, last out' basis when the last cut-back came but he was a skilled man and had no difficulty in finding another job. Another Pole, a good worker, went off to a lumber-camp in Canada, where his friends were earning fabulous wages. Then there's Mrs. S., the cleaner. She's been with us for years and likes to talk about her pre-war glories. Her son works with us as an electrician.

This firm's experience with coloured Commonwealth workers had been more satisfactory than that of Firm A. The Anglo-Indians were the 'favoured nation'. I was told:

> Our chief clan are the Anglo-Indians. It started with one and he brought his friends in. Now we have half a dozen men. One is a 'progress chaser': that's an important job that needs a grasp of detail and enough personality and tact to talk persuasively to foremen. This one is a charming character, darkish, good-looking, and with a soft, pleasant voice (he

does some singing in the social club). The other Anglo-Indians have various sorts of jobs down to one labourer. I've no complaints about their working capacity, though most are a bit slower than the average. There are no Anglo-Indian women except for one on the office staff, who doesn't show it or admit to it.

Management at this smallish firm took a friendly interest in the personal lives of its employees and my informant knew a good deal about the Anglo-Indians' social relations and problems both on and off the job:

They stick together and most live together; they don't seem to have any trouble in finding lodgings. Most are touchy over their colour and chi-chi accents. Some call England 'home' and others look towards India. But they all join in the activities of the social club we have here and they also go out with local girls. Most local people aren't prejudiced and don't think about it, though they wouldn't like their daughters to marry an obviously coloured man.

The firm's personnel officer told me of an incident which illustrated both local women's varying attitudes to colour and Anglo-Indian touchiness (certainly justified in this case)—the sequel also showed the extent to which the Anglo-Indians had been accepted as part of the stable labour force:

One of the older women befriended a girl who'd already had one illegitimate baby and been thrown out by her family. Mrs. G. is usually very nice to the coloured workers but she's sharp-tongued and very possessive. When this girl took up with one of the Anglo-Indians she objected and told her she shouldn't be 'going around with a nigger'. The girl passed this on to him and naturally all the Anglo-Indians were up in arms at once. We finally managed to smooth the incident over and the girl left.

In earlier years Firm B employed three or four coloured West Indians or West Africans at a time but few stayed for any length of time, either because they were students on temporary work or because they left to get higher wages elsewhere:

There was no definite decision to take them on—a darkie simply turned up one day. There was no opposition from the men, probably because the Anglo-Indians had broken the ice. We've had no particular problems with the few we've employed—there's only one labourer at the moment. One who was sacked for poor work accused us of 'colour bar' although I and the shop-steward spent hours trying to explain the real reason to him. None of the foremen are anti-colour. If one of them put off a bad coloured worker he'd often take another on at once if there's one applying just then.

Firm B's policy and practice in the employment of immigrants seemed both expedient and liberal: 'We have not experienced much difficulty, first because the proportion is not very noticeable and second because we try to persuade ourselves that the colour bar does not exist.'

As in Firm A, but more easily, the adaptable immigrant could gradually win a considerable degree of acceptance. This was another firm whose management expressed satisfaction with the relations between immigrants and local workers and was unwilling to agree to a more detailed study 'for fear of starting a disruptive train of thought where at present I do not think it exists'.

(b) *Other Heavy Industries*

Croydon's heavy industry was small, and consists of rather a mixed bag. Information was obtained about four firms employing a total of just over 1,000 in all: a brick-works, a die-casting firm, a rubber manufacturer, and a foundry. All but the rubber manufacturer (with 300 employees) fall into the 101–250 employee category.

These manufacturing processes have in common the fact that they involve a considerable amount of heavy, hot, and (in the case of rubber production) smelly work which makes them relatively unattractive to British workers. Brick-making is one of the industries into which post-war immigrant labour was directed and in my earlier South London inquiry I found that the other industries mentioned above also relied heavily on immigrant labour. In Croydon, however, this was not the case. The foundry had never employed European or coloured immigrants, the chief reasons being that it was highly mechanized, had a stable labour force, and had experienced no particular labour shortage. When asked about the possibility of taking on immigrant labour in the future, a spokesman said that he was 'not sure how the men would take such a move'.

A similar situation was found in the case of the rubber manufacturers, which employed only a handful of West Indians or other immigrants in its labour force of 300. More detailed information could not be obtained direct from this firm, but it was learned from another source that one out of the three West Indians was employed as a laboratory assistant and not on manual labour.[1]

In this industrial group only two Croydon firms, the brick-works (A) and the die-casters (B), employed large numbers of immigrants: the respective percentages were 14 and 49. In contrast to the heavy engineering firms the immigrants in this group were drawn almost entirely from two ethnic groups, the West Indians and Italian immigrants who came in on Ministry of Labour permits.

Firm A was old-established but went out of production during the 1939–45 War. It started up again in 1946 with only a few pre-war workers but soon built up a large stable nucleus of local workers: 'About 85–90 per cent. of the chaps have been with us since the late 1940s, but the turnover with the other 10–15 per cent. is absolutely terrific.'

Although the work was less heavy than in pre-war days as a result of increased mechanization, it was described as 'still a man's job which needs a certain amount of stamina'. Earnings averaged about £11 for a 44-hour week, overtime was fairly regular and there was a profit-sharing bonus which increases with each five year of service. A minority of workers, especially the lorry-drivers, were thought to belong to a union but none was recognized. The director commented:

> There's a works committee and labour relations are pretty good. They don't seem to want a union. Five or six years ago one of the main unions approached us and asked for permission to address the men. We arranged a secret ballot with two tellers and the men voted four to one against having the union, with no prompting from us. We operate through the works committee. For instance when the labour situation got difficult we got our own chaps together and put it to them about taking on Poles and later Italians. After the odds and sods we'd been having who used to walk out in the middle of the job the men rather welcomed the idea of having decent solid workers, as most of them turned out to be.

Poles from the Resettlement Corps and E.V.W.s were the first immigrants to come to Firm A. About thirty Poles were taken on, but only three 'labouring types' still remained.

[1] This firm provided a considerable contrast to a rubber manufacturer some miles to the north which I visited in 1956; there one-eighth of the male labour force of 400 were immigrants (Poles and West Indians) (*Dark Strangers*, pp. 118–19).

Most of them were directed here and treated the job as a stepping-stone to more suitable work (one was a lawyer before the War). Many went to the States or Canada when their visas came through but six went in a bunch to work with British Railways nearby. They like to get together in a gang and the railways offer security even though they get less money.[1] They were good types and quite good workers, better than the Italians by and large, and more responsible. On cleanliness they taught our chaps a lot. The two dozen showers which the army put in during the war were more or less an ornament until the Poles came. Their example slowly took effect and we've had to put in another dozen.

The next immigrant group was Italian, recruited and brought in since 1950–1 under a bulk scheme operated by the brick industry. About two dozen had been employed by the firm since then and one dozen or so were still there. With the exception of one, who was returned home as unsuitable, the remainder drifted to other employment (mainly hotel work or tailoring) after their contracts had expired.

They're good at repetitive work and have adequate stamina for the current demands of the job, although they wouldn't have stood up to the pre-war work. Like the Poles they work better in a gang of their own countrymen and they're out to earn as much as possible. Many send as much as £4 or £5 home to Italy each week. There's been no trouble between them and our chaps. Most of those who are still with us have finished their contracts but they've settled locally and some have already brought their wives and children over. Among the local landladies there's actually a waiting list for Italians—they have such a good reputation as lodgers.

Firm A had no migrant Southern Irish in its labour force—it is thought that they found the building trade proper more attractive. Its remaining immigrant workers consisted of two Canadians and five West Indians. The former were completely accepted but the latter had only recently become acceptable at all:

A few years ago the foreman wouldn't look at them. He said they were lazy. Now we've got five Jamaicans who are settled and quite good. But they're geared to work over a twelve-hour day and we have to split them up for good results, unlike the Poles and the Italians. We have no particular personal problems with them. There's only been one bit of fisticuffs and that was between two of them—one nearly bit the other's finger off.

[1] See pp. 100–4. The desired security was to prove less real than it seemed in the immediate post-war years.

Redundancy had been an abstract problem in Firm A since it reopened in 1946. The management was confident that a mild trade recession could with foresight be handled by normal wastage and a brake on hiring. Non-British immigrants should in theory go first if there were any redundancy, but my informant considered that 'all the outsiders are so well accepted now that redundancy would probably apply to all workers on the same basis'. Only over the question of promotion were some reservations expressed: 'The Italians and Jamaicans don't aspire to it and we'd have some hesitation over taking such a step. With the Poles it was different. They were responsible types and they had their own leaders.'

Firm B, the die-casters, seemed to be the single exemplification in Croydon of that old bogey of trade unions and local labour, the management that uses immigrant workers to weaken the power of organized local labour. This was a small, efficient, paternalistically run firm which was established just after the end of the Second World War. The work was dirty, rough, and hot, and required considerable skill in practice. Firm B had to compete with two other local firms for the few available skilled men, found trainees virtually unobtainable and had since its founding suffered from an acute and increasing shortage of all male and female labour (women formed a quarter of the labour force): 'As far as the women are concerned it's a dirty job and they'd rather go to one of the light industrial plants. As for the men the only available white labour is trash and the turnover is enormous.'

Firm B's local labour difficulties were intensified some years ago when there was a dispute with the union to which 80 per cent. of employees belonged. One of the directors described the sequel:

> The local union man threatened to withdraw all *his* labour if we didn't give way on several points. We had three months' reserves so we sacked the lot and closed down. Then we took back twenty or thirty men we could trust and started to build up again. I wouldn't take the rest back so we had to look around for other sources of labour. The Poles were no good—we'd tried a few but all they wanted to do was court the girls and fight. So we decided to try a few brown boys.

Within a year of this 30 per cent. of Firm B's labour force was coloured and at the time of interview nearly half were coloured, in the proportion of three men to one woman. Most of these women had been recruited by the management asking West Indian employees to bring along their wives or women friends.

A number of the West Indians were thought to have been brought along by one of the early arrivals, who owned three lodging-houses in Croydon and was believed to provide loans to pay fares from the West Indies.

The firm was well enough satisfied with the working ability of its West Indian employees. My informant said:

> We had to sort them out at first but they're a jolly crowd now. We had one who was a real bad character. He pulled a knife when he was fired but the foreman got him first with a heavy casting on the jaw. There are good and bad among them like the whites, but they're more willing to work and they work happily and have a lower turnover. They adapt themselves amazingly quickly to our techniques considering that they probably didn't know anything before except picking bananas. It took some of the monkey-shine out of our skilled casters, who are as temperamental as ballet dancers, to find that a big chap just down off the tree could learn to do their job as well as they do. I don't find the Jamaicans slow but patience is needed to get the routine into their heads. They're particularly good for routine work, whereas the whites tend to get bored and start introducing so-called improvements.

Management at Firm B was less concerned than most with the reactions of its local labour force but did not overlook these altogether:

> There have been no major troubles over canteen or toilet habits or sex and generally speaking relations are happy though they do 'pong' a bit and some eat Kit-e-Kat sandwiches. But the percentage is now reaching danger level. This place is called 'Little Jamaica' and the English are a little resentful, mainly because they are afraid that the coloured workers will bring down the rate for the job. In fact, we pay a higher rate to maintain the present coloured level, but we've put up a 'no vacancy' sign and aren't taking on any more. I'd like to have more diversity, perhaps by bringing in some trained North Italians—they're very industrious and would set a good example.

The West Indians seemed to be more or less fully accepted by management as part of Firm B's labour force. Redundancy was obviously an academic question but it was said that colour would play no part in any redundancy policy, which would be based on seniority and efficiency. Several West Indians had also become team leaders, in some cases with white youths under them, but none were regarded as of sufficient intelligence for higher promotion. On the other hand the single non-West Indian immigrant employee, a Pakistani, was considered exceptionally able and had been promoted to floor inspector 'without any trouble from the other men'.

Firm B resembled Firm A, the brick-works, in that it suffered from a chronic labour shortage and employed a large percentage of immigrant labour. On the surface the immigrant workers seemed to be further integrated and accepted in Firm B than in Firm A, but the process in this particular firm had certain rather singular features. In Firm A, as in most other firms, the absorption of immigrants was taking place through interaction between three main interest-groups, the management, the local labour force, and the newcomers themselves. The management needed the labour of the newcomers but was also concerned to maintain the character and keep the goodwill of its stable labour nucleus. In consequence the absorptive process was a gradual one, achieved by consultation and trial and error rather than by management *fiat*. In Firm B, on the other hand, the management relied heavily on tough supervision and clearly regarded its labour force, with the partial exception of the minority who were taken back after the mass sackings, as a set of more or less interchangeable human working units. The absorption of the newcomers had so far been largely a two-way process between them and management, without much consultation with or consideration of local workers' views; such a situation could clearly have wider repercussions among local organized labour.

(c) *The Building Industry*

Building and contracting constituted Croydon's third largest industry group, employing over 9,000 workers. About half of these workers were employed by the dozen '100-plus' firms.[1]

The building industry, being both seasonal and particularly sensitive to general economic trends, has a very high labour turnover. Most firms keep only a small permanent nucleus of craftsmen and take on other labour as it is required. Wages are good but settled family men do not always care for the job's insecurity, for the frequent need to travel long distances, or for the climatic conditions of winter work. This is, therefore, an industry that has always

[1] Three of these firms employed over 500 workers, four between 251 and 500 and the remainder from 101 to 250.

attracted, and indeed welcomed, large proportions of mobile migrant workers. In London and many parts of the British Isles it has for many decades been something of a preserve for a particular migrant group, the Southern Irish; their grip is often strengthened by the presence of Irish foremen, who prefer to hire their own migrant countrymen rather than other newcomers.[1]

As we have already noted, Irish labour played quite a part in the development of Croydon in the nineteenth century and there was a considerable Irish settlement, both old-established and migrant, in the area at this time. The twelve '100-plus' firms in the Croydon building industry employed a considerable number of Irish, and indeed the Irish were so fully accepted as part of the regular labour force that only one informant (Firm B) had any observations about the 'migrant' as opposed to the 'settled' Irish.

Rather contrary to expectation it was found that only three of these twelve firms had ever employed any significant numbers of immigrants of other origins. On further inquiry several reasons emerged for this state of affairs. Some of the firms were not builders but builders' merchants, with a stable local labour force and a low labour turnover. Others were engaged mainly upon specialized, skilled engineering work or upon government contracts involving a security clause which precluded the employment of foreigners. Others, again, were situated in outlying southern districts of Croydon which were not very accessible to immigrant work-seekers, particularly the West Indians, most of whom still lived north of Croydon. Moreover, three firms were found to consist mainly of office staff and working *cadres*, the bulk of whose contracts and the associated labour recruitment were carried out outside the area.

The three Croydon firms which had some experience of immigrant labour were all building contractors. They were also family firms, although they differed considerably in size and scope. The largest, Firm A, had its head office in Croydon and at the time of the interview employed something over 1,000 men (about 7 per

[1] In 1951, 5·48 per cent. of the total male labour force in the building industry in England and Wales (and 10·4 per cent. of all builders' labourers) were Irish-born, while 17·85 per cent. of all occupied Irish-born males in this country were in this industry (*Census of England and Wales* 1951, Occupation Tables, Table 26, pp. 603–13). J. A. Jackson (op. cit., pp. 81, 105–7) writes of the building industry as the 'ultimate aim' for many unskilled Irish male migrants, of the leading contractors' long tradition of direct recruitment of Irish labour and of the way in which some Irish move about in gangs from contract to contract.

cent. of them immigrants) on a number of sites in the South London area. Of this total about 60 per cent. were employed on a special 'staff scheme' arrangement which was designed to reduce the high turnover and mobility that had long been a feature of the industry by giving certain workers some security of job tenure ('otherwise it's two hours' notice on a Friday'). This arrangement also enabled the employer to build up stable and efficient working groups and gangs with a low labour turnover and created a certain feeling of solidarity between management and men.

Many of this firm's building workers were Irish, but the latter were a fully accepted component of the labour force and my informant had little to say about them. The earliest post-war immigrant group represented was Polish:

> Some have been here eight or ten years—they're accepted as part and parcel of the organization and a number are on the 'staff scheme'. Most work in their gangs under a Polish foreman. Though most are middle-aged, with several ex-officers among them, they specialize in heavy erecting jobs. They're pretty well accepted and one is actually a foreman over an English gang. He's pretty outstanding, though; to get such a supervisory post a Pole doesn't just have to be as good as a local but better.

This firm had had little experience of other European immigrants ('we interviewed a few Hungarians, but they seemed unsuitable because of the language difficulty'). One or two 'darkish' Anglo-Egyptian refugees who had worked for affiliated firms were taken on to the clerical staff after the Suez crisis, but in general it was felt that coloured fellow-employees would not be accepted by the clerical or technical staffs, nor by some members of top management.

The only other immigrants employed by Firm A were West Indians. These had been taken on for about a year, following an acute labour shortage:

> I don't remember taking any decision about it—the exchange simply began sending them along. Nor was there any formal consultation or special arrangements with the unions, though we're fairly well unionized here. The Jamaicans tend to be rough carpenters—what we call 'shuttering hands'. Some are stimulated by working in gangs and the high bonuses available but others simply can't adjust themselves to the pace of this organization, which is particularly fast-moving. Then again, coloured workers seem especially susceptible to bad weather conditions

and tend to stay away sick for long periods. So they're more apt than others to fall into the redundancy group every January to March.

There's a certain amount of feeling against coloured workers but it varies from site to site and no site refuses them altogether. We are employing about forty-five at present—that's nearly 5 per cent. of the total—but there may be up to 10 per cent. on a particular site depending on how much carpentering work there is at the time. We don't favour a higher concentration than that. As for friction over social habits, there's more of that with the Irish than with the coloured. But this is a rough-and-ready sort of job, often in the open air, and you don't get as much trouble of that kind as you would in a works where everyone's shut up together for years on end. I can only recall one serious bit of trouble with a Jamaican and that wasn't over his colour. One of the unions accused us of taking on defaulters, of whom he was one, and made quite an issue of it.

Firm B, which was engaged in general contracting and maintenance, was more localized and smaller than Firm A, with a labour force that varied between 300 and 500 according to the season. It was even more of a family firm than Firm A, several of the specialized working departments being in charge of family members; it was also far less highly unionized than the larger firm.

Unlike most building firms, Firm B employed few Irish, mostly what were described as 'the settled type'. On the other hand, it had employed West Indians for seven or eight years, together with Poles and E.V.W.s. At the time of the interview nearly 10 per cent. of the labour force consisted of immigrants (twenty West Indians, five Poles, and four Cypriots). Of these only two Poles, a craftsman and a labourer, were 'retainers' on the permanent labour force.

Several of the working directors were present at the interview and it was thus possible to get an idea not only of the varying aptitudes of different groups of immigrants but also of variations of atmosphere between the different departments. There was general agreement about past and present Polish workers: 'Good all-rounders but there have been some language difficulties in the past and their English is still poor. A year or so ago we had a painter whom we thought good enough for a foreman's job, *despite his marked accent*,[1] but he left to go to the university.'

The four Cypriots were all carpenters; the head of this department considered them satisfactory workers and had no other comments to make about them.

[1] Author's italics.

The experience and views of the different departmental chiefs about West Indian labour showed considerable variation. One department with a 75 per cent. skilled labour force, including the two Polish 'retainers', had no coloured workers at all; its chief said: 'None of the Jamaicans are any good as tradesmen in this particular craft [mechanical]. I don't like employing them and if I do I'll only take on one at a time. Otherwise they gang up and their discipline gets bad.'

In the maintenance department, however, with an 80 per cent. skilled labour force, the director took a less restrictive line:

I never take more than eight or ten Jamaicans at a time. The labourers are all lazy and the tradesmen don't come up to our 'fair standard', according to the foremen. We have to be careful as some clients object, and I imagine many more might, to coloured men being used on maintenance work when housewives are at home on their own.

In the decorating and carpentry sections, where the proportion of skilled labour was about 60 per cent., West Indian craftsmen were held in better esteem, though with some qualifications: 'The painters are bad at setting out their tools and planning and the carpenters are fairly rough.'

The carpentry section was, incidentally, the one which contained the largest number of immigrants: two Poles, four Cypriots and about a dozen 'Jamaicans'. Neither here nor elsewhere in the firm, however, was there anything in the nature of an ethnic working-group. In the case of the West Indians, indeed, deliberate efforts were made to separate and disperse them; they were believed to 'gang up together' and 'slow down' if allowed to work in a group.

The main observations and criticisms about West Indians voiced by informants in this firm referred to their working ability, but one departmental head met with general approval from the others when he said: 'They're best treated as grown-up children.' Relations between West Indians and other workers on the job were said to be reasonably good, although local workers had sometimes been heard to complain about the 'garlicky food' brought by the West Indians and the spitting indulged in by a few of them.

Poles and West Indians had been working for this rather clannish local firm for roughly the same length of time. No discriminatory redundancy or other agreements existed and both groups would therefore seem to have started level. Nevertheless, while the Poles were fairly well absorbed, the West Indians were clearly still regarded as outsiders of rather poor working quality. No West Indians were yet 'retainers' on the permanent labour force and the question of promotion remained academic since none were considered remotely suitable for it; on the other hand, a Pole achieved this degree of acceptance some years ago.

The smallest of the three firms which admitted to any appreciable experience of immigrant labour was Firm C. This specialized in civil engineering and had a labour force of some 250, most of them skilled men. This firm employed a considerable number of Irish workers but only three West Indians, all labourers. It had had no experience of other immigrant workers; but some years ago, in a period of acute labour shortage just before the 1956–7 recession, it took on about twenty-five West Indian labourers. These were all laid off during the credit squeeze and the labour situation had not since then been sufficiently acute for the firm to consider further large-scale recruitment. West Indians were regarded by this management simply as casual labourers. None had ever been employed or considered for the particular kinds of skilled work carried out here.

It was difficult to draw any far-reaching conclusions from the experience of these three firms. On the whole, however, it would seem that the main consideration of employers had been with recurring labour shortages and applicants' skills and working capacity, and that other considerations, such as, for instance, the views of the permanent labour nucleus or the unions, had played a less important part than they did in some industries.

The presence and full acceptance of a large proportion of Irish labour in this particular industry has certain implications which merit more detailed study. On the one hand, it has accustomed employers to a steady stream of non-local and highly mobile labour. On the other, the fact that so many supervisors and foremen are Irish obviously favours the continued entry of Irish newcomers into the industry, whereas it may work against the entry of other immigrant groups. The experience of some Polish building workers whom I questioned rather tended to support the latter suggestion, although one of them considered that this did not always apply, nor with all groups:

For instance, we don't get on too badly with most because they know we're fellow-Catholics and they think both our countries have had a bad deal from their big neighbours. The main trouble comes when they're anti-clerical and when there's a lot of militant left-wing activity on a site. Then of course, we're branded as Fascist landlords and the lot.

(d) *Public Utilities*

Public utilities are included in the 'heavy' industries sector because the bulk of the employment they provide is heavy manual or unskilled work for men and because it is in this type of work that the great majority of immigrants in the public utilities are to be found, in Croydon as in many other British industrial areas.

The public utilities do, however, offer a much wider range of employment than the other 'heavy' industries. This includes not only heavy manual labour such as shunting, navvying, and stoking but skilled work of various kinds (e.g. engine-driving, telephone and electrical installation, and repair-work) and responsible white-collar and technical jobs, many of which involve contact with the public. The public utilities also differ from some of the private 'heavy' industrial firms in the degree of security they offer and, until recent years, in the good wage-scales and high status enjoyed by most employees, and in the fact that each service has, in past generations, built up links with a nucleus of families, most of whose members have automatically sought employment and lived out their working lives in it. This applies particularly to the railways and the Post Office.

There are thus certain important aspects of the public utilities which could well be considered in the later section which deals with professional, white-collar, and associated occupations, including local government services. The latter would indeed have been considered in conjunction with the public utilities but for the fact that they employ proportionately much larger and more varied administrative, professional, technical, and clerical staffs in which a certain number of immigrants are included; these local government services, therefore, present a picture of rather specific interest which is best considered from the viewpoint of professional and white-collar employment.

At the time of this inquiry no immigrants were, so far as could be ascertained, employed locally by the Post Office, in the offices of national government departments, or in the police force. Except in the case of the Post Office this was hardly surprising, since most immigrants of all groups would be debarred from entering these types of public service by such matters as nationality restrictions, language difficulties, age, and lack of the appropriate qualifications.

The Post Office presents rather a different picture because it provides a large number of semi-skilled and marginally white-collar jobs, and has since 1948 been recruiting West Indians and other coloured workers in the London area. There would seem to be two main reasons for the lack of coloured postmen in Croydon at this time. In the first place relatively few West Indians and other coloured immigrants were then resident in the district. Secondly, the recruiting position was not so difficult in the outer suburb postal districts as it was in Central London and there was no acute shortage of local recruits, who might be considered as more acceptable because of their familiarity with local topography and local people.[1]

The public utilities investigated in this inquiry were the local Electricity and Gas Boards, the road transport services, and the local stations and depots of British Railways (and they are the only ones enumerated in Appendix 3).

(e) *Electricity and Gas Services*

The electricity board in Croydon was concerned with distribution and maintenance. In mid-1958 it employed 386 staff (255 male, 131 female) and 448 manual workers (433 male). The latter included only a few labourers, the heavy work of cable-laying being given to outside contractors. It claimed to have little trouble in recruiting the needed staff. At the time of this inquiry only two immigrants were employed, a Polish electrician and a Nigerian student on clerical work. The fact that so many of the staff come into regular contact with the public, either over the counter or on repair and meter-reading work in homes and offices, seemed to be a major consideration in the selection of staff:

> The Pole's a first-class chap: no objections or troubles there. We did take on some coloured labour, including one West Indian electrician who was a very good worker—but there were complaints from members of the public about his going into private houses. The colour of their skin is all the same to me but that's a personal opinion and not everyone feels that way. We can get all the labour we want so why look for trouble.

[1] See *Dark Strangers*, Chapter 5, pp. 89–91, for an account of the absorption of coloured staff in the London area. Even as late as 1959 coloured postmen were still concentrated in three Central London districts with a particularly acute and chronic labour problem.

The picture at the Gas Board was very different. Apart from its clerical and technical staff, on which no immigrants appeared to be employed, it employed between 450 and 500 manual workers on production at the local gasworks. There is a seasonal aspect to this production and traditionally the gas-works drew the additional labour which they needed in winter from building workers laid off during this period.

There was a stable nucleus of long-term local labour and even a strong family tradition at this gas-works, although most fathers were said to aim at apprenticeships rather than labouring jobs for their sons. Labour turnover was very low before the War but since 1945 there had been a chronic labour shortage and a high labour turnover among all but the stable nucleus. The labour shortage was attributed less to the wage-scales, which compared well with those in other public utilities, than to the hot, heavy, and seasonal nature of the work and the fact that considerable shift-working was involved.

The gas-works were well unionized and the unions were consulted before new sources of labour were taken on. The main immigrant group represented in the post-war labour force here was in fact the West Indian one. A few Hungarians were taken on in 1956–7, but they did not stay for long. A handful of Poles had also been employed at various times. There was, however, no large-scale intake of Poles during the post-war resettlement period, apparently because the local unions objected. This refusal would seem to reflect a specific local situation because the principal union concerned has at top level consistently adopted a helpful and sympathetic attitude to Polish and other anti-Communist exile workers from Europe.

Coloured workers, most of whom were West Indians, had been employed at the gas-works since 1952, but there was no large inflow until 1956. There was a high labour turnover among earlier arrivals but most of the 1956 entrants had stayed, probably because the subsequent recession made work more difficult to get. At the time of my interview some fifty, or 10 per cent., of the total manual labour force were coloured (mainly West Indian), although it was stressed that no quota was involved. Most of them had two years' service or more. All coloured workers began work on the purifiers. This was shift-work on a piece-work basis, bringing in about £13 a week. It had for years been unpopular with local workers because of the unpleasant smell associated with it. West Indians were, however, said to tolerate this and to find the work easy:

It's an agricultural sort of job. Over two-thirds of the men there are coloured but there's no trouble and they don't gang up among themselves. At the beginning we tried them out in the retort-houses—that's semi-skilled work involving the use of crude tools. But they proved unsuitable for that and strange to say they suffered from the heat there as well. Now they're improving and some have graduated from the purifiers to stoking, which is the best of the manual jobs and brings in £15 a week. Some are also working as bricklayers' mates but we've no coloured tradesmen. At first some of the foremen were biased against the West Indians but this changed after a few had proved themselves as good workers and now none of the foremen refuse to take them.

Relations between West Indians and other workers were said to be good at this particular gas-works; this was in contrast with the situation reported at some others in South London.[1] There was little friction on the job or in the canteen or cloakrooms:

The West Indians usually eat together but no one objects to that. They're also exceptionally clean in their habits; they usually bathe and change into good clothes here, instead of dashing off like our chaps. They were slow to join the union but most are members now. We've never had any suggestion that they should be dismissed before others. This might have happened a few years ago if we'd failed to handle the seasonal redundancy by means of normal wastage but I doubt if it would today—they're more or less integrated themselves now.

Thus it would seem that West Indians were accepted as part of the regular force at the gas-works. This acceptance was, however, confined to manual work and no West Indians had yet been promoted to positions of any authority or skill. Even this modest degree of accommodation on both sides could, however, be largely attributed to the tolerant, firm and sympathetic policy of the local management.

(f) *Public Transport*

Before the outbreak of war in 1939 the road and rail services were more of a vocation than merely a job for the majority of their employees. They offered security, status, and opportunity in a world of economic uncertainty, and also the satisfaction of belonging to a close confraternity which provided an indispensable public

[1] Cf. *Dark Strangers*, p. 98–9.

service. Each local bus or tram company, and to a greater extent each regional railway company, could recruit from a nucleus of families whose lives had been linked with the company's fortunes, or those of the smaller companies that were merged into them, for two or more generations.

Since the end of the Second World War, however, this situation has undergone rapid change. The advent of full employment and the disproportionate forward leap of private industrial wages have caused the transport services to suffer from a chronic labour shortage and have also undermined the economic and social status of the job. During the London bus strike of the summer of 1958 two busmen expressed their view of the change succinctly:

> Before the War it was a hell of a job to get on the buses, but once on you were set for life. The job's not what it was, we were the second best paid on the industrial list and now we're the fifty-seventh. The trouble started during the War when we accepted a wage-freeze to help the war effort. Before the War the police and the buses were the two best jobs in London. Now it's deteriorated out of all recognition. . . . And the types on the buses. Before the War it was definitely respectable.[1]

Since the post-war years both the London Transport Executive (now Board) and British Railways have become large-scale employers of immigrant labour in an endeavour to bring their labour force up to adequate strength. In Croydon, however, the situation at the London Transport garages was at the time of this inquiry similar to that in the local Post Office. There was a large nucleus of long-term local workers and the few vacancies that occurred were easily filled by local recruitment. An informant at head office had no knowledge of any immigrants working in the Croydon garages, with the exception of three West Indian conductors in one garage several miles from the centre.[2] Nor was there any record of

[1] *Observer*, 4 May 1958. See also the leaflet issued to 'Members of the Travelling Public' by the T. and G.W.U. No. 1 Region, during the London bus strike in 1958. This showed the wage increases received by bus drivers and five other classes of skilled workers in other industries since 1939, with the bus driver lagging behind the next lowest paid to the tune of 26*s*. 8*d*. per week.

[2] This situation changed radically within the next two to three years, probably because recruitment of local staff became more difficult during the minor boom that followed the 1956–8 recession and because more coloured migrants had settled locally and were applying for work on the buses. By April 1961 (another year of recession, which usually exacerbates local workers' views on immigration) enough coloured busmen had been taken on, particularly in South Croydon, to induce a delegate conference of Croydon busmen to pass by a narrow majority

Poles being employed in the Croydon area; but this was attributed mainly to the fact that Polish applicants usually preferred and applied for work on the underground, which of course meant that they worked mainly in the central and northern areas of London.

By contrast, British Railways had been substantial employers of various immigrant groups in the Croydon area for years. At this time immigrants were employed at each of the three main stations and in a large railway workshop. The situations in these four establishments were, however, far from identical. Unlike London Transport, British Railways is a fairly decentralized organization in which station-masters have considerable autonomy and do their own recruiting in the starting grade. Each station or depot tends to have its own individual character, imparted by a clannish nucleus of 'old-timers' and by the station-master and supervisors, themselves usually long-service employees who have risen from the ranks.[1] Old-timers and supervisory staff alike have strong local or regional affiliations and are bound together by old loyalties to the smaller private lines in which so many began their service and which were gradually swallowed by the Southern Railway and ultimately by the nationalized organization.

Stations A and B in Croydon were both fairly large stations which handled both passenger and goods traffic. Each had a staff of something over 100, some members of which worked at smaller

(37 to 35) a resolution asking for restrictions on immigration and on the recruitment of immigrant busmen in the area. This was reversed in June by a vote of 65 to 14, but it provoked a flurry of protests and counter-protests (mainly against the earlier decision) in the *Croydon Advertiser* (30 June, 7 July, 11, 25 August) and *Croydon Times* (14 July, 18 and 28 August). After some weeks the trouble seemed to have died down and in October the *Croydon Advertiser* (16 October 1961) reported that one Croydon garage had about forty-five coloured staff out of a total of 617 (over 7 per cent.) while another had half a dozen out of 210 (about 3 per cent.).

[1] A check through earlier press cuttings revealed the fact that coloured railwaymen had found one energetic sponsor, an N.U.R. member who wrote at least four letters to the Croydon press and the *Railway Review* (the N.U.R. journal) in 1956 and 1957 following reports that shunting staff in a local goods yard were objecting to coloured labour. His defence of the right of coloured workers to come to Britain included the following passage: 'We in this country have lived on the backs of the colonial workers for well over a hundred years and even now we stand in debt to colonial people. . . . Don't you think brothers that they have suffered enough, without some of you trying to make their lives unbearable when they come here. Most of them don't really want to leave their homes (such as they are) and loved ones, but they are forced to, because imperialism takes everything out and puts very little back' (*Railway Review*, 28 September 1956).

branch stations, and each suffered from a considerable labour shortage and a high turnover. Neither station had a large nucleus of old-timers. At A the old-timers were mostly porters, while at B they were signalmen. This meant that they were isolated for most of their working day and consequently did not form very vocal pressure-groups in the station working community as a whole.

At both stations the number of immigrant railwaymen was so small (three Barbadian porters at A, two Anglo-Indians, a Pole, and a Barbadian at B) that they tended to be regarded and judged as individuals rather than members of an outgroup. The station-master at Station A made the following comments:

> The Barbadians are not the nigger type but well-educated, intelligible in their speech and able to write good reports. They've all been here for two or three years. As workers one's reliable, the other medium and the third's a monkey unless he's watched all the time. They don't seem particularly touchy or difficult—certainly not with me. There was a little feeling among the other men at first and some talked of leaving. One man was particularly against having them. The three coloured chaps stuck together at first as a result but the trouble blew over and now they mix in.

At Station B the processes of absorption seemed to have gone further, probably because of the very positive and helpful attitude of the station-master. The immigrants were in a variety of jobs; one Anglo-Indian was a goods guard, the other a clerk; the Barbadian was a porter and the Pole worked in the engineering department. There were also three Southern Irish porters, but they were not regarded as immigrants:

> I've had a few coloured men in earlier years but they've moved on—two were actually promoted on my recommendation. They take a bit of time to settle down but I've several good inspectors who cope well and help them at the beginning. A lot of them turn up for jobs but I don't take them unless they look smart and intelligent. I can't take on too many coloured workers as I don't want to spoil the good relations that have prevailed from the start. The Anglo-Indians may seem a better proposition as so many of them were on the railways in India. But here the work is much more intensive and they can't all keep up. One of them is first-class, like the Pole; the other's lazy and resents taking orders. He's got a bit of a chip about his colour.

Station C, whose staff was distributed about several sub-stations, was situated in an area of fairly intensive coloured immigrant settlement. All its labour force was locally recruited and this was probably why nearly 17 per cent. of the small passenger and goods staff at the station itself consisted of coloured immigrants. They included one Anglo-Indian leading porter, who was an engine-driver in India, another Anglo-Indian and two Barbadian porters, and a Jamaican clerk; all of them had been employed for some years. The station-master had had other coloured staff in the past, one of whom, a Barbadian, was up-graded to another station as a signalman on the station-master's recommendation. There had been no European immigrant staff at this station.

The small size of the station made it easy for the station-master to maintain close and direct contact with every individual member of his staff. His picture of working relationships was, therefore, considerably more detailed and first-hand than those given at the two larger stations:

> We've very few old-timers here now. The pay and conditions are such that the railways are no longer a vocation. But we get a nice local type applying, coloured as well as white, and there's never been any overt trouble here, although there was a bit of feeling at the beginning, and though there's still an undercurrent among local people outside. But it's not like the types that are recruited around some of the main-line stations in Central London. I'd expect to have trouble there. Our chaps share a common staff-room and get on all right. The West Indians don't eat different food in this station. The Anglo-Indians are a bit quick-tempered but the Barbadians are very placid. They're decent-living men with wives and families. They've no intention of going home and are settling down fast and saving up to move into a nicer district. I've been to see them at home several times and helped them with their family problems. I'm interested in their welfare and find them interesting people.

The satisfactory working relations at this station were clearly due in large measure to the firm, tolerant, and kindly personality of the station-master. This rather cosy situation exemplified the view which was expressed to me at the regional office at about this time, that coloured railwaymen were absorbed in the service most successfully when they were placed in twos and threes in the smaller suburban stations or depots.

The process of absorption had, however, some way still to go even at Station C. The station-master expressed some doubts about the newcomers' working potential and also about the degree to which the rest of the staff had accepted them as fellow-railway-men[1]

The coloured men are much the same on the job if they're taught properly, though they're a little slower. There's sometimes a problem of intelligibility on both sides and this can be dangerous in some railway jobs. They also lack geographical knowledge and are a bit limited altogether. We must take on some staff who can be up-graded according to the general railway policy. This is one reason why I don't feel I could take on any more at present. The other is that I don't want to provoke any bad feeling among the rest of the staff. In my view the coloured chaps aren't sufficiently accepted yet to have too many or to put them in authority over others.

At none of the three Croydon stations did there appear to have been any adverse reaction from the public to the presence of coloured railway staff, although the stations were extensively used by middle-class suburban commuters. This contrasted with the situation that was reported to have prevailed for some time in one London main-line passenger station falling under another regional administration.[2]

The fourth of the British Railways establishments in the Croydon area—the railway workshop—was not strictly comparable to the three stations. It employed some 120 'shopmen', not 'railwaymen', and here the N.U.R. has to compete for members with at least four non-railway craft or general unions. The local workers were described as 'rather a rough, uncouth crowd—we employ people we wouldn't have looked at in the past'. Although there was a nucleus of old-timers the general turnover was higher than in the stations and depots.

This workshop was proportionately one of the largest employers of immigrant labour in Croydon: of its 120 shopmen about thirty

[1] The problems of maintaining an inflow of suitable recruits and of providing the public with safe and good service are a major consideration with both the railway administration and the unions (see *Dark Strangers*, pp. 91–95, and p. 151 f.).

[2] See *Reynolds News*, 18 June 1961. When it was reported that no coloured workers at all were employed at this station and relatively few in the region as a whole a staff officer is said to have commented: 'Quite wealthy people travel from . . . and they expect good service. All things being equal we prefer taking on white people. . . . they are preferred to coloured men for reasons of intelligence and education.' See p. 273 f. for a more detailed discussion of the apparent discrepancy between public reactions, actual and anticipated, to coloured and other immigrant workers in a variety of situations.

were Poles and fifteen to twenty West Africans, while there were about half a dozen West Indians and a score of Pakistanis and Anglo-Indians. At the most conservative estimate, therefore, over half of the workshop staff consisted of immigrants, at least one-third being 'coloured'. Poles had been working here since the re-settlement period and West Africans since 1948. Indeed, this was one of the few Croydon establishments in which the latter group was found in any numbers.

A major element in the situation at this workshop was the colourful personality of the Superintendent himself. Lively, enthusiastic, tough, well-read and travelled, an ex-naval officer, a Fabian, and a member of many and diverse committees, he emerged during the course of a four-hour interview as a law unto himself in the railway world and as very much of a 'sponsor' type: 'Some of the local lads call me the "Patron Saint of Poland" and "Jesus Christ for the Negroes". I'm a mixture of Irish and Jew myself so I'm more inter-racially minded than the locals.'

The Superintendent had formed a fairly clear picture of the general characteristics of the various minority groups which he had employed over the last decade or so. Of the Poles he said:

They can be divided into two main castes [*sic*]—a minority of ex-officers and a majority who belonged to the urban working-class in Poland, mainly railwaymen from Silesia. Both groups have a high standard of work and discipline and a low turnover. The finest and fastest tool-maker I ever had was a Pole; he became a shop-steward. But he emigrated to the States some years ago. The local men know the Poles can lick them hands down at the job but this doesn't mean any of them are fully accepted. You might say they're 'with us' but not 'of us'.

The working-class types (especially the Silesians) fit in far better socially than the ex-officers but even those who are naturalized keep aloof from off-the-job activities. The Poles are clannish and tend to drift together at work but I restrict this to working in pairs. Several of the ex-officers have high educational and professional qualifications and I've been able to place some of them in more suitable work. They keep aloof from the working-class Poles and from the other men. Their children usually get back to professional status again.

Only six out of the whole lot are naturalized but they're beginning to apply now there's a threat of redundancy. The unwritten law is 'no promotions and first out for foreigners'. Until now they've taken promotions in the normal way because there were few British applicants. Now they feel insecure *vis-à-vis* black British subjects because a depot's just been closed down and we've had to displace some Poles here to make room for coloured men who are British subjects.[1] Apart from this the Poles often object to working with Negro shopmen, apparently because they think it lowers their status in British eyes.[2]

Off the job I find most of the Poles—the ex-officers and the others alike—circumspect and old-fashioned in their behaviour. They're very thrifty and the first thing that most of them buy is a house. But a few drink heavily; they save up and have one glorious burst.

No other European immigrants were working here at present but the Superintendent had employed Germans and Hungarians in the past. The Germans he regarded as 'easier to handle' than the Poles. Of the Hungarians he commented, rather unexpectedly: 'They're very like the English and fit in easily.'

My informant had little to say about Pakistani workers but characterized the Anglo-Indian staff as 'sub-county class, Catholics, with almost English standards'. Most had been civil servants or clerical workers on the Indian railways and they were doing worse jobs and had lost status since they came to this country. Speaking about Anglo-Indians in general the Superintendent made an interesting comment: 'They tend to get clerical and nursing jobs more easily than the Negroes because the margin of colour is tolerable.'

The workshop was one of the few establishments in Croydon where West Indians and Africans were employed side by side. The Superintendent held very definite and detailed views about the working capacity and general characteristics of these and other coloured groups. In some cases such views seemed to pre-date his

[1] From Polish sources it was learned that further displacement at about this time was averted by an initiative of the local N.U.R., which apparently took the view that long service constituted some sort of honorary citizenship, even for those who were not formally naturalized (see *Polish Daily*, 11 and 23 April 1959).

[2] A Polish ex-officer employed in this particular workshop described his reactions to Negro fellow-workers in a letter to the *Polish Daily* published on 8 June 1959. Claiming that the problem was less one of colour than of cultural differences he wrote: 'There are some decent and fairly knowledgeable fellows amongst them but the vast majority are still, to put it delicately, completely primitive; they are also burdened with many complexes, above all with an inferiority complex, hence they are exceptionally touchy and difficult. Qualities such as decency, ambition, honour, accuracy and responsibility are completely foreign to them. They irritate and upset one with their noisiness, their shamelessness and their arrogance—they are extremely lazy and prone to malingering. The Poles also object to these new arrivals because the Negroes as British subjects have priority in jobs and promotion over the Poles, regardless of length of service and qualifications.'

railway service and be based on pre-independence experiences in Africa and Asia and also on a correlation between the amount of 'white blood' possessed by an individual and his 'cultural level':

As far as working ability is concerned Africans are good carpenters but not so good as fitters. The West Indians are extremely good craftsmen (70 per cent. come in at the skilled level) but it's difficult to get them to take advanced classes, as the railways like their men to do. The craft unions sometimes challenge these skills but I make the West Indians take a trade test to prove themselves and they usually suceed in this. I attribute the West Indians' superior know-how to the fact that they have a lot of white blood.

They're also rather Americanized to start with but adapt themselves easily to English ways. In fact, their standard of behaviour and hygiene are usually better than those of the local English lads, although the latter did make a few complaints at first about dirty toilet habits and some refused to wash after coloured workers, saying that they were afraid the colour might come off. There are fights from time to time but they're usually between coloured men. Knives and chisels have been involved and once some paint-work got damaged and I had to call out the fire-brigade and have a hose turned on the fighters. Otherwise I deal with these *fracas* myself, being a judo expert.

I handle the West Indians by leg-pulling, but as a rule I find Africans easier to handle and prefer to deal with them. I prefer Muslim Africans to the 'mission boy' or 'Liberian type'. They're held back by their living conditions in London. Most live in rooming-houses owned by English-speaking Africans or Anglo-Coloured who exploit them. These boys live wrong and eat wrong. Very few of them drink, it's true, unlike the Irish, but most have white mammy trouble. There are girls on call in those houses and sometimes two will call for the same man's wages. One West African was rumoured to have V.D. I called him in and he admitted it. 'I get it from my wife—she a prostitute,' he said, apparently taking it as quite normal.

In the Superintendent's view no immigrant workers were fully accepted by the small, old-established nucleus of local workers. He summed up the prevailing attitude among the latter as 'equal but not accepted':

A number may accept the coloured workers 'against the Poles' but on the other hand some responsible union men have been aggravated by the coloured workers. The Poles have taken promotion in the normal run but when I made one coloured man a charge-hand the N.U.R. men said they wouldn't take orders from a 'bloody Negro' and I had to rescind the promotion, although officially the union has no colour bar. It's not a closed shop here and there are several unions but inter-union rivalry doesn't seem to help the immigrant workers. The craft unions are strong but the T. and G.W.U. is a West Indian bloc. But the real background to working relationships is the terrific insecurity now—the happy days are over and many of the workshop men are unemployable elsewhere on the railways. There's also the widespread feeling of lost status among the old-timers.

Job insecurity and anxiety over status indeed appeared to characterize the entire working community in this workshop. They were felt not only by the old-timers but also by the Poles and Anglo-Indians. The prevailing undercurrent of uncertainty and frustration could not fail to affect the West Indians and West Africans, who had perhaps less reason to be anxious over lowered status but who were passing through the difficult early stage of accommodation not only at work but also in society as a whole.

Conclusions

In the 'heavy' sector several industrial groups were considered together on the somewhat arbitrary grounds that much of the work involved was 'heavy', that most of the labour force was male and that the great majority of the establishments surveyed were rather static and traditional in character. In a number of other aspects, appreciable differences emerged between industries and firms, and the numbers and degree of absorption of various immigrant groups was also found to differ widely from industry to industry and firm to firm.

In the 'heavy' sector, as elsewhere, labour shortage was undoubtedly the main factor in promoting the entry of immigrant workers into an industry or firm. In the subsequent processes of accommodation, however, less utilitarian factors, arising out of established management–labour relations, tradition, status, and other intangibles, would seem to have played a more important part than they did in the dynamic, labour-hungry, light engineering sector. It was not necessarily the industries and firms with the greatest labour shortage, nor indeed those with the largest proportion of immigrant workers, in which accommodation could be said to be proceeding most smoothly and satisfactorily.

It was in the two heavy engineering firms and the public utilities that the absorption of one or more groups of immigrants had proceeded farthest, though not necessarily for the same reasons. The two heavy engineering firms had a larger nucleus of long-service labour and a less chronic and urgent labour problem than the various public utilities (other than the Electricity Board). Moreover, they continued to offer their workers relatively good wages and conditions, job security and high status in the local industrial hierarchy. Both the firms involved were well-integrated working communities with good labour relations, communities in which all newcomers, immigrant or not, had to be both efficient and adaptable and to expect only gradual acceptance. Once this acceptance was won, however, it was likely to be satisfactory and complete, and to contribute greatly to similar acceptance in the wider community. In both firms there had been some kind of sponsorship—in Firm A by a pre-war Hungarian immigrant on the staff, in Firm B by an Anglo-Indian who had himself 'made the grade' and had introduced a number of his friends.

By contrast with these two private firms, the public utilities had since the war steadily lost status in relation to other industries. In recent years, moreover, even the 100 per cent. job security, which helped to counter-balance such disadvantages as long working hours, week-end and night work, had been increasingly eroded. Management and supervisory staff, which had been largely recruited from the ranks, tended to share the anxieties of the rank and file and to be even more concerned with the possibility of lowered standards of public service and deterioration in the quality of the personnel and the status of the industry. On the other hand, the chronic labour shortage in most sectors and areas provided a considerable incentive to experiment systematically with the recruitment, training, and absorption of new and suitable sources of labour.

In Croydon at this time there was no great shortage on the buses or at the Electricity Board but the labour-hungry gas industry and railways were employing a considerable number of immigrants, mainly West Indians and other 'coloured' people. In both cases their entry into the labour force was agreed in principle by the strong general and industrial unions concerned, though such agreement was not always whole-hearted or without reservations, and some pockets of resistance and hostility remained at the lower levels, in particular depots, workshops, or working gangs. In the public utilities, however, both the administration and the representatives of organized labour could not in principle differentiate against any groups of British nationals and any deviations from this in practice tended to attract more public attention than would the actions of management and labour in private firms. This consideration was obviously a factor that could assist the entry and initial absorption of Commonwealth immigrants in the public utilities.[1]

Efficiency and adaptability were as essential for immigrants in the railway service as they were in the heavy engineering firms. Moreover, as in all establishments in which employees had dealings with the public, a pleasant and equable temperament was of advantage for passenger station staff. Here the 'decent-living, family men' specially recruited by British Railways in Barbados often achieved the most satisfactory accommodation in the railway service and were adequately equipped for gradual up-grading according to its routine promotion policy.

In the other two industrial groups (building and the miscellaneous heavy industries), the process of absorption of recent immigrants had not gone so far. The Irish monopoly of the building trade was an important factor restricting the entry of more recent immigrants in the majority of Croydon's twelve '100-plus' building and construction firms. The three firms investigated employed quite a number of other newcomers, but only the Poles had so far entered the more or less permanent cadre of retainers in the two larger firms. The West Indians, who constituted the largest single group of immigrants in this industry with the exception of the Irish, were generally regarded as poor craftsmen or, more usually, as casual and expendable unskilled labour inferior to Southern Irish labour. The utilitarian approach of employers in this industry was another important factor in the absorptive process, whereas the reactions of unions and the local labour force seemed much less important than they were in the public utilities or the well-unionized heavy engineering firms.

The heavy industrial sector would seem to constitute a characteristic 'transit-camp' type of industry into which newcomers to the labour market traditionally go or are directed and which tends to rely on a small established labour-core and a continued supply of transient newcomers. Only two of the four firms involved in Croydon in fact employed any considerable number of immigrants. The brick-works did, however, afford a classic example of

[1] For an exception, see p. 102, n. 1.

the 'transit camp'. Most Poles and European Voluntary Workers (E.V.W.s) had already passed through, as had a number of Italians as soon as they were free to do so. A dozen Italians had, however, settled in the locality and appeared to be prepared to regard the firm as a 'permanent billet'. The West Indians had become acceptable only in recent years and it was not yet clear whether they regarded the firm as a transit camp or a permanent billet.

The other firm with a considerable proportion of immigrant labour provided a classic exemplification of the nightmare stereotype of organized labour: that of the tough employer who uses immigrant labour to prevent the unionization of his labour force. It was because of the possible outside repercussions of this employer's action that the situation in this firm could not be regarded as entirely satisfactory, although a large West Indian contingent had been absorbed, there had been some promotion and there was no indication of any cutting of wage rates as a consequence of the taking on of so many immigrants.

(3) *The 'Consumer' Industries*

The 'consumer' sector includes light industry, garment and associated trades, laundry and dry cleaning, and food processing and distribution. All these industries or firms provide consumer goods or services; they were also grouped together for discussion here because (with the exception of some rather specialized light industrial firms) the bulk of the work involved is not only fairly light but also not particularly skilled, and because many firms employ a considerable number of women.

In many cases, yet another common combination or cluster of factors is present, which helps to produce a particular industrial climate. Most of these industries and firms operate in highly competitive conditions and are subject either to seasonal fluctuations or to changes in public taste and demand; there is therefore a tendency to cut labour costs by working with a small, permanent cadre combined with seasonally recruited, low-wage labour. This tendency, in conjunction with the high proportion of women workers, keeps unionization low in most firms. There are, however, as in the other sectors surveyed, certain differences between industrial groups and individual firms in such matters as labour supply, wage levels, and job security and status.

(a) *Light Industry Proper*

The light industrial group proper includes, as has just been said, some firms which were different in character and culture from those described above, and rather nearer to some firms in the skilled section of light engineering.

Of the nine '100-plus' light industrial firms in Croydon, one was a manufacturer of toilet articles, a second produced specialized office and stationery goods, three made various types of furniture and upholstery, two were engaged in producing a wide variety of insulating or packing materials, and two more on the production of plastics.

Firm A, the toilet goods manufacturer, was an old-established, rather traditional firm which moved to the new industrial area in Croydon some years before the War. The work was light, pleasant, and performed in exceptionally agreeable conditions and surroundings. Jobs were secure for full-time workers and there was a pension scheme; the atmosphere seemed easy-going and friendly and the works manager, who had himself been with the firm for forty years, stressed the congenial nature of the work and the 'nice type of women' who formed the bulk of the labour force. Since 1945, however, the firm had had to compete for female labour with the neighbouring light engineering firms, which paid higher wages and offered more overtime opportunities. It had solved this problem fairly satisfactorily by building up a steady labour force of older local women ('the young girls have a much higher turnover') and using part-time student and other labour when necessary. There was little or no unionization at this firm, although facilities were said to have been given to the appropriate union to approach the workers just before the War: 'But they'd nothing to offer our people and nothing came of it.'

At the time of my visit Firm A employed about fifty men, mainly on dispatch and maintenance, and 230 women, seventy of them part-time, on production. The men included one Pakistani, one Anglo-Indian, and a Nigerian; a West African student also had been doing vacation work there for several years. There was also a Pole who had been with the firm for eight years: 'He's an export packer and worth two men to me. We've had one or two other Poles here since the War and they've all been good workers. I took a Hungarian on in early 1957, though, and his attitude to the work was very off-hand so he didn't last more than a couple of months.'

Firm A's main experience with women immigrants had been with West Indians, but none were employed at this time. My informant said:

> They come and go. We've had them before and we'll probably have them again. They're very good workers and we've no grumble about their slowness or anything else. They always leave of their own accord. Like the young local girls they use us as a stop-gap until they get work with an engineering firm at higher rates.

The next establishment in the light industrial group, Firm B, was about forty years old, produced specialized stationery articles and was situated in an older industrial area not far from one of the areas of recent coloured settlement in Croydon. It was a smallish 'family' firm employing approximately 240 workers, of whom all but fifty were women.

The situation here is a very individual one, influenced greatly by the dominating personality of its managing director, an ex-officer with strong views on most subjects. During the discussion he emerged as very much of a paternalistic, 'sponsor' type for certain classes of people, this sponsorship being balanced by an equally strong hostility to other groups, notably Roman Catholics and the Catholic hierarchy. In the earlier part of a long interview this informant cross-questioned me rather sharply as to the motives and aims of the survey: 'What's the real purpose? A lot of people are trying to get information to use against the coloured people. I wouldn't want anything I say to be misquoted and destroy their trust in me.'

Later the managing director's suspicions abated and he became very communicative about his employment policy and relationships between coloured and white in the firm. To the end, however, he made it clear that he did not wish to answer questions about processes, production, wage-levels, unionization, and similar routine matters:

> This is an unusual type of firm. You'll notice that we don't have the name on the gate and we don't advertise. There's no union and we don't belong to the local Chamber of Commerce. We don't keep any statistics. Our processes are secret, the products sell by the way they're made and we don't fix the price until the article's made. It works well enough. We've never had any redundancy in forty years.

Despite his reticence over general facts and figures, this informant was willing to hazard the estimate that about 15 per cent. of the firm's labour force at that time consisted of coloured immigrants, mainly West Indian and Anglo-Indian women. When describing his general personnel policy and working relations within the firm, my informant was considerably more vocal than on earlier subjects:

I came home after the War and tried to bring in the war-time spirit of comradeship. There's a wonderful team spirit all through the factory. We're all one family and I know everyone personally, but there's no coddling. If they're malingering they don't get sick pay. The others know it too and tell them off, as they're working on various bonus systems and stand to lose.

Coloured workers had been employed by Firm B for about five years. The managing director was quite willing to discuss his reasons for taking them on and his methods of influencing relations between coloured and white workers:

I consider it my Christian duty to help others as far as possible. I believe in the principle 'do as you would be done by'. I take on ex-convicts, cripples, applicants of all ages and immigrants, coloured or not, judging them only according to their personality. I failed with the Poles for some reason—I would have taken Hungarians after the Rising but there were none available.

I started taking coloured people when the Labour Exchange sent one along. They're no different from anybody else. I believe in environment, not blood. There's good and bad in all races. They're not particularly slow workers and they fit in well enough with the others. No coloured worker would dare to accuse anyone here of being anti-coloured nor would a white dare to be anti-coloured while I'm around. I've forced tolerance on the whites, though Croydon's a tolerant place and they have the roots of tolerance in them. As for my relations with the coloured workers, I find the odd one has a chip on the shoulder about his or her colour. I reason with them and I usually win. Some can't put up with it and leave but the others become different people. Some are a bit suspicious of me but most trust me, though they probably think I'm a harmless nut.

This particular informant displayed so many strong prepossessions and prejudices in relation to a wide range of topics and groups that it was difficult to take his account of the situation and relationships in his factory at face value. His secretive and suspicious attitude at the beginning of the interview and his reiterated aversion to unions also seemed to argue against his credibility. Nevertheless, later observation of the cordial relationship between him and various employees suggested that his account was reasonably correct, although clearly workers who could not come to terms with his personality did not stay long with this firm. On the whole this appeared to be a 'good' firm for the absorption of coloured immigrants. The reported failure with Poles could perhaps be attributed to the informant's hostility to Roman Catholicism, perhaps to the fact that such European exiles might have less been willing to accept the particular paternalistic régime that prevailed in this firm.

Of the three furniture and upholstery firms, C and D employed something over 400 workers each while E was smaller, with about 200 workers. They differed from most of the other firms in this sector in that they employed a large long-term labour force consisting of about three men to every woman operative, and that the majority of their labour force had to be, skilled, mainly as cabinet-makers. Firms C and D were old-established family firms in the older industrial areas of Croydon. They drew on local labour, had a low labour turnover and were therefore under no particular pressure to seek new sources of labour. Firm E was situated in and drew its labour force from a peri-urban housing estate some miles from the centre of Croydon. No immigrants lived in this area and few non-residents of any kind applied for work because of transport difficulties. In consequence only three immigrants had ever worked for this firm: one Pole who left some years ago and two West Indians who were doing unskilled jobs there at the time of this inquiry. The management's attitude was helpful, but beyond saying that it was satisfied with the work of these individuals it had no particular comments to make about them.

Of the two larger firms, Firm D was unwilling to grant an interview but wrote, somewhat stiffly: 'We have a comparatively small number of coloured workers here with whom we are satisfied that they give us fair results in their labour. It must be understood however that we prefer to employ our own people when available.'

Firm C, on the other hand, employed eight skilled immigrants, four Indians and Anglo-Indians, two Cypriots, one Pole, and a German. All of them were regarded as part of the permanent labour force by management and fellow-workers, but none were so far in positions involving responsibility or direct supervision over others. Other Asians and Europeans had been employed in the past, but the firm had not so far engaged or indeed had many applications from West Indians or West Africans.

Of the two producers of insulation or packing materials, Firm F was part of a nation-wide industrial group, which took over this particular factory after the Second World War. Here again three out of every four workers in the 400-strong labour force were men. The work was not, however, particularly skilled, unlike that in the furniture factories. The factory was heavily mechanized, most of the work being organized on production lines in three eight-hour shifts. The personnel manager described its nature and requirements thus:

> Our main requirements are speed, concentration and unflagging diligence. The workers are tied to the machine and subject to its speed, which varies according to production requirements. It's crew work with bonus schemes and a worker who can't keep up is useless to us and unpopular with the men.

Firm F had a fairly high labour turnover but no particular labour problem: 'In fact we have a long waiting list of our own people. The firm has a good name in the district and the wages are a little over average. There's also a pension scheme and a social club.'

In keeping with this firm's general efficiency its personnel department had tried out various groups of immigrant workers as they became available. At this time the firm employed something over 2 per cent. of immigrants (five Polish men, five Italian men, two Italian women, and two Hong Kong Chinese women married to Englishmen). There were also a fair number of Southern Irish, of whom it was said: 'They're usually good workers, especially the women, but the unsettled recent arrivals present a problem because of their practice of working for a year and then disappearing for several months or altogether.'

About the other immigrant workers my informant commented:

> We're satisfied with their work, and particularly with that of the Poles. The majority are ex-professional officers and two have been promoted to more skilled and responsible work after starting as labourers. The majority are now married to local girls and all have taken British nationality and got into the pension scheme, which is restricted to British

subjects. They and all the others mix in well socially and participate in the social club outings. The other workers accept them—when one of the Italian girls had some financial trouble all her work-mates rallied round to help her.

Firm F had tried other groups of immigrants with less success. Several Hungarians who were taken on after the Rising were found 'capable of doing the work but unsatisfactory for a variety of other reasons, language difficulties, truculence, etc.'. None were now employed. Coloured workers had also been tried, but found wanting for a different reason: 'They simply can't keep up with the production-line and even if they get used to one speed they can't adjust themselves when it's suddenly altered.' In fact, their unsatisfactory performance had only confirmed the unfavourable stereotype of coloured workers' capabilities reached by the personnel manager when he was an officer in the Regular Army: 'I served for many years before and during the last War in India and Egypt and I had a good deal to do with coloured labour. As for Anglo-Indians some have applied here but after my experience in India I'd be the last person to take them on at all.'

Despite his 'wog complex' this informant was prepared to state not only that the firm recognized no colour bar but also he thought that local workers would be willing to accept coloured workers provided that they met the necessary standards of efficiency and so did not threaten group bonuses. Firm F was an open shop, but nearly half the workers were union members; neither the workers nor the unions had objected to the employment of any groups of immigrant labour. The main factors affecting immigrant absorption in Firm F seemed to be the absence of any drastic labour shortage, the demands of the work process itself and, in the case of coloured immigrants, the unfavourable attitude of the personnel manager.

Firm G was, like Firm F, part of a large international combine. It had been operating in Croydon only since the War and was even more loosely linked with the area than Firm E. A good deal of the work involved installation of the product all over southern England and labour was still taken on at an office on the other side of London, much of it being drawn from areas other than Croydon. The labour force of about 300 was almost entirely male, in the proportion of one apprentice to two trained workers.

The work was fairly skilled and very well paid; it offered considerable variety and opportunities for travel but could also involve working in uncomfortable and dirty conditions. The firm was well unionized and entry was through a routine, five-year apprenticeship scheme which was accepted by firms and unions throughout the industry. This set of circumstances undoubtedly affected the intake of immigrant workers.

> The only jobs for newcomers over the age of sixteen are labouring or warehouse work, and there's not much of that going. We haven't had any immigrant lads applying for apprenticeship so far as I can recall. The immigrants we've had are adults who came in during the post-war years when there was a frightful manpower shortage and the union apprenticeship scheme was relaxed until a short time ago. We took on men anywhere then. We had a lot of Cypriots at one time (not recruited in Croydon) but only three or four are left new. Most of them are awkward customers—they won't work but prefer letting off rooms at exorbitant rates, driving posh cars, pimping and so on. Most coloureds are like the Cypriots—they don't like to work. If you get one of these chappies who really wants to settle, then he will work. The rest of the Negroids are messers and cost more to chase than they're worth. All the same there's no automatic bar against anyone and we get a lot of coloured applicants when the word goes round on the grape-vine that we're recruiting.

At this time only three other immigrants (two Poles and a man rather loosely described as a 'light-coloured chappie—Filippino or Eurasian') were still with Firm G. All three had achieved skilled status and one of the Poles, a war-time airman, was a charge-hand. The three men were described as good workers, who got on well with their fellow-workers.

Both of the two firms engaged in plastics production were owned or managed by immigrants. In such firms one might reasonably expect to find a greater readiness to employ immigrant labour and in fact well over half of Firm H's staff and labour force (350-strong in mid-1958) were non-British born (mainly Poles, like the managing director) while Firm I employed over 11 per cent. of immigrants. Firm H was unique among Croydon firms in that many of the senior staff posts with the exception of the works manager, personnel manager, and administrative and sales staff, and the great majority of the supervisory jobs in the works were held by Poles. Local English manual labour was at the bottom of the works hierarchy and showed a high labour turnover. The situation in this 'vice versa' firm is described and analysed in more detail in Part IV.

Firm I was ten years or so older than Firm H, having been started by an Austrian refugee in the 1930s. Its employment policy was, as has been said, a tolerant one so far as immigrants were concerned but there was no similar clustering of employees of the same origin as the managing director, probably because this group is fully absorbed in either the professions, commerce, or white-collar work.

The labour force at this firm consisted of ninety men and sixty women. Ten per cent. of the work was skilled, 70 per cent. semi-skilled, and 20 per cent. unskilled or labouring work. Some of the semi-skilled work was hot or monotonous but wage rates were said to be extremely good by local standards. There were no group bonuses and little automation, so that speed was not as important as it was in, for instance, Firm F. Firm I's labour force was not highly unionized, with the exception of the skilled minority.

This firm had employed a Pole and now had a Ceylonese in the office and one Indian on semi-skilled work, but its main experience had been with West Indian immigrants. Recruitment of West Indian work-seekers began in 1955–6, at a time of considerable labour shortage. My informant said:

> We just started employing them without any formal consultation—but there were no objections except from one foreman, so we avoided putting any under him. We had up to 15 per cent. at one time but thinned them out when there was a bit of redundancy following the credit squeeze. There was no demand for coloureds to go first but we got rid of all those who were least use.
>
> Those we have now (about a dozen men and four women) are quite satisfactory. They're slower but will stay on at a monotonous job that would bore most English workers. They've a lower turnover than the average, perhaps because they realize the difficulty of getting another job (they're much better in this respect than the Southern Irish, who are very irresponsible and sometimes flit off after two or three weeks). The West Indians are good time-keepers and they'll work overtime and all sorts of hours because they know the value of money. They're not skilled in our terms and none are on skilled work. We've no training scheme so the semi-skilled stay in that category. One man claimed he was not being accepted as a skilled carpenter because of his colour but the foreman was right that he hadn't got the skills.

On the subject of informal relations with other workers he commented:

They don't mix with the other workers off the job nor outside but then neither do the English workers. The social club had so little support that we closed it down some years ago. There's not much friction. We're happy to employ them but I'd be very careful about placing and promotion. For instance, one coloured man applied for the job of gate-keeper recently. I didn't give it him because a gate-keeper has to exert some authority and sometimes to turn applicants away. If it were a coloured man turning away locals there might be trouble.

(b) *The Garment and Associated Trades*

The garment industry in Britain, as in many other countries, is traditionally a domain of immigrant labour and enterprise and there is usually no very strong resistance by management or labour to the entry of newcomers.

There were only four '100-plus' firms in this group in Croydon. One of them had never employed any immigrants at all; it was small (only 100 or so workers) and had to reduce its staff in recent years. A second establishment, Firm A, differed from most garment manufacturers in that it manufactured a product which required certain specialized skills and in its reliance on a stable labour force of about 100 (mainly women). This included several Polish and two Indian (or possibly Anglo-Indian) women. The welfare officer commented: 'There really isn't much I can tell you. They're all thoroughly accepted. The two coloured ladies seem to have settled down in our factory as if they had been here all their lives. They are both very popular with the other girls.'

Firms B and C were small, old-established firms, each employing about 100 workers. They were fairly close in type to the many small garment firms found in central and east London. Each had a handful of male tailors, pressers, and others, and a solid nucleus of highly trained women power-machinists augmented by additional workers before peak seasons (notably the summer months in preparation for the Christmas trade). Speed and efficiency were all-important in this highly competitive, marginal-profit industry, and machinists who could not reach a minimum target or standard after a trial period were usually dismissed. Unionization was low, particularly among female labour.

Both firms began to take on immigrants, particularly women, in the early 1950s, as a result of a grave shortage of trained power-machinists. Most of their experience had been with West Indians, although a handful of European and Asian women had also been employed. Neither of these two firms had, however, employed or indeed had any applications from Polish or other East European women workers.

At this time Firm B had no immigrants in its labour force. The manageress described her past experiences:

We've tried Cypriots, Southern Irish and West Indian girls but they all have a high turnover; in addition the Irish were slow and clumsy and the Cypriots didn't seem keen to work. The West Indian girls certainly tried hard but they weren't really a satisfactory proposition. Some were youngsters just arrived in this country and they hadn't a clue. They would tell me they'd done machining at home, but it was hand-machining. Here the work is arranged so that each machinist makes the whole garment and that was too difficult for them. We pay the Board of Trade minimum rate but a top machinist can earn £9 to £11 per week. None of the West Indians even got up to the minimum. One girl might have learned if she had stuck it for a year, but her family wanted her to earn more at once and took her away. I never tried any of them on pressing. I think they would have found it too difficult. Most of them left of their own accord. I would still take on West Indian applicants, but they're not turning up now. I think they go to the local light engineering firms and laundries.

Firm C was on the northern boundary of Croydon, in an area with a large floating population, and drew some of its labour from such areas as Brixton. It had suffered from an even graver labour shortage than Firm B:

The Brixton exchange was offering us coloured workers for years, but we only began to take them in 1951. We were taking anyone who came then, because of the labour shortage. First, however, we called our own people together and said: 'Look here—don't let's have any trouble. We need workers badly.' We've had more coloured workers than we've got now—at present it's about 5 per cent, mostly West Indians. There are one or two Dutch and German women but they present no problem. With the West Indians the main trouble is slowness. They claim to know how to operate power machines but that's usually exaggerated. Not all of them can achieve the minimum output we require. Some work well in a team but most slow down output and are therefore difficult to match with others.

Working relations between coloured immigrants and local workers were said to have been cordial in Firm B and my informant, the manageress, was a friendly and helpful person who had clearly gone out of her way to assist the newcomers. In Firm C, on the other hand, considerable initial resistance from the 'hard core' of local labour was reported: 'We had to get them used to the coloured workers, but now any coloured woman who's normal and pleasant is accepted and included in birthday parties and other sprees.'

Firm C's works manager had a far more utilitarian, no-nonsense approach than the benevolent manageress at Firm B; none the less this firm still continued to employ coloured machinists although it was not entirely satisfied with their performance, while Firm B had given up altogether. It would seem that labour shortage and immigrant working efficiency were the over-riding factors in Firm C, whereas mild sponsoring attitudes on the part of management and acceptance by the long-service nucleus in Firm B were insufficient to ensure the retention of West Indian immigrants who were unable to achieve the required speed and efficiency. It could also be that Firm C, which because of its location had had more coloured applicants and more experience of coloured workers, had evolved better methods of selection for this particular source of labour than Firm B.

(c) *The Laundry and Dry-Cleaning Industry*

The laundry and dry-cleaning industry resembles the garment trade in many features. It is highly competitive and has a low profit margin. Most of its labour is female (including many married women and part-time workers) and unionization is consequently low, except in co-operative laundries. The chronic labour shortage from which the industry suffers is even graver than in the garment trade because although the work requires less speed and skill many work-seekers are deterred by the nature of the work,[1] the relatively low wages,[2] and the low prestige of the job.

[1] An unattractive stereotype of laundry work is still widely held, although it may represent a more or less outmoded image. At a careers conference held in Croydon by the Croydon section of the Institute of British Launderers, with the object of informing headmasters and headmistresses of local secondary schools of openings in the laundry industry for school-leavers, the chairman of the section pointed out that, while people were still inclined to think of laundries as dark, dank, steamy places, this was a false impression. Laundry work was changing and most of the heavy work was now done by machinery (*Croydon Times*, 4 December 1959).

[2] At the careers conference referred to on p. 118, n. 1, the Croydon Youth Employment Officer drew an unfavourable comparison between the minimum

The Croydon employment exchange listed only three laundry and dry-cleaning firms among the '100-plus' establishments. One of these failed to reply to several requests for an interview for information. Of the other two, Firm A was associated with and located in the same district as garment Firm C, and drew much of its labour from Brixton and other South London areas north of Croydon. The labour force contained about 10 per cent. of coloured women (West Indian, Indian, and Anglo-Indian) and a few European women.[1] Some West Indian men were taken on in past years, but they were found to be unsatisfactory workers: 'We have plenty of coloured men applying, but we don't take them any more. Now that the labour situation's eased a little we can get more suitable applicants. But we still take on coloured women for laundry work.'

The laundry manager distinguished between the working abilities of various groups: 'The women have a high turnover but seem better than the men and I regard the Indians as generally better than the Jamaicans, who are often lethargic. In fact, you can usually tell by the way applicants walk up the yard whether they're going to be any good or not—that applies to white as well as coloured.' Questioned about promotion, this informant said:

> Filling supervisory posts is a general headache because most women don't want to take on any responsibility. Once I was so desperate I decided to try out a very good Anglo-Indian girl who'd been with us for several years as a charge-hand on the evening shift. But it didn't work out. I don't think the others were willing to take orders from her and she was unsure of herself—neither fish nor flesh. I wouldn't be anxious to try the experiment again.

Firm B was much larger than Firm A, with a total labour force of some 400, of whom nearly three-quarters were women; it was said to be one of the biggest and most modernly equipped laundries in Britain. The firm was old-established and drew much of its labour from the central working-class area in which it was situated.

wages offered to school-leavers going into laundry work and the wages obtainable in commerce or shop-work. He did not add that the latter occupations also fall into a higher-status, white-collar category, which would constitute an additional attraction.

[1] There were no European men in this 'transit-camp' firm; the manager recalled a Polish storekeeper (a very good worker) who had left some years earlier to take on a better job.

There was a 20 per cent. nucleus of local old-timers and families, but otherwise labour turnover was high.

To meet the post-war labour shortage this laundry had tried various immigrant groups in succession.

We had Poles after the War, but they were on the move up and didn't stay long—I found them educated, intelligent and industrious. We haven't had many other Europeans. So far as coloured workers are concerned we started with Anglo-Indians. They were good workers and I liked them but you can't hold them, they're going up all the time. We may still have one left but no more. We also regularly take African government trainees to learn the job.

Two years ago we started taking West Indians and since then we've had about a dozen men and a dozen women at a time.[1] I wouldn't take them if I could get whites but few whites are applying now. Nobody wants to work these days but the blacks are the worst. It's not that they're lazy but they don't know what real work is. They keep on all day, slow and steady, and you can't hurry them up. I don't think you could, even if you used a whip. Some of them are bright enough off the job though —they have cars and good suits. One is a real little capitalist, coining money out of housing his own people. We have managed to train some of the men to do a fair job as pressers. Another difficulty is that we find some of them virtually unintelligible. There's one good point—since the recession their turnover has been lower than that of the other transients.

Working relations between local workers and the West Indians were reported to be good in this firm and the main reservations and objections came from the management.

I didn't consult our own people before taking them but they're not particularly biased—Croydon is famous for having no colour bar and there's been no feeling locally about coloured infiltration. I wouldn't expect it really. The black people we have here are working people, unlike those in Notting Hill. There they stand about on the street corner all day and live on National Assistance. You can't blame the locals for feeling badly about it. We haven't had much friction here and no bad incidents between white and coloured—that I wouldn't allow, I'd toss them out. The West Indian men tend to be truculent—they've got a chip on their shoulders about colour and won't take instructions or reprimands. The coloured women in particular mix very well with the local women. They chat away together on the job, go to each other's weddings and on the firm's outings. I think we could take a

[1] About 6 per cent.

larger proportion without any of our own people objecting—they're only too thankful for the help on the job. I wouldn't mind promoting West Indian workers and I don't think the local people would but the coloured people don't seem any keener than the whites on taking responsibility.

You asked about redundancy policy. Redundancy is highly unlikely but if it were to happen we'd get rid of the coloured workers—not because of any demand by the other workers but because of their low working ability and their aggressiveness.

Clearly West Indian workers were far from being accepted as a part of the permanent labour force by this management. Another reason for this, one which was not stated explicitly, could have been connected with the management's very definite concern for the status of their firm and their pride in its success and efficiency.[1] There was, however, a hint of increasing acceptance in the favourable comparison drawn between 'the black people we have here' and the 'bad types' in Notting Hill.

(d) *Food and Soft Drinks Manufacture and Distribution*

Nine '100-plus' firms in Croydon were engaged in the manufacture or distribution of food or soft drinks. They consisted of: three sweet factories, one canning factory, two bakers, one wholesale grocer, one multiple fishmonger, and the local distribution agent of a large ice-cream firm.

The last three of these and one of the bakeries had not employed any immigrant labour, with the possible exception of Southern Irish workers. The main reasons seem to be that these establishments were relatively small, had a low turnover, and had no great difficulty in recruiting more labour locally. The work they offered was, moreover, not particularly attractive to immigrants in search of high rates and overtime and there was the additional consideration

[1] At about this time a representative of one of the laundry trade organizations told me: 'Laundries generally do not like to publicize their use of coloured labour. We are still at the stage of regarding its use as a stop-gap, and are not ready to treat it on equal terms. The whole problem is very difficult because, although we may be very sympathetic, we cannot overlook the fact that they have different standards of living, which make their full acceptance into British life rather difficult. An employee, and I know many such intimately, may be very happy with Tom or Harry in the wash-house. In one instance, a West Indian established himself in the eyes of the manager as one of the best wash-housemen he has ever had. But apart from the prejudice which many people still feel against colour, there is the fact, as one supervisor said to me very recently, that their ways of living are very different from ours and on a lower scale.'

that much of it involved contact with the public, a factor which often deters employers from taking on coloured applicants.

Like the garment trade, sweet-making is a seasonal trade with a heavy intake of labour from August to December for the peak Christmas trade. As a result it has a high labour turnover, many firms relying on a steady nucleus of women workers and a large number of part-timers or temporary workers (married women, students on vacation, and so on). There is little unionization, as in other industries with a similarly constituted labour force. The work is pleasant, light, clean, and reasonably well-paid (at least in so far as women's wages are concerned). It requires no formal skills, but dexterity and personal cleanliness are essential qualifications.

All three of the Croydon sweet firms employed considerable numbers of immigrants, mostly coloured. Unfortunately no interview could be arranged with the smallest of the three, which was in the process of reorganization and could only provide figures of its labour force. Firms A and B were much larger, employing respectively up to 650 and 550 full and part-time workers in the high season; both were visited.

The situation in Firm A is described in more detail in the case study at the end of this section. This firm had long and wide experience of various immigrant groups and had come to accept them as part of the permanent labour force. Such firms tend to be something of a transit camp for ambitious younger immigrant workers, particularly men, and most of the Poles and other European exile workers employed here in former years had drifted away to other industries. When this firm was first visited nearly 15 per cent. of the male labour force of 180 consisted of immigrants: four Poles, one Anglo-Indian, and twenty 'coloured' workers (West Indian or West African). Of the 450 women only something over 2 per cent. were immigrants (one German, four Anglo-Indians, five West Indians). There were also a dozen Southern Irish men and the same number of women, this firm being located in an area of fairly heavy Irish settlement.

Firm B was on the near-rural periphery of the Croydon employment exchange area, in a council housing estate district where few or no immigrants had settled. It had, consequently, little experience of European immigrants other than the German, Austrian, or Italian wives of ex-servicemen. The recruiting of West Indians began only three years ago in an attempt to meet the chronic labour shortage, which in this firm was accentuated by the fact that the generally unpopular three-shift system was operated. West Indians now formed about one-quarter of the entire female labour force, and the build-up had been so rapid that there were certain signs of strain.

We've become nervous about having too many and have just asked the labour exchange to go slow. I don't want the firm to get known as a coloured firm and so lose our regular local applicants. We have to take on up to 300 each year for the peak months. The dark women all sit together at meals and don't mix. They've got some embarrassing habits which upset the other women. They eat differently, spit a lot and there are some sanitary troubles.

Despite these reservations the management at Firm B was fairly satisfied with the working ability of its West Indians:

They create an impression of slowness, but in some ways actually work better than the others. Some have managed to speed up on piece-work even though we can't, with such a large proportion, split them up to any extent. We're fairly experienced at selection now and turn down some applicants. I can tell at once if they're going to be dirty. When the slack season comes we put off all workers on a basis of relative efficiency. Some of the dark girls are kept on. We've had some pretty experienced girls now and a couple of them help us with any problems that arise among the rest. We've none in charge, however; I can't see them taking on supervisory jobs, which need paper work. There were a couple who were good enough, but they were only marking time here and went on to train as nurses.

Firm C was a small, old-established family firm run on rather authoritarian lines. It manufactured preserves and canned foods, and, as with the sweet manufacturers, there was considerable seasonal fluctuation in the labour force. There was a solid labour nucleus drawn from local families ('We get girls coming straight from school to join their mothers'). For the rest there was a chronic labour shortage and a high labour turnover. Some Southern Irish were employed, but they were described as 'settled Croydon residents'. Otherwise the firm reported little or no experience with immigrants other than West Indians. According to the manager:

We started taking on West Indians in late 1955 because of the labour shortage. I don't know what we would have done without them then. We have over 50 per cent now (about twenty men, thirty-five girls).

The worst labour shortage is over, but we're still taking coloured workers on by recommendation from those already working here. There's usually a job they can do. I take on more than I need and then sort them out. There's no question of a quota here. They are good on routine jobs but slower. We have to use four dark girls to every three white on the machines. You have to watch them all the time, and very few show any initiative. But they're good time-keepers, especially the men. Those we have now don't leave easily. Quite a number get paid the long-service bonus for two years' service or more. They seem to appreciate working here, with the exception of a few. I have a few who were skilled in other trades (one is a tailor) but can't get a job over here.

The West Indians seemed to have won more complete acceptance from the management than from fellow-workers at Firm C, but there had been little overt friction with the latter:

There's no union (they tried some years ago but we've got good pension schemes and services and they had nothing to offer). But before we decided to take on dark labour I consulted our own people. There were no objections and nobody left as a result. There were a few language difficulties at first and also some complaints over the cloakroom. Both the men and the women have different cloakroom habits but we can't have segregated toilets. Only one or two are really dirty and I've had to threaten them with dismissal. Occasionally there's a bit of trouble, as when last week one of the coloured girls refused to take her turn in sweeping and cleaning; she apparently thought it was demeaning. They don't mix much—there are so many of them that they can keep to themselves and they usually sit in a group in the canteen.

The lack of full acceptance of West Indians by the local nucleus, among which must be included the supervisors and foremen, all of whom had worked their way up from the floor, emerged in the manager's admission that he is 'generally regarded as being too soft with them' and that some foremen and supervisors occasionally get impatient with coloured workers' slowness. He also commented: 'I don't think you'd get white men to work under a black. Anyway I wouldn't like to try it. If I get an intelligent one I try to give him an independent job. But I do have one coloured boy in charge of a section with dark labour under him.'

At this factory the management valued its West Indian workers sufficiently to make certain special arrangements for them:

I noticed that they have different canteen habits. (They used to eat in all the odd corners, but the regulations don't allow that so I sent them up to the canteen.) They won't eat the meat we provide in the canteen so we give them sausages, which they like, and special rice. We try to meet their needs in other ways. One girl goes off at four on Fridays and another an hour before sunset, both for some religious reason. Some of them come to me with their personal and housing troubles—I'm shocked at the rents their own people charge them.

The manager accepted West Indians as a permanent part of his labour force, but found their 'touchiness' a bar to fuller acceptance:

They tend to be touchy although they shouldn't—they get the same treatment as our own white people. I make a point of saying good morning and calling each one by his Christian name. But they're colour-conscious and that makes it difficult for people to accept them fully. In a factory there's a lot of leg-pulling but with them you have to think what you're saying and can't make a joke. I'll give you an example. The other day I passed a coloured man who was standing under a ladder helping the painter who was putting a coat of whitewash on the wall. I said: 'Good morning Henry. If he tips that over it'll make you white.' I meant no harm and wouldn't have said it if I'd thought. But he bristled up and said: 'I'm quite satisfied to be black, sir.' One or two of the men are very hot-headed—the agitator type—but there's really very little of that.

The way in which this large and relatively isolated and unassimilated group of West Indian workers was organized and controlled was not entirely clear. There were clearly one or two potential 'protest' leaders, but there did not seem to be any West Indian go-betweens or informal leaders of the type used in Firm B and some other establishments with a large immigrant labour force. The answer probably lay in the small size and rather informal organization of the working community and in the paternalistic, rather authoritarian control exerted by the manager himself.

Firm D, the bakers and confectioners, was another small, old family firm (about 250 employees). The situation here was, however, very different from that in Firm C. The work was more skilled and had a higher status, although wage-scales were low in relation to those offered locally in light engineering firms .The atmosphere was traditional and the core of local old-stagers very large ('many of the women have been here since they were girls and some have daughters and granddaughters working alongside them. We're proud of this record'). Apart from this long-term nucleus Firm D had, like most Croydon firms, suffered from high turnover and labour shortage since the War:

It was at its worst in 1956. Even skilled bakers were leaving the industry for the 37½-hour week and overtime in the light engineering firms. Another reason was that their wives didn't like the week-end work. We had one excellent tradesman who left after twenty years, forfeiting his pension rights, and went over to make radio parts. Now the credit squeeze has hit overtime these fellows are coming back. They can do better here than on the engineering minimum rate.

In 1956 we tried some coloured labour but we never had more than half a dozen men employed on rough-and-ready labouring jobs and one or two coloured women on cake-making. We haven't got any now that the labour situation has eased. I prefer to employ white labour. Quite a number of Irish drift in and out in the winter when they're off the building. The darkies were slow and inefficient and there were some hygienic troubles and complaints over odour. There was no overt animosity but the men didn't like sharing men's rooms and so on. We also had one dark chap—a good worker and popular—who'd been with us for twelve years. I don't know what he was but he also kept well away from the West Indians. We haven't had many other immigrants. We had one or two Poles but the difficulty there was language and the foreman used to get a bit irritated. One of them was an excellent bread-baker but he was what I call a floater. He could always get a job and never stayed anywhere for long though I believe he still lives round here.

While there was no absolute bar against outsiders in this firm it was the kind of traditional close-knit, status-conscious working community in which only the most skilled and adaptable individuals were likely to find acceptance. The manager shared the insular views of his labour force and his unfavourable attitude to coloured labour could also have been influenced by war-time experiences: 'I was out East and worked native labour for several years so I know how to handle them. I suppose there must be some intelligent ones—after all, there are coloured doctors and lawyers—but I've never come across any.'

Conclusions

Looking back over the industries and firms grouped together in the 'consumer' sector, we find that once again labour shortage has been the most important factor in inducing firms to try new sources of labour.

With four exceptions all firms in this sector had experienced a period of acute labour shortage; the majority, indeed, continued to do so either because of low wage-rates or because they had to rely on a regular seasonal intake of labour. The four exceptional firms (the three rather atypical furniture manufacturers in the light industrial group (C, D, and E) and one specialized firm (A) in the garment-trade group), on the other hand, could all rely on a steady, skilled local labour force; one, Firm A, had come to accept a few immigrants as part of its regular labour force, but its experience was limited to skilled Europeans and Asians.

Three other firms in this sector (F and G in the light industrial group and the bakers (D) in the food manufacturing group) had a somewhat different experience. All three experienced a grave labour shortage during the years before the 1956 credit squeeze, but after that had much less difficulty in recruiting the skilled or efficient labour (mostly male) which they required. Firm F had accepted European and some Asian immigrants but discarded coloured workers on grounds of slowness and lack of adaptability (the personnel manager's 'wog complex' bias could also have played some part in this); Firm G, while accepting its European and Eurasian workers, had reverted to its normal system of recruitment by apprenticeship, which did away with any further recruitment of adult immigrants. The bakery had with relief and alacrity re-established its former insular policy and atmosphere, preferred by workers as well as management, although no rigid barrier was set up and an able and adaptable outsider could conceivably still be accepted.

Unionization was considerably higher in these seven firms than in any of the other establishments in the consumer sector. It was, however, difficult to say how far and in what direction the unions had influenced the employment and absorption of immigrants. The fact that management informants made no attempt to attribute any responsibility for restrictions or rejections to union intervention suggests that such decisions had usually been made within each establishment by an informal consensus of management and the local labour-core, which might in some cases have included settled members of earlier immigrant groups.

The remaining firms in this group were compelled by chronic labour shortage to continue taking immigrants. The newcomers' skill or working ability remained, however, an important factor; particularly so in the initial phase when the pioneers of each new immigrant group entered an industry or factory. For most employers tended to generalize from a few particular instances, while few firms in these marginal-profit, seasonal industries had the time, facilities, or resources to embark on long or specialized induction or training schemes for a minority. Thus of the two garment firms we found that one had, despite considerable goodwill on the management side, come to the conclusion that West Indian women were too slow to meet their requirements for machinists, while the other firm continued to tolerate them, but with considerable reservations.

In laundry-work, where such speed and precision are not required, managements expressed similar criticisms and reservations. In the sweet-making and canning firms, on the other hand, where much of the work would seem to demand greater dexterity and precision than laundry-work, informants were satisfied with West Indian workers ('there's usually some job they can do'). This greater acceptance could be attributed to a number of factors, including the attitudes of management or workers in particular firms and the presence of especially able and adaptable pioneers from a particular immigrant group. Such pioneering could come about accidentally, or it could be decided by selection, whether by the employment exchange or by the immigrants themselves.

In this connexion, it should not be assumed that every immigrant group shares the receiving society's views on the relative desirability and prestige of various occupations and types of work. For instance, lower-class West Indian immigrants have a particular aversion to work (like laundry-work) resembling the domestic and menial jobs which were all that most could hope to get at home, and the more capable are therefore unlikely to accept laundry-work or to stay in it. On the other hand, many older middle-class European exiles are willing to accept occupational down-grading and to do such work without regarding it as lowering to their social status within the refugee community.

The immigrant's degree of skill or working ability may of course operate differently against the employer, particularly in relatively low-skilled, low-paid, low-status industries. For these represent only a 'transit camp' for the able and ambitious newcomer, as I found in the larger of the two laundry firms. Here my informant referred nostalgically to Polish and Anglo-Indian workers who had been with the firm in past years, but 'they're on the way up—you just can't hold them'. In one or two firms (notably the toilet-goods manufacturer—Firm E—in the light industrial sector) there were also reports of West Indians having treated the work only as a 'transit camp' to better-paid work in the mass-production light-engineering firms. Elsewhere the possibility of West Indian workers moving on to greener fields was not seriously considered and they were accepted as part of the available local labour force. It was not always clear, however, how far they were seen as a source of unskilled, or semi-skilled seasonal or stop-gap labour or to what extent they had become part of the small, long-term local labour-core on which most of these firms relied to keep production going all the year round. In so far as West Indians or other recent migrants were concerned, such fuller acceptance would be unlikely until they had themselves settled down locally and made the psychological 'about-turn' or reorientation towards the country of settlement which turns an immigrant into a settler.

At the time of this survey just under 600 immigrants were employed in a total labour force of approximately 7,000 in this group of 'consumer' industries. This proportion would have been considerably lower but for the presence of the Polish-owner plastics factory; this accounted for all but four of the Poles working in this sector, for all the Hungarian and other East European refugees, and for a number of the other Europeans.

Otherwise, the survey showed that European immigrants had worked in this industrial sector in past years but that the majority had moved on to work offering better money, conditions, or opportunities.

The situation of the Anglo-Indians seemed to be evolving in the same way and it was the 305 West Indians (66 men, 239 women) who now formed the main immigrant source of unskilled and semi-skilled labour in this sector. They were not, however, evenly distributed but were clustered mainly in two firms in the light industrial sector and four firms in the food manufacturing sector. They were fairly well accepted in these firms, which were by no means those with the lowest wage-levels, conditions, and working status.

(4) *The 'White-Collar' and Professional Sector*

In the three industrial sectors so far surveyed the inquiry has been focused rather on the large labour force than on the smaller clerical, administrative, and technical staffs, although information was collected about these wherever it was possible.

The final sector, however, the next largest after light engineering, covers a set of industrial groups and establishments in which non-manual or salaried employees, whether professional, administrative, technical, or lower white-collar, outnumbered manual workers by nearly two to one. It is a sector in which considerations of occupational training, economic security, and social status play a particularly important part, and also one in which contact with the public is frequently involved.

In this part of the report we shall be concerned less with the minority of manual workers than with the majority of non-manual, salaried workers; most of them are people with middle-class affiliations or aspirations, drawn from the social and occupational class groups which are popularly, and not without statistical justification, regarded as forming a large proportion of the population of the 'middle-class' town of Croydon.[1] We shall also be looking for any special factors that could influence the absorption of outsiders in high-status or status-conscious occupations and working communities.

The economic classifications 'non-manual' and 'salaried' are not of course coextensive with each other or with the social classification 'middle-class'. Virtually all staff in the retail and distributive trades, for instance, are paid by the week, but many are doing obviously manual work. Indeed there are even some non-manual shop-workers who would not claim lower-middle-class status for themselves or be classified as such by others. On the other hand there are many hourly-paid skilled or semi-skilled manual workers in industry who are better paid, have a higher standard of living and are better educated and more securely middle-class than the lower-grade white-collar worker.

Nevertheless it may be said that the terms 'non-manual' and 'salaried' still carry social class implications and that the great majority of white-collar workers to whom they refer are highly status-conscious and either class themselves as 'middle-class' or have aspirations to move up into the 'middle classes' by virtue of their occupation.

(a) *The Retail and Distributive Trades*

Two centuries ago the economic and social status of London's journeymen shopmen seems to have been higher than that of the

[1] See p. 13–14.

usher or assistant teacher and equal to that of merchants' clerks.[1] In 1814 they lost the monopolistic protection afforded by the Elizabethan statute confining skilled crafts by law to regularly apprenticed workers, but their continuing lower-middle-class status was confirmed by Dudley Baxter's classification in 1867.[2] Later H. G. Well's novel *Kipps* gave a vivid picture of the status-consciousness and pretensions of the assistants in a south coast drapery establishment towards the end of the nineteenth century.[3] Kipps (like the writer himself) is brought up by an uncle who is a small shop-keeper and an aunt who was in domestic service; they are concerned with proper behaviour, fear 'low' people, and 'keep themselves to themselves'. They have ambitions for Kipps, who is sent to a private 'middle-class' academy and is thereafter apprenticed to a draper. In this establishment Kipps tries to conceal his aunt's past occupation and later aspires to enter the 'good' middle-class society of Folkestone with the backing of a windfall legacy.

The entry of the 'young lady assistants' certainly undermined the economic status of the male shop-assistant. It may, however, have helped to maintain the genteel associations of the job[4] since it was one of the few non-manual jobs open to untrained girls and thus tended to attract the better-spoken, more prepossessing, and more socially ambitious daughters of the lower-middle and upper-lower or 'respectable' working class.

At the present time it is difficult to generalize about the occupational status of the vast and heterogeneous army of shop-workers; they range from the Roedean-educated managerial candidate doing a temporary spell as counter-assistant at a 'Knightsbridge store' to the South London girl in the canteen of a Southwark chain-store. The larger retail establishments of today also employ a

[1] G. D. H. Cole and Raymond Postgate, *The Common People*, 1746–1946, University Paperbacks 22, (London, Methuen, 1961), p. 69 f.

[2] Ibid., pp. 353–4.

[3] 'Now, such is the sweetness of human charity that the shop young lady in England has just the same horror of doing anything that savours of the servant girl as the lady journalist, let us say, has of anything savouring of the shop-girl, or the really nice young lady has of anything savouring of any sort of girl who has gone down into the economic battlefield to earn herself a living' (*Kipps*, London, Collins, 1952, p. 51).

[4] These associations were in any case strong. 'Never forget,' wrote P. D. Hoffman in *They Also Serve* (London, Porcupine Press, 1949), an account of the organized struggle for better pay and conditions and the growth of unionization in the retail trade, 'T'was but a span since the time when shop-assistants wore a top hat and frock coat.'

considerable behind-the-scenes staff in workshops, canteens and restaurants, warehouses and maintenance, many of whom are only members of the white-collar group marginally or by virtue of their association with the retail trade.

The shop-assistant is, however, still the most important element in the retail trade's working force and it is his or her occupational status that sets the general tone. Pay-rates and conditions of work were made more secure when the Trade Boards were extended to the distributive trades by the Labour Government after 1926. The job had, however, already lost any claims to its eighteenth-century parity with teaching and clerking, both of which required increasingly specialized training. And since the 1939–45 War it has lost ground and status in the eyes of school-leavers by comparison with light industry.[1] To quote one of my informants from the retail trade:

> There's little or no shortage of applicants at present because of the industrial recession. But the status and attractiveness of the job has slipped in recent years. There's competition both from the factories and from the offices with their five-day week. The newer light engineering factories offer not only higher pay and fringe benefits but pleasant working conditions, canteens, clubs, and so on; these attract the better type of girl who would have gone for a white-collar job before the War. On the other hand the work here's not so stereotyped and you're dealing with people instead of doing the same mechanical action all day and listening to 'Music While You Work'. Then they don't have to get to work so early here and there's the cachet and greater security of being weekly-paid, and greater opportunities of working one's way up for women than in most large factories.

Thus it seems that shop-assistants, particularly those employed in large stores, can fairly be classified as white-collar workers. But the marginal and precarious status of this occupation is suggested by the variety of classifications made by contemporary social historians and sociologists. In their study of the *English Middle Classes*[2] Roy Lewis and Angus Maude, writing from an upper-middle-class standpoint, distinguish explicitly between small shop-

[1] In 1959 20 per cent. of Croydon's 3,400 school-leavers entered the retail trade but the 5½-day week and the lack of adequate training facilities for boys were said to be putting off the best candidates (*Croydon Times*, 13 November 1959). This figure fell in 1960 (York Employment Service Report, 1955–63, op. cit., p. 6).

[2] London, Penguin Books, 1953, p. 17.

keepers[1] and shop-assistants and uncompromisingly include the latter in the working class. On the other hand Richard Hoggart, describing his own northern working-class childhood, writes: 'Foremen are included (in the working classes) but office-clerks and employees in *large* shops [my italics], though they may live in these areas, are on the whole better regarded as members of the lower middle classes.'[2]

Cole and Postgate, writing of the 1930s, class shop-assistants as 'black-coat workers' along with hotel and restaurant workers.[3] David Lockwood's excellent study, *The Black-Coated Worker*, contains no reference to shopworkers and is restricted to clerical workers; the writer indeed uses the terms 'black-coated worker' and 'clerical worker' interchangeably, on the grounds that clerks make up the greater part of the black-coated group.[4] Young and

[1] The great majority of retail establishments in this country are still small, independent units whose owners may be financially as insecure as the semi-skilled labourers living in their neighbourhood, but they are distinguished by the fact that they are by intention 'their own bosses', thereby having a different set of values and what Lewis and Maude call 'a broad pattern in their lives and behaviour, of profit-seeking and risk-taking, of a sense of responsibility and habitude to decision, of self-improvement and social ambition' (op. cit., p. 144).

[2] *The Uses of Literacy*, London, Penguin Books, 1958, p. 9. Working-class people may regard shop-assistants, clerks, and other lower-grade non-manual workers as middle-class, but their attitudes can also be ambiguous, hostile, and even contemptuous (cf. Michael Young and Peter Willmott, 'Social Grading by Manual Workers' in *British Journal of Sociology*, Vol. VII, No. 4, December 1956). The 'normal' respondents graded shop-assistants in 24th place out of 28, with dock and agricultural labourers above them and only carters, railway porters, barmen and road sweepers below). See also Zweig, *The British Worker* (London, Penguin Books, 1952, p. 206) for the British working-man's dislike of the lower-middle-class persons whom he encounters in shops and offices. There is of course a distinction between the manual worker's view that white-collar workers are 'only fit for licking stamps' and a judgement as to social class. They may be despised as effeminate, artificial, lacking in strength and courage, but are none the less regarded as of higher social status. The contempt also includes the higher *bourgeoisie*.

[3] Cole and Postgate, op. cit., p. 629. A discussion of the comparative status of waiters and other skilled workers in the hotel and catering trades raises some rather complex issues which are not to be examined here as no hotel or catering units of sufficient size were listed in the Croydon employment exchange area. Catering and hotel work do, like shopwork, impose certain standards of appearance, dress, speech, and behaviour. They are, however, more obviously associated with manual crafts and also with a cosmopolitan tradition and staff. The recent instance of an English *restaurateur* who was required to take an Italian name on being promoted in one of London's luxury hotels constitutes a situation that would be hard to parallel in the retail trade.

[4] D. Lockwood, *The Black-Coated Worker*, London, George Allen and Unwin, 1958, p. 13 n.

Willmott, in their study of another 'middle-class' London peri-urban area, do, however, equate 'manual' with 'working-class' and 'non-manual' with 'middle-class', and their list of occupations falling under the latter head include all those occupations in Group III of the Registrar General's Socio-Economic Groups 6 ('Clerical workers') and 7 ('Shop-assistants, including also all salesmen, commercial travellers, canvassers and insurance agents').[1]

In their chapter on 'The Social Grading of Occupations' in *Social Mobility in Britain*,[2] C. A. Moser and J. R. Hall, allocated shop-assistants (along with policemen, routine clerks, fitters, carpenters, and brick-layers) to Class 5 (out of seven classes), comprising 'Skilled Manual and routine grades of Non-Manual' in their Standard Classification of Occupations; they found that the public's ranking of thirty occupations was much the same. In another chapter of the same study, however, subjective social-class ratings by informants showed up the marginality of the shop-assistant's occupation, particularly in the eyes of manual workers.[3]

Probably the most important view of the shop-assistant's status and prestige is that held by shop-workers themselves; more particularly by the long-service nucleus of staff in large stores, including those men and women in managerial positions who have worked their way up from the ranks. From the Croydon evidence the occupation would appear to be regarded as definitely 'middle-class', its social selectness and fringe benefits being stressed by way of compensation for lowered economic status. The inquiry also indicated a certain connexion between the clientèle and staff, both established and newly recruited, of a particular store. There are 'select', 'middle-class', and 'popular' stores, and there is also an obvious tendency for such stores to attract or select incoming staff of a type to fit in with their long-service local staff and to conform to the views of their steady clientèle.

The importance of the status aspect and the insecurity over status felt by many shop-assistants are also brought out in the findings of one of the few recent published studies of shop-workers, Joan

[1] P. Willmott and M. Young, *Family and Class in a London Suburb*, London, Routledge and Kegan Paul, for Institute of Community Studies, 1960, p. xi, and Appendix 3, p. 159.

[2] D. V. Glass (ed.)., London, Routledge and Kegan Paul, 1954, pp. 32–35.

[3] F. M. Martin, 'Some Subjective Aspects of Social Stratification', op. cit., p. 62.

Woodward's *The Saleswoman*.[1] She notes that while selling staff appear to resent the low status afforded them by the community, one of the strongest motives for taking up such work is the status it is felt to confer. Much of the working force is assumed by them to be drawn from people without higher and educational qualifications or professional training who nevertheless feel socially superior to the rank and file of factory workers.[2]

Four department stores in Croydon were listed as employing over 100 workers and of these one (with a total staff of 700) did not employ immigrants at all. This was a firm catering for a popular trade and situated in the less select, predominantly lower-class end of the main shopping street. The absence of immigrant employees was attributed to the fact that none had applied.[3]

The three other firms all employed some immigrant workers in various capacities at the time of this inquiry. These establishments differed in character, organization, and clientèle, as did their policy and their experiences with immigrant employees.

Store A was situated in the more elegant section of the main shopping centre and catered for a discriminating, upper-middle-class clientèle from Croydon and its southern suburbs. It was a large, old-fashioned 'family' firm, employing a staff of more

[1] London, Pitman, 1960. Published under the auspices of the Retail Distributors' Association, this synthesizes the results of four loosely co-ordinated but independent pilot studies of staff relations in retail stores (two in the London area, two in the provinces) carried out by three University Social Science Departments in 1957. Among the findings it is noted that emphasis on and anxiety over status are intensified by rigid status systems operating *within* the store. See pp. 72–3 and (b) 'role' inferiority in relation to the customer, particularly in upper- and middle-class areas (p. 75).

[2] Op. cit. pp. 7, 15–16, 26, 29, 74. The latter section contains a table showing the relative prestige given to work in retail distribution by those interviewed in one store, in relation to alternative employment in factories or offices:

Comparison with	*Factory*	*Office*
Higher status than	177	109
Lower status than	12	65
Neutral	16	29
No views	—	2
Total	205	205

[3] The minority of immigrants qualified for and seeking such work (mostly Europeans and Anglo-Indians) in this area would be more likely to apply to the more select stores (A, B, and C) which were also considerably nearer to the districts in which these groups congregated residentially.

than 700, over 500 of whom were women. There was an apprenticeship scheme covering about forty girls; only a few part-time workers were employed. The labour situation, though difficult, was said to have improved in the past two or three years: 'We don't have to take on the Teddy-boy type of youth any more; but it's still hard to get good, reliable porters and manual workers. They can always get higher wages and a five-day week in industry.'

Though there was a high turnover among young employees and labourers, there was a solid nucleus of middle-aged old-timers, both men and women, on the office and sales staff.[1] The manageress herself had been with the firm nearly fifty years, having started on a two-year apprenticeship[2] and worked her way up. Most other members of the supervisory staff had also worked their way up in the firm's hierarchy. Staff relations were said to be good and an atmosphere of friendly efficiency prevailed.

This store had employed European and Asian immigrants for at least a decade. At this time its male staff included one Pakistani youth and an Anglo-Indian porter, while among the women sales or workroom staff there were several Germans or Austrians, one Greek, and a Pole. The personnel manager, a quiet-voiced, sympathetic north-countrywoman, viewed the employment of non-British workers, whether on the counter or behind the scenes, from a practical and relatively unbiased standpoint:

> Good workers with a nice manner go down well on the counter and looks don't count particularly, either with other workers or customers. The Polish woman is a funny little thing but an excellent saleswoman and her broken English hasn't held her back—customers find it attractive. The other Europeans are in the workshops and we had a coal-black Negro girl there too some years ago. She had a lovely figure and wore gay clothes, but some of the old dears up there were very prejudiced against her and she soon left.

[1] Woodward (op. cit., pp. 10–11) points out that even among recruits the proportion of older women seems higher than in most other trades and industries. This could also have an influence on the absorption of immigrant workers, since the attitudes of such women are likely to be less flexible than those of younger staff.

[2] During this period my informant received 4*s.* a month plus her lunch and tea each day. Hours were from 8.45 a.m. to the time when the last customer left at 7 or 8 p.m. and most assistants lived in. After the apprentice period pay rose to 2*s.* 6*d.* per week. The increased pay rates that came into effect from 3 August 1959 for shop-assistants in provincial centres were £8 16*s.* for men and £6 4*s.* 6*d.* for women.

As for coloured workers, we won't have them in the front of the shop as a general rule if they're obviously coloured. The firm has no prejudice but we must bear in mind possible customer reaction. I've had an Anglo-Indian counter-assistant till recently but I had to dismiss her as unsuitable—she was casual and touchy like the three or four other Anglo-Indian women I've had. They've got a poor attitude and are liable to walk out without warning. But there's one good saleswoman here now who certainly has a splash of Asia in her. She's immensely popular and highly successful in the gown department. She's plump and cheerful and dumpier; older women customers prefer to go to her than the lean, model type of saleswoman. As for the Pakistani boy, we're trying him as relief in the food hall and watching customer reaction very carefully to see whether he's acceptable.

This particular informant shared the widespread, usually untested view still held by many store managements[1] that a minority of the public might react adversely if served by a coloured counterhand or waitress; she had, however, been gently testing out public reactions by what might be termed a 'thin-end-of-the-wedge' method. Having tried out light-coloured saleswomen without any adverse reaction she had proceeded to experiment with the 'deeper-hued' Pakistani youth, placing him in the rather tricky job of food-handling, with its associations with cleanliness and therefore possibly with whiteness,[2] in the peak shopping period of Saturday morning.

Unlike a number of informants this personnel manager had not encountered adverse reactions to the employment of coloured workers from her clerical staff, nor did she seem apprehensive about the possibility:

I'm quite prepared to give them a try but I get very few applicants. Recently one Jamaican girl did write in to apply for a clerical job but the letter was so ill-written and ill-spelled that I wouldn't normally have considered interviewing her. I didn't want her to attribute her rejection to colour-bar on our part, however, so I asked her to come in. Unfortunately she proved quite unsuitable—never stopped giggling for a moment and obviously found life one great big joke.

According to my informant, Store A would be willing to employ more 'Jamaicans' and other coloured workers behind the scenes in

[1] Cf. an unpublished study-group report on the employment of coloured workers in London (London Council of Social Service, 1959).

[2] For white South African views on this, see S. Patterson, *Colour and Culture in South Africa*, London, Routledge and Kegan Paul, 1953, p. 264, n. 77.

lower-status jobs such as canteen-work, portering, and labouring jobs:

I watched some Jamaicans from a Wimbledon firm running at the last A.A.A. contest and I thought we might try them as porters. They looked young and strong and all we can get locally are the halt and the blind. But very few apply because they can do better in the factories. I had one in here yesterday, an ex-R.A.F. type who'd been in a sheet-metal works but found the work too heavy. He was a real black Jamaican, and with his pink protruding tongue and rolling, bloodshot eyeballs I could understand how some people might feel squeamish about working alongside him.

Possibly the 'thin-end-of-the-wedge' policy was only beginning to work on this informant as well as on the public, but on the whole the situation in this firm seemed to be one of increasing tolerance and acceptance of immigrant employees. The interview ended with the informant asking for information about organizations that might be able to send along suitable West Indian applicants for manual work.

Store B presented a rather different picture. Situated at the lower-class end of the main shopping street, it was part of a large, old-established co-operative society with over 250,000 members and branches all over South London and Surrey. As a co-operative, the moralistic and co-partnership aims inherited from its Christian Socialist founders and its political association with the Labour Party would in principle prevent it from applying or countenancing any sort of racial or religious discrimination in its employment policy. This principle could, however, be modified by the fact that co-operative store customers were also members who could register their views at quarterly meetings and also by the fact that the establishment was a closed shop and therefore susceptible to union pressures.

The total staff, excluding a large office force of 350 or so which will be considered in the clerical section, numbered about 3,000, in the proportion of two men to every woman; of this total only a couple of hundred worked in the Croydon branch, along with the bulk of the clerical staff.

The total number of immigrant workers now employed in all branches of Store B was sixteen (Croydon figures could not be singled out but the majority of immigrants were said to work in the Croydon co-operative or in neighbouring branches). Of the total, four worked in the general office. The remaining twelve were widely dispersed: two (an Indian and a West Indian woman) worked on dispatch or packing in the grocery department; there were three male refugees from Eastern Europe[1] working as yardmen or inside workers in the dairy; one Indian semi-skilled mechanic in the traffic department; four Jamaican male operatives in the bakery; and two Jamaican labourers.

After these details had been provided by the personnel office my informant expressed surprise at the low number, saying that it was usually higher, quite apart from seasonal and temporary student workers; and in fact a year later there were nineteen immigrant employees, eight of whom remained from the preceding year.[2]

It will be noticed that none of these immigrants were employed on counter-work or in contact with the public. This was attributed mainly to supervisors' anxiety about public reactions, particularly in relation to coloured staff:

> We've several coloured bakery operators but we might find it more difficult to put them on rounds. The bakery manager has his doubts. Some sections of the membership might object and voice their opinions at the quarterly and half-yearly meetings.
>
> Ask for reactions from the old-timers—whole families work with us—by and large they raise no objections. I haven't heard of any hygienic complaints and *they* always come up quickly enough, whoever's involved. The question of promotion doesn't arise as they aren't of sufficient calibre. It might come up in the bakery at a later stage. Any redundancy would be according to a set of established priorities, with length of service and ability taken into account.

It was rather difficult to assess the real position in this large, multiple-branch establishment. The few immigrants seemed to receive egalitarian treatment in unskilled and semi-skilled work, and the interest and sympathy shown by my informant in the inquiry also indicated an unbiased approach to the question at higher management level.

Store C was intermediate between Stores A and B, both geographically and in the social status of the majority of its clientele.

[1] A Ukrainian, a Lithuanian, and a 'Czech' who was subsequently found to be Latvian. The store employed Poles in the bakery and warehouse in earlier years, but these had since moved into industry or emigrated.

[2] Southern Irish were also employed in fair numbers from time to time, but were regarded as too mobile for 'full confidence'. There were no immigrant apprentices, and my informant could not recall having received any applications.

It employed about 700 staff, mostly women, of whom some 300 were sales staff and the remainder engaged on behind-the-scenes work (work-rooms, warehouses, maintenance, portering, cleaning, etc.) Of these, eight were immigrants (four Europeans and four Anglo-Indians). The Europeans were all women: a Latvian cleaner ('She never learned to speak English and works in the kitchen'), one 'little German-Jewish lady', and a Frenchwoman and an Italian working as waitresses ('but Latins are temperamentally lazy'). Of the four Anglo-Indians one was a clerical worker; the other three were members of the same family—two, a mother and son, were sales staff and the second son was a packer.

My informant, the personnel manager, discussed the matter of public reactions:

No one objects to light-coloured sales staff. Ours just look well-tanned. Darkness and negroid features are what people are likely to object to. Appearance, manner and voice are important. We don't have an apprenticeship scheme any more but we give all our junior staff a six-months' training including voice training. Here the European women present a problem. With their accents they're more difficult to train and the European currencies, weights and measures are also different. They find it difficult to advise customers and to cope with complicated invoices, H.P. and so on. Then most of them are too old to be apprenticed and once they're over twenty-five we have to pay the full rate though their knowledge and background may be nil.

Store C had also employed Polish men in past years, but all had moved on to other work (one requalified as a doctor, another got a radio job). It had never employed West Indian or other dark-skinned workers and my informant clearly thought of them only as unskilled labour and not as potential counter-staff:

We've very few labouring jobs and have had our own porters for a long time. It's nothing for people to work here for forty or fifty years. In general we haven't suffered from a large labour shortage and we've no difficulty in getting part-timers and pensioners for cleaning and washing up and such jobs.

Anglo-Indians seemed to be the 'favoured nation' in this store:

They had to get out of India and choose which side to cleave to. They've got enough white blood to get on and they're here to stay. They're well-educated though they do have some difficulty over money differences, like the Europeans.[1] I think they could be promoted and be quite acceptable.

This informant had travelled widely in the tropics and had very decided views on immigration and the coloured question in general —which might possibly have had a bearing on the fact that this store employed no coloured workers other than the 'white-blooded' Anglo-Indians:

I don't think the emigration authorities should paint such a glowing picture and allow them to come over here. They should improve conditions in their own countries and let them stay there with their own food and ways and a siesta in the afternoon. I think in a hundred years the coloured race will rule the world but now they're just not up to it. These things go in cycles and we've nearly reached our peak. Now the coloured people are beginning to come up. They're very clever when they get an education. Half the trouble has been that we've educated some, instead of leaving them in their old ways, and then tried to refuse them independence.

I think Little Rock was a disgrace and I don't have any other prejudices but I do disapprove firmly of mixed marriages. It's all right if they would only agree not to have children. Look at Seretse. Even his children won't be accepted.[2] The best people on both sides don't countenance mixed marriages.

(b) *Automobile Distribution and Repair*

An industrial group which was surveyed separately in Croydon was that concerned with automobile distribution and repair. Only three firms were, however, listed as employing 100 workers or more. Such firms usually have a work force consisting of salesmen, clerical staff, and a small number of skilled motor-mechanics (a trade possessed by a considerable number of Polish ex-servicemen and West Indian immigrants). None of the three in Croydon had ever employed immigrants of any kind on the sales or office staff. On the works side, one of them had never employed any immigrants, and the second reported that it had employed one West Indian and several Southern Irishmen in past years. The third replied briefly to the inquiry: 'We have had two coloured mechanics; they are the only immigrants we have employed since the War and there doesn't seem to be anything of interest to say concerning them.'

[1] i.e. pounds, shillings, and pence and the non-metric system generally.

[2] Cf. p. 35, n. 2. This comment was difficult to reconcile with the approval conferred on the Anglo-Indians.

(c) *Office and Clerical Work*

Within the non-manual group the occupational status of clerical workers would seem to be generally higher than that of shop-workers; like the latter, however, it has declined in recent decades in relation to the status of the skilled or better-paid manual worker. The main reasons for this are similar—lowered income differentials, the spread of literacy to the working classes following the introduction of compulsory elementary education in 1870, loss of prestige as a result of the increasing entry of women into clerical work since that time,[1] the intensified routine and mechanization of much office work,[2] and the improvement in industrial wages and working conditions since the 1939–45 War.[3] In recent years the rise of the affluent or 'bourgeois' worker has begun to blur the frontier between middle and lower class,[4] and the status of clerical work has been increasingly questioned from below and above.[5] At the same time, growing insecurity over status has led many clerical workers, especially those who themselves are only a generation away from the working class,[6] to stress and exaggerate their middle-class membership. As with the shop-workers, therefore, concern with status and prestige is likely to be an extremely important factor influencing local clerical workers' attitudes to the entry of outsiders, particularly those from groups commonly associated with inferior or lower-class traits, into their offices.

The importance of this factor has already emerged in a number of those offices attached to industrial establishments in which there

[1] See S. M. Lipset and R. Bendix, *Social Mobility in Industrial Society*, London, Heinemann, 1959, pp. 14–17. The prestige of most clerical work done by females is also lower than that done by males.

[2] With the introduction of mechanization the basic distinction between manual and non-manual work may become blurred; most routine work done by girls requires as much manual dexterity and is also as stereotyped and as lacking in opportunities for promotion as a factory machinist's job. On the other hand, routine male clerical jobs (and the supply of workers) are moving towards extinction, although there are increasing opportunities for able young men on their way up to management level.

[3] See Lockwood, op. cit., Chapter 4 *passim*.

[4] See S. Zweig, *The Worker in an Affluent Society*, London, Heinemann, 1961, pp. 133–8 and 206–12. In an earlier study, *Life, Labour and Poverty* (Gollancz, 1948, pp. 88–89), Zweig observes that the 'office worker of lower rank regards himself and is treated as belonging to the working class, but with a difference'. Immediately after this, however, he says that all those whom he came across in fact belonged to the lower middle class.

[5] See Lewis and Maude, op. cit., pp. 125-6.

[6] Ibid., p. 242.

had been or were any immigrant staff, particularly coloured people. It was, indeed, one of the most important influences after the factor of immigrant skills and general suitability for clerical work.[1] We have seen the 'thin-edge-of-the-wedge' principle at work in some firms, with a fairly widespread acceptance of well-educated, light-coloured Anglo-Indians, a rarer acceptance of Pakistani, Indian, and even West African students, preferably on a temporary basis, and a general avoidance of West Indians, especially men. In the case of West Indians, however, the situation in Croydon had also been conditioned by the virtual absence of suitable clerical applicants.

At the time of this survey the redevelopment of central Croydon and the southward move of large insurance and other offices from Central London had barely begun. Only three '100-plus' private clerical establishments were listed: a pools firm some miles from the centre of Croydon (Firm A); a finance company which had only just moved into the Croydon area (Firm B); and the clerical section of the co-operative society just described in the retail section (Store C).

Firm A was started in the late 1930s and moved to the Croydon area nearly ten years ago. The staff consisted of rather more than fifty men, working either as clerks or security officers (the latter were usually ex-policemen), and of about 650 women (half of them part-timers), engaged on routine clerical work. The main requirement for the latter work was said to be a good understanding of written and spoken English, as all work was done by address orders and instructions were given out over loudspeakers. The basic wage was not high but there were additional incentives such as a service increase, Christmas bonus, and frequent overtime opportunities. Working conditions were pleasant and turnover was not high. There was no recognized union.

With the exception of some higher supervisory staff all employees had been taken on since the move to Croydon. The manager said:

> The main basis of the staff is the nearby housing estate [locally regarded as 'select' or 'respectable'—S.P.] The girls are a fair cross-section. Some of the part-timers even pay golf-fees. We're prepared to give anyone a try. At present we've eleven European girls, eight West

[1] On the persistence of this traditional 'collar-bar', or industrial caste system based on the colour of the employee's collar, see also an article by Richard Denman in the *Western Daily Press*, 21 August 1962.

Indians and three Australians. There was also an Anglo-Indian girl, who left recently. The first West Indian girl appeared in 1954. We took her on and she was quite exceptional. We did wonder what the local girls' reaction would be but we've never had any trouble then or since. The coloured girls are split up and it's all very smooth. That West Indian is now 'head of table' over nine other girls. There's no crabbing over that—she's very popular and mixes in the canteen and off the job socially (she lives locally). Length of service counts towards promotion and another West Indian girl will probably be promoted soon. There's also a Polish woman who's 'head of table'. I think it would be possible to promote either the West Indian or the Pole to the next two higher supervisory levels, where they'd be in charge of forty or 300 girls.

The smooth and tolerant relationships disclosed at Firm A were in contrast to the declared policy of Firm B. The latter had brought most of its highly specialized staff from Central London and had as yet no local links or sentiments. Only a few staff had so far been taken on in Croydon and it was learned from another source that the firm had not been very co-operative about finding posts for retired or redundant older clerical workers living locally. A management informant stated quite categorically that the firm did not employ any European or coloured immigrants and was not prepared to take them on. An exception appeared to be made in the case of white, Anglo-Saxon applicants from the Commonwealth: 'We have employed a few Canadians, South Africans and Australians but only one could be described as an immigrant [*sic*] and our experience from the few involved has been entirely satisfactory.'

A perhaps not unconnected piece of information about Firm B came to light a year or so later when it was reported in the Press that the firm was pulling out of investment in newly independent Commonwealth countries in the Caribbean and Africa.

Firm C employed proportionately more immigrants on its office staff than on the retail and distributive side. The forty or so males on the office staff included a West African and an Indian clerk; among the 300-odd female office staff there were one Malayan-Chinese typist and an Indian shorthand-typist. From time to time, by arrangement with the International Co-operative Alliance, the firm also accepted overseas students from all parts of the world for part-time work during their studies. My informant commented on the immigrants' working ability, temperament, and social acceptability:

The standards of the coloured immigrants vary considerably but all those that we have are giving satisfactory service. One of the male clerks is well-liked but rather lazy and in general most African and Asian male clerks give the impression of lazing a bit. Some of the Anglo-Indians we've had in past years were unpopular with the other clerks because it was felt they weren't doing their fair share of the work. There's been no adverse social reaction fom the staff, male or female, and one West African student lodged with a supervisor. But one of the Asian women is a bit difficult though she works well. She lost her husband and had a bad time during the War—she tends to be over critical, almost anti-British, and she upsets the balance in the office. As for promotion, the question doesn't arise as none of those we've employed are of the required calibre.

(d) *Local Government Offices*

Writing about Britain's 150,000 or so Local Government Officers in the immediate post-war years, Lewis and Maude said:

The Local Government Service, while it has never welcomed university graduates with any show of enthusiasm, offers reasonably good prospects to secondary school leavers. There is a fair chance of promotion to the highest offices, and opportunity to secure a professional qualification while earning a living as a clerk. The Service also induces another metamorphosis in its employees. In addition to turning clerks into professional men and women, it also turns professional men and women into administrators. . . . The middle and lower grades (we are not considering for the purposes of this book, the dustmen and other manual employees of local councils) recruit a type not greatly dissimilar to that of the junior civil servants whom we have been considering. There has never been any serious difficulty in recruiting numbers, though quality has not always been so easy to secure. But plenty of young people regard the prospects as attractive. . .[1]

Because of its local associations and relatively low recruitment problem, local government service is not a sphere in which one would expect to find many outsiders or immigrants. The majority would also be unacceptable because of nationality, language, or educational shortcomings, while some of the minority with all the requisite qualifications might find this service less attractive than private industry. For it offers a modest, long-term security rather than the immediate financial rewards for which most recent immigrants strive.

At this period the Croydon employment exchange area covered

[1] Op. cit., p. 90.

Croydon County Borough and two less concentrated suburban areas,[1] and the three local government offices employed a total staff, including manual workers, of nearly 5,500, excluding teachers. The two smaller offices, which employed respectively about 500 and 220 people, were in areas which had few immigrant residents of any kind and were not readily accessible for non-residents. Their white-collar staffs were fairly small and on the whole locally recruited. Council A employed one Anglo-Indian accountant some years ago. He was described as a 'good fellow who worked in well with the staff. In fact, he married one of the girls in the office and after some years moved on to a higher post in a town in south-west England.' This individual seemed to be accepted on his own merits and was not identified with any particular outgroup. Indeed, his ethnic origins clearly counted for little, since my first informant spoke of him as a Pole (he was apparently very light in colour) and it was only when a colleague joined in that his true ethnic origin was determined.

The only serious manpower shortage experienced by these two councils was one of unskilled labour in the Highways or Public Engineer's Departments.

Despite the relative remoteness of the middle-class sub-rural area administered by Council A, West Indians had been applying at the depot for labouring jobs since 1956: 'Quite a number aren't used to our class of work and we have to turn them down.' Some thirty or so had, however, passed through the appropriate department since then. The council did not employ more than a dozen at any one time (this would constitute 3 to 4 per cent. of the department's total labour force). At this time six Jamaicans were employed; all of them had been with the council for a year or more. There were only a couple of Southern Irishmen, although quite a number had passed through the department in earlier years.

The superintendent gave a detailed picture of the immigrants' working performance and relations with local workers:

> Four of the six are good working chaps while the other two are only fairly satisfactory. All but one need a good deal of supervision and they

[1] The area covered by the Ministry of Labour's Croydon Exchange has remained unchanged; it includes the new G.L.C. Borough (excluding Farleigh and Alderstead Heath) plus Mitcham Junction, Wallington, Beddington, and Hackbridge. The new Borough takes in the former Urban District of Coulsdon and Purley (formerly part of the Administrative County of Surrey), as well as the whole of the former County Borough of Croydon.

work best apart. Our object is to put only one in a gang. Another reason for that is that when they get together we can't tell what they're talking about. They're all right on one particular job but most we've had would be lost if they were put on something new. They get on all right with our own white men and there's been no objection from them from the beginning although there's quite a lot of unemployment locally. There was no objection from the union [T. and G.W.U.] either. Our relations there are good. As for promotion, in the lower grades it usually goes by seniority—one coloured chap has moved out of the lowest grade and another—a dark fellow who's a jolly good worker, in fact the best we've got—was put in charge once when the foreman was away, without any kicks from the rest of the men.

Many local government labourers are in contact with the public in the sense that they are on view in parks[1] and on the highways. Dustmen (or refuse-collectors, as they should now more properly be called) do, however, come into more direct contact with the public on their weekly rounds. No adverse public reaction had been noted by Council A except for a complaint received from a nervous housewife that a West Indian dustman appeared to be 'hanging round the house on a couple of occasions'. This complaint was not taken very seriously as the man in question was known and trusted.

The departmental head, who rarely came into direct contact with individual labourers, expressed the view that the West Indians 'keep themselves apart' and that it was 'difficult to get through to them'. The superintendent, on the other hand, was a bluff and kindly man who had established such close and friendly relations with several of his West Indian labourers that he could be classed as a 'sponsor':

At least five are married. None live locally—they are either in South Norwood, Dulwich or Peckham. I've visited two families in their rooms to check up on conditions and rents. One has his own house now and none regard themselves as visitors. They're here to stay and they appreciate a steady job with security. None of them has any chip-on-the-shoulder and we've never had any episodes or fights between them or with my own chaps. They use the canteen and social club like anyone else and participate in the men's annual outing, where they seem to enjoy themselves. I've had a few of them over to my house for the last two Christmasses and one couple in particular I regard as especial

[1] No coloured men worked in the parks in this area but the main reason seemed to be that this work, being seasonal, was largely done by casual labour.

friends. My foreman was best man when they got married again [*sic*] over here and my son fixed up the formalities for Mrs. J. to have her baby in hospital.

Like Council A, Council B administered a semi-rural, mainly middle-class residential area with few immigrant residents. An informant could not recall having received any applications for white-collar or technical posts from European or Commonwealth immigrants. The Parks and Highways Department had employed two Poles and several West Indians in recent years but no Southern Irish: 'There's a local Irish builder and he probably mops up all the available Irish labour.'

The superintendent expressed great satisfaction with his former Polish workers:

> One worked as a driver about 1952 and he was marvellous. Too good in fact, though his English was a little difficult. Finally he moved on to a better job elsewhere. The other chap was here for years and is missed by everyone. His wife came over from Poland to join him, didn't like it here and made him go back with her. He cried as he left. I shall never forget him.

The department was acutely short of labour in 1956 and the superintendent decided to try two Jamaicans (something under a hundred labourers were employed in all):

> They were exceptionally good but unfortunately they didn't like the climate and went back home after a year or so here. I was sorry to see them go. The next two were different. They knew all the rules and regulations and went sick a lot. Finally one left to work in a laundry and the other was dismissed. He was abusive to a householder when he was on a dust-collection and cheeked me when I reprimanded him. I wouldn't mind considering Jamaicans if any vacancies arise, particularly if they were like the first two, but at present we have a full staff with a lower turnover, and we take on students for the extra summer work.

My informant said that the coloured men had been 'well received' by the local workers and had not evoked any complaints from the local public: 'There was only that incident when one dustman was rude and the woman wrote in about it. Otherwise nothing, though it's a toffee-nosed area. But they're not interested in colour because no coloured people have moved in here to live.

This informant, like a number of other managerial spokesmen, had spent some years working in Africa. Unlike many, however, he displayed no trace of 'wog complex' and seemed to be entirely sincere when he said: 'I find coloured workers O.K. if you treat them properly, just like anyone else.'

Council C had much more extensive experience of overseas employees in various grades and occupations. This was the largest independent local government service in the south of England and it provided an excellent and popular place for local government students from all over the British Isles and the Commonwealth to get practical training.

Commonwealth students are accepted by arrangement with the Commonwealth Relations Office or the British Council for periods ranging between three months and one year. The majority so far had been West Africans with a handful from the West Indies and various Asian countries.

The arrangement works very well, thanks to the co-operativeness of the permanent staff, who've been gradually acclimatized for twenty years and do everything they can to help. There's been no objection from N.A.L.G.O. or the other unions involved. The students vary in intelligence but most get good posts later. There is no problem about finding suitable lodgings as most of the students stay at the International Language Club.[1] Most stay too short a time to form any social ties with the permanent staff outside the office. I only know of one who was invited to people's homes. He was outstanding and very personable—dark brown but not negroid. He didn't live with the others in the Club but had a flat of his own just outside Croydon. He was also a keen Oxford Group man, which may have helped. Unlike some of the others, who seem to feel it's our duty to help them, he wrote afterwards to thank us.

Apart from the students, who were accepted in all the appropriate departments, Council C employed a fair number of European and Commonwealth staff (non-manual as well as manual) in its main administrative offices and also in some specialized departments. There was no uniform policy, so that the position in each department varied according to such factors as the availability of suitable immigrants and the views of the departmental head and permanent staff.

As might have been expected, the non-student immigrant staff, other than clerical workers, were mostly to be found in the specialized departments concerned with town planning, education, welfare,

[1] See p. 35.

and so on. The purely administrative side of local government tends to attract local candidates, who for their part are often more suitable for the work because of their local upbringing, knowledge, and associations. It may also be that in some local authorities the general administrative departments are more conservative and insular in atmosphere than the specialized professional ones, and are therefore less receptive to the entry of outsiders. In this particular council, the steady flow of temporary Commonwealth students had probably modified insular feelings, but in fact only one non-student immigrant, an Indian shorthand-typist, was working in the main office at the time of the survey. Of her it was said: 'She's been here nearly a year. She's not quick but accurate and painstaking. In character she's quiet and retiring but generally well liked by the other girls.'

The situation in the different technical departments varied considerably. Apart from one midwife 'of African extraction' in the Public Health Department, all the rest of the non-student immigrant staff were concentrated in the Borough Engineer's Department, two welfare departments, and the Education Department.

The Borough Engineer's Department employed some 250 officers and about 1,200 manual workers. Since the War it had employed four permanent officers from overseas (a naturalized Pole, two Anglo-Indians, and an Indian). It had also had two temporary assistant officers, both West Africans, and two students, a Pakistani and a West African. Of the permanent officers the Pole and the Indian were still with the department:

> The two other permanent officers have gone to other local authorities. There's always a lot of coming and going amongst younger professional people. Both the two we have are well liked by their fellow-officers. Most of our staff are professional people and they don't feel strongly about race or colour. The Pole had some language difficulty at first, especially with the pick-and-shovel men, but that passed. I think you could probably promote him in the normal way in due course. The Indian has a law degree and is very ambitious. He feels he rates a better job but he's agreeable and doesn't display any bitterness about it.

This department had employed two Poles and about two dozen coloured[1] workers on its manual labour force since the late

[1] Most of these seem to have been West Indian, but a rather vague reference was made by one section informant to 'some Cypriots, West Africans, and Indians' under the general heading of 'coloured'.

1940s. One Pole left some years earlier to emigrate to the United States. The other was still with the department, working as a tractor driver. Both were described as very good workers.

No coloured workers were left at the time of this survey:

> Neither the local men nor the union [N.U.G.M.W.] raised any objection but they all left of their own accord after a short period. Most of them were not particularly satisfactory workers and required considerable supervision. There are always vacancies for a good, strong labourer but few coloured men apply here. We don't employ them in two out of seven sections, where the men come into regular contact with the public, to avoid any possibility of householders objecting. We're a bit timid about possible reactions where coloured men have to go on the premises.

The Education Department had no shortage of teachers, this being an attractive area for applicants. Nevertheless it usually had twenty to thirty temporary male and female teachers from outside Britain each year, some of these appointments being exchanges arranged by governments or teaching associations. Among the countries of origin named were: France, Poland, the Scandinavian countries, Egypt, Burma, South Africa, Australia, New Zealand, India, and the West Indies. The number of such teachers varied from year to year. There were twenty-nine in 1958 and twenty-four in 1959. An informant commented on the working ability and reception of these newcomers:

> All applicants have to meet certain qualifications so their work is fairly satisfactory. There are some difficulties over language, of course. Teachers are a tolerant lot on the whole and they accept them. We haven't even had trouble between white South Africans and coloured teachers.

Only one of the many temporary teachers from overseas had so far been taken on to the permanent local teaching staff: 'She's an Anglo-Indian. We'd probably consider others, if they wanted to stay and had the qualifications.'

The 'thin-end-of-the-wedge' principle seemed to operate in the matter of public reactions, in this case those of pupils and their parents:

> The local residents are a pretty tolerant lot and have been used to having a fair number of foreigners and coloured students about the place for a number of years. The arrival of a very dark American Negro woman on exchange did cause some fuss among parents at first. So did a really black West African woman who was sent in from London as a

temporary replacement during a 'flu epidemic. We were a bit hesitant in both cases but it worked all right. It's probably just a question of people getting used to it as they have got used to the Anglo-Indian and Indian teachers and also to coloured fellow-pupils. There's an Indian boy at school with my son and he brings him home a lot.

This department also had a Burmese girl clerk and two Indian male clerks. Of the former it was said: 'She has a charming personality and after a while her colour just doesn't arise. Everyone forgets about it. She's well qualified and has been promoted. Of course she and her family are here for good. They're Christians and have a British outlook.'

Two welfare departments in Council C had employed and continued to employ fair numbers of European and Commonwealth staff, most of them as orderlies or in domestic work. There were also three European house-mothers and an Anglo-Indian assistant warden. For orderly and domestic work the Europeans were regarded as excellent workers despite some language difficulties. Coloured workers were considered to be 'difficult' in their relations with the rest of the staff.

In the course of half a dozen interviews in various departments of this council a picture emerged of a tolerant and agreeable working community, in which newcomers with adequate professional and personal qualifications were on the way to achieving a fairly satisfactory accommodation in their work and relations with colleagues and superior officers. The degree of absorption differed according to the climate prevailing in particular departments and sections; it seemed further advanced in the more specialized and professional sectors than in the general administration or even in the manual labour force.

(e) *Printing and Bookbinding*

The few '100-plus' establishments concerned with these ancient and well-guarded crafts constitute a separate and very different occupational grouping. They could have been included in the skilled engineering group, but they were surveyed in this section for two reasons. Firstly, one of the establishments was attached to a local authority. Secondly, despite the manual nature of the work, its traditional character, intellectual content, and the high pay-rates and occupational status associated with it seemed to bring it closer to white-collar or even professional work than to even the skilled industrial occupations surveyed in the three earlier sections.

There are, of course, certain conspicuous differences, the most notable ones being found in the relationship of printing workers to their unions and in their social class attitudes. Whereas unionization is weak among the lower, less-qualified white-collar workers, partly because of its working-class associations, printing workers have no such reservations. Unionization is very high in this craft and the printing unions, traditional journeymen's descendants of the medieval guilds, are the source and guarantee of their members' high economic and occupational status.[1] Printers tend to be the intellectual aristocrats of the skilled working-class and are often very militant in wider trade-union activities.

All craft unions are selective and exclusive in their attitudes to would-be entrants and the various printers' and allied unions would seem to be more so than the rest. This is so despite, or perhaps because of, the fact that printing and bookbinding are traditional crafts whose standards and rules apply in at least some of the countries from which Britain's post-war immigrants have come. To quote the vivid illustration given by the manager of a bookbinding department: 'Binding hasn't altered much in 400 years. A bookbinder of Caxton's day could come in here and start work, given half an hour's instruction.'

In this case, therefore, it appears that the acceptance of proved craftsmen from other countries would not necessarily contribute to any lowering of British craft standards, as it might be held to do in such trades as carpentering, where the apprenticeship period and standards may be considerably less demanding in, for instance, the West Indies than they are in Britain.

Croydon had five printing or bookbinding establishments in the 100–250-employee range, but three of them (A, B, and C) employed no immigrants at all. In all cases the reason given by management was that the firms were 'closed shops' and that they recruited all their labour through the unions. No coloured workers had ever been submitted, either for printing or for the few labouring jobs,

[1] There is an abundant literature on the origins, traditions, and development of the printing craft unions, which were among the first craft unions to be set up in Britain. It ranges from histories of the unions themselves (e.g., those of the Typographical Association, and the Scottish Typographical Association) to general works on the history of trade unionism (Webb, S. and B., *The History of Trade Unionism*, London, Cass, 1968, and Lujo Brentano's works, representing the opposite poles of interpretation of the nature of the links between guilds and craft unions).

which were also covered by the 'closed shop' agreement. Some years ago a Polish printer was sent down by the union to Firm A but I was told that 'the Communists in the local chapel objected on political grounds and refused to let us accept him'.[1]

The information given about these three firms indicated that union rejection was the principal reason for the absence of immigrant workers. There was no evidence of management objections. One informant said:

> We have great trouble in filling the few labouring jobs but it was quite difficult to persuade the union to let us take on a few non-union workers as cleaners. Even then they made the condition that we must only employ pensioners. We have a constant trickle of coloured applicants at the door but in the circumstances can't consider taking them in any capacity. In the office, where the union writ doesn't run, we had a Pakistani typist for a while. She was a nice little girl but had a terrible inferiority complex over her colour. One couldn't correct her like the others.

Firm D was also a closed shop, but it had for some years employed a West Indian craftsman. His entry and later acceptance were attributable primarily to the firm persistence of the manager in his dealings with the union chapel. By the time of my visit the foreman could speak of the West Indian as a 'good craftsman' and 'one of us', and had helped him over a number of housing and personal problems.

Firm D's manager described his printing workers in the following terms:

> They're the aristocrats of labour—touchy to handle, critical of unskilled labourers, of the Southern Irish and so on. In my view they've accepted the West Indian more readily than they would accept some Europeans. The question's only arisen once, when the union sent a Polish member down for a vacancy. The chapel refused to accept him, saying: 'We don't want any bloody Polish counts in here. They're too

[1] There is a considerable group of skilled Polish printing workers in Britain and over the years many or most of them have been accepted as members of various printing unions. Most work in small Polish printing houses, but even there the British unions sometimes make their power felt. At times this has ludicrous consequences, as when Polish firms printing Polish-language publications are forced to take a quota of English compositors and even proof-readers who speak not a word of the language, and to apprentice a proportion of English boys if they wish to train further Polish apprentices.

good for us.'[1] There may well have been some political considerations behind this as well. As for the West Indian, he's nice-looking, very light in colour with European features, and he's happy-go-lucky and likes a bet, which makes him popular.

Firm E presented a very different picture from the other four. It was the only non-union shop, relying to a large extent on high mechanization and non-union female operatives. Its labour policy was therefore dictated by management and not by the unions. The firm had a low labour turnover and no great labour difficulties. Out of a total works staff of about 100, it employed one Polish male, three Anglo-Indian or Indian women, and three Southern Irish women. My informant had no particular comment to make on their performance but regarded them as part of the permanent labour force; he expressed willingness to take on other suitable immigrant applicants if a vacancy were to occur.

The situation in this last firm illustrates the very real threat to the privileged position of the skilled printing worker, a position which has been so long maintained and guarded by the craft unions. For there are many processes in printing which could, but for union restrictive practices, be rationalized, mechanized, and entrusted to semi-skilled workers, particularly women, with their faster and more delicate touch. This is one of the main reasons for union exclusiveness and resistance to the entry of all outsiders to their closed circle.

(f) *The Hospital Service*

The antecedents of the twentieth-century nursing profession[2] can be sought both in the work of certain specialized religious orders and in domestic service. The first seems to have contributed to the 'vocational' mythology that is still accepted by most senior members of the profession[3] as well as by the lay world, and thereby to the perpetuation of unattractive and uncompetitive rates of pay, hours, and conditions of work. The second association was ana-

[1] A year later at least one Polish compositor (with pre-war training) was working in a closed-shop printing works in Croydon. He was a Silesian miner's son and thus, like virtually all Polish craftsmen, of working-class origin.

[2] Out of the whole range of medical and lay personnel that staff the hospital service, this survey was mainly focused on the professional staff and particularly on the nurses.

[3] This general introduction is based on material from Brian Abel-Smith, *A History of the Nursing Profession* (London, Heinemann, 1960), and R. Lewis and A. Maude, *Professional People* (London, Phoenix House, 1952)

thema to the 'ladies' and educated women who entered and dominated[1] nursing after its dramatic reform and re-creation by Florence Nightingale; hence the traditional determination to ensure that this manual profession should remain a high-status job for educated women.

The combination of an austere and almost cloistered discipline, increasingly uncompetitive salary rates and over-high educational standards for entrance has since the 1920s helped to produce a chronic shortage of nursing staff. The shortage has been only partly eased by the entry of an increasing number of Southern Irish girls,[2] and made more acute by the introduction of the National Health Service. This situation, combined with earlier marriage, the opening up of a greater number of alternative careers for women and perhaps a certain loss of social prestige for the profession, has led to some dilution and relaxation of educational standards, and also to the employment of an increasing number of foreign and Commonwealth nurses, student nurses, and pupil assistants.[3] The process has in recent years reached a point where many smaller and more remote hospitals would be unable to function without them, as without the junior medical staff from overseas. Such a rapid and radical change in the sources of recruitment has not, however, as in some other professions and occupations, produced an equivalent change in the status and prestige of nursing, either within the profession or in the public esteem; probably because of the very rigidity of the profession's standards and also because of the special nature of a nurse's work, with its continuous and intimate association with people who are suffering pain and anxiety, and who may be in fear of death.

The three '100-plus' hospitals in Croydon consisted of a large training hospital with an attached midwifery department (A), a smaller hospital training for the general register (B), and a small

[1] They dominated but never entirely filled the profession, for the simple reason that the supply of female secondary-school leavers has always been inadequate to fill the needs of nursing and teaching combined (Abel-Smith, op. cit., pp. 149–54).

[2] In 1951, 11 per cent. of the nurses in England and Wales were Irish-born.

[3] In 1959–60 for instance, there were nearly 6,000 overseas student nurses and another 2,000 trained nurses from overseas among the 200,000 hospital nurses in Britain. Their numbers have increased considerably since then. Recruiting literature is issued by the Confederation of Health Service Employees in French, Italian, German, and Spanish, and some hospitals post notices in several languages.

hospital for the old and chronic sick, which trained assistant nurses (C). They employed between them a total of over 1,350 people, more than two-thirds of them on the staff (mainly in nursing).[1] Of this total, over 15 per cent. of the staff and 18 per cent. on the manual side were immigrants (not including the large number of Southern Irish, who were found mainly on the nursing and medical staff). The percentage of European and Commonwealth immigrants working in the hospitals was in striking contrast with the 1 per cent. or less found in all other groups in this 'white-collar' and professional sector. It was, however, similarly low in the small clerical sections in each hospital, where considerations of vocation, personal service, and professional training do not apply as they do in the medical, nursing, and specialist technical departments. The large number of West Indian female immigrants found in domestic work and catering in the hospitals was also striking in view of their normal dislike of such work; it may be attributed mainly to the fact that among West Indians any kind of work in a hospital confers prestige and status.

The ethnic breakdown of the immigrant nursing contingent varied from hospital to hospital, as did the distribution of various groups over the nursing hierarchy. Hospital A had 600 beds and a nursing staff of 378, including students. The precise ethnic breakdown of the nursing and auxiliary staff is given in Table 1.

This showed that under 60 per cent. of the nursing staff at this time were from the United Kingdom, while nearly one-fifth came from Southern Ireland. In this particular profession, however, the Irish were already fully accepted as an integral and permanent component of the British nursing force. As the matron of Hospital A said of them (and the other two agreed): 'Of course you don't include the Irish nurses in the category of immigrants, do you?'

The twenty-nine European nurses were mainly from Western and Southern Europe, with the exception of eight Finnish student nurses and auxiliaries. No representatives remained of the post-war East European exile groups; but there were several German and Austrian nurses, whose position in the hospital hierarchy suggested that they had been in this country for a number of years.

[1] Information on the nursing, nursing auxiliary, and domestic staffs was provided by the matron in each hospital, and on the professional, technical, administrative, and clerical staff by the administrative officer.

TABLE 1

Ethnic Origins of Nursing and Auxiliary Staff

	Total	United Kingdom	Irish	European	Commonwealth (Colonial) and other
General Wards and Departments					
Nursing Administrative Staff	8	6 English	1	—	1 Indian
Sister Tutors	4	3 English 1 Welsh	—	—	—
Night Superintendent	1	—	—	1 Austrian	—
Night Sisters	7	5 English 2 Welsh	—	—	—
Theatre Superintendent and Sisters	7	6 English	—	1 German	—
Ward and Departmental Sisters	23	15 English 1 Scottish	6	—	1 Jewish (born Calcutta)
Staff Nurses	22	13 English	2	1 German 1 French 1 Dutch	1 Anglo-Indian 3 Colonial
Student Nurses	171	71 English 1 Scottish 1 Channel Islander	51	2 Spanish 2 Swiss 1 French 1 Dutch 1 Swede 1 Greek 1 German 1 Austrian 1 Italian 6 Finnish	18 Colonial 6 Iranians 6 Chinese
Male Nurses	10	7 English	—	1 Spanish	2 Colonial
Assistant Nurses	3	3 English	—	—	—
Nursing Auxiliaries and Cadets	16	9 English	2	2 Finnish 1 Spanish 1 Italian	1 Iranian
Part-time Nurses (all grades)	39	38 English	—	—	1 Colonial
Maternity Department					
Administrative Staff	3	2 English	—	1 German	—
Sisters	9	5 English 1 Welsh	2	—	1 Colonial
Staff Nurses and Midwives	8	5 English	—	—	3 Colonial
Pupil Midwives	27	13 English	3	1 German	10 Colonial
Nursing Auxiliaries	4	1 English	1	—	2 Colonial
Part-time Nurses (all grades)	16	15 English	—	—	1 Colonial
	378	217 English 4 Welsh 2 Scottish 1 Channel Islander 224	68	8 Finns 5 Germans 4 Spanish 2 Austrians 2 French 2 Dutch 2 Italians 2 Swiss 1 Swede 1 Greek 29	41 Colonial 7 Iranian 6 Chinese 1 Indian 1 Anglo-Indian 1 Jewish (born Calcutta) 57
Ancillary Staff					
Ward Orderlies	43	33 English	2	2 Italian 1 Austrian 1 Spanish	4 Colonial
Resident Housemaids	14	3 English	—	5 Spanish 4 Italian 2 Dutch	—
Domestic Assistants—day duty	70	52 English	1	1 Italian	16 Colonial
Domestic Assistants—evening duty	14	14 English	—	—	—
Ward Porters	3	2 English	—	1 French	—

Just over 10 per cent. of the nursing staff of Hospital A were classed as 'colonial', the great majority of them being West Indians. The unofficial term 'colonial' apparently referred primarily to the sponsored trainees from colonial (or former colonial) territories who were placed in hospital training schools by arrangement with the Colonial Office or the Ministry of Labour. In addition there were seven Iranians, six Chinese (from Hong Kong or Malaya), and three Indian-born nurses.

This hospital could afford to be selective and demanded G.C.E. or Senior Cambridge School Certificate level from all applicants:

> We don't take all those who apply by any means, and there are more colonials at other local hospitals, where the standards are less demanding. I've no complaints about their work but we try to spread them out thin over the wards to discourage slowness and the formation of cliques. . . . The nurses all get along well with each other and I've never had any complaints from patients.

The various ethnic groups were by no means uniformly distributed in the nursing hierarchy. Most senior posts were held by United Kingdom nurses, together with some Irish and a handful of Germans and Austrians. There were two coloured nurses, an Indian and a West Indian (described as 'very charming, quite dark') in senior positions, but the bulk of 'colonial' nurses were staff nurses, students, or auxiliaries. This was not necessarily due to any resistance to their promotion: 'colonial' nurses began to enter the hospitals several years later than the Germans and Austrians; in addition, many of them were likely to return to excellent positions in their own countries soon after training.

The table shows that a considerable number of Europeans, 'colonials' and others were employed on the ancillary staff. Immigrants were also found among the 240 or so non-nursing staff. Five out of the forty-five medical staff were newcomers (one Pole, one Greek, one Indian, two Pakistanis) and there was an Indian pharmacist. A Pole and a West Indian were also employed in the catering department. Their presence appeared to be taken entirely for granted and my informant had reservations only about employing more than one or two West Indian manual workers in the same department, following one incident of 'ganging up'.

Hospital B was considerably smaller than Hospital A and had a nursing staff of 140, seventeen of whom came from outside the British Isles. Apart from a Belgian sister, an Indian staff nurse, and a part-time nurse from Scandinavia, all the rest were student nurses (one German, thirteen 'colonials'). In the immediate post-war years this hospital had some Polish and other East European refugees but after that only northern and western Europeans. Like Hospital A, this hospital accepted about 10 per cent. of 'colonial' nurses:

> The nursing profession regards 10 per cent. of coloured nurses as reasonable. If there are more the tempo of the work drops. We've been taking them as students since about 1950 and the number of West Indian applicants has steadily increased since then. I find colonial students about two years behind British applicants in education and like them to have the Senior Cambridge Certificate. On the whole they're slow but after a few years some quicken up and a few even reach prize-winning level. They're pretty good on the whole and not lazy. Many are keen to make good and return home, where there are good jobs waiting for them.

As at the other two hospitals relations between white and coloured nurses were said to be satisfactory:

> White nurses are quite used to the presence of coloured nurses. There've been occasional complaints about B.O. and different cooking smells in the nurses' home but nothing serious. Most coloured girls seem much more conscious of their colour than the whites and one was very anti-white when she came. They are often quick-tempered and don't readily take criticism or reprimand. As for promotion, I've had two as night staff nurses and that worked well. I don't know how acceptable they'd be in higher authority yet.

More friction had been noted between West Indian and West African nurses:

> The Africans are down on the West Indians and call them descendants of slaves. I've noticed that the West Indian nurses don't fraternize much with the West Indian domestics and they usually differ in appearance and colour. The nurses have a middle-class background and it's only occasionally you get a real blackie or negroid type among them.

As in the other two Croydon hospitals there were far more immigrant nurses than patients at this time. Relations between patients and coloured nurses were said to be good: 'The patients are quite accustomed to them. I only once remember a patient being difficult —she refused to let a coloured nurse give her a bed-bath. The coloured nurses are particularly good with children and the children like them.'

Three of the eight medical staff at this hospital were Indians;

there were also four Europeans, one West African, and two Indian-born staff employed on unskilled work in the catering and maintenance departments. The number of immigrants in all professional, technical, and non-nursing occupations varied from year to year and they were definitely accepted as a permanent element in the labour force. There were not, however, and so far had never been, any on the administrative and clerical staff.

Hospital C's situation was very different from those at A and B. Being a 400-bed hospital for the aged and chronic sick it required fewer fully trained nurses. From the assistant nurses who were trained here no specific educational qualifications were demanded. They were, however, required to write a short essay and take a simple arithmetical test to ensure that they would be able to deal with reports and charts.

Out of a male and female nursing staff of 155, twenty-seven were coloured (nine Anglo-Indians, one Pakistani, sixteen West Indians, and one West African) and six were European (two Austrians, a Pole, a Latvian, a Dutchwoman, and an Italian). Most Anglo-Indians and Europeans were fully trained nurses in more responsible positions but the great majority of the West Indians were pupil assistant nurses.

> We began to train coloured pupils about 1953. Since then increasing numbers have applied, as we're known to accept them. The Colonial Office prefers hospitals to take only recommended students [i.e. those recommended by their home governments] but if a particularly intelligent applicant presents herself here I bypass this. On the whole I find they haven't much stamina and they are generally slower and stay that way. This upsets working relationships and some of our other girls have slowed down to their speed. Relations between white and coloured nurses are good, however, and I wouldn't hesitate to put any who are good enough in positions of authority over others. The Anglo-Indians are good but seem particularly prone to carry a chip on their shoulders. There is sometimes friction between West Indians from different islands and I also find that Barbadian girls seem more suited to nursing than Jamaicans, perhaps because of more careful selection at the other end.

Relations between coloured nurses and the 'public' (i.e. patients) in Hospital C were more difficult than in the other two: 'This is chiefly because the patients are old and set in their ways. Most of the trouble is made by people who have lived in India or Africa.

Two elderly women who were memsahibs in India were particularly unkind and I had to tell them that if they didn't like being nursed by coloured nurses they would have to go elsewhere.'

Hospital C had a Polish and an Austrian doctor on its medical staff of five, three Jamaican porters out of a total of seventeen, and a 'coloured lady' among the twenty laundry-workers.

The material from these three Croydon hospitals indicated that, compared with some other skilled occupations and professions, the nursing profession is relatively tolerant of all outsiders who have the required educational and social background and who accept the ideals, ethical standards, and ways of behaviour which are held to characterize the profession.[1] For many decades the profession has tolerated the entry of a considerable minority of upwardly mobile entrants[2] from the British Isles and has conferred higher status on them. In the absence of sufficient local candidates this tolerance has since the War been cautiously extended to European and Commonwealth entrants.[3] Despite the fact that nurses' pay (at

[1] Florence Nightingale wrote: 'My principle has always been that we should give the best training we could to any woman, of any class, of any sect, paid or unpaid, who had the requisite qualifications, moral, intellectual and physical, for the vocation of a nurse. Unquestionably the educated will be more likely to rise to the post of superintendent, but *not* because they are ladies, but because they are *educated*'. (Cecil Woodham Smith, *Florence Nightingale* (London, Constable, 1950 1951), p. 483, quoted by Lewis and Maude, op. cit., p. 27.)

[2] See Abel-Smith, op. cit., Chapter X. Trained nurses are classified as Social Class II. A report on student nurses in the Oxford area showed that one-third of entrants were making an upwardly mobile occupational choice. Twelve per cent. of all entrants were 'Non-European', mainly West Indian, but there is no break-down by ethnic origin and educational level to show how many of them were upwardly mobile (*From Student to Nurse*, Oxford Area Nurse Training Committee Report, 1961, p. 29).

[3] 'As for those who come here to be trained, to learn their nursing, we must "hold out our hands in welcome to them", if only for the purely selfish reason that without them many hospitals would be hard put to it to nurse their patients. But there should be more to it than that. Although these girls have usually no nursing tradition to offer, they have some of the gifts of their trained sisters—the new background, the different outlook, and often a genuine talent for nursing—certainly a gift for the patient. And they offer one priceless opportunity to all of us growing up in this new world-in-the-melting-pot, when Britons can no longer live within their encircling water, secure from any interest in peoples and places beyond. In the happiest way (if we will take it), the way of living and working together as colleagues, we can learn something of their background and tradition, a gift for every nurse who hopes, as well as being a good nurse, to be a good citizen.

The gifts, however, are not all on one side. We can learn from our colleagues from overseas, but they can also learn from us—and that is what many of them have specifically come for. The British way of life, the British standards of nurs-

the time of this survey) compared unfavourably with that of untrained domestic labour in the same hospital,[1] senior members of the profession appeared to feel no such fears of lowered status or prestige as were encountered in white-collar occupations with a less demanding training and less rigid standards. Here at least it was still the profession that conferred status on the individual and not vice versa.

From the Croydon material it appeared that Irish nurses had been entirely absorbed into the profession while European nurses, who began to enter nursing in increasing numbers in the immediate post-war years, had moved a considerable way up the hierarchy, followed by Anglo-Indians and Indians. The acceptance of these lighter-coloured nurses was not, however, necessarily associated with their lower visibility but could arise out of their generally higher qualifications and the fact that most of them had entered the profession some years before the large-scale entry of West Indians and West Africans. In recent years the latter influx had caused most matrons to apply a rough 10 per cent. quota. Some teaching hospitals with very high standards of selection and long waiting lists in fact took very few or no students from outside Britain at all.[2] At the other end of the scale came such hospitals as Hospital C, about one-fifth of whose female nursing staff were coloured, (mainly pupil assistants). Hospitals A and B each had about 10 per cent. of 'colonial' nurses, the main reason for this being not only a shortage of suitable applicants from other sources but also a willingness to comply with the authorities' request for co-operation in training nurses from 'colonial' (now 'Commonwealth') areas.

Some doubts appeared to be entertained by matrons about the speed, efficiency, and intellectual capacity of West Indian and West African nurses and about their suitability for promotion to senior posts. These doubts were, however, expressed not in racial or even social terms but in terms of known educational background and

ing, or so we believe, are worth showing forth to the guests in our midst. We hope they will find in them much that is worth noting, worth adopting, worth taking home with them, if and when they return. So it behoves us to show them, in our living and working, only the best, and if with it we offer the genuine friendship and respect of colleagues all working in the same field, they will be able to accept our gifts, as we do theirs, to the mutual profit of us both, and the ultimate benefit of all our patients' (*Nursing Mirror*, 27 April 1962).

[1] Cf. *Time and Tide*, 15 March 1962.

[2] See London Council of Social Service, *Report on the Employment of Coloured Workers in London*, 1959, p. 7, and Oxford report, op. cit.

observed working ability. Such reservations are fairly characteristic of the early phase of experience of a new source of staff. The slight reluctance to promote 'colonial' nurses to senior posts could also be attributed, in part at least, to the fact that senior posts tend to go to nurses who are likely to remain in the profession in Britain, whereas many of the 'colonial' nurses return home to work shortly after their training is finished.

The views and staff policy of individual matrons, whose authority over their nursing staffs is virtually supreme, are very important for the employment of immigrant nurses. All three matrons interviewed in Croydon were willing to accept applicants from various immigrant groups. The matron in Hospital C had, in practice, become something of a 'sponsor' in relation to coloured nurses and assistant nurses; she had no reservations about promotion and did not countenance biased or hostile behaviour towards them by patients.

By contrast with most informants in the white-collar group sector and the other industrial sectors, the matrons seemed concerned almost exclusively with the working ability and potential of their nursing staff and very little with personal characteristics and behaviour. None of the three had much to say about off-the-job behaviour or frictions between nurses,[1] nor did any of them know precisely how many of the 'colonial' nurses[2] came from the West Indies or West Africa, nor what particular problems or difficulties might confront these newcomers. This single-minded approach has, as has already been noted, a positive as well as a negative side, since it means that matrons are less prone to turn down applicants simply because of their ethnic origins or any assumptions about social and cultural differences.

Like the other occupations in this sector, nursing involves con-

[1] One well-qualified young staff nurse from a suburban middle-class family who had returned to her old hospital after some years of working abroad and on passenger liners commented: 'I came back to find the place full of coloured and Irish. The place seems neglected and scruffy, although the atmosphere's friendly enough. They won't stand the strict training we used to get. If you tell the little students what to do too strictly then off they go to Matron. The West Indians seem more intelligent than the West Africans. The Anglo-Indians are a good mixture. You can't get the right type of girl any longer. I didn't go out nursing with the thought of money but the pay situation's dreadful compared with private industry.'

[2] Cf. London Council of Social Service report (op. cit.), p. 9, for a similar impression gained by a study group member reporting on the situation in some London hospitals.

tact with the public. Indeed, it is hard to imagine a more close and prolonged contact than that between nurse and patient.

It was, therefore, of particular interest that in the two large general hospitals matrons could recall only one or two instances of white patients[1] objecting to the presence of coloured or other immigrant nurses (or doctors) over a period of up to ten years. This may seem surprising when the same patients would probably be hesitant about welcoming the families of the coloured nurses or doctors as neighbours or tenants, and even more reluctant to tolerate the same individuals as marriage partners for close relatives. The explanation would seem to be that most people's behaviour towards strangers and outsiders in a given situation is determined by the nature and requirements of that situation. In a well-defined area of association such as is found at work or in religious, political, and other organized associational life, roles and relationships are governed and limited by generally accepted rules and conventions. In informal and intimate personal relationships the rules and conventions are less firmly defined and there is a greater tendency, particularly among the reserved, mildly xenophobic British, to avoid contact with strangers who may not know the unwritten rules and the values behind them, particularly if these strangers are associated with an alien culture and a low social position.

The nurse–patient relationship and the doctor–patient relationship are two of the most firmly defined of all professional relationships. This may explain why, for instance, a woman patient accepts without protest a coloured nurse or even a coloured male doctor because they conform to her image of a nurse or a doctor, whereas she may be apprehensive if a coloured electrician or a coloured dustman arrives at her home to repair a fuse or collect the garbage, or a coloured medical student knocks to inquire after the vacant room in her 'select' suburban house. Another element involved here is that of *force majeure*. A sick patient is not usually in a position or a mood to bargain about the nature of the treatment he receives or the identity of the trained personnel who give this to him. On the contrary, he is more likely to accept it with relief and to appreciate those who minister to him. This consideration, of course, applied much less in Hospital C, where old and chronic

[1] At the time of this survey these Croydon hospitals reported only a handful of coloured or other immigrant patients, unlike most hospitals in London boroughs further north.

sick patients were waiting for death and often required more domestic than proper nursing care. Such patients are more likely to infuse their everyday biases and antipathies, often magnified by age and crotchetiness, into their hospital relationships with assistant nurses and orderlies, who themselves may come from a different background than the more highly educated immigrant nurses and doctors.

Yet another important element in the patients' (as in the junior nurses') acceptance of immigrant nurses is the attitude of the matron. Unlike most employers or supervisors in the other professional and white-collar 'contact' occupations surveyed here (for instance, some public and local government services, shop-work, clerical work, teaching), matrons did not seem particularly concerned with the possible reaction of the 'client' or patient to the presence of foreign or coloured nurses in the wards. Their main concern was rather with the maintenance of professional standards and the continuation of efficient service to the community, with the aid of any and every source of suitable recruits.

On the lay side of the hospital, working relationships seemed to approximate more closely to the patterns found in offices and local government, although they were perhaps modified and mellowed by the general association with the work and values of the hospital service. There were some immigrant professional and technical specialists but no coloured or foreign-born people on the administrative and clerical staff, which was appointed by the local group administration. There were a fair number of European men and women in various indoor and outdoor manual occupations but few West Indian males, presumably because similar work in industry was better paid. There were, as has been said, an appreciable number of West Indian women in catering and the domestic work which they are usually so unwilling to accept; this was probably because their customary aversion to such work had been overcome by the prestige attached to working in a hospital, even in a non-nursing capacity.

Conclusions

In this white-collar and professional sector the total work force of about 11,600 included some 364 immigrants, 209 on the staff side (including all retail workers) and 155 manual workers. The great majority of immigrants on the staff were found, as we have seen, in the hospitals, rather few immigrants having actually applied for jobs in the other industrial groups. This could be attributed to the newcomers' fear of rejection, but seemed more likely to be due to such factors as language difficulties, lack of local knowledge or vocational training, and preference for well-paid industrial work with overtime, rather than the modest security afforded by retail and clerical work and local government. The low percentage on the 'manual' side was also due in the main to the unskilled immigrants' preference for better-paid work in private industry, even if it offered less security.

Of the four industrial groups surveyed, the hospital service was the only one that had taken in and accepted large numbers of immigrants from all over the world at the professional and technical as well as the manual levels. The main reason for the initial decision was undoubtedly a shortage of suitable local recruits, but the rapid and relatively easy absorption of Irish, European, and Asian and more recently West Indian and other coloured Commonwealth recruits, particularly in the nursing profession, should probably be attributed to the highly institutionalized character of the work, including the long, exacting, status-conferring training, to its vocational or 'service' orientation, and to the nature of the nurse–patient relationship.

Professional training and status also appeared to be associated with a greater tolerance of suitably qualified outsiders. This was seen not only among the nursing and medical staffs in the hospitals but also among professional staff, particularly teachers in the largest local government education department, the only other section in which professional outsiders were found in the local government sector. Here again the public service aspect of teaching and local government work could also have contributed to acceptance.

Where occupational training was less rigid and exacting than in the professions, as in clerical and shop-work, there was greater status insecurity. This was found in association with considerable resistance to the employment of immigrants, especially darker-coloured people, in offices and shops, particularly in jobs involving contact with the public. The Croydon store in which immigrants were being most satisfactorily absorbed was the most 'select' establishment of the four, with the most 'select' staff and the most 'select' clientele.

In general, labour shortage was the major factor that had induced most establishments in this sector to start employing immigrants on a regular as opposed to a student basis. The presence, over a decade or more, of a considerable number of students in various professional and technical departments had, however, accustomed their colleagues to the idea of their permanent presence, even where the labour shortage might not be very grave, and had dispelled or modified a number of second-hand notions about various newcomers' intellectual inferiority or cultural backwardness. The number of immigrants entering professional and 'white-collar' jobs in Croydon was, however, limited, because of the majority's inadequate socio-economic and educational background, qualifications, and aptitudes, and, in the case of Europeans, by language difficulties, foreign nationality, and so on. In several establishments which employed no non-manual immigrants, however, it turned out that none had in fact even applied. The fact that an establishment employed no immigrants did not therefore constitute automatic evidence of discrimination.

The universal preference of local managements for local workers was particularly and understandably strong in the purely administrative departments of local government, especially at recruitment stage. Local employees were also preferred in other sub-sectors, with the exception of the hospitals and professional departments, where recruitment was country-wide or even wider.

In this sector the unions were weak and played little part in influencing the absorption of immigrants, with the notable exception of the 'closed shop' printing and bookbinding industry. Here the unions were the major influence hindering the entry and acceptance of outsiders, and apart from one exception, which was under public control, and where sponsorship had also been at work, it was only in the solitary non-union firm that any immigrants were found.

In this sector, as elsewhere, particularly in the white-collar occupations, a shortage of local labour has usually been associated with a decline in the employee's comparative rates of pay and occupational status. The immigrant 'white-collar' worker is often concerned less with occupational status in the new society (or with security, pensions, and fringe benefits), than with getting an immediate high wage and the prospect of overtime. This consideration seems to have kept some former 'white-collar' immigrants from seeking work in offices and shops; a number of them were, indeed, found in semi-skilled industrial work.

Another factor that had influenced the entry and absorption of immigrants into this sector was sponsorship. This had played a clear part in the public establishments, where student nurses and other students from the Commonwealth were sponsored by their Governments and placed by the British authorities in co-operation with the hospitals and local government authorities. In the manual department of one of the local authorities, a sponsoring supervisor had also stopped the outward drift of immigrant labourers to better-paid work and had built up a settled West Indian contingent.

PART III

FINDINGS AND CONCLUSIONS

CHAPTER 6
THE MAIN IMMIGRANT GROUPS

(1) THE NUMBERS AND DISTRIBUTION OF THE MAIN IMMIGRANT GROUPINGS IN CROYDON INDUSTRY

A summary is given in Table 2 of the numbers and distribution of the three main classes of immigrant workers in Croydon industry (partly-selected European refugees, selected European economic migrants, unselected Commonwealth and other economic migrants), by ethnic origin and sex, at the period of this survey. Appendixes 3 and 4 also give more detailed breakdowns by industrial sectors and sub-sectors, and by ethnic groups.

These figures must be approached with caution, for the possibilities of error were considerable. Where different people in a firm gave differing figures, I accepted those given by the informant who was in closer touch with the labour force (for instance, a personnel officer, works manager, or supervisor, instead of a managing director). In a few cases, especially in the larger firms, informants could give no more information than 'a few', 'a lot', or express the numbers in terms of a percentage of overall numbers.

Another possible source of error lay in some informants' inability to ascribe the correct nationality or ethnic origin to their employees. This was infrequent in the case of European workers, but more frequent in the case of the more recently arrived Commonwealth immigrants, particularly those with dark skins. Indians, Pakistanis, and Anglo-Indians were often classed together,[1] Anglo-Indians usually being distinguished only if they had light skins or

[1] It seems probable that there were more Indians than Pakistanis. The fact that employers were not compelled to take more account of national, ethnic, religious, and cultural differences suggests that these were mostly the pioneer type of immigrant who strikes out on his own, away from the self-segregating settlements (Desai's 'deviants': *Indian Immigrants in Britain*, London, Oxford University Press, 1963, pp. 122 f.). On the other hand, it could well be that the Indians and Pakistanis had tended to scatter or cluster in small groups on the basis of such differences in a manner not perceived by management.

clearly dissociated themselves from the others. For this reason, Indians and Pakistanis are enumerated together on the table, while Anglo-Indians are listed separately only when their identity was definitely established. In a few cases there was confusion between West Indians and West Africans, and in two firms between

TABLE 2

Statistics of Immigrants in Firms in Croydon employing more than 100 people in 1958–9, by National or Ethnic Origin and Sex

(a) Numbers and Percentages in each Ethnic Group and Immigrant Category

1. *Europeans*

(a) *Refugees*	Male			Female			Total		
		%	%		%	%		%	%
Poles	370	83·9	95·6	17	43·6	4·4	387	80·6	100·0
Hungarians	31	7·0	75·6	10	25·6	24·4	41	8·6	100·0
Others	40	9·1	76·9	12	30·8	23·1	52	10·8	100·0
Total	441	100·0	91·9	39	100·0	8·1	480	100·0	100·0

(b) *Economic Migrants*	Male			Female			Total		
		%	%		%	%		%	%
Germans & Austrians	8	9·8	13·1	53	30·8	86·9	61	24·0	100·0
Italians	19	23·2	35·8	34	19·8	64·2	53	20·9	100·0
Others	55	67·0	39·3	85	49·4	60·7	140	55·1	100.0
Total	82	100·0	32·3	172	100·0	67·7	254	100·0	100·0

2. *Commonwealth Coloured and Other Immigrants*

	Male			Female			Total		
		%	%		%	%		%	%
West Indians	438	61·4	42·8	585	87·6	57·2	1,023	74·1	100·0
West Africans	64	9·0	86·5	10	1·5	13·5	14	5·4	100·0
Indians/ Pakistanis	86	12·1	86·9	13	1·9	13·1	99	7·2	100·0
Anglo-Indians	79	11·1	66·9	39	5·8	33·1	118	8·5	100·0
Others Coloured	34	4·8	79·1	9	1·3	20·9	43	3·1	100·0
Others	12	1·7	50·0	12	1·8	50·0	24	1·7	100·0
Total	713	100·1	51·6	668	99·9	48·4	1,381	100·0	100·0

(b) Numbers in each Immigrant Category and Percentages for each Category in relation to total Immigrants, by Sex

	Male		Female		Total	
1. *Europeans*		%		%		%
(a) Refugees	441	35·7	39	4·4	480	22·7
(b) Economic Migrants	82	6·6	172	19·6	254	12·0
Total Europeans	523	42·3	211	24·0	734	34·7
2. *Commonwealth Coloured & Other Immigrants*	713	57·7	668	76·0	1,381	65·3
Total Immigrants	1,236	100·0	879	100·0	2,115	100·0

Total estimated labour force in 100-plus firms—47,850

Cypriots and Maltese. One informant even talked about a 'Polish' accountant who turned out to be an Anglo-Indian.

Occasionally, too, the uncertainty seems to have been provoked by the immigrants themselves. Light-coloured Asians in search of clerical work were known to represent themselves as Anglo-Indians, Anglo-Burmese, and so on, while Germans sometimes tried to pass as Austrians. In one rather unusual case a Pole who had campaigned with the Polish Armoured Corps in Holland and spoke fluent Dutch 'passed' as a Dutchman in a firm under Anglo-Dutch management.

The greatest difficulty was encountered in enumerating the quasi-Commonwealth Southern Irish, as most informants spoke of 'a few', 'a lot', or said 'they come and go'. In the end it proved impossible to give the exact numbers of Irish present in various industries and industrial sectors. This situation did, however, indicate a considerable degree of acceptance of even the migrant Irish as a regular component of the local labour force.

The table shows that nearly 2,000 immigrants were to be found in Croydon's '100-plus' firms, that is to say nearly 4½ per cent. of the total labour force employed in them. Of this immigrant total, about two-thirds were from the Commonwealth. The overwhelming majority of this group were 'coloured', that is to say from the West Indies, Africa and Asia—and about three-quarters of them came from the West Indies.

The number of Anglo-Indians revealed by the survey at first

seemed surprisingly large, but their presence in the area in considerable numbers was subsequently confirmed by an English business man who had, during his years in India, been closely concerned with educational and welfare work in the Anglo-Indian community.[1]

The refugees and exiles made up nearly two-thirds of the European total, the Poles being by far the largest single group. Under the heading of 'other refugees' were included some members of a refugee group which initially I had not intended to enumerate. These were Austrian and German Jewish refugees from Nazi Germany in the 1930s. I came across a pocket of them in one large plant: most had arrived here as young children or in their teens and had received all or much of their education in Britain. They were all salaried employees at various levels of the managerial and technical hierarchy. The total given here is a nominal one; there was certainly a considerably larger number of such people in Croydon industry, but their presence was revealed only towards the end of the general survey and it was not possible to check back with all the firms already visited. The fact that no earlier informant had mentioned their presence indicates how thoroughly absorbed they were.

The other European 'economic' immigrants included over fifty German women, some of them married to local English workers, fifty-three Italians, the men concentrated in brick-making, and fifty-five men and eighty-five women from various northern, western, and southern European countries. The majority of the women were found in the hospitals, either as nurses or as domestic staff; most of the men, who included a fair number of Dutch, were found on the managerial and technical staffs of two large light engineering plants with extensive international links.

(2) THE SITUATION OF THE MAIN IMMIGRANT GROUPS

When we examine the situation in more detail from the standpoint of the immigrants we find, as might be expected, considerable variations not only in their distribution by industry and occupation but also in the degree of industrial absorption achieved by the different groups.

[1] See p. 36

(a) *European Refugees and Exiles*

The 87 Poles were by far the largest national group in this class. All but seventeen of them were men, a proportion that did far more than reflect the disproportionate sex ratio within this exile group. A number of firms reported that they had employed Polish women in earlier years and their virtual disappearance from the industrial scene before 1958–9 was, as has already been said, an index of the Poles' increasing economic and residential adaptation.

Nearly one-half of the Polish men in Croydon industry worked for Polplastics. Twenty of the office staff of forty were Poles, at the time of my first visit, mostly employed in the technical departments concerned with design; these were under Polish management and were virtually Polish preserves. On the works side, including monthly- and weekly-paid employees, there were about 145 Poles, including a young assistant production manager, the production foreman, the charge-hands and assistants on all three shifts, the tool-room supervisor and half of his skilled staff,[1] all the supervisors and charge-hands in non-production departments, and over half of the male labour force.

Apart from those Poles who had staff or supervisory jobs in Polplastics, there was a tendency for younger and better-qualified men to leave the works side in search of better-paid work and greater opportunities elsewhere. The large stable nucleus consisted of older men, mostly ex-officers or ex-N.C.O.s, who spoke little English and preferred the modest security and Polish climate of this firm to the risks of the wider industrial society.

There were only fourteen other Polish men working in the 'consumer' sector; most of them were in firms in the light industrial group, which offered more skilled jobs, more security and better wages and working conditions than the other three industrial groups. All had been with their firms for years, were doing skilled jobs and were fully accepted as part of the permanent labour force; one had been promoted to charge-hand.

In the rest of the 'consumer' sector, more Polish men had been employed in the past, but they had either gone to Polplastics or

[1] The situation in this open-shop tool-room contrasted strongly with those found in most engineering closed shops in many other Croydon firms, where Polish and Hungarian craftsmen were usually excluded on political grounds by A.E.U. left-wingers.

moved out to better-paid work in other sectors. Like the laundry and dry-cleaning industry and some light industrial establishments, the sweet-making and canning firms were 'transit camps' for younger, better-qualified, and more ambitious newcomers. There were however, four Poles working in Chocolac, the sweet-making factory included in the case-histories. An informant described them as 'a hangover of the days when we had a lot of Poles. They have all been with the firm for a number of years, are doing skilled or responsible jobs, and are thoroughly accepted by management and work-groups.'

The 'consumer' sector was the largest employer of Polish men only because of Polplastics. Next came the light engineering sector. Except for seven working in the 'intermediate' group, they were fairly evenly divided between the 'skilled' firms (52) and the two large mass-production firms (62). There were, however, forty Poles on the staff in professional and technical jobs in the two mass-production firms and only two in supervisory work in one of the 'skilled' firms. Most of the remainder were clustered in skilled work in a few of the skilled firms. In almost every case, the Poles had been with their firms for years and were well accepted and in line for up-grading. In a few firms, the sons of Polish employees had begun to work, either as apprentices or staff trainees, with the opportunity of reaching a higher level in the economic hierarchy than their parents.

The 'intermediate' group of six engineering firms proved to have been a transit camp for Polish workers. All reported having employed one or more in earlier years, but most had drifted either to the 'skilled' or to the mass-production firms. At this time seven only were left in two factories. All were in skilled and responsible jobs.

Many Poles had passed through the two mass-production firms, but only a score of Poles remained on the works side; here again most of them were engaged on skilled or responsible work. Several were shop-stewards and most were well enough accepted in all departments except in the militant left-wing A.E.U. engineering closed shops. Several had been or were shop-stewards, but like many English fellow-workers, most had refused to be made up to charge-hand because this would mean a drop in earnings.

The Poles on the staff in these two firms were salaried technicians at medium and lower levels. A few had come up from the shop floor, while others had come straight in after receiving at least their secondary or vocational education in Britain. Poles in this group were rather younger than the ex-servicemen on the works side and most seemed to be accepted in positions of responsibility and authority by virtue of their professional qualifications (fluency in English and a not too pronounced accent were also important here). Those who had come up from the shop floor had a low ceiling of promotion, because this depended basically on higher technical qualifications which are difficult to acquire after years away from school.

In the 'heavy' industrial sector there were sixty-five Polish men, all but eight of them employed in building or public transport and utilities. The great majority were actually working for one building firm or in the railway workshop. A number of other firms in this partially 'transit camp' sector reported the presence of Polish P.R.C. or E.V.W. workers, mostly directed, in earlier years, but the majority had long since passed through to lighter, better-paid work. Only three Polish 'labouring types' were left out of the earlier total of about thirty in the brick-works.

The die-casters, one of the few firms to report dissatisfaction with Polish workers,[1] tried a few out in earlier years but they soon left or were dismissed. None remained on the buses, but there were still five in the two heavy engineering firms. These factories were old-established and had a low labour turnover and a strong community spirit. For former professional, technical, or 'white-collar' refugees or exiles, however, they presented a 'transit camp' situation and most Poles employed there earlier had passed through.

The twenty-five Poles in the building industry were all accepted as members of the regular labour force in two family firms of building contractors. The larger firm had twenty: most of them were long-service men on the 'staff scheme', which gave considerable security of job tenure. Two were foremen, one over a Polish gang, the other over English workers. In the other smaller firm, two out of five were retainers on the regular labour force.

In public transport and utilities, the local electricity board had one Polish electrician and there was one Polish railwayman at a

[1] One reason for dissatisfaction given by management was that they only wanted to 'court the girls and fight'. 'Messing about with girls' was a familiar charge against service-men during the War and for some time after. This was the only time it was mentioned during the Croydon study, presumably because so many Poles were by then middle-aged family men.

local station. The remaining thirty were all in the local railway workshop, where many had worked since the post-war resettlement period. They were well enough accepted by management and organized labour, as an incident arising out of threatened redundancy showed.[1]

In the 'white-collar' and professional sector, language difficulties, lack of local knowledge, and nationality restrictions had barred some avenues to non-British entrants. Only ten Poles were working in this sector, although a large number had been employed in the hospitals, retail work, and among local government manual workers in earlier years. Of the four women, two were nurses, one a clerical supervisor, and one a saleswoman. The six men consisted of a doctor, a male nurse, and a cook in the largest hospital, a local government officer with technical qualifications, a tractor-driver with the borough council, and a printer in a non-union firm. All had been in their jobs for some years and seemed fully accepted.

To sum up, the Poles, who came to Croydon only after they were free of employment restrictions, had gradually moved into lighter, better-paid work or work that was congenial for some other reason, such as the possibility of speaking Polish or working with fellow-countrymen.

Of the other post-war East European refugees and exiles who entered the British economy at about the same time as the Poles, there were only a handful in Croydon's '100-plus' firms. In general, their industrial absorption had followed a pattern similar to that of the Poles, with whom they tended to cluster.

Most Hungarian immigrants resembled the Polish group in socio-economic background and political motivations, but differed in being a rather younger group and in having entered the British economy between seven and ten years later, though under rather more favourable auspices. Croydon was, as has been said, one of the main reception centres for Hungarians in the autumn and winter of 1956–7, and a considerable number were placed in local industry, although some firms were already feeling the effects of the 1956 credit squeeze and were unable to take on any more workers. The survey showed that few Hungarians had remained in their first placings and that a considerable number might have found work elsewhere or even have moved out of the area altogether. Several informants spoke of language difficulties, unsatisfactory working

[1] See pp. 101–2 and p. 217.

performance, problems of personal adjustment, restlessness, and other features characteristic of the earliest stage of accommodation at work.

Forty-one Hungarians (thirty-one men, ten women) were working in the '100-plus' firms at this time. Of these the ten women and ten of the men were operators in one of the mass-production firms; another four men worked in the other, which was some miles farther from the centre of Croydon. The fact that some Hungarian women were found in full-time work was characteristic of the early years of immigrant absorption. Another ten men were in Polplastics, where their initial entry was sponsored by a local Englishwoman with Hungarian connexions. They were well accepted here and showed a lower labour turnover than elsewhere. This was probably because they felt at ease in the 'Polish' atmosphere. In addition, the initial selection was good; the personnel office was unusually well-informed about the circumstances of the Hungarian Rising and avoided taking on many of the spivs and freed prisoners, usually common criminals, who came out with the earliest waves of refugees: '. . . the genuine revolutionaries . . . usually turn out to be the good workers . . . I just ask them the date of their arrival in Britain. If it was the autumn of 1956, the presumption is that they're no good; if the winter, they're usually all right.'

A Hungarian former E.V.W. was doing skilled work in one of the skilled light engineering firms, but those taken on in 1956–7 had all left. One of the small intermediate firms also had a Hungarian draughtsman ('the best in the firm'), but some others who were taken on for semi-skilled work were found unsatisfactory and had gone. The remaining three men were employed in a large, rather traditional, heavy engineering firm on the edge of the Croydon industrial area. This firm had a Hungarian-born chief designer who sponsored the entry of about eight of the 1956 exiles; three still remained, but for the others it was a 'transit camp'.

(b) *European Economic Migrants*

In Croydon industry, this group was represented by rather modest contingents of Germans, Austrians, and Italians, mostly women, and others from west and south Europe and Scandinavia. Most had come in on Ministry of Labour permits for specified work, but there was a minority of women married to Englishmen. There was an overall preponderance of women, but certain differences emerged between the employment patterns of Germans, Austrians, and Italians on the one side and the rest on the other. The women in the latter group were usually more recent arrivals than the original nucleus of Germans, Austrians, and Italians, (some of whom could even have been in Britain in the war years as prisoners-of-war); they were found almost exclusively in the professional and 'white-collar' sector, most of them as teachers or student nurses.

The sixty-one Germans and Austrians were found in light engineering, the 'consumer' and the 'white-collar' sectors. There were none in the 'heavy' industrial sector. Despite their small overall total, there was a certain amount of clustering: three skilled men in a watch-making firm, four women in a small 'skilled' engineering firm, two men and two women in an 'intermediate' light engineering firm, five women in each of the two mass-production firms, four women in a laundry and dry-cleaning firm, five in a sweet factory, and four in one retail store. One light industrial firm had employed more in the past, but only one man was still there. The fact that only this and one other firm reported having employed more Germans and Austrians in earlier years suggests that Croydon industry drew rather little on this particular source of labour.[1] In the hospitals, however, earlier comers from Germany and Austria had moved well up the nursing hierarchy and they were also found on the ancillary staff and among the student nurses.

Wherever they were working, the Germans and Austrians seemed to be very well accepted; this was particularly true in nursing, where they had attained positions of direct authority, apparently without any noticeable comment, protest, or reservations. One or two were also reported in supervisory jobs in industry; the only sort of comment reported about some German and Austrian workers was that some of them annoyed fellow-workers by working too hard and by norm-breaking. Otherwise, they seemed to be well on the way to assimilation in industry.

The Italians in Croydon followed a pattern similar to that of the

[1] With the possible exception of the hotel and catering industry. None of these establishments in Croydon were included in the Employment Exchange list of '100-plus' firms, but from personal observation it was evident that they employed a considerable proportion of European and Commonwealth immigrants.

Germans and Austrians, but usually at lower and less-skilled levels in the economic hierarchy. They appeared to be fairly well accepted as individuals in semi-skilled or unskilled work. Only in one firm, the brick-works which employed Italians under a bulk scheme operated since 1950–1 by the brick industry, were any particular views expressed on their working qualities. Here they were accepted by management and local men as part of the regular labour force, particularly those who had settled locally and brought over their families. The management, however, still retained some reservations about putting them in direct supervisory positions and added that in any case 'they don't aspire to it'.

The other Europeans were found mainly in the 'white-collar' sector and mass-production firms, where there were ten operators and another forty men on the executive, administrative, and technical staffs. Over half of them were Dutch, some in very senior positions in one of the firms, which was associated with a giant Dutch industrial concern. Most of these people were well on the way to complete assimilation. Indeed, in the case of the firm with Dutch connexions, English informants suggested half-jokingly that the assimilatory process was reversed: 'If an Englishman wants to get right to the top in his firm, his only hope is to go over to the Dutch plant, put a "van" before his name and try to marry a director's daughter.'

In the 'white-collar' sector, the other European newcomers were mostly found either as clerical workers in a pools firm, in the hospitals as nursing staff, students, or domestic workers, or in local government employment, as temporary teachers (often on exchange), welfare, and domestic workers. The nursing students and domestic workers included a considerable proportion of Spaniards, another European economic immigrant group which began to enter the British labour force rather later than the Italians. Not many of them were enumerated in the survey of '100-plus' firms, but employment exchange and other informants suggested that a considerable number were working in hotels, restaurants, and in private domestic service.

(c) *Commonwealth Economic Migrants*

In Croydon industry this group was represented by West Indians, most of them from Jamaica, smaller groups of Anglo-Indians, Indians and Pakistanis, and West Africans, a handful of immigrants from other Commonwealth territories, and a group of 'quasi-Commonwealth' Southern Irish migrants, numerically undetermined but sizeable. The fact that there were so few Asians and Africans meant that Croydon industry had not, at least at this time, been compelled to face the additional problems of absorption that confront some northern and Midlands industrial areas with large Asian settlements, or to evolve special techniques for absorbing large numbers of immigrants who come from a very different economic, social, and religious environment and who speak little or no English. Where Indians, Pakistanis, and West Africans were found, it was usually in ones or twos in each department or firm; and most of them were either students with higher educational qualifications and some knowledge of English, or energetic, 'assimilating' pioneers, who had struck out for themselves away from the main centres of Asian and West African migrant settlement in London.

The West Indians

(*i*) *West Indian Women:* The 1,000 odd West Indians working in Croydon's '100-plus' firms formed almost one-half of the total immigrant labour force, and made up three-quarters of the 'Commonwealth mass migrant' class, excluding the Southern Irish. In striking contrast to the Poles, but like the European economic migrants, there were more West Indian women than men workers. The fact that almost all were working full-time suggested that the group was still in the early stages of economic accommodation.[1] The great majority of West Indian women were concentrated in a few firms in three industrial groups—mass production, light engineering, food manufacture, and the hospitals.

In the 'skilled' light engineering sector, two firms employed West Indian women: Firm A, with thirteen on work requiring excellent eyesight and great manual dexterity, and Firm L, with one clerical worker and one West Indian operative. Both firms seemed satisfied with these women, but Firm B, which had taken West Indian applicants since 1948, no longer employed the wo-

[1] In the West Indian case, there is the additional complication that many women live alone with their children and must therefore be full-time wage-earners for longer than most other immigrant women. As the men achieve economic security, however, there is a greater tendency to contract legal conjugal unions, but the wife is still likely to continue working for some years, like other economic migrants.

men: 'About 50 per cent. . . . have been satisfactory . . . but they're all rather slow. Recently applicants have been no good—unskilled and truculent when we tell them there's nothing for them.' There were none in the 'intermediate' group; Firm B had tried them but found them too slow. The two mass-production firms, however, employed about 100 and 120 West Indian women respectively. They had been recruited in large numbers for only three to four years by these firms, but were on the whole accepted by management and unions as part of the regular labour force, on a quota basis. Recently this quota had been somewhat exceeded without any protest from unions or other workers, an indication of increasing acceptance. Special selection, training, and placing procedures had been evolved for them and they were accepted in most departments, except for some of the smaller women's working-groups, as semi-skilled operatives and in the better-paid grades. The question of promotion to positions of direct authority did not arise, as all supervisors, including charge-hands, were men.

The only immigrant women on the works or manual side in the entire 'heavy industrial' sector were twelve West Indians in a small firm of die-casters (B); most of them were wives, consorts, or relatives of the three dozen or so West Indian men working there. Another firm, the large heavy engineering works (A), had tried out West Indian women some years earlier in a *bloc* experiment. Faced with a shortage of women applicants, they broke down one job into a number of simple, easily learned processes; thirty West Indian women were then taken on in a batch from the Brixton employment exchange. Not surprisingly, this procedure led to considerable friction between local women workers and the newcomers, who remained 'ganged-up' on the job and off it, and the management took advantage of a redundancy period to 'clear the lot out'. There was not a total bar, however; coloured girls were still being interviewed for clerical work and there were a few skilled West Indian men in the works.

In the 'consumer' sector most of the 239 West Indian women were working in the highly seasonal food manufacturing firms: about 115 were employed in a single large sweet factory[1] (Firm B), and thirty-five in a small canning factory (Firm C). In Firm B

[1] The largest sweet factory, Chocolac, which employs a considerable number of immigrant workers, had only five West Indian women at this time. See Part IV, Ch. 10, for a more detailed account of this.

only a nucleus of the West Indians were on the regular labour force, others being taken on as seasonal workers for the peak season only. Two or three acted as unofficial leaders and interpreters, but none were in supervisory positions, principally because they were thought to be unable to do the necessary paper work. In Firm C West Indians formed over half the labour force and were thoroughly accepted by management as workers (to the extent of providing their preferred dishes in the canteen and making other special arrangements), but not as supervisors over local workers. The interview material suggested that the West Indians were still holding aloof from the local people, neither seeking more complete acceptance nor being accorded it: 'There are so many of them that they can keep to themselves and they usually sit in a group in the canteen.' In Firms B and C West Indian women were regarded by management as slow workers either in fact or in seeming, but as good time-keepers with a low labour turnover.

In the light industrial group of this sector, there were thirty West Indian women; four worked in a plastics firm (Firm I) and the remainder in a small stationery manufacturers (Firm B). Two other firms had employed them in the past, but no longer did so; in one case poor performance was cited, in the other it was said that they were good workers who had left of their own accord for better-paid work. Firm I had employed larger numbers in the past, but cut down during the credit squeeze. They were considered slow, but good at routine, monotonous work and excellent time-keepers. In Firm B nearly 15 per cent. of the women workers were West Indian; they appeared to be well on the way to absorption into the labour force, mainly because of the forceful sponsorship of the managing director.

Of the four small garment firms in Croydon, two had no labour shortage and a low labour turnover; neither of these employed West Indian women. The two remaining firms had experienced a grave shortage of trained women machinists in the early 1950s and tried out all immigrants who applied, including West Indians. Both firms found them slow and unfamiliar with power machines. None were left in one firm, but the other still had four; despite management reservations about their working speed, and initial resistance from the 'hard core' of local workers, they were by this time accepted as part of the regular labour force.

Most laundry and dry-cleaning work is less demanding than

power machining. Twenty West Indian women were employed in two out of the three laundries in Croydon. In neither case, however, did the management accept them fully, regarding them as stop-gap labour, slow, generally unsatisfactory and with a high turnover.

In the 'white-collar' and professional sector, eighty-two out of the ninety-four West Indian women enumerated were working in the hospitals. Of the remainder, the co-operative store employed two, a clerical worker and a packer, and eight were doing routine clerical work in a pools firm, where one was already in a direct supervisory post.

The 'clustering' and degree of absorption in the pools firm seemed atypical and differed considerably from the situation in most retail and clerical establishments surveyed, and from that in the clerical sections of most industrial firms. At the time of the survey, very few applications were being received from West Indian women or girls for retail or clerical jobs, and still fewer of the applicants were suitably qualified.

This lack of suitable West Indian applicants for retail and clerical work has helped to perpetuate the situation in which status-conscious local employees are reluctant to accept their entry and most managements still cherish the notion, usually untested, that there may be adverse reactions from the public if they are served by a coloured counter-hand or waitress. The position could change in Croydon, as it has in such earlier areas of West Indian settlement as Brixton, when West Indian local school-leavers with adequate qualifications begin to apply for such jobs. Their entry and acceptance could be eased by the 'thin-end-of-the-wedge' process that had already begun in Croydon shops and offices, either by deliberate decision or unconsciously, with the employment of Anglo-Indians and light-coloured Asians in offices and also on the counter.

In the three Croydon hospitals there were about fifty West Indian women on the nursing staff and another thirty doing catering and domestic work. Apart from one nursing sister and a few staff nurses, most of the fifty were student nurses in the two larger hospitals, where a quota of roughly 10 per cent. was observed, or assistant nurses in the third hospital for the aged and chronic sick. The West Indian nurses seemed to be well enough accepted by matrons, colleagues, and patients, but not so completely as the Irish, European, and Anglo-Indian or Asian nurses who entered nursing some years before them. The matron of one hospital expressed some doubts about their acceptability in higher authority; on the other hand, many who might have proved suitable for such posts were returning home soon after training to vacancies offering greater opportunities for promotion.

(ii) *West Indian Men:* West Indian male workers in Croydon were found mainly in semi-skilled or labouring jobs in the light engineering mass-production firms and in the heavy industrial sector. There was also a small handful of 'white-collar' workers or students doing temporary or part-time industrial work.

In the two large mass-production firms, West Indian men had been taken on since the post-war years, but they had only been employed in large numbers since 1955, at which time the unions asked for and got a quota of 3–4 per cent. of coloured immigrants. This had since been somewhat exceeded, though by lower margins in the case of the men than in that of the women. Like the West Indian women in these two factories, they were passing through the early stages of industrial absorption and were accepted as part of the regular semi-skilled and unskilled labour force by management, unions, and fellow-workers, except in some sections and groups, which remained 'lily-white', often because they contained a prejudiced 'anti-sponsor'. A few West Indian men had become shop-stewards and a few pioneers had been tried out as charge-hands. On the whole, however, they were not yet acceptable in supervisory positions, particularly in sections and groups with a female labour force.[1] There were no West Indian men on the staff side in either of these two firms; a few engineers with qualifications acceptable to the unions were, however, working in the closed-shop engineering shop and other engineering sections.

In the 'skilled' group of light-engineering firms, there were twenty West Indian men: about half were doing skilled work, the rest semi-skilled work or labouring. They were employed by five firms out of the twelve. Four others had tried West Indians in earlier years, but no longer employed them, usually because applicants lacked the necessary skills and qualifications. The three remaining firms had never taken on West Indians, one because it has experienced no great labour problem and the other two because no West Indian practitioners of the particular skill required, glass-blowing, had applied. An alternative for smaller precision

[1] See p. 250.

engineering firms faced with a continuing shortage of skilled workers is to improve techniques and increase mechanization, and some Croydon firms had done this. One of the earliest firms in this group to employ West Indian skilled workers was Firm B, which began recruiting R.A.F. ex-servicemen in 1948. About fifty men and women had passed through this firm since then, but only one of the original skilled recruits was still there. The remainder had moved on to better-paid work, while more recent applicants had been found unskilled and unsatisfactory.

The other West Indian skilled workers were found in two open-shop firms, which employed some West Indian women and a number of immigrants from other groups. On the whole, they appeared to be settled and accepted as part of the working community, though not yet in supervisory positions. The smaller of the two firms (L), while it was willing to take West Indians in skilled jobs, refused to recruit them any longer as labourers; the reason given was that they had proved unsatisfactory workers with a high turnover, and the Irish were preferred for any casual labouring work that was required. In two other skilled firms, however, West Indians were employed and regarded as unskilled labourers *par excellence*. At Firm C, where care was taken over selection, they were preferred to the Irish as having a lower turnover.

Firm D regarded West Indian workers as 'unskilled or semi-skilled at best' and unlikely to settle, because labouring work in the engineering industry is poorly paid by comparison with the rates in building and road-work.

Of the six 'intermediate' light engineering firms, the largest (A) had tried West Indians on semi-skilled work but discarded them as being too slow, although it continued to employ Anglo-Indians on skilled and unskilled work. An old-established medium-sized firm (C) employed half a dozen West Indians (five labourers, and a paint-sprayer). Management and supervisors considered them slow workers and were unwilling to take on more. One of the smaller firms (E) employed six West Indian labourers and regarded them as 'of poor working quality, slow, and only suitable for labouring', while another had only one West Indian, doing semi-skilled work; although he was well accepted, the management would only employ one at a time for fear of 'ganging-up' and slowing down of work.

To sum up, the absorption of the few really skilled West Indian workers seemed to be proceeding with reasonable ease in the whole of the light engineering sector, whereas the semi-skilled and unskilled men were far less settled and accepted, except in large firms which had the resources, time and will to evolve special techniques of selection, training, and placing, or in a few small firms where they could be treated as individuals. There was considerable evidence to show that more West Indian men had been employed in this sector in past years; a number of labourers had drifted into better-paid labouring work in building and elsewhere, while the credit squeeze of 1956 and the easier labour situation between 1956 and 1958 enabled several firms to get rid of semi-skilled West Indian operatives whose working performance they found unsatisfactory.

Over half of the West Indian men in the heavy industrial sector were employed in a single firm; this was the small union-busting die-casters (B), in which they, together with a dozen West Indian women, constituted nearly 50 per cent. of the entire labour force. The management had evolved special selection and training techniques and was well satisfied with the West Indians' performance in what is skilled but somewhat routine work. In this firm, West Indians had also been promoted to the rank of team leader, with white youths under them; but none were considered suitable for higher promotion, although an 'exceptionally able' Pakistani had been promoted to the post of floor inspector. The management was less concerned with local workers' reactions than most, but was sensitive to the fact that 'the percentage is now reaching danger level', and was no longer recruiting coloured workers.

In the rest of the heavy industrial sector, West Indian men were found in considerable numbers only in building, the gas-works, and on British Railways. There were also five at the brick-works, two semi-skilled men and a technician at the rubber-manufacturers, and three and one respectively in each of the two heavy engineering firms. In the traditional and clannish larger firm (A), the period of initiation was long and rather rigorous for all newcomers, and only efficient and adaptable individuals survived it. Three West Indian skilled men had done so, but others had been found slow and otherwise unsuitable. Acceptance of the three seemed to have been promoted by the fact that they participated in the firm's sporting activities.

Only three of the '100-plus' building firms had ever employed any noticeable number of immigrants other than the Southern

Irish, one of whose traditional preserves this is. A labour force in the building trade varies immensely in size and composition, according to the work in hand, but at the time of this survey some sixty-eight West Indian workers, mostly semi-skilled men and some labourers, were employed by three Croydon building contractors. The largest firm (A) had been taking on West Indians for only a year, following an acute labour shortage. At this time there were forty-five out of a total labour force of 1,000, mainly 'rough carpenters', distributed unevenly over all sites to a maximum of 10 per cent. None of the West Indians was as yet on the regular labour force, the main reasons given being slowness or proneness to stay away ill in bad or cold weather. Though no particular friction with the other men was reported, top management still clearly regarded West Indians as part of the semi-skilled, seasonal labour force, rather than of the more efficient regular cadres.

The medium-sized family firm (B) had been employing West Indians for seven years, much longer than Firm A. At this time they had twenty but none were 'retainers', as the permanent labour nucleus was called. The majority were carpenters and painters in the carpentry, decorating and maintenance departments. The departmental heads were not unduly impressed by their level of skill and took pains to separate and disperse them to prevent them 'slowing down' and 'ganging-up together'. The position of the three West Indians in the third and smallest firm (C) was even less secure than in Firms A and B. They were all that remained of a group of twenty-five West Indians taken on because of acute labour shortage in the mid-1950s. All the rest were laid off during the credit squeeze and the firm continued to regard West Indians simply as labourers.

In Croydon's public utilities, West Indians were, at this time, found only in the gas-works and on British Railways. West Indians formed about 10 per cent. of the manual labour force of 400–500 at the local gas-works, and had been employed since about 1952 by agreement with the unions. They appeared to be fully accepted by management and fellow-workers as good workers in manual and semi-skilled work, but there were none in skilled jobs or supervisory positions.

Each of Croydon's three main railway stations had one or more Barbadian porters and one had a Jamaican clerk. The Barbadians were from the specially selected class recruited by British Railways in Barbados and were fitting into the working community as individual settlers rather than undifferentiated outgroup members. Two station-masters had recommended earlier West Indian employees for promotion, but informants at all three stations entertained certain doubts about most West Indians' educational and general qualifications for promotion to direct supervisory posts and about their acceptability in such posts by other railwaymen.

About half a dozen West Indians worked in the small railway workshop in Croydon, over half of whose labour force consisted of Commonwealth or East European (Polish) immigrants. The superintendent regarded them as good craftsmen but found West Africans easier to handle. Coloured shopmen were not so fully accepted by the small nucleus of local old-timers as by the superintendent; N.U.R. men refused to take orders from one who had been up-graded to a charge-hand and the promotion had to be rescinded.

In the 'consumer' sector, there were only sixty-six West Indian men to 39 West Indian women. They were mostly found working in the same firms as the women, in light industry, laundry work and food manufacture. In one case (Laundry A), however, management had ceased to take West Indian men since the labour shortage eased, although it continued to take women. West Indian men were also no longer being recruited in several other 'consumer' firms employing mostly male labour, usually because they had not shown themselves to be sufficiently good workers before the labour shortage eased and local applicants became available. In another firm (A), on the other hand, redundancy led to the laying off of all but one of the West Indian women, on the grounds that they had not proved so satisfactory as the men.[1]

In another light industrial firm (I), twelve West Indian men and four women were employed on semi-skilled work. In earlier years up to 15 per cent. of the labour force had been West Indian, but when redundancy came management dismissed the least efficient. It was quite satisfied with those who remained, because, though slow, they were considered to be good at doing monotonous work, were good time-keepers, and willing to work overtime and extra hours. They were, however, prevented from rising in the firm's hierarchy because there was no training scheme and all semi-skilled workers would stay in that category.

[1] See Chocolac case study, Ch. 10.

Slow working speed and low turnover were also mentioned by the manager of a large laundry (B), who employed West Indian men and women up to about 6 per cent. of the total labour force, because local labour was very difficult to get. Although working relations were said to be good, this management had not accepted its West Indian workers as regular rather than transient labour; redundancy was clearly unlikely, but it was said that, if it were to occur, the West Indians would go first, 'because of their low working ability and aggressiveness'.

In the 'consumer' sector, West Indian men seemed to have achieved the best accommodation in the small light industrial firm (B), where the managing director had acted as 'sponsor'; in Chocolac; and in the small canning factory (C), where West Indians formed over half the labour force. Only in the first two firms did they seem to have reached the stage of acceptability in direct supervisory positions; in most of the other firms in this sector, they were tolerated as stop-gap or seasonal labour, but had not been accepted as part of the regular labour force. This could be due in part to the fact that the more able and skilled men had moved out of this sector into better-paid work elsewhere.

Over the whole range of occupations and professions covered by the 'white-collar' and professional sector, there were forty-three West Indian men; most of them were employed as manual labour, although in recent years a handful of West Indian students had worked in local government offices or done temporary vacation work in shops. There were no West Indian men in professional posts, nor could informants recall having received any applications from West Indians for such posts. This situation contrasted with that of West Africans and Asians, of whom a much larger proportion were in professional or white-collar jobs.

West Africans and Asians

The seventy-four West Africans (sixty-four men, ten women) working in Croydon at this period fell into two quite distinct occupational groups: professional and 'white-collar' on the one side (including students and trainees, totalling fifteen men and eight women), unskilled or manual labour on the other. There were no African skilled workers.

Of the former group, Telelux employed five scientists and technicians and there were also five male local government student and temporary officers working in Council C. West African male clerks were employed in one railway station, in a toilet-goods factory and in the co-operative store. Small batches of African and other Commonwealth trainees and students were also taken from time to time by the large laundry and the co-operative store, and whole- or part-time students were taken for vacation work by several private firms needing seasonal labour. The women were found in local government (in welfare and domestic work) and in the hospitals (mostly as student nurses).

Most West African professional and clerical workers were employed singly in a department or firm, and were accepted as individuals. Among scientists and technicians the working climate tended to be cool and impersonal and difficulties were more likely to arise out of differences in approach to the work; for instance, in Telelux a qualified African objected on status grounds to the routine amount of 'manual' bench-work and he was finally dismissed. The initial resistance by status-conscious, marginally middle-class clerical workers and shop-workers to the idea of the entry of dark-skinned, negroid-featured outsiders has usually weakened or disappeared where it has been tested in practice. So far, however, this had been infrequent in Croydon because of the small number of applicants for such work. In firms where there had been a regular succession of trainees, their presence was accepted by the local staff and it also accustomed the latter to the idea of having coloured colleagues on a more permanent basis. Any cases of individual friction that arose were eased by the fact that the students and trainees were transients, not permanent employees. On the supposedly vexed question of employing African male immigrants with female staff, little adverse reaction was reported.

The West Africans employed on various kinds of manual work showed a tendency to cluster in a few firms. The main 'clusters' were found in a skilled light-engineering firm (K) in Hackbridge, where the management recruited them in preference to West Indians, because of their lower turnover; in the two large mass-production plants; in the largest building contractors; in the railway workshop; and in Chocolac, the sweet factory. In the engineering firm and the railway workshop, management expressed a preference for West Africans over West Indians: in the first case because they were good workers and had a lower labour turnover; in the second because they were said to be easier to handle. In the

Hackbridge firm, the West Africans were also reported to be very popular with the other workers.

Indians and Pakistanis

As with the West Africans, a considerable minority of the Indian and Pakistani group in Croydon industry were employed in professional and 'white-collar' work. Of the remainder, however, over two-fifths were in skilled jobs, whereas not a single West African was found working in a trade. There were also proportionately far more Indian and Pakistani semi-skilled workers. Both ethnic groups were alike in that they contained few women workers; this reflected their general patterns of migration and the fact that most of the professionals were here only to finish their training; for their part, most manual workers might not yet be in a financial position to bring over wives, who customarily do not go out to work.

In both the West African and Indian–Pakistani groups, most of the women actually working were nurses or student nurses. Certain Indian nurses had, however, moved higher up the nursing hierarchy than any African, perhaps because they entered the profession earlier and had decided to stay on in Britain. There was, however, less similarity between the professional distribution of Indian men and that of Africans, the West Africans being concentrated in technical jobs in light engineering while the Indians were also found in medical practice. In professional and 'white-collar' occupations, moreover, Indians and Pakistanis in Croydon appeared to be more easily accepted than West Africans, apparently because of their intermediate position in the colour-class and colour-culture hierarchy which many people in Britain still seem to accept and apply to newcomers from the Commonwealth.

Most Indian manual workers were found in light engineering. The large watchmaking and scientific instrument firm, which employed immigrants from many other groups, had about half a dozen skilled and two semi-skilled Indians as well as an Indian labourer. One of the oldest and most traditional skilled engineering firms in Croydon had two Indian craftsmen, and there were four Indian craftsmen in a smaller, highly skilled, closed-shop firm and two in another, which is well-unionized. Indians were the 'favoured nation', together with Anglo-Indians, in the large, highly unionized 'intermediate' firm (A), which had organizational links with India. There were semi-skilled Indians in the two giant mass-production plants, a handful of individuals in consumer firms (there were more in the past), ten Pakistanis in the railway workshop, and a few women in one of the laundries, and a non-union printers. One Pakistani youth was being used as a 'pioneer' on counter work in a select Croydon store. There were no Indians and Pakistanis at all in the labour forces in building or heavy ndustry.

Most informants had not a great deal to say about their Indian and Pakistani employees, other than that they were usually satisfactory workers and less slow than the West Indians. They were so sparsely distributed over Croydon's industries and firms that most of them had been obliged to adapt themselves and be accepted on an individual basis; the skilled workers in particular seemed thoroughly accommodated and accepted by management and unions alike. Whether they would yet be acceptable in supervisory posts was less certain, but the question of such promotion was often academic in the 'skilled' firms, with their large nucleus of long-service workers and low labour turnover.

Anglo-Indians

The Anglo-Indians differ from most other post-war immigrants to Britain in that they came with the firm intention of settling here permanently and of being assimilated into British society as rapidly as possible. This initial settler-orientation can be a tremendous 'push-factor' towards absorption, particularly when it is combined, as generally in the Anglo-Indian case, with certain shared cultural values and norms, notably, English as a first language, adherence to the Christian religion, and similar family, educational, occupational, and general social patterns.

The predominantly 'white-collar' or skilled manual background of the Anglo-Indians proved a useful springboard for their entrance into and accommodation in Croydon industry, although (often as a result of the lower standards arising out of their virtual monopoly of certain occupations and industries in British India) they experienced some occupational down-grading, even in firms and industries with Indian connexions and sympathies. Their rather modest ambitions and expectations would also appear to have been a factor promoting their acceptance in 'white-collar' and skilled or semi-skilled jobs, for which there was still a shortage of suitable applicants in Croydon. Initial accommodation and adjustment off the job was also fostered by the presence of family groups and by the newcomers' ready participation in local religious life and recreational activities, particularly sports.

As for the colour factor, many members of this marginal group were visibly distinguishable from the 'pinko-grey' local population, but this difference seemed to be more than counterbalanced, at least in most industrial situations, by the Anglo-Indians' relative lack of cultural 'strangeness' and by their usual unobtrusiveness and adaptability (although 'chip-on-the-shoulder' attitudes were sometimes reported). Dark skin colour, with all its associations, has contributed to slower acceptance in some cases involving promotion to supervisory posts; but it was only one of a number of diverse factors at work and, as we have seen, several Anglo-Indians had already achieved such up-grading.

Seventy-nine Anglo-Indian men and thirty-nine women were working in the '100-plus' firms. Like the Indians and Pakistanis, they were concentrated in light engineering, with rather smaller contingents in the 'consumer' and 'white-collar' sectors, and no representatives at all in building. Among the Anglo-Indians, however, there were proportionately fewer professionals and skilled workers and considerably more semi-skilled workers; there was also a larger proportion of women. The two groups were alike in having hardly any unskilled workers or labourers; in Croydon, if immigrant labour was taken on, such jobs were customarily filled by Irish or West Indians. Some informants considered that Anglo-Indians and other Asians lacked the stamina for heavy manual work.

Though Anglo-Indians and Indians or Pakistanis were concentrated in the same industrial sectors, they were not always found in the same factories, departments, or working-groups. It seemed possible that there might be an element of avoidance here. For many of the Anglo-Indians who have migrated to Britain appear to have rejected the Indian part of their ethnic and cultural heritage; thus they do not seek to be reminded of it or to be associated with Indians in the eyes of the British receiving population. As one informant said: 'The Anglo-Indians look upon themselves as English and white and join the cliques as individuals.'

Well over half of the Anglo-Indian men were employed in light engineering, and they were a 'favoured nation' in four firms. Those with the appropriate qualifications were in skilled jobs and there were several 'white-collar' workers, staff trainees, and apprentices. Anglo-Indians were also the 'favoured nation' in a large 'intermediate' firm (A), together with 'lighter-coloured' Indians. In this case the preference could be attributed in part at least to the firm's Indian affiliations. In two small firms (E and F) in this group, Anglo-Indians were also thoroughly accepted; in the second firm the managing director felt that Anglo-Indians might be acceptable to local workers in supervisory posts.

In British India the railways were a job preserve for Anglo-Indians. This fact was generally known among higher-level staff in British Railways and may have helped to produce a favourable climate for the reception of those Anglo-Indian former railway staff who sought similar work in Britain. In Croydon there were four Anglo-Indians at two of the three stations: a clerk, a goods-guard, a leading porter, and a porter. In the railway workshop, there were about ten Anglo-Indians. In most cases, there had been occupational down-grading for a variety of reasons. For example, the leading porter had been an engine-driver in India, and most of the shopmen were said to have been civil servants or railway clerks before they migrated.

Firms in the 'consumer' sector reported varying experiences with Anglo-Indian workers. At this time almost all the men were employed in the light industrial group, which offered lighter, better-paid, more secure work than did the other industrial groups in this sector. Laundry-work had been a 'transit camp' for Anglo-Indians as for Poles. In the white-collar sector, there were Anglo-Indian counter-assistants: one store had got rid of all but one, on the grounds that they were 'casual and touchy', but in another they were the 'favoured nation' and there was no apprehension about public reactions.

A few Anglo-Indian professional people, mainly teachers, local government officials, and nurses, had worked in Croydon in earlier years, but of these only a woman teacher and eight nurses were left at the time of this survey. The teacher was the only one of the many temporary immigrant teachers to have been taken on the permanent local teaching staff as yet. All but one of the Anglo-Indian nurses were in the hospital for the chronic sick, but most of them were fully trained and in more responsible positions than the West Indians.

In general, the Anglo-Indians appeared to be well on the way to industrial absorption in Croydon. Most were in lighter, better-paid, skilled or semi-skilled work, a few had been promoted to modest supervisory posts, and some of the younger or second generation had already been accepted as apprentices or staff trainees. They were also a 'favoured nation' in quite a number of firms. In situations involving promotion and work in contact with the public, they seemed to be acting as the thin end of the wedge to open up opportunities for people and groups of darker colour.

Other Commonwealth and Coloured Immigrants

With the exception of a few clusters in the hospitals or firms connected with particular overseas areas, these immigrants had entered Croydon industry as individuals, on their own merits, and seemed to be accepted on this basis in the firms in which they were working. Most were doing 'white-collar' or skilled work, in which they seemed able to meet local standards. Most belonged to ethnic and cultural groups which are not very numerous or highly organized in Britain, and they tended to associate themselves with the local working community rather than with other immigrants in the same firm. Some of the women had married local men, in which case their home circumstances were also conducive to easy absorption. Others were post-colonial settlers, like the Anglo-Indians, often from marginal groups such as the Cape Coloured People of South Africa, the Anglo-Burmese, and Anglo-Ceylonese. These are usually people who have rejected the non-European or non-British part of their ethnic or cultural heritage, people who no longer see a place for themselves in the country of their birth.

Clusters of such immigrants were found on the staff side of one of the large mass-production firms and of a large building firm. In each case their presence was attributable to the firm's links or former links with a particular area: Indonesians in the case of the firm with Dutch connexions, Anglo-Egyptians in the building firm.

Of the twenty-four persons listed under the heading of 'Other Commonwealth Immigrants' the majority were Maltese and Cypriots; they were scattered in twos and threes in clerical, skilled, and semi-skilled work in light engineering, light industry, building, and the retail trade. Most managements seemed to be reasonably satisfied with their working performance, but few had any particular comments to make about either group. In some cases, indeed, informants were not entirely sure whether the workers referred to were Maltese or Cypriot.

As for white immigrants from the 'old' Dominions (Australia, Canada, New Zealand, and the former Union of South Africa) the 1961 Census showed that 1,255 Croydon residents were born in these territories. It would be reasonable to assume that a fair number of them also worked in the area, but it was rare for informants to mention them. Where they were found, they were usually in professional, 'white-collar', or skilled work, and the comment would be: 'Of course, I don't count them as immigrants.' (See p. 41, n. 1, for the common assumption that 'Commonwealth' immigrants meant 'coloured' immigrants.)

The Southern Irish

For well over a century Southern Irish immigrants have been working and settling in Croydon. Local informants distinguished two groups, the 'settled' majority, who were more or less absorbed in the local population, and the 'migrant' minority, a highly mobile group consisting mainly of young single men, most of whom were believed to return home for a break after each two-year stretch of work in Britain, in order to avoid paying income tax.

The 'settled' Irish were accepted in industry in the same way as other local people, according to their aptitudes and qualifications. The migrants were rejected in some industries and occupations, accepted in others, usually on the basis of traditional associations and their suitability and individual qualifications. The fact that most informants could not give precise figures of their Irish migrant labour force at a given time gave an indication of the extent to which such acceptance had gone.

In general, the Southern Irish are the 'favoured nation' in the building trade, which relies on a considerable proportion of mobile and seasonal labour; their position is strengthened by the fact that many builders and foremen are Irish and give preference to Irish applicants. For their part, Irish migrants gravitate to building because they are surer of acceptance and because of its relatively high wages compared with labouring work in engineering, local government, and other industries. In Croydon most of the '100-plus' building contractors and builders' merchants employed Irish and regarded them as an integral part of their labour force. In one firm, however, a medium-sized family firm with a large stable labour nucleus, mobility was not regarded as an asset, and only a few 'settled' Irish were employed.

While mobility is usually an asset in the building trade, it is less so in many other industries. While there were very few Croydon firms or establishments offering labouring or semi-skilled jobs which had not employed some Irish men or women in the post-war years, several firms no longer recruited them because of their high turnover, preferring West Indians. In most cases, where they were accepted, it was in labouring or, occasionally, in semi-skilled jobs. They were rarely taken for skilled or precision work.

At the upper end of the occupational scale, in medicine and nursing, however, the Irish had established themselves and been fully accepted as doctors and nurses in Croydon as elsewhere. As one matron said: 'Of course you don't include the Irish nurses in the category of immigrants, do you?'

SUMMARY

In the following sections we shall be examining in greater detail the indices of the various phases of industrial absorption and the major factors that speed or impede such absorption. Here we may briefly summarize and compare the situations of the principal immigrant groups (Poles, Irish, Anglo-Indians, and West Indians) which entered Croydon industry after the end of the 1939–45 War, in terms of these phases and indices.

The Poles, despite the lack of any industrial pre-selection, were well on the way to industrial assimilation (or integration in the case of Polplastics), while the younger, British-educated generation was fully assimilated in a wide range of firms and industries for which their elders were not professionally or linguistically equipped. Most of the older generation were found in skilled, responsible, or congenial work, having moved out of the heavier, less secure, 'transit-camp' firms and industries years ago. Few Polish women still needed to work, most men were long-service employees and a fair number had been promoted to positions of direct authority over local English workers.

The other main immigrant groups in Croydon were drawn from the class of Commonwealth or quasi-Commonwealth economic migrants—West Indians, Anglo-Indians, and Southern Irish. As migrants the latter are traditionally accepted for certain work and in certain industries in Britain. If they turn settler they are usually accepted fairly quickly on the same basis and criteria as other local workers, although except for the medical and nursing professions the majority still tend to be concentrated in heavy manual work and labouring.

The Anglo-Indians, with their 'settler' and assimilationist intentions, and their British-oriented educational, occupational and cultural background, had accommodated themselves to Croydon industry fairly rapidly, in some cases having established themselves as 'favoured nation', and were moving into the phase of assimilation. Like the Poles, most had moved out of 'transit-camp' industries and uncongenial firms to establish themselves in light engineering and, to a lesser extent, the 'consumer' and 'white-collar' sectors. Unlike the Poles, however, the younger and second generations of Anglo-Indians were tending to follow in the footsteps of their elders, whereas most young Poles were strongly upwardly mobile, whether or not their parents were of the professional or managerial classes before 1939.

The largest and (by a few years) the most recently arrived group in Croydon, the West Indians, were the least accepted, being for the most part in the earlier or later phases of accommodation, mainly in semi-skilled or unskilled work. There was some evidence of movement of the better workers out of 'transit-camp' industries, firms, and jobs, followed by lower job-mobility and increased settlement in congenial, better-paid work. But there was also evidence of rejection of West Indian workers by employers or of their toleration only as casual, expendable labour. Some individuals had become more or less assimilated in their places of work, but the majority were accepted as at best a regular component of the available unskilled and semi-skilled local labour force, generally suitable for slow, regular work and best handled by such measures as special selection and training devices, dispersal, and quotas. In many cases, first-hand experience had on the whole tended to support rather than dispel current pejorative stereotypes about West Indians' working capacity and this fact, combined with notions linking dark colour with strangeness and low class, was helping to maintain resistance among local workers as well as employers to putting West Indians into white-collar work or positions of direct authority or even responsibility.

As for the second West Indian generation, most were still in primary school and it was too early for any evidence to be available about its representatives' fortunes in industry. The material on Poles and Anglo-Indians indicates that in these groups the older generation has won sufficient acceptance to sponsor the younger ones in industry. For instance, young Poles might get apprenticeships or, more likely, technical or staff openings in firms where their parents had become a part of the working community. This generational sponsoring of course applied to the children of all settled local workers—but in the case of immigrants, there could also be an additional 'push' given by ambitious or frustrated parents. Such a push factor might well be present among West Indians, but it remained to be seen whether the majority of first-generation immigrants would have established themselves sufficiently as part of the working community to be able to sponsor their locally educated children by the time the latter entered the economy.[1]

These four groups differed considerably in socio-economic and cultural background, intentions and other important criteria. As a result, their entry and absorption into Croydon industry had not been characterized by the simple chronological 'pecking order' found in some countries of immigration. The Poles and Anglo-Indians had moved well ahead of the Irish, and settled West Indians might be preferred to unsettled Irish, depending on the requirements of the job. Moreover, the 'economic man' approach was perhaps less in evidence in Croydon than in some New World areas of large-scale immigration.[2] Instead, there was a gradual and individualized process of sorting, self-selection, and dispersal that had helped and was still helping to spread the newcomers through the four industrial sectors and up and down the occupational hierarchy, in the main according to their working qualifications and general suitability. In practice this process had tended to draw Anglo-Indians into industries and jobs similar to those in which most Poles and other East European refugees were found, though not necessarily into the same firms. On the other hand, West Indians had tended to move into sectors and jobs traditionally associated with the Southern Irish, from nursing to labouring.

It seemed possible that the West Indians might indeed follow

[1] For further discussion of this aspect, see R. Hooper (ed.), *Colour in Britain*, London, B.B.C. Publications, 1965, pp. 83–84.

[2] Cf. Brewton Berry, *Race and Ethnic Relations*, Houghton, Mifflin Co., Boston, 1958, pp. 304–10; and Orvis, Collins, 'Ethnic Behaviour in Industry', *American Journal of Sociology*, Vol. LI, January 1946, p. 294.

the same course as the Southern Irish, and becoming a second traditional source of migrant workers, who become acceptable, at least in industry. The factor of distance and expense was of course always a difficulty, and a year or so later the growing influx of other 'coloured' immigrants and the move towards restrictions effected a radical and adverse change in the situation.

CHAPTER 7
THE PROCESSES OF INDUSTRIAL ABSORPTION: (I) PHASES, INDICES, ASPECTS

(1) *Accommodation—Two Sub-Phases*

The fact that over 2,000 immigrants (not counting Southern Irish migrants) were employed in Croydon's '100-plus' firms at this time shows in itself that industrial absorption had begun. From the survey findings it was clear that immigrant labour was on the whole accepted by most larger firms as part of the available labour force. In certain sectors, industries, firms, and occupations, however, some individuals and immigrant groups were, as we said, accorded considerably more than a minimal acceptance. We should now go beyond the distribution and situation of the various immigrant groups to a more general examination, firstly of the processes and indices of industrial absorption, and then of the major factors involved in these processes.

In the introduction I defined three phases of immigrant absorption—accommodation, assimilation, pluralistic integration—and the sort of indices which, so the results of a previous investigation had suggested, could be associated with each phase in the industrial situation. As the Croydon inquiry proceeded, these concepts became more detailed and precise and the initial phase of accommodation, through which most of the immigrants are still passing, appeared to fall into two sub-phases. An attempt is made in Table 3 to represent the various phases and sub-phases and the indices associated with them, from the standpoint and in terms of the interaction of the three main groupings involved: management, local labour, and newcomers.[1]

The table is intended to show the interaction that takes place in

[1] See pp. 6–9. It should be stressed once more that we are concerned only with industrial absorption—not with overall absorption of immigrants in the wider society, which is a longer and more complex process. Similar processes apply, though to a lesser degree, to all new entrants to a working community.

P

TABLE 3

Indices of Industrial Absorption

	(1) MANAGEMENT	(2) LOCAL LABOUR	(3) IMMIGRANTS
INITIAL CONTACT	Do not employ (various motivations).	Refuse to work with (various motivations).	Arrive in area and seek work.
ACCOMMODATION Earlier phase	Agree to try (usually as unskilled or semi-skilled stopgap labour, casual or seasonal).	Agree to accept (usually resist acceptance in skilled work)—often with conditions, quotas, special redundancy agreements, etc.	Start work. Learn job and begin to acquire 'culture of the factory'—join unions where this is the custom, but 'gang up' where possible.
	Tries out various methods of selection, training, and placement (gangs, dispersal, etc.).		Become good time-keepers, with low labour turnover, but still tend to keep together in groups.
			Some begin to feel sense of community with local labour, loyalty to firm—decide to settle locally—begin to dress and talk more like locals (or to learn adequate colloquial English).
	Immigrants accepted as part of available labour force.		
ACCOMMODATION Later phase	Increasing tendency for employers and local labour to stretch quotas, overlook special redundancy provisions, etc.		
	Acquire special expertise in selection, training, placement.	Accept male immigrants working with women.	
	Begin to think of some immigrants as belonging to 'our own people'. May evolve a 'favoured nation' policy.		Begin to behave as individuals, to break away from ethnic cliques—seek to acquire greater skills—begin to introduce suitable applicants for vacancies ('clustering' may begin).
	Cease to associate with particular kinds of work (unskilled, manual, etc.). Try out in wider range.	Begin to regard newcomers as 'one of us', mingle in canteen and recreation clubs, accept in cliques.	Start to mingle in canteen, sports and social clubs, to enter local cliques to share some outside activities (outings, socials, weddings, etc.); to be more active in unions, to teach newcomers factory *mores*, and act as sponsors.
		Feel able to tease or joke with newcomers without self-consciousness or special consideration.	
	Begin to upgrade suitable individuals.	Accept in responsible jobs and as shop-stewards.	Decide to settle in Britain. Non-British may seek naturalization. Tendency for some women to stop working.
ASSIMILATION	Some adaptation may occur of factory culture to include newcomers and their modified cultures.		
	Increasing tendencies not to know exact numbers or ethnic background.		
	Willing to start promoting; and to accept children as apprentices, even as trainees.	Accept in direct supervisory posts over locals—and in higher union offices.	Capable of performing and willing to accept supervisory posts.
	Willingness to promote to higher supervisory levels.	Accept as foremen and supervisors.	Some immigrants become employers or enter higher management, thereby aiding acceptance of group.
	Accept at all levels as individuals.		Sufficiently adapted and qualified to aspire to all jobs on basis of individual merit.
PLURALISTIC INTEGRATION	If ethnic gangs have been found satisfactory in earlier phase, this may persist and may be extended, thereby changing the whole formal and informal structure of the factory, with the possibility of occupational segregation developing.	May either have little say in situation or else occupy privileged position.	Individuals emerge as: (*a*) informal leaders of work-gangs and groups; (*b*) formal supervisors.

a factory,[1] rather than the more complex processes of absorption in professional and 'white-collar' establishments. Nor does the table show the occasional intervention of the fourth element—the public at large—since this is so often a matter of untested supposition rather than actuality.

Of necessity the table presents the processes of industrial absorption in an ordered and regular form, which does not reflect the pauses, checks, and irregularities of industrial reality. Certain additional comments and qualifications are therefore required to illustrate the variety of situations and relationships which were found in Croydon industry.

In the first place, the absorptive process differs not only in speed and regularity but also in depth and quality, according to the particular 'culture' of the industrial sector, industry, firm, or work-group. Whereas it may take decades to achieve full assimilation in a traditional, well-integrated firm, the process will be faster and the relationships less profound in most departments of an expanding mass-production firm. The process also differs according to the characteristics and general adaptability of the particular immigrant groups involved.

Secondly, pluralistic integration does not follow assimilation, as the table presents it. Where it occurs, it is more likely to follow the first sub-phase of accommodation and it may be final or may lead on to assimilation; but in Croydon industry, where the prevailing ethos seemed to be 'assimilating' rather than 'pluralistic', this phase was infrequently encountered.

Of the two sub-phases into which industrial accommodation appears to be divided, the first is one of trial, error, and impermanency; management and local labour accept the newcomers only as stop-gap labour and in limited numbers, usually with special curbs and restrictions, and the newcomers are unsettled, only just beginning to adapt themselves to the job and the working community. The transition into the later sub-phase is characterized by a swing from mobility to stability, transience to permanence, in all three groups involved. The immigrants gain seniority, and those with adequate qualifications are up-graded to more skilled or responsible work. But such a transition does not necessarily take place in every establishment. If a management is dissatisfied with the immigrants' working performance, or if their presence causes excessive friction

[1] With rare exceptions such as the Polish-owned Polplastics.

in labour relations, the experiment may end in their dismissal. Again, the newcomers may treat the firm as a transit camp and remain only until they can find higher-paid, more congenial work elsewhere. (In itself, such a move can represent the transition from the first to the second sub-phase for the immigrant.) In such cases, however, the pattern of employing immigrant labour may have become established and management will continue to take on new arrivals from the same or other ethnic groups.

The motives and viewpoints of management and local labour differ considerably. Management's approach is generally more utilitarian; refusal to take immigrant workers tends to be based on the absence of any labour shortage, on unsatisfactory experience, or on the existence of a closed-shop agreement. Refusal or unwillingness on the part of local labour usually has a heavier emotional load of economic fears and status anxieties; this and the face-to-face, frequently intimate nature of the relationship between fellow-workers are among the principal reasons why workers usually accept newcomers more slowly than management, apart from the fact that the latter almost invariably takes the initiative in trying out immigrant labour.

As Table 3 indicates, management usually reaches the stage of including immigrants among 'our own people' rather sooner than workers accept them as 'one of us'. In some cases, indeed, management–worker relations in a particular factory are such that the workers' viewpoint plays little or no part in the initial processes of absorption. These proceed mainly through interaction between management and immigrants, and can lead rapidly to an integrative situation, as in the die-casters.[1]

On the other hand, there may be cases in which local workers have reached the stage of accepting immigrants as 'one of us', while management rejects them on grounds of performance or continues to accept them merely as inferior, stop-gap labour.[2]

In the more stable, close-knit working communities, however, the reactions of management and local labour force to the entry and acceptance of newcomers seem to approximate more closely, whether they are in favour of accepting and absorbing newcomers or not. Here one should note that a 'good' factory in this sense is not necessarily 'good' for the absorption of all or any immigrants. The factory 'culture' can be self-sufficient, traditional, and insular; on

[1] See pp. 84–6. [2] See pp. 117–19 (Firm C); p. 121 (Firm B).

the other hand, it can be tolerant, expanding, and contain sponsors who promote the entrance and acceptance of newcomers, as in some of the larger, more progressive factories.

The time-lag between management's and labour's acceptance of immigrants is likely to be longer in firms with bad labour relations, in jobs which involve team-work in close proximity, and in the case of immigrant groups about which the receiving society has built up a large corpus of second-hand notions and stereotypes that link them with the alien and inferior. This time-lag or reluctance to accept is particularly evident in work-situations involving extra-industrial relationships (for instance, work-groups of mixed sex or jobs involving contact with the public) or superordinate–subordinate roles (as in cases where newcomers are promoted to a position of direct authority over others).

On occasion, as accommodation proceeds, acceptance of the newcomers by local labour and management may run ahead of the newcomers' degree of adaptation. This is because some adaptation is beginning to occur in the working community itself, a change or modification of the factory 'culture', a widening of horizons, to include certain 'favoured nation' groups of newcomers or certain individual 'characters'. This adaptation on the part of the receiving community differs only in degree from the changes and modifications that occur in the individual 'culture' of a factory with the coming and going of personnel and with the introduction of new ideas and techniques.[1] In both cases, the changes and modifications are limited by the general character and culture of the wider society of which the factory is a part, although the society may itself be undergoing change and modification as a result of large-scale immigration.

From the immigrants' standpoint the early phase of accommodation is characterized by high mobility and instability; in the later one they begin to develop a settler-orientation in the wider society as well as at work. Almost all the Poles and former E.V.W.s had been settled in one firm for several years. The withdrawal of women from full-time work (for instance, the Poles and to a lesser extent the Anglo-Indians) is also likely to be an indication that accommodation is well advanced.[2]

[1] Cf. Jaques, op. cit., pp. 252–3.

[2] This may not apply in the case of the West Indians, unless there is an accompanying change in their conjugal and family patterns.

(2) *Assimilation*

When management promotes an immigrant to a position of direct authority over local workers and those local workers accept him this affords the clearest indication that industrial assimilation has begun for a particular group in a particular firm. Such promotion is usually carefully planned (several informants stressed that the individual who is to be promoted must be 'better than the locals') and the views of supervisors, shop-stewards, and work-groups are canvassed. Initially it may take the form of promotion to a supervisory job over a group containing some members of the immigrant's own group, just as immigrant skilled workers are often put in charge of immigrant apprentices instead of local boys. But in the absence of any large number of ethnic teams, this may be regarded as a transitional phase to fuller assimilation, not the beginning of a segregated hierarchy of immigrant employees alongside the local one.[1]

Promotion of a male immigrant to a supervisory post over women presents certain special problems, since the relationship involves not only efficient supervision but also what one informant described as a 'father-confessor role'. The newcomer must therefore be acceptable to women workers in this quasi-paternal role, that is to say acceptable outside the purely industrial situation. As assimilation proceeds, qualified individuals become acceptable at all occupational and supervisory levels. Promotion can, however, only be achieved by a few employees in any concern, and in the smaller, traditional long-service firms it may take decades. Nor is it the aim of all immigrants, many of whom, like most local workers, do not desire the extra responsibility or the inevitable alienation from the rest of the working-group, and are deterred by the fact that promotion can mean a lowering of actual earnings (cf. Telelux p. 329).

Meanwhile, the process of assimilation will also begin for other immigrants who have decided to settle and are achieving fuller acceptance on the shop floor. Even though they may not be fully acculturated, factory memories of the earlier frictions are blurred

[1] The Croydon situation afforded a considerable contrast with that of Negro employees in some American industrial concerns, as reported by Hughes, op. cit., pp. 173–4. How the situation in firms elsewhere in Britain which make extensive use of ethnic gangs will develop is still uncertain.

and overlaid, and the immigrants' distinctive traits and ways of behaving are increasingly accepted as part of their individual personalities, rather than as outgroup characteristics, and as a contribution to the life and culture of the working community. Though there is little perceptible change, the culture of the factory is subtly enlarged and enriched, through such partly assimilated individuals, with such elements as an Irishman's convivial humour and love–hate view of England, a Pole's normalcy in the face of loss and exile, an Anglo-Indian's rose-tinted or bitter nostalgia for the vanished days of British India, an Italian or Caribbean peasant's yearning for sun and his own piece of land—elements that may in earlier years have irritated the same local workers.

The first immigrants to move into the phase of assimilation are usually 'pioneer' types, individuals of special ability, drive, and adaptability. Once they have been accepted, the way is eased for others of the same group and the evolution of a 'favoured nation' is encouraged. This is often perpetuated in the second generation by the firm's acceptance of immigrants' children as apprentices, staff trainees, or clerical workers. As the assimilation of one group of immigrants proceeds, however, this tends to ease the entry and assimilation of other groups, again on a 'thin-end-of-the-wedge' basis. This process is particularly evident in nursing, where the Irish have been followed by Europeans, Anglo-Indians, and West Indians, all groups but the last being more or less fully assimilated and accepted in senior positions.[1]

(3) *Integrative Situations*

The survey afforded few instances of firms that had reached or were moving towards the phase of pluralistic integration in the industrial sphere, that is to say, a situation involving the employment of ethnic gangs or of particular ethnic groups on particular kinds of work.[2] This was in contrast to the situation reported in some industries and firms in the Midlands and North of England where considerable use seems to be made of ethnic gangs (generally

[1] Assimilation at work does not necessarily imply that the individuals concerned are seeking assimilation in the wider society. This may follow, but many were found to be moving, with their minority communities, into the phase of pluristic integration.

[2] An extreme and institutionalized form of this would be the industrial *apartheid* and job reservation practised in the Republic of South Africa.

Pakistani or Indian) under English-speaking leaders or 'go-betweens' ('straw bosses' in American parlance).

This kind of practice is probably to be associated both with the organization and needs of particular industries and firms and with the fact that most recent Indian and Pakistani migrants speak no English and are self-segregating by intention; on arrival they gravitate to their own village-kin group already established here, looking to them for work as well as lodging and the satisfaction of social needs.[1] In Croydon, however, there were few Asians at this time, and the West Indians, who constituted the largest immigrant group in industry, were English-speaking and not particularly self-segregating by inclination. So far from favouring their employment in self-segregating gangs or teams, moreover, most management informants were emphatic about the need to disperse them as widely as possible. Some managements had experimented with the employment of West Indian ethnic gangs in the early years of their employment, but for the most part these failed, and only a few all-West Indian work-groups were still to be found (e.g. in a sweet-making factory, a canning firm, the gas-works, and a die-casters).

Like the Irish gangs in the building industry, however, the members of these West Indian work-groups in Croydon were not isolated from the rest of the working community by the barrier of language, as are so many Pakistanis and Indians. Thus the Croydon ethnic work-groups seemed less permanent and opportunities for individual mobility and advancement were greater. The Italian and Polish work-groups showed some permanency, but even here there had been a considerable streaming-off of the younger, more energetic, better-qualified pioneers, the Italians mostly to catering, the Poles to better industrial jobs or entrepreneurship, their children to technical and professional posts.

For the older generation of political exiles, the ethnic work-group (like the ethnic firm) provides a form of shielding from the full impact of exile and occupational down-grading. This kind of arrangement is usually acceptable to employers, so long as it is found to have no adverse effect on production or even to stimulate it. In such situations, the main interaction tends to be two-way rather

[1] See Desai, R., *Indian Immigrants in Britain*, pp. 80, 84–87, and Peter Wright, Research Note on 'Go-Betweens in Industry' (Institute of Race Relations *Newsletter*, January 1964, p. 28).

than three-way, between management and the immigrants, with local labour playing a minor part. In some cases, the unions are also excluded from participation; in others, they may succeed in entering the relationship either to represent the views and interests of local labour or to protect the newcomers and act in an intermediary role between them and local labour.[1]

The ethnic firm of Polplastics presented a rather special case of industrial integration, in which management, lower supervisors, and the main labour nucleus were linked by minority in-group ties *vis-à-vis* not only the host society but the transient outgroup of local workers. The perpetuation of such an integrated working community depends on a continuing supply of Polish recruits. The main source has, however, been drying up as the older exiles die or reach pensionable age; the community receives very few reinforcements from Poland; and the second generation is English-educated and equipped to seek employment anywhere in British industry. Professional, technical, supervisory, and skilled jobs could continue to be a Polish preserve in Polplastics, but it seemed probable that the firm would have to look farther afield in recruiting operatives for semi-skilled shift-work in the years to come.

No comparable instance of a fair-sized ethnic working community was found in Croydon, although there were a number of small catering, retail, and other businesses based on ethnic ties, often reinforced by kinship links. Similar situations could in theory arise, if members of other recent immigrant groups become large-scale employers, but the example of the light industrial firm started by a pre-war European refugee (Firm I, p. 156) and the Dutch-affiliated mass-production firm Telelux, suggests that a more likely development would be, at the most, a 'favoured nation' policy at management level and a fairly tolerant attitude to the recruitment of all newcomers. Polplastics therefore seems likely to remain an industrial curiosity in an industrial society whose climate, unlike that of South Africa and many former colonial territories, does not in general favour the development of self-segregating or segregated units. As Jaques wrote of the British factory in general:

[1] See the railway workshop (p. 102). In one South London firm (*Dark Strangers*, p. 103) there was an entire night-shift production line of elderly ex-officers with a Polish shop-steward.

Patterns of behaviour and organization within the concern must remain consistent with the patterns of behaviour and expectations of a community that carries this culture. Too wide departures would rapidly bring into operation those subtle forces which cause an organization to become unacceptable and to be rated low on the scale of places where employment is sought (p. 261).

(4) *Some Aspects of Industrial Absorption*

(a) *Quotas and Special Redundancy Agreements*

When a large group of newcomers enters industry over a short space of time, the local labour force usually demands the maximum safeguards for its wage levels, working conditions, and employment possibilities against possible undercutting, dilution, and other threats to its economic status. In the case of non-British immigrants, such safeguards have since 1920[1] been statutorily enforced for the first period of the immigrant's stay; even in the immediate post-war period of labour shortage the entry into industry of the Polish ex-servicemen and the E.V.W.s was negotiated between Government, employers, and the trade unions, and was strictly controlled.[2]

Most of these workers were directed to certain undermanned industries and remained subject to Ministry of Labour direction for about three years. Placings were subject to the condition that no suitable British labour should be available, and there was usually a clause providing that foreign workers should be the first to go in the event of redundancy. Wages were to be at least at British minimum levels, and the foreign workers were to be advised, encouraged, or even, according to some agreements, obliged to join the appropriate trade unions as soon as possible. Some industries also imposed a quota for each department, which was often in the neighbourhood of 10 per cent.[3] The employers favoured this be-

[1] The Aliens Order, 1920, S.R. and O. 1920/448 (later replaced by the Aliens Order, S.I. 1953, No. 167, section 4(1)(c)).

[2] See Tannahill, op. cit., Chapter V.

[3] As J. A. C. Brown writes: 'There is some evidence that when foreign workers must be used in a factory, their number should not exceed 10 per cent. of the total and that they should be divided up and spread evenly throughout the various groups in the firm' (p. 115). See also J. Egginton, *They Seek a Living* (London, Hutchinson, 1957), p. 100, for the widespread acceptance by employers of a 10 per cent. quota for West Indian workers.

cause of the need to train the newcomers and teach them English, while the unions wished to promote assimilation and prevent group rivalries within the labour force.

Until the Commonwealth Immigrants Act of 1962, immigrants from the Commonwealth and Eire were subject to no restrictions or controls of this kind, and even then the restriction was only on entry to the country, after which the immigrant was free to apply for any job in any area and to change jobs or move about as he chose.

Local labour has therefore attempted to set up its own safeguards, either by a flat refusal to admit such immigrants (in some industries, firms, or trades where the unions were strong) or, more frequently in recent years, by an informal and unpublicized agreement between unions or the long-term labour-core and the employers in a particular factory that recruitment would be limited to a quota. In Croydon such quotas were usually fixed at about 3 to 5 per cent. of the total labour force, except in the two larger hospitals, where a quota of about 10 per cent. for 'colonial' nurses was applied. In one or two firms organized labour, in suggesting a quota of 3 per cent., associated it verbally with the minimum percentage of disabled persons which larger firms are statutorily obliged to employ.[1] (This implied association of the newcomers with disability was, incidentally, so disliked by the management at one of the large light engineering firms that it insisted on substituting a 4 per cent. quota instead.) As for special redundancy agreements to apply to coloured Commonwealth workers, there was little concrete evidence of their existence, although some employers could have committed themselves unofficially on this.

The imposition of a quota is generally interpreted in a negative sense, as discriminatory, especially when it applies to coloured workers. Yet it has its positive economic and socio-cultural aspects, which can be assessed more objectively in relation to the post-war European exiles and refugees. Working techniques are communicated much more rapidly and thoroughly if newcomers are dispersed over the labour force, and there is less opportunity for the 'ganging-up' and inter-group friction feared by management and unions alike. But over and above these considerations, a quota or informal limitation is a mechanism often adopted by management and the long-term local labour-core alike, whether deliberately or

[1] Cf. Stephens, op. cit., p. 111.

unconsciously, to protect the character and 'culture' of the factory. Since awareness of the need to preserve the character and 'culture' of the factory is stronger in stable, well-integrated working communities, such firms are more likely to apply a limitation on intake than are managements which operate on the 'rabble hypothesis'[1]—that an industrial organization is an aggregate of individuals each of whom is seeking his own gain, and that one pair of hands is as good as another. In this connexion one can compare the situation in the light engineering Firm L (pp. 57–9) with the rapid build-up to nearly 50 per cent. by the die-casters (Firm B, pp. 84–5).

As the later stage of accommodation proceeded in Croydon, many of the firms which had applied a modest initial quota for coloured workers and then promoted their absorption by special selection, training, and placing methods, had reached a point where precise quotas had been exceeded without protest from the unions,[2] or had been superseded by an informal consensus about the 'right number'.[3] This consensus was often shared by the more settled immigrant workers, who no longer brought along all new arrivals for jobs, but only those whom they considered suitable. On the other hand, in the few firms which permitted a rapid build-up, most management informants spoke of 'having too many', or 'reaching danger level' and had limited or stopped further recruitment of coloured workers.[4]

Where special redundancy agreements have been negotiated prior to the entry of certain groups of immigrant workers into an industry or firm, the manner and severity of their actual application in case of need affords an opportunity to see how far the processes of adaptation and acceptance have gone. It was, however, difficult to test this particular index of absorption, since there was little redundancy in Croydon at this period, except for the usual seasonal cut-backs in such industries as food-processing, building, and gas-production. Apart from the migrant Irish, who accepted and indeed preferred the seasonal pattern, the West Indians were the only group to be noticeably affected by such seasonal redundancy, particularly in building, because they had not proved them-

[1] Elton Mayo, *The Social Problems of an Industrial Civilisation*, Boston, 1945, Chapter II and *passim*.

[2] See for instance, p. 92.

[3] Increasing vagueness about numbers may be regarded as an indication of increasing acceptance—the Irish were the supreme example of this in Croydon.

[4] See p. 123.

selves sufficiently skilled to be accepted by management in the regular cadres of 'retainers'. In the gas-works, however, West Indians were more readily accepted by management and fellow-workers; there had been no demand from the latter for West Indians to go first and seasonal redundancy was handled by means of normal labour wastage.

One instance of non-seasonal redundancy in Croydon was found in the railway workshop. Here an attempt was made by management to apply the long-overlooked redundancy agreement providing for non-naturalized Poles and other Europeans to be made redundant, however long their service, so as to make room for more recently arrived British nationals, West Indians, displaced from another depot. Much of this displacement was averted by union intervention, an example being thereby afforded of worker-solidarity and the extent to which the labour core's informal acceptance of these particular foreigners had proceeded beyond the minimum of the initial formal agreement to work with them.[1] The incident, as it happened, pushed the Poles farther towards formal integration and there was a sudden upsurge in applications for naturalization.

Most of the information on redundancy practice in Croydon came retrospectively from firms which had suffered from the mild recession of 1956–8. Some had taken advantage of the opportunity to 'weed out' the undesirables, although this applied not only to immigrants, but to local workers (for example, Firm I). In one or two firms, there was a wholesale clear-out, as in one 'traditional' firm (Firm A, p. 77); here a *bloc* of West Indian women engaged on a particular process were dismissed, although other male immigrants were retained. In some cases, West Indians, Hungarians, and others were displaced simply through the normal operation of the 'last-in, first-out' rule.

Even though recession and redundancy might not lead labour to demand that immigrants go first or management to dismiss them as being less satisfactory than local workers, they could create a situation in which employers became less willing to recruit more immigrants, either because more local labour was available (Firm D, p. 126), or because they did not wish to upset the local labour force (Firm E, p. 66).

[1] Cf. Tannahill, op. cit. (pp. 64–65), for a similar elasticity and equitability in operating textile redundance agreements during the recession of 1952.

A considerable number of Croydon firms had not, however, had any redundancy for years. Informants' views on redundancy policy and possible practice therefore tended to reflect the degree to which various immigrant groups had been absorbed in the firm at that time; in the event of redundancy occurring later, the immigrants could well have become more acceptable and the firm's redundancy practice would be found to differ correspondingly.[1]

As an immigrant group moves through the later stages of industrial accommodation into the phase of assimilation, quotas are overlooked and exceeded, but it may be asked whether the idea of limitation and balance ever disappears completely, at least in the first or second immigrant generation. The situation of the Poles in Croydon provides no clear answer to the question; they were fully accommodated, scattered in small groups all through Croydon industry (except in the special case of Polplastics), and had ceased to receive any large accessions of new immigrants. Yet, although the Poles were included among 'our own people', they and their older children were still a separate and culturally distinctive group and at least one local management spoke of the need to limit the intake of second-generation Polish technicians on to the staff to a 'reasonable proportion'.

On the other hand, it would also be difficult to imagine a local factory recruiting a majority of recent arrivals from Scotland, Wales, or the North of England, although individuals and clusters of workers from these areas are likely to be found at all levels of the factory hierarchy.

One may speculate as to whether the particular visibility of coloured immigrants is likely to lead to a prolongation of quotas and limitations; absorption must, however, proceed much farther before any answer becomes available, and such factors as numerical concentration and continued immigration must also be taken into account. So long as an immigrant group continues to receive considerable reinforcements from its country of origin, (e.g. West Indians, Pakistanis, and Indians) it seems likely that some sort of quota or limitation on numbers will persist in industry, however well accepted older settlers may be. Indeed, the earlier arrivals sometimes favour such limitation, for fear that their own progress may be retarded and that they themselves may lose the individual

[1] See *Dark Strangers*, p. 141, for a similar disparity between management's stated intentions and later practice over redundancy.

status which they have acquired and be sucked back into the faceless outgroup of newcomers.

(b) *Immigrant–Host Relations On and Off the Shop-Floor*

In his work-place the immigrant has to adapt himself to the demands of the job, on the one hand as it is seen by the employer, and on the other to the work patterns and conventions established by the local labour-core. These two sets of patterns and expectations are not always identical and can differ considerably, and the newcomer who fails to conform to one or the other is unlikely to attain a satisfactory accommodation. For instance, 'rate-busting' is unlikely to displease management (unless it leads to industrial disputes), but it contravenes and shows up the work-group's estimate of a 'fair day's work', and will therefore antagonize fellow-workers. At the other extreme, slowness, inefficiency, and carelessness are a more immediate source of dissatisfaction to management than to the labour force. But where the immigrant is working not on his own but in a closely integrated working group, such working behaviour is likely to be regarded as a failure to do one's fair share of the work. In cases where bonus payments are involved, resentment is even stronger.[1] Similar reactions are evoked by bad time-keeping and absenteeism, which are most often found in the earliest phase of immigrant accommodation.[2]

As well as the more formal aspects of working relations, immigrants, like all new entrants, have to try to learn a whole set of informal conventions about social behaviour (language, comportment, demeanour, dress, etc.) in the factory.[3] These involve relationships with fellow-workers on the floor, during the breaks, in the

[1] On the other hand, a long-service, fully accepted member of the working-group may be 'carried' despite his inadequacy. This does not happen in the early stages of immigrant accommodation, but one or two instances were found of Poles and other old-timers who were tolerated in this way, by management as well as by labour.

[2] As Everett Hughes points out (op. cit., p. 177), such 'non-economic behaviour' may not be due merely to unfamiliarity with the ways of the new working environment, but also constitute a reaction to covert but effective rejection by the established labour-core.

[3] On the whole question of informed organization and working cultures, Miller and Form, op. cit., pp. 231–44, 262–87. J. A. C. Brown (op. cit., pp. 147–8) also stresses the importance of the correct use of 'bad language', private jokes, even similar articles of clothing to demonstrate the unity and solidarity of the working-group.

canteen, cloakroom, recreational club, and so on; they vary according to the individual factory but are part of the behaviour norms of the same socio-economic group in the wider society.

The emotional content and level of informal relationships at work is not uniform but varies according to the general climate of the establishment, its size, status, traditions, degree of stability and integration, and its links with the local society outside. It also varies at different levels of the hierarchy and in different occupational groups. For instance, scientists and technical workers in Telelux spoke of the 'low level of co-existence' prevailing among the research staff; this they attributed to the fact that most scientists are less interested in personal relationships than are other professional workers.[1] In nursing and 'white-collar' jobs, on the other hand, people are more interdependent and there is likely to be more intensity in personal relations in the ward, nurses' home, office, or shop. Thus the pressure on newcomers to adapt themselves to the network of informal relations in a given establishment or occupation will obviously vary considerably in intensity.

First, however, the immigrant worker is mainly concerned with getting and learning a job; later he begins to learn the more formal and general elements of the working culture, and seeks acceptance as a fellow-worker, perhaps a fellow trade-unionist; only later still does he seek to enter the informal community of a working-group or clique, in the canteen, club, and pub outside the gates where the men assemble for a beer after work. On their side, local workers start by according newcomers a wary and limited acceptance as part of the labour force, though not necessarily a permanent part. Where accommodation proceeds fairly smoothly, this acceptance becomes more profound and less formal, until individual newcomers are accepted as team-mates and companions in canteen, club, and pub. At this stage, an individual immigrant may well be more acceptable to his working group than a local newcomer. An index of this thoroughgoing degree of accommodation, approaching the phase of assimilation, is the growth of an easygoing, bantering relationship on both sides; only when such informal social acceptance exists, are local workers likely to accept an immigrant in any sort of direct supervisory post.[2]

[1] See p. 343.

[2] See Firm A (p. 144), for an instance of the importance of 'mixing in' if an immigrant is to be accepted in a position of authority.

This is the manner in which absorption proceeds in most firms employing immigrants. Exceptions were found in firms where the build-up of immigrants has been rapid and large-scale (as in Firm C, pp. 123–5). In such cases the newcomers can and often do form their own in-groups and cliques and there is less need for or compulsion on them to conform to local informal patterns or to seek acceptance in established local working groups and cliques; this kind of situation tends to be accompanied by resistance on the part of local workers to the promotion of immigrants, or pressure to limit such promotion to supervision of ethnic groups or gangs.

(c) '*Visibility*' *and* '*Audibility*'

In the case of newcomers who are visibly or audibly conspicuous and different from the local labour force, the development of informal relations with fellow-workers is understandably restricted and hampered until the biological differences are overlooked or the linguistic and cultural gaps narrowed. In the latter case, this is brought about mainly by the immigrants adapting themselves to local norms of dress and behaviour, learning the language, and so on, or by the local community accepting as no longer outlandish certain conventions of appearance and dress, such as turbans and beards in the case of Muslims and Sikhs.

In the matter of learning the English language, local expectations vary according to the newcomer's working role and his status in the working community. It is generally understood by management and fellow-workers that most older immigrants, such as the Poles and some of the Hungarians, are unlikely to learn more English than they will need to do their work properly and to maintain minimal informal relations in the working environment.[1] But for those who aspire to supervisory, technical or administrative posts, poor English and a heavy accent are drawbacks if not definite blocks.[2] This can also apply to Irish and West Indian immigrants; indeed, higher standards may be demanded because English is known to be their first language.

The local demand that the newcomers be intelligible does not spring merely from insular caprice. It has an important utilitarian justification, particularly in work where speed and precision of

[1] See p. 65 (Firm E).

[2] For some instances of situations involving proficiency in English, see Council C (p. 150); Telelux (p. 347); Firm L (p. 58); Firm B (p. 88).

communication are essential. This applies, for example, in complex technical processes and in administrative and office work, while the health services, railways, and mining afford good instances of the sort of work where lack of intelligibility between local and immigrant workers can actually be dangerous.[1] In professional, 'white-collar', and contact-jobs, moreover, not only intelligibility is required but also the kind of vocabulary, enunciation, timbre, and accent that are considered appropriate to the particular role.[2] Appearance, dress, and manner are, like language and accent, more important in high-status or status-conscious occupations, particularly those involving contact with the public, than they are on the factory floor, although even there most working communities have fairly definite expectations in this connexion.

So far, we have been discussing more or less acquirable characteristics. In the case of immutable biological traits, such as pigmentation, and negroid or mongoloid features, the newcomers cannot adapt or change themselves, and absorption must proceed through their increasing acceptance by the local working community as being no longer different but 'one of us'. This process of acceptance was clearly under way in a large number of Croydon factories, but was less evident as yet in non-manual work and contact-jobs.

In situations of the latter kind, a 'thin-end-of-the-wedge' process usually seemed to be at work.[3] Light-coloured Anglo-Indians (and other Anglo-Asians) were the first to be tried and accepted; then came darker-skinned Indians and Pakistanis, still with non-negroid-looking West Indians or Africans, and lastly dark-skinned negroid people. In most Croydon cases this process had not yet gone beyond the stage of 'getting used to' and accepting Indians and Pakistanis.

In a few establishments, this kind of sequence was part of a deliberate policy by management. In most, however, it seemed to have arisen from a combination of two factors: the received belief of the host society in a socio-ethnic hierarchy with English-white at the top and Negro-black at the bottom, and the fact that many of the newcomers actually fitted into such a hierarchy. Most Anglo-Indians

[1] See Patterson, *Dark Strangers*, p. 93, for an instance of this on the railways.

[2] See Stores A and C, p. 136, 139.

[3] For various examples of this process at work, see Firm B (p. 79 f.), Stores A and C (pp. 136–7, 140), Council C (p. 152), Hospital A (p. 160).

and Indians in Croydon were better-educated and better-qualified for non-manual and even for skilled manual work than were the bulk of the West Indian immigrants. Thus West Indians who sought such jobs were doubly handicapped, although in a number of instances individuals had been taken on and won full acceptance. On occasions, however, such acceptance was described in a somewhat revealing manner. Comments such as the following: 'He's so English that everyone forgets he's coloured'[1] seemed to imply that colour is still the badge of the stranger and the undifferentiated outgroup, a badge that is forgotten or overlooked only in the case of a known few. A coloured Englishman is not yet a generally accepted notion, either at work or in the wider society.[2] There is, however, no reason to assume that this cannot come about, and indeed the evidence from Croydon indicated a potentially 'assimilating' situation, in which coloured people were gradually breaching the industrial stranger-bar and entering the working community.[3]

(d) *Teaming, 'Ganging-Up', 'Clustering', and 'Favoured Nations'*

The grouping of immigrants and newcomers in a working-group generally goes through certain phases. In the initial sub-phase of accommodation groups of newcomers try to keep together or 'gang up', both on the shop floor and off it, and most managements and unions regard this tendency with disfavour and take steps to prevent it. In earlier years, as we know, some Croydon employers did attempt to translate the tendency into formal terms by experimenting with ethnic work-groups or teams: successful teaming was reported from some firms for Southern Irish, Poles, and Italians, particularly in building and brick-making. The organization of the building industry, with its extensive use of teams or gangs of specialized craftsmen and assistants, favours this process, provided

[1] See p. 78.

[2] As Dr. Ruth Landes wrote in 1952, contrasting the situation of coloured people in the United States and Britain: 'Britons could not follow the logic of black men profoundly integrated into the American social system because, in their system, black men are not so integrated. . . . Since such understanding does not bind the Briton and the Negro, the Negro's civil status and significance are similar to those of a foreigner.' 'A Preliminary Statement of a Survey of Negro–White Relations in Britain' (unpublished communication, Royal Anthropological Institute, 6 May 1952.)

[3] See pp. 255–8 and p. 290, for further consideration of the importance of colour as a factor in influencing industrial absorption.

that those in a team or gang work well and efficiently together. In most cases, however, the experiment failed and the firm either ceased to employ immigrants altogether or switched to a policy of dispersal.[1]

Such failures were particularly frequent in the case of West Indians. In almost every case informants reported that, if teamed together, their working tempo would slow; some added that such grouping led to unco-operative and aggressive behaviour, which caused friction within the working community.[2] In earlier years a few firms had tried teaming West Indians and West Africans together, apparently on the assumption that coloured negroid peoples were alike;[3] these reported not only poor working performance but friction within the team. Similar friction was also noted in some cases where West Indians from different islands and environments were teamed together.

This undiscriminating tendency by employers to lump all coloured workers together in the early days could indeed have contributed considerably to the poor working performance and unco-operative attitudes reported in a number of cases. The fact that, by the time of this inquiry, many employers had learned to distinguish between West Africans and West Indians, and even between West Indians of different regional origins, could in itself be regarded as an index of increasing accommodation.[4]

Apart from the instances of the use of ethnic working-groups just mentioned, the survey showed that most Croydon 100-plus managements were employing such mechanisms as quotas and deliberate dispersal of immigrant workers in order to preserve the existing culture and character of their establishments. Thus, whereas a considerable body of opinion, both well and ill grounded, had grown up about the working qualities and general characteristics of

[1] See p. 74, for an instance of the first solution, the light engineering, mass-production plants, pp. 70–4, for the second.

[2] See Hospital A, p. 160.

[3] Informants sometimes failed to distinguish between Indians and Pakistanis, but rarely spoke of them as 'coloured', a term which, if it was still used, was generally reserved for West Indians and West Africans.

[4] When managements have a precise and detailed knowledge of the ethnic origins and characteristics of their immigrant employees, this may be regarded as an index of increasing acceptance. When they display vagueness, this may be indicative of an 'economic man' approach by management; on the other hand, it may indicate an assimilative situation (as with the Irish in a number of firms and industries).

the various immigrant groups, there was little tendency for firms to allow certain types of job to become the province of particular groups, even in the case of West Indians and other coloured workers. Although there was a fairly widespread notion that West Indian workers were unskilled and slow, few firms had allowed menial or unskilled jobs to become the special province of West Indians, that is to say, to permit the development of something like a 'Kaffir work' complex to develop.[1]

Certain managements, indeed, showed a lively awareness of this possibility and its undesirability. For instance, one light engineering firm took coloured skilled men but not coloured labourers (Firm L, p. 68), and both of the two large mass-production light engineering plants were careful to disperse coloured newcomers as widely as possible and not to take on large numbers as labourers or canteen workers.

In the second sub-phase of industrial accommodation, management, and local workers cease to criticize the newcomers for 'ganging-up'. This can mean that the immigrants are beginning to break away from their own little out-cliques and to enter the informal life of the factory. It can also mean that, although they continue to maintain close relations with one another, they realize that it is not well regarded and are therefore more discreet about it.[2]

At about this time what may be called the 'clustering' process begins. The more established and accepted immigrants begin to recommend later arrivals from their own home town, village or kin for vacancies.[3] Having a fair idea of the requirements of the job, such established workers act as a preliminary selection-mechanism; this is often welcomed by managements, in contrast to the indiscriminate mass applications which occur as soon as it is known over the grape-vine that a factory is accepting a particular immigrant group.[4] These older-established immigrants are also able to sponsor the newcomers in the working-group. In this way, there evolve the 'favoured nation' groups that were found in a number of establishments, particularly in smaller and medium-sized factories with little time or scope to experiment with every new source of labour.

[1] For 'Kaffir work', see *Colour and Culture in South Africa*, p. 65.
[2] See p. 329. [3] See p. 79. [4] See p. 72.

A 'favoured nation'[1] does not evolve in an establishment unless the newcomers have shown that they are suited to the work. Its evolution can come about by chance, experimentation, or as a matter of policy. In a few firms, the 'favoured nation' was drawn from nationals and trainees from a country with which the firm had business links, such as India.

In medium and smaller firms, the 'favoured nation' system was clearly advantageous, since it opened up a new recruiting source and involved only a simple process of accommodation between a single group of newcomers and the receiving community. Once established, therefore, a 'favoured nation' tended to be self-perpetuating through the recruitment of new arrivals and the second generation, except in transit-camp industries and jobs, such as sweet-making, laundries, brick-making, and some labouring work. The factor of chance could, of course, work the other way. Several firms tried out one or more individuals from various immigrant groups, found them unsatisfactory and decided to recruit no more from that particular group.

A 'favoured nation' policy naturally works mainly to the benefit of the particular group or groups concerned. It does, however, have an indirect 'thin-end-of-the-wedge' effect by accustoming management and local labour to the presence of immigrants; it thus makes them more ready to accept other newcomers, or at least those who are not too dissimilar, and likely to be congenial to the established group. For example, the presence of Poles sometimes paved the way for the entry of other refugees and Europeans generally, and perhaps for the entry of Anglo-Indians. Again, the presence of an Anglo-Indian 'favoured nation' seemed likely to facilitate the entry and acceptance of darker-skinned Asians, and possibly later of other coloured people.

Employers do not always consider the preferences of their 'favoured nation' when taking on other immigrants, but there was some evidence in Croydon that established groups resented the entry of certain later comers, either because of traditional enmities or on status grounds, the latter often being related to local norms and values. For instance, Polish ex-officers and N.C.O.s were resigned to doing unskilled or manual work, but objected to the recruiting of coloured people for the same work; this was not be-

[1] For this process, cf. L. Stephens, *Employment of Coloured Workers in the Birmingham Area*, London, Institute of Personnel Management, 1956, p. 2.

cause of any racialist notions or colonial associations (few Poles had ever seen a Negro before 1939), but on cultural grounds and because the association would lower their own status in British eyes.[1] Anglo-Indians sometimes seemed anxious to avoid too close association with darker-coloured Indians, still more with negroid people. How far a 'favoured nation' is in fact able to make life difficult for, and ultimately to force the departure of, unwanted newcomers from other minority groups is uncertain; if it happens, it is presumably through the operation of the same informal mechanisms and controls as are used by local work-groups in the first place to keep out or remove unwanted outsiders.

Poles and Anglo-Indians were the 'favoured nation', together or apart, in quite a number of Croydon firms.[2] The Southern Irish were the principal 'favoured nation' in the very different occupations of nursing and building. The West Indians were preferred to migrant Irish as manual workers in some firms, but they could hardly be said to have established themselves as a 'favoured nation' anywhere, except in the few establishments where they constituted nearly half the labour force. This failure to establish themselves could be attributed to a combination of factors, notably their comparatively recent arrival, their large numbers and their lack of working skills, local antipathy or ignorance, and also, perhaps, the operation of the 'favoured nation' principle on behalf of groups that had entered the labour market earlier.

[1] See p. 102, and Polplastics, Ch. 11, in which no coloured people were employed, except for a few Anglo-Indians.

[2] See pp. 65–6.

CHAPTER 8

THE PROCESSES OF INDUSTRIAL ABSORPTION: (II) FACTORS AND INTEREST GROUPS

The manner, speed, and ease of industrial absorption are, as the survey material has shown, affected by a considerable number of differing factors. In this chapter the operation and interaction of the major factors and sets of factors is reviewed; it concludes with an evaluation of their relative importance in the situation under study.

One major set of factors is of a different order to the rest. It consists of economic, ecological, demographic, and other quantitative factors that are often external, antecedent, and sometimes preconditioning in relation to the process of immigrant absorption in industry. They are concerned with such things as labour shortage, availability of housing and the size, speed, and density of settlement, and the demographic composition of an immigrant group or groups.

The other sets of factors may be termed 'internal' factors: they are basically socio-economic and cultural[1] or qualitative, and they operate concurrently with the processes of absorption. As they are associated with the needs, values, norms, objectives, and interaction of the main interest-groups involved in the work-situation, they have here been classified under the following headings: employers and management; the labour force; the immigrants; the specific and often widely differing working cultures and communities which are the product of the interaction of the first two interest-groups; and, finally, the public and the wider society.

[1] There is also the environmental factor of climate which, in conjunction with such social and cultural variables as old-country living patterns and diet, can have a considerable effect on the physical health and endurance of the immigrants and consequently upon their working ability. This effect was not particularly marked in the case of Irish, Poles, and other Europeans; but it was more evident among West Indians, Anglo-Indians, and Asians.

A more individual and unpredictable kind of variable is also discussed—the intervention of individuals or small groups belonging to any of the major interest-groups in sponsoring, 'blackballing', leadership, or similar roles. Such interventions seem to take place more often at work than is generally realized, and they are frequently responsible, at least in part, for the wide range of variation and the differing forms and degrees of immigrant absorption found in otherwise similar industrial situations.

(I) 'EXTERNAL' FACTORS

The 'pull' factor of labour shortage is likely to operate most freely not only in dynamic and expanding areas but in dynamic and expanding industries and firms. New immigrant groups do not settle in large numbers in areas of long-standing depression, nor would they be likely to get work easily if they did. This 'pull' factor is likely to be particularly strong in large mass-production firms; in firms that have recently moved into an area and thus lack an old-established core and source of local labour; in marginal-profit or low-status industries; and in services and firms with a high labour turnover or large seasonal fluctuations in their labour requirements.

The Croydon survey indicated that the existence of a chronic, large-scale labour shortage was likely to be far and away the most important single pre-conditioning factor in 'pulling' migrants to this area and in inducing local employers to try out new sources of labour. Apart from the few establishments with overseas connexions or exchange arrangements, only those firms which suffered from labour shortage had ever taken on any newly arrived immigrants, although settled and part-assimilated newcomers might be accepted elsewhere. In most cases, though not all, labour shortage also appeared to have weakened the resistance of local labour to the entrance of immigrants.

The permanent shortage of skilled labour in such areas as Croydon would have constituted an even greater 'pull factor' but for the fact that few immigrants possessed the required skills or were young enough to acquire them after arrival. When skilled immigrant workers were available in Croydon they seemed to have had no real difficulty in getting skilled jobs somewhere, though not necessarily in the first firm they approached. The same applied to the few young or second-generation immigrants, mostly Poles, Anglo-Indians, and Asians, who had sought apprenticeships. At the time of this study the West Indians were only just setting up residence and family life in the area and there was no evidence that any West Indian school-leavers were seeking apprenticeships. Whether the widespread assessment by local employers and local labour of West Indian adult immigrants as suited only for semi-skilled, unskilled, or labouring work would prejudice the second generation's chances of being accepted as potential skilled workers by apprenticeship committee has remained a question that can only be answered in the next decade or so, as English-born, locally educated school-leavers begin to enter the local labour market in fair numbers.

The 'pull' of a labour shortage is also limited in another way—by the nature of the work. There is a chronic labour shortage in mining and agriculture, but these hold little attraction for most immigrants. Few coloured Commonwealth immigrants ever enter them, while most of those Europeans who were directed there after the 1939–45 War have (except for a minority who were miners or farmers by profession) moved to lighter and more congenial work in the towns. Even in manufacturing industry there are jobs that are more or less congenial, as we noted in the case of 'transit-camp' industries and firms.

Labour shortage is an all-important antecedent factor in inducing employers to take the plunge and try out immigrant labour; but it does not at a later stage always exert an equally strong influence on employers to persevere with immigrants whom they have found unsatisfactory or unsuitable. Most likely to persevere are large firms with sufficient resources and facilities to experiment with special selection, induction, and training techniques for workers who would otherwise be unable to meet their requirements, or low-status, seasonal firms which have no other choice. Other firms and industries may be in a position, before or after trying immigrant labour, to meet their labour problems by other means, such as the use of part-time women workers, or increased mechanization and automation. Thus labour shortage, although it can be the most important initial 'pull factor', does not invariably lead to a steady inflow of outside or overseas immigrant workers.

The choice of a solution is basically associated with the nature of the formal organization and job requirements in a particular firm, but as these are closely involved with the main interest-groups in industry they will be discussed later in this chapter.[1]

The free operation of the 'pull factor' of labour shortage can be impeded, not only by a variety of socio-economic and cultural factors but also by one major environmental factor. A labour-hungry area can only attract immigrants if cheap housing is available locally or near by. For instance, few immigrants are as yet found in the New Towns, where the available housing is linked with the job, and the greater difficulty of getting residential accommodation in the more 'select' suburbs of Carshalton and Purley at the time of this survey limited the numbers of immigrant workers in those areas.

Croydon, on the other hand, contained its 'zones of transition' or 'twilight areas', into which the immigrants were gradually moving from Brixton, Battersea, and Camberwell after finding work in the Croydon industrial area. Indeed, the fact that most recent immigrants only came to live in Croydon some time after they had found work there may have eased the process of their acceptance both at work and in the wider local community, since frictions over housing developed only after the newcomers had begun to establish themselves as part of the labour force. The size and rate of the build-up was roughly though unintentionally regulated by the requirements of industry and was proceeding relatively slowly because of the widespread operation of informal quotas. This could be contrasted with the rapid build-up that seemed to have occurred in some other areas, particularly in the case of Asian immigrants employed on the ethnic gang system in certain industries, when the proportion of immigrants could be considerably higher. This unofficial regulation of intake by individual managements, acting in conjunction with organized labour or their established labour-cores, was usually combined with a deliberate policy of dispersing the newcomers (particularly West Indians) as widely as possible over the departments and working units. On the whole, it seemed to have promoted absorption and to have kept tensions down; on the other hand, in most of the small number of firms that permitted a rapid build-up there were reports of friction, ganging-up, numbers 'reaching danger level', and so on. To this extent the Croydon material supports the hypothesis that there is a rough optimum proportion and rate of intake for newcomers in a given

[1] See pp. 289–90.

firm or work unit, although this can and does vary according to a considerable number of variables, qualitative as well as quantitative, and is based on considerations less of economic than of cultural absorptive capacity.

The only two immigrant groups in respect of which concern over numbers, rate of build-up and concentration had been felt in Croydon industry in the post-war period were the Poles (along with other East European refugees and E.V.W.s) and the West Indians. Concern over East European numbers was, however, confined to a few firms and had ceased to exist years before the time, as absorption progressed and the inflow of newcomers dried up. Concern over the West Indians persisted and this could be associated with the fact that the inflow into Britain was continuing, while those already here were in only the early stages of absorption.

The whole question of the size, rate, and density of settlement and the demographic composition of an immigrant labour force and an immigrant group in any locality would seem to merit further comparative inquiry in the British context, in which the necessity for constructive planning, as well as for immigration controls, is being increasingly recognized. How far is the absorption, economic and overall, of immigrants influenced by their numbers, rate of arrival, density of settlement, and demographic structure? Is there an optimum quota for a working or a local community, an optimum sex and age structure, an optimum density and degree of dispersal and an optimum rate of build-up?[1] And if such optimum rates exist, do they differ, and if so, how far, and according to what criteria, for different groups of immigrants, and in different kinds of working community and area and at different stages in the processes of absorption?

Whatever the answers to these questions, it seems clear that they cannot be simple quantitative ones nor based only on calculations of 'economic absorptive capacity', that is to say on the economy's capacity to absorb a certain number of immigrant 'economic men'. Undoubtedly the existence of favourable economic circumstances promotes economic absorption, but social and cultural absorption are at least equally important.

[1] Length of settlement is another factor influencing the degree of absorption; but its importance may be diminished by the continued arrival of large batches of newcomers, which may have the effect of slowing adaptation and also acceptance by the receiving society, which may not differentiate between the earlier arrivals, however far acculturated, and the outgroup as a whole.

W. D. Borrie, discussing the theory and practice of 'economic absorption' and 'cultural integration', stresses the complexities of the social and cultural interactions involved in the processes of integration, including the differences between countries of immigration and between host and immigrant cultures, and the impossibility of divorcing economic from social and cultural factors even in the sphere of employment, especially in contemporary urban industrial settlements. The writer is, of course, discussing the planning of migration, whereas this Croydon study was concerned with mainly uncontrolled immigration into a particular industrial area. Nevertheless, in view of the fact that all economic immigration to Britain, with the exception of the Southern Irish and the dependants of those already here, has since mid-1962 been subject to some measure of control and selection, it may not be inapposite, by way of conclusion to this section on external factors, to quote Borrie's comments on the large-scale, post-war international migration schemes:

> . . . The relative success of post-war planning in regard to immigration does appear to have been due, in considerable measure, to a much more realistic view of the inter-relationships between economic and cutural factors in the processes of adjustment, to greater care in the selection and placing of immigrants, to greater co-operation by governments of receiving and sending countries, both directly and through international agencies and to better understanding of the techniques of promoting economic growth.[1]

(2) SOCIO-ECONOMIC AND CULTURAL FACTORS AND INDUSTRIAL INTEREST-GROUPS

(a) *Employers and Management*

Of the three principal interest-groups involved in the process of industrial absorption in British industry, the most important one is that composed of employers or management, whether it is interacting with other interest-groups in the working community or operating on its own. The simple and obvious reason for this is that employers and managers have more power than the labour force. They may co-operate with or be checked by the labour force to a

[1] *The Cultural Integration of Immigrants*, U.N.E.S.C.O., Population and Culture series, 1959, Chapter V *passim*. This chapter includes a valuable set of references to research done in this field in a number of countries of migration.

greater or lesser degree, but ultimately it is they who make the major policy decisions and plan or are responsible for the firm's formal organization. Perhaps most important, it is they who hire and fire, and they who, in a situation of chronic labour shortage, take the decision whether to try out a new labour source or to reduce the need for human labour by mechanization or other forms of reorganization.

For four or five decades before the end of the Second World War, the idea of immigrant labour (other than Southern Irish) as a regular part of the British industrial labour force was not part of management thinking, despite the presence of large pockets of coloured or Jewish immigrants in specialized occupations and industries, notably in the merchant marine, the garment trade, and commerce. Notwithstanding the considerable historical contribution of successive immigrant groups to her economy, Britain, unlike the United States and Canada, has not by intention been an immigrant country. Nor has her industrial strength been based on large accessions of immigrant labour from outside to anything like the same extent as the Americas, although she has of course depended greatly on internal migration from the country to the city.

Despite some initial reactions of caution and suspicion, the approach of most Croydon employers and management to the novel idea of trying out immigrant labour was found to be a pragmatic one, particularly given the existence of a chronic labour shortage; it was thus more likely to promote than to impede the entry and absorption of newcomers. As for the handful of existing immigrant employers or managers, they were on the whole less cautious and more favourable to the employment of at least some groups of immigrants.

We have been referring to employers or management as if they formed an undifferentiated group. In fact, it emerged clearly from the interviews that the viewpoints and behaviour of management were not only the outcome of personality differences but were influenced by such factors as the size of the organization and the degree of personalization within it, the informant's position in the management and supervisory hierarchy, the type of managerial training received, and so on.[1] For instance, both in giving information and in actual working relations there was some variation in approach and influence between the boss of a small, highly per-

[1] See also pp. 45–7 for a more detailed note about management informants.

sonalized or family firm and the managing director of a large, multiple, or mass-production concern; and between upper and lower management and face-to-face supervisors, as, for instance, an old-style works manager, a trained personnel officer, a foreman promoted from the ranks, and a technically trained, new-style supervisor.

The theoretical ultimate in depersonalization in an industrial establishment occurs when it is publicly as opposed to privately owned. The kind of ownership clearly has some effect on management policy and practice. In the public sector in Britain this means greater uniformity and universal recognition of trade unions or professional bodies. In so far as the entry and absorption of immigrants is concerned, the views of organized labour have in general had more influence, and those of management less influence, on the process than in most private firms. In some parts of the public sector, notably the postal and transport services, this relative weakness of management can also be attributed to the fact that at all but the very highest levels managers have been promoted from the ranks and tend to sympathize with or share the views of the rank and file.

Apart from a minority of individuals with strong prejudices or predispositions, which they injected into the work-situation, the majority of employers and managers in all industrial sectors in Croydon appeared, as has been said, to approach the employment of immigrants from a pragmatic viewpoint. Many could have been influenced by preconceptions or second-hand reports about the characteristics of certain immigrant groups, and where these were widespread, derogatory and of long-standing, the entry and acceptance of such immigrants was undoubtedly rendered more difficult because they did have not only to prove their own merits but also to dispel existing notions and expectations.

Basically, however, most managers and supervisors were primarily concerned with the newcomers' working ability, and also with their general suitability for membership of a particular working community.[1] In a few cases managers in Croydon seemed to be acting on the 'rabble hypothesis' of economic absorptive capacity.

[1] Here again, especially in the smaller firms, there was an understandable tendency to generalize about the working qualities of various immigrant groups from a few instances. Thus a firm's first experiences with a particular immigrant group were very important for future policy and practice. Cf. Hermann Feldman, *Racial Factors in American Industry*, New York, Harper and Bros, 1931, p. 192.

In the majority of firms, however, management spokesmen had a well-defined idea of their particular working community and its culture, which in large firms could of course vary considerably between one department, section, or unit and another.[1] Their views on the entry and absorption of immigrants therefore tended to include social and cultural as well as economic considerations.

Extremely important in the absorptive process were the methods adopted by management for introducing immigrants into the establishment and for promoting their absorption. The method of introduction was naturally conditioned by and indeed reflected the overall state of management–labour relations. In some cases the entry had been imposed without consultation (e.g. Firm B, p. 80); in others it was said to have 'just happened', either because they turned up at the gate or because the employment exchange began to send them along (e.g. Firm A, p. 88). In yet other firms, there was prior consultation, which could have been informal, as in light engineering, Firm A (although the latter firm was well unionized, it was small and management–labour relations were particularly friendly and informal, see p. 50) or formal (see the two light engineering mass-production firms: light engineering, p. 71).

Although the method of imposing entry is less likely to be satisfactory, none of the other three can be singled out as being likely to prove the most satisfactory. The method of introduction should be and usually is geared to the general pattern of management–labour relations in an individual establishment. Whether the prior consultation is formal or informal, however, it would appear that if upper management takes a positive and forthright line from the start over the entry and acceptance of immigrants the outcome is more likely to be successful. This is in line with findings based on experience of introducing Negro workers into industry in the Northern United States.[2] As Everett Hughes wrote in his classic paper on the *Knitting of Racial Groups in Industry:*

[1] These differences were usually self-perpetuating, but a few of the larger firms seemed to be adopting a definite policy of 'scrambling' the labour force by switching people about, so as to prevent the crystallization of cliques and rigid 'cultures'. The fluidity thereby created could of course help the absorption of immigrants, since few working units would contain old-established cliques powerful enough to resist their entry.

[2] See Herbert Blumer, 'Recent Research on Race Relations in the United States', *International Social Science Bulletin*, Vol. X, No. 3, 1958, pp. 416 and 427. Cf. also Stephens, op. cit., p. 15.

Recent experience suggests that this grid of relationships, and the manner in which Negroes are introduced into it, are more significant in the success of a policy of hiring Negroes than are the generalized racial attitudes of the white workers concerned.

He went on to say:

Polling of white workers to find whether they favor the hiring of Negroes as their equal and close fellow-workers would almost anywhere result in an emphatic 'No'. Workers generally prefer not to have any new kinds of workers introduced among them equal to themselves. But Negroes have been successfully employed among white workers; and many other new kinds of workers have been introduced among older kinds of workers who were not enthusiastic about them. Polling of attitudes, on this simple basis, gives little clue to the probable behavior of the old workers to the new. The simple 'No' of the workers to many proposals of management is not to be taken at face value; for industry has not been run by majority vote of the workers, and a 'No' is often no more than a demonstration of protest. In fact, workers more or less expect each other to object to changes proposed by management.[1]

In British industry an outright 'No' from workers might not be so general as in the United States,[2] but unwillingness would be probably fairly widespread. In Croydon, as has been said, the reception given to immigrants by workers seems to have been influenced considerably by the degree of firmness shown by management in their initial consultations with supervisors, shop-stewards, or key old-time employees. The most successful consultations have often included an appeal for solidarity in the face of an insoluble labour problem and, in the case of trade unionists, a reference to the T.U.C.'s condemnation of discrimination against coloured Commonwealth brothers-at-work. Almost invariably in such consultations, management has conceded safeguards, including quotas and trade tests, to meet the workers' reservations and anxieties.

[1] Everett C. Hughes and Helen McG. Hughes, *Where Peoples Meet*, Free Press, Glencoe, Illinois, p. 176.

[2] In 1958 a Gallup Poll showed that, asked 'Do you think that coloured people from the Commonwealth should be allowed to compete for jobs in Britain on equal terms with people born here?', 48 per cent. of respondents answered 'Yes', 37 per cent. 'No', and 15 per cent. 'Don't know' (London percentages 36 and 14 respectively). The percentage answering 'Yes' rose appreciably among those who had personal acquaintance with coloured people. By 1961 the proportion answering 'Yes' had risen to 60 per cent., while the 'Noes' had shrunk to 29 per cent. and the 'Don't knows' to 11 per cent.

The least successful consultations seem to have been carried out in the spirit of the Latin question form that expects the answer 'No'. In several cases managements reported having received a negative answer from one or more departments—most refusals having come either from superintendents and foremen, in the case of coloured workers, or from trade-union 'closed shops', usually with reference to anti-Communist East European refugees. A fair number of refusals were also reported from white-collar working units; these were usually expressed by the manager or superintendent in the familiar, status-conscious phrase that 'the staff wouldn't like it'.

While the method of introduction is important in securing the initial entry of newcomers to a working community, it is not enough to guarantee final success. For such success, managements often found it necessary to evolve special techniques of selection, induction, training, limitation of intake, dispersal, or special placing, special handling of redundancy or promotion and up-grading and personnel problems on and off the shop floor. In the smaller firms this process developed informally, almost unconsciously, often because of the activities of a sponsor or by the evolution of a self-regulating 'favoured nation' policy. In larger firms the development of techniques was stimulated by the continuing need for labour, and was usually more deliberate. The painstaking trial-error-and-reappraisal methods adopted by the personnel departments in the two light engineering mass-production firms afford an excellent example of the working of this process (light engineering, pp. 72–3). The findings on which the final techniques evolved in relation to West Indians were based included the following (which indeed seem to have been reached by most successful employers of West Indian labour in Croydon):

(i) That they could not be treated simply as 'coloured economic men' but must be distinguished in placing and treatment not only from non-West Indian coloured workers but also according to their regional provenance (e.g. Jamaicans and Barbadians do not always work well together).

(ii) That they worked badly in ethnic teams and best when dispersed as widely as possible through the factory.

(iii) That their learning curve during training for semi-skilled work might be longer but that, given patience, they would ultimately reach the same point, although they might still *appear* to be slower.[1]

(iv) That special induction courses stressing hygiene or personal habits were not necessary and might well evoke unnecessary hurt and resentment in the hearers.

(v) That labour turnover among them was lower than average, particularly after the 1957–8 recession (this would not necessarily apply in 'transit-camp' industries or jobs).

(vi) That a quota agreed by joint consultation could be exceeded (within reason) without protest from local labour as the newcomers adapted themselves and became increasingly accepted as part of the regular labour force.

(vii) That West Indian newcomers were not accustomed to the large-scale, impersonal machinery of the modern industrial establishment and had problems of adjustment not only in the factory but also in the unfamiliar urban world outside. They welcomed and responded well to sympathetic advice and assistance from personnel welfare and medical staff on problems ranging from housing to family difficulties, schooling for children, sickness, and taxation.

(viii) That up-grading of immigrants on merit and seniority could be carried out without undue difficulty, provided this was to posts of extra responsibility; but that promotion to any direct supervisory position needed special diplomacy and caution, and the selection of an outstanding pioneer-type candidate.

(b) *The Labour Force*

The second major interest-group involved in the industrial absorption of immigrants are the workers—particularly those who belong to a trade union or to the stable, long-service core of workers found in most firms. With some exceptions and qualifications, notably in closed-shop departments, labour generally has less to say than management about the entry and even the subsequent

[1] Some firms had a rigid training system which could not easily be adapted to suit the needs of immigrant workers. An instance of this was Firm A (p. 62) which after instruction put newcomers straight out on to the shop floor, where they could rely only on a few hints from the supervisor. Under this system Poles and East Europeans failed to cope because of the language problem, West Indians were found too slow and only the Indians and Anglo-Indians had made the grade and became a 'favoured nation'. There were also many marginal, seasonal, or small firms, notably in the 'consumer' sector, which had not the time, facilities, or resources to embark on special training schemes for newcomers, even if they would have liked to do so.

employment of immigrant workers; workers can nevertheless influence developments either by subtle unco-operativeness in face-to-face working relations or by informal pressure on management in firms where labour and management are part of a tight-knit working community.

Much of the material on the reactions and behaviour of Croydon workers was provided by informants at various levels of the managerial and supervisory hierarchy. Even allowing for a certain bias on their part, it was clear that here, as elsewhere in Britain, labour's approach on the employment of immigrants has tended to be more emotional and negative, while management's viewpoint has usually been more positive and pragmatic. It has been management, not labour, that has taken the initial decision to try out a new labour source. And labour's reactions has varied from antipathy, apprehension, and resistance to a rather limited and grudging acceptance of most newcomers, at least in the first years after each group has entered the industrial sphere.

Such reactions are hardly surprising. No body of workers welcomes outsiders, and in Britain, as in most industrialized societies, workers have a traditional and well-grounded fear of 'foreign' labour, since more than once over the past century foreign workers, often encouraged by management, have threatened their security and working conditions, undercut their wages and living standards, and weakened industrial organization and action. These economic fears are augmented by the mild antipathy to foreigners that is widespread in England; by preoccupations over status, which are at least as strong as their economic motivations; and by various second-hand notions attributing various derogatory or inferior traits to particular groups of immigrants. But such feelings of apprehension, anxiety and antipathy are not as strong among workers in expanding industrial areas as they are in the regions of long-standing industrial depression farther north. In Croydon, indeed, they actually seemed less pronounced than in such nearby London districts as Brixton, Battersea, and Bermondsey, which have a more traditional and static industrial climate.

(i) *The Trade Unions*

Most unions in Croydon did not, as we said earlier, take a very restrictive line about the employment of immigrants, particularly at district level. To this extent their attitude was likely to help the early processes of immigrant absorption in Croydon industry—but in fact their writ was a limited one in all but the light engineering sector, heavy engineering, the public utilities, printing, and, to a lesser extent, local government.

How did the unions influence the absorption of immigrants in those industries and firms where they were strong? And were they able to bring any influence to bear elsewhere?

In the well-unionized, and skilled sub-sector of light engineering, between 3 and 4 per cent. of all skilled workers were immigrants; two-thirds of them were from Europe (mostly Poles), the remainder from the Commonwealth (mostly Indians or Anglo-Indians). But, in fact, the majority of these immigrants were employed either in four of the larger firms, firms which maintained an open shop, although they were well unionized, or in three small non-union firms. Two of the latter and one of the large firms were also concerned with rather unusual skills (glass-blowing and watch-making) and arrived in the area only after the 1939–45 War, so that they had had to build up a local labour force from scratch. There were few or no immigrants in the five remaining medium or small precision engineering firms, all closed shops or highly unionized, but this seemed likely to be due less to any union resistance than to the fact that these particular firms had not suffered from any appreciable labour shortage and could cope with their staffing problems by accepting local apprentices and by increased mechanization.

Despite the high degree of unionization in the whole light engineering sector, there was no large-scale evidence of effective resistance to the entry of skilled immigrants by craft unions in this sector, other than in some closed-shop departments. In the semi-skilled sub-sector there was rather lower unionization in most firms, except for the A.E.U. closed-shop tool-rooms. In these there was definite evidence in three firms (A, D, and F)[1] of some bias and resistance. This took the form either of reluctance to accept outside qualifications or of hostility towards anti-Communist refugees. In most other departments, however, acceptance or rejection depended on supervisors or management.

Both mass-production light engineering firms were highly unionized and the entry of each new group of immigrants was

[1] On the other hand, a charge-hand in Firm E's open-shop tool-room was a Pole (see p. 65).

negotiated with the unions; the latter asked for, and got, prior redundancy agreements (for non-British workers) and quotas of 3 to 4 per cent. (in the case of coloured workers). They also favoured dispersal. Except for the A.E.U. little resistance to the acceptance of outside qualifications or of skilled anti-Communist refugees was reported. On the other hand, the prevailing A.E.U. attitude had kept the tool-rooms in both these firms more or less free of immigrants, those with craft qualifications being found in skilled work elsewhere in the plants, or having moved out of the sub-sector altogether.

The two heavy-engineering firms were well unionized, but the intake of immigrants had been influenced, not by any formal consultation with the unions as such but by an informal agreement between management and the long-service core of local workers. There was no evidence of any union resistance—but each newcomer was sized up by the core-community and only those who could make the grade on the job and fit in socially have lasted.

There was a high degree of unionization at all levels in the public services (professional, staff, craft, and general unions). No evidence was, however, found of official resistance by professional bodies or unions to the entry of immigrant employees, although some resistance at branch level was to occur later, after the recruiting of coloured busmen began in the area (see pp. 96–7). At this time, however, the fact that there were no coloured postmen or busmen should be attributed not so much to resistance by organized labour as to the following considerations: firstly, that the local recruiting situation was not so acute as it was to become, and secondly that hardly any had applied, probably because few as yet lived locally.

On the other hand, immigrants were already being employed in fair numbers by the Gas Board and British Railways. In each case there had been full prior consultation and agreement with the N.U.G.M.W. and the railway unions. And although some pockets of resistance and hostility remained at low level, in a few depots or working units, these were not approved by the unions. The newcomers were joining the unions, and there was growing evidence of satisfactory working relations and even of solidarity between local workers and newcomer *vis-à-vis* management.

On the whole, it must be said that the general and industrial unions have put up a less effective resistance to the entry of immigrants into British industry than have the craft unions. This does not mean that all general and industrial unions have always shown a more welcoming attitude,[1] nor that the craft unions have been uniformly hostile—Poles and Hungarians were found in quite a number of the less leftist A.E.U. tool-rooms, and skilled Indians, Anglo-Indians, and West Indians usually found a niche in some skilled job. The most probable explanation for the craft unions' greater effectiveness is that in a society with a chronic shortage of skilled men they have manoeuvred themselves into a position where they can, if they wish, dictate employment policy to many managements. This was found in many A.E.U. tool-rooms in Croydon,[2] and was even better exemplified in the printing firms. With the exception of one non-union shop using special techniques and female labour, the four others were closed shops (and 'closed shop' means everybody from compositor and reader to labourer and cleaner). There was only one immigrant craftsman in any of these firms, a West Indian, while the left-wing chapels in two of the firms had each rejected Polish craftsmen sent down by their own union.

The power of the craft unions makes itself felt everywhere except in the building industry, where the seasonal nature and mobility of the work limit the extent to which closed or exclusive working units can survive or be organized by a union. In Croydon building firms immigrants with the appropriate skills seemed to have experienced less difficulty in being accepted, perhaps because the decision usually rested with management or supervisors, rather than with a shop-steward and the members of a closed shop.

(ii) *The Labour-Core*

In most of Croydon's '100-plus' firms the viewpoint of the established nucleus or core of long-service workers appeared to have

[1] Perusal of T. and G.W.U. and N.U.R. discussions of the subject in earlier years will rapidly dispel this notion. The N.U.G.M.W. has been more circumspect in its public discussions, although there has been some local friction in South London (for references, see *Dark Strangers*, pp. 154–60). In Croydon's gasworks, on the other hand, while there was considerable resistance to Poles in the resettlement period, there had been no official N.U.G.M.W. objection to the intake of West Indians, who numbered about 10 per cent. of the manual labour force.

[2] No evidence could be obtained about similar activities by the E.T.U. or other craft unions.

considerable importance and to be taken into account by management, whether or not there was a high degree of unionization. Indeed, such informal labour-cores usually played a more important part in the actual absorption of newcomers at local level than did organized labour. This influence was frequently exerted in conjunction or consensus with management or supervisors and we shall have more to say about it when we come to discuss the interaction within a working community as a whole. Here we may consider some aspects of formal and informal organization in industry and some characteristics of particular local labour-cores.

(iii) *Formal and Informal Organization*

The formal requirements and organization of a job, in the sense of the skills and aptitudes required, and the established techniques of production, influence or even determine the composition of the entire labour force and the climate of the working culture and community. Such formal organization can range from integrated teamwork, involving a high degree of skill, interaction, and understanding, verbalized or not, between members (high team bonuses may also be a feature here), to individual operations, individually paid, in which operatives have little contact or interaction with others on the floor. At one extreme formal requirements and informal organization virtually coincide, and there is little chance of any newcomer staying on or entering unless he is acceptable to the established team. At the other extreme, there is a considerable divergence between formal and informal organization; the formal organization is less cohesive and the informal organization is composed of cliques, solitaries, and, sometimes, if immigrants are introduced, of cliques of outsiders.[1] In the latter kind of situation, 'mixing in' with other workers is desirable, but a solitary can retain his or her job, given a minimum conformity to workshop practice and a working performance satisfactory to management. The second type of formal organization, which is found in many mass-production firms, is likely to afford an easier entrance for immigrants. This is particularly true of firms like Telelux, where there has been a steady expansion, enlargement of production departments, fairly

[1] Cf. Hughes, op. cit., pp. 180–8 and Lipton, op. cit., p. 188–9, for a discussion of two extremes of formal and informal workshop organization in the American and English contexts. On informal organization generally, see Miller and Form, op. cit., p. 224 f., and for the types of worker participation, see ibid., pp. 498–501.

frequent transfer and up-grading of workers, and a high labour turnover.

Contacts and relationships between workers are usually more intimate and continuous than those between management or even supervisors and labour. They are therefore likely to be influenced by certain aspects of the formal organization of the work. For instance, some jobs are performed in the open air (like building); others at close quarters (e.g. some offices, laboratories, and factory team-jobs). Where people work at such close quarters that they can talk to their neighbours, some compatibility of interests and personality is obviously desirable. Then there is the kind of work which needs strong team spirit and awareness, such as the partnership between bus-driver and conductor, or the close, security-conscious co-operation needed in a railway shunters' gang. Some jobs involve working in heat or steam (for example, gas-works, laundries, or rubber manufactories). Where the process is dirty or where the atmosphere is hot and steamy, physiological factors also gain in importance and wide divergences in dietetic and hygienic practices may be more noticeable. Moreover, where canteen and cloakroom facilities are already inadequate or cramped the introduction of newcomers may provide a focus for existing discontent.

The acceptance of newcomers by the local labour-core, as by management, depends to a great extent on the capacities and characteristics of the particular immigrants whom choice, chance, or sponsorship introduces into their midst. Skills and working ability are respected as much by the labour-core as by management, although there are often different expectations about the ways in which these should be employed.[1] On the other hand, as has been pointed out,[2] personal characteristics are usually more important to local workers than they are to management, because of the greater intimacy of relations within the working group. And the manner and degree of acceptance depend to a considerable extent on the character of the labour-core. In most working units in Croydon, other than a few where ethnic teams and integrative situations were found, acceptance was on the basis of individual merit and traits, and there was little indication of the formation of established industrial minority groups of lesser acceptability, such as are found on the

[1] See J. A. Banks, 'The Sociology of Work', *Listener*, 2 May 1963.

[2] See pp. 219–20.

American industrial scene. A number of instances were found where an immigrant was more accepted as an in-group member than a local newcomer, or where a coloured individual was less of a stranger than a white person.

(iv) *Some Features of Labour-Cores*

The size, life-span, and demographic composition of a labour-core vary considerably from industry to industry and firm to firm, and even working unit to working unit. At one extreme we have the traditional close-knit working community of heavy engineering Firm A, with its 'Quarter-Century Club' and the close identification between its large, long-service labour-core and its managerial and supervisory hierarchy and also between the firm and the neighbourhood; at the other the temporary working unit that is often found on a large building site, with only a small nucleus of supervisory staff, craftsmen, and old-timers having any links with the firm.

The presence of a large, established core of local labour in an establishment does not usually speed the entry and absorption of immigrant workers. But those individuals who finally do 'make the grade' will find themselves satisfactorily and thoroughly absorbed as part of the working community. In such firms some form of 'sponsorship' often helps to speed this process.

In the few Croydon firms in which the labour-core was of considerable vintage, perhaps dating back to pre-war days, with the possibility of reinforcements on a local and family basis, the 'culture' of the factory was usually so complex and inflexible that any and all outsiders had difficulty in winning acceptance. The absorption of immigrants seemed to progress more easily in firms where the labour-core was not quite so traditional: for instance, in firms which had moved into the area since the War and had to start building up a labour nucleus from scratch. In some cases individual immigrants might even have become members of such a labour-core; this did not necessarily mean that the labour-core would be more willing to accept newcomers from other groups.

The survey material provided some indications that a labour-core which is not only older-established as a group but 'older' in the average age of its members tends to be less receptive to the entry of outsiders. This was noted in a small foundry-works, in some small precision engineering firms and in the older women's working groups in the mass-production factories.

The relative size of the labour-core also seemed to affect the entry and absorption of newcomers. In the rare cases when it was large enough to meet the firm's labour needs and self-perpetuating through the apprenticeship system and family or local connexions, there was little or no opening for an outsider. At the other end of the scale, particularly in seasonal or marginal industries, there was a small labour-core, sometimes linked closely with management and supervisors'; here immigrants would be permitted to enter as 'economic men, for instance as seasonal or casual unskilled labour, but not necessarily as part of the long-service core. In between there were a considerable number of firms with a fair-sized labour-core but a labour shortage, where immigrants were acceptable on their merits and general suitability, and might ultimately expect to become part of the labour-core.

(v) *Women's Working Groups*

The sex of the majority of a given labour force was one of the factors that helped to differentiate the four major industrial sectors in Croydon. It seemed probable that the sexual composition of the labour-core might also have an influence on the absorption of immigrants, particularly if women workers do, in fact, have a different attitude to industrial work than their male counterparts.

It is widely believed by management and male workers that women workers are more docile and have less capacity for collective action than men because of such reasons as the following: most do not rely entirely on industrial earnings for their support, they are often industrial 'birds of passage'; their main interests lie in the home; they have tended to occupy a subordinate role in working-class family life, and are accustomed to male dominance, which makes them more submissive to management dictates; and they lack experience of collective action. On the other hand, Lupton has recently suggested that this is not a complete explanation of women's attitude to and behaviour at work, and that whereas women workers in our society show a tendency towards individualism and away from collective controls, they may also be influenced by the customs and conventions of the industry (or firm) which they enter, whether these tend towards individualism or towards collective action.[1] This conformity could also include acceptance of prevailing attitudes to immigrant workers. This inquiry provided instances of both general tendencies, but it also brought out another feature of women workers' behaviour in all kinds of working culture that seemed of particular importance for the absorption of immigrants. For in most cases those women workers who formed the established core of a working group were less interested in the financial and more in the 'sociable' aspects of work than were the male workers or even the young women who would spend a few years working before they settled down to family life.[2] This was understandable because most women are not the sole breadwinners of their families and also because their salaries or wages are usually lower and their prospects of advancement limited. The desire for sociability was particularly noticeable in the married women's part-time shifts, many of whose members' main motivation was the wish to escape from the loneliness and boredom of domestic routine for a few hours of budget-augmenting work in congenial company. There was also rather more evidence of social contacts between full- and part-time workers outside the factory.

So far as the reception of immigrants was concerned, in general it seemed that women workers, even in some of the more cliquey groups,[3] accepted the entry of immigrants of their own sex

[1] For further discussion of these points, see T. Lupton, *On the Shop Floor*, Pergamon Press, 1963, pp. 91–92, 190–1. J. H. Smith has reported on a situation involving married women workers with only a limited 'desire to control' at Peek Frean's Bermondsey factory, *British Journal of Sociology*, Vol. XII, No. 1, March 1961, pp. 12–22. More recently E. Hopper has described the expectations and concerns of married women returning to work, in the light of a number of studies of working women. ('Some Effects of Supervisory Style', *British Journal of Sociology*, Vol. XVI, No. 3, September 1965, pp. 199–200.)

[2] In his inquiry into family life and industry (*The Worker in the Affluent Society*) Ferdynand Zweig interviewed a random sample of sixty-seven (nineteen part-time, the rest full-time) in one of the two Croydon mass-production light engineering firms. He found that the majority would prefer to work than stay at home, one of the most important incentives being companionship; that they disliked being transferred from one work-group to another even more than men; that only one in four were working because of economic necessity, the rest being motivated by a wish to achieve a higher standard of living for the family and a variety of other reasons. Regular contacts with fellow-workers outside the factory were also found to be far more frequent than among the men, especially among women in their thirties.

[3] For instance, Telelux, pp. 222–3. The married women's part-time shifts contained no immigrants, but this was due mainly to the fact that they were part-time, whereas most immigrant women wanted full-time work. There could

rather more easily than do the men, judging them less as a potential economic threat and more in terms of their sociability. Complaints about their behaviour, appearance, and personal hygiene were more often raised by women than by men, but in many units women workers were also quicker to befriend newcomers. The development of relations would also appear to have been strongly influenced by the way in which the work was organized (e.g. on a team or an individual basis), and the general conditions and degree of intimacy involved, but this was a factor that also operated in the case of male working groups.

The tendency to introduce off-the-job values in women's working groups was seen most clearly in particular status-conscious establishments or jobs, or when there was a question of introducing male immigrants into a predominantly female work-group.[1] It was not, however, always clear whether these values were introduced by the employees alone. In many cases where resistance was reported on either of these grounds, it seemed to be shared, if not actually imputed by management, particularly in situations which also involved contact with the public.[2] In cases where managements had promoted or even sponsored the entry of immigrants into white-collar units, employees usually seemed to have accepted them, although there were a few exceptions. The survey material suggested that where women employed on non-manual work had objected to the introduction of immigrant employees their objections were based on considerations of general socio-economic status and referred to both sexes, rather than to male immigrants on sexual grounds. On the shop floor the introduction of male immigrants into a department did not usually meet with any active resistance from the female labour-core.[3] This may be because the women usually worked and went to the canteen and cloakroom in all-female groups, while any men in the department would be doing different work and in general kept their distance (though a male supervisor might sit with his 'girls' in the tea-break). This routine sex segregation could, of course, lead to misunderstandings. For instance, after the introduction of the first West Indian labourer

also be a generational incompatibility, since many members of the part-time shifts were middle-aged or older women, where most immigrants were younger.

[1] See Telelux, pp. 310–11.

[2] E.g., Firm B, p. 318.

[3] See Telelux, p. 316, for a rather exceptional instance of such toleration.

into a particular unit in Telelux[1] it was noticed that the women operatives avoided sitting near the newcomer in the tea-break. This was at first interpreted as prejudice but further inquiry elicited the fact that the women liked to gossip among themselves in the break and avoided all masculine company; when coloured women were introduced to the group they mixed in and were accepted quite easily.

It seemed possible that local women workers would put up a much stronger resistance if immigrant men were to be put in a supervisory position over them. This issue was frequently discussed at Telelux; but again it was difficult to determine whether the resistance was actually felt by the women concerned, or whether it was, in part at least, a projection of the resistance felt by most supervisory informants (all male) to the idea of such up-grading.[2] In any case, it was clear that few if any of the immigrant candidates for up-grading to charge-hand conformed at all to the paternalistic model of a supervisor of female workers evolved by this firm, so that the chance to test actual resistance was unlikely to arise for some time to come.

(c) *The Immigrants*

(i) *Working Capacity and Demographic Criteria*

Whereas labour shortage is the most important antecedent external factor in providing newcomers with an entrée to particular industries or firms, the working capacity or potential emerged as one of the most important, if not *the* most important, of the internal factors influencing their subsequent absorption into Croydon industry. Immigrants with technical skills had little difficulty in finding appropriate work somewhere in Croydon, although they they might have encountered difficulties in fitting into the specific cultures of some firms or working units.

Most managements and unions are sceptical about the working qualities of any new group entering the labour force; these doubts

[1] See p. 313.

[2] For instances of ideal and actual relationships between male charge-hands and women workers encountered at Telelux, see pp. 309–11, 331–2. See also E. Hopper, op. cit., p. 200, for women workers' attitudes to supervisory behaviour.

may deepen into adverse stereotypes as a consequence of unsuccessful experiences, or they may be dispelled by successful ones. Even when an adverse stereotype is created, however, there is often a willingness to make an exception for individuals, particularly if their claim to consideration is backed by a good reference from a British employer or, better still, a local one, or by possession of some verifiable craft credentials.

With an immigrant's working capacity or potential is associated the question of his or her general suitability for a particular working community. The degree of suitability is associated with a number of qualitative and quantitative criteria, such as the newcomers' numbers, demographic structure, rate of arrival and length of stay, social and cultural background, degree of adaptability, attitudes to and expectations of the host community.

As we have shown, there were considerable differences between the principal immigrant groups found in Croydon industry in respect of most of these criteria. The East European refugees, and particularly the Polish ex-servicemen, were less strictly selected for specific work than the Central European economic migrants; most had been forced to accept economic down-grading but had sufficient resources of education, background, and character to start moving up the industrial ladder, to achieve a modest economic security and social status, and to encourage their children to rise still higher in the economic hierarchy. In some cases they had clearly been found more acceptable by management than by fellow-workers; this could be because of a widespread tendency among them to work harder than the norm established by a particular labour-core, or because of feelings of social distance induced by such features as a poor knowledge of English, different educational and social class background, voluntary self-segregation or the strongly anti-Communist views that prevail among almost all East European exiles.

Unlike the refugees, the European economic immigrants were selected for entry on strictly economic grounds, without the intrusion of humanitarian considerations. Most of them were thus people who have been selected for their general suitability as workers;[1] apart from some 'rate-busting' by zealous individuals they had

[1] The only exceptions were the European wives of local Britons, but these women had at least been individually selected as marital partners and thus could be seen as potentially assimilable in the local community.

on the whole been accepted as individuals in the various working communities where they were found, particularly in nursing.

With few exceptions the 'coloured' Commonwealth migrants lacked the educational and industrial background of most European refugees and immigrants. And, like the Southern Irish, the overwhelming majority had not at the time of this survey gone through any official selection process to determine their general suitability for employment in Britain. Any selection that occurred was either self-selection (which often meant the migration of the more enterprising and those with sufficient resources or credit to raise the fare) or, after arrival in Britain, the selective processes resulting from the requirements of particular areas, industries, and firms.

In the Croydon industrial area this latter kind of selection had been at work, and had brought in mostly West Indians, with relatively few Africans, Asians, and Anglo-Asians. The latter groups had mostly been 'white-collar' workers and professionals, or energetic 'pioneers' striking out on their own away from the main African and Asian migrant settlements. There had been further self-selection, as indeed with all immigrant workers to Croydon, in that many of them did not arrive by chance but chose to come and work there after being in other parts of London or Britain. The later arrivals were also often joining friends or relations already working in Croydon.

While the Southern Irish migrants are not officially selected, they have a long tradition of migration to Britain and the self-selection process is more efficient than it has yet become among the West Indians. Before they leave home the Southern Irish migrants know far more about the requirements of British industry and about the industries and firms where they can expect to find work. They are also frequently sponsored by relations or friends resident here or, as in the building industry, by Irish foremen who give them preference.

The general suitability of various groups of immigrants in the working context is, as has just been said, associated with a number of differing quantitative and qualitative criteria. The broader demographic aspects have already been mentioned at the beginning of this chapter, but some more detailed comments may be added here. We have seen how in Croydon the dimensions and rate of the industrial intake of immigrants were being regulated, not by government, but by a more or less informal imposition of quotas.

The informal industrial controls had also influenced the numbers and rate of build-up of immigrant settlement in Croydon, since most immigrants moved into the area only after finding work there. At this time there was a fair amount of residential concentration, but settlement was not so dense as in most immigrant reception areas; a major reason for this would seem to have been that for many immigrants, particularly the Poles, residence in Croydon represented a later phase of residential adaptation, in which they were moving into 'better' housing and 'better' areas.

The size and degree of concentration of an immigrant settlement, and also its possibilities of reinforcement, are important not only for their influence on the receiving society but also because they can affect its members' need and will to adapt to local *mores*. For instance, the West Indians were beginning to move into Croydon in sufficient numbers and concentration to permit the majority, if they so wished, to make only a minimal accommodation to local *mores*. Their numbers were being steadily reinforced and the stability and cohesiveness of the settlement was being increased by the arrival of women and children from home. It also seemed likely that their high visibility might make the settlement seem larger and more conspicuous in local eyes.

As the Croydon inquiry showed, age and sex distribution are two other demographic criteria which can affect the general 'suitability' of immigrants in industry, as in the wider society. Younger immigrants are usually more adaptable; on the other hand they may also be more unsettled, and those who are taking their first job may be handicapped by a different or curtailed education. Older immigrants are generally more stable, but they may find it difficult or impossible to requalify in their professions or crafts or, as in the case of the older Poles and other European exiles, to achieve sufficient fluency in English to qualify for anything but unskilled or semi-skilled work. As for women immigrants, their presence in a factory can ease off-the-floor sexual jealousies and fears; an immigrant family's budget is also enlarged by the contributions of a woman wage-earner, and the family's security, standard of living, and acceptability in the neighbourhood are thereby increased.

(ii) *Socio-Economic and Cultural Criteria*

The working ability or potential required in British industry is more likely to be found among immigrants from developed societies. Thus the Poles, the European economic migrants, most of the East European refugees and a minority of the Asians start well ahead of most West Indians. And even where educational and specialized training cannot be put to direct use in British industry, they often induce a flexible approach and an adaptability that help the immigrant to adjust and be accepted in his new job.

In the overall processes of immigrant absorption, religion and language are among the most important cultural elements; only the second of these seemed, however, to be particularly important in industrial absorption, at least in Croydon.[1] Knowledge of English is obviously important at work, and indeed essential in technical and professional positions, in work involving some element of danger, and in jobs involving communication with the public.[2] Moreover, up-grading and promotion are usually contingent on fluency in English, not only because it is directly necessary for communication but because poor English identifies its speaker audibly as a 'stranger', and thus as a person who is not acceptable in such a position.

In this study, poor English and problems of communication were frequently reported in connexion with the older Poles and other East European exiles and refugees. The barrier of audibility and intelligibility seemed, however, less marked in the case of the European economic immigrants, perhaps because most of them were younger, and thus found it easier to learn English; also because they were few in number and so dispersed that they were compelled to learn the language as soon as possible. Most Germans, Austrians, Dutch, and Scandinavians had also learned some English at school.

Those Commonwealth and other immigrants whose first or main language is English obviously start with an immense advantage in British industry. They include Australians, New Zealanders, Canadians, South Africans (white and non-white), Rhodesians,

[1] This might be less true in such areas as Glasgow and Liverpool. Religious problems are more likely to arise in factories in the case of non-Christians, who have a holy day other than Sunday, who must observe certain hours and periods of prayer or fasting, and who are bound by certain rituals relating to diet, personal cleanliness, and so on, which may conflict with the behaviour and patterns of the majority. In Croydon such problems were rarely mentioned—the only instances were in the case of a few sectarians who observed the Sabbath from Friday at sunset.

[2] See pp. 221–2, for a discussion of this aspect of 'intelligibility'.

East Africans (white and Asian), West Indians, Anglo-Indians, Irish, and North Americans. Most of the white English-speaking immigrants are identifiable by certain differences of accent and sometimes vocabulary, but this makes them seem no more or only a little more 'strange' to South Londoners than are the Scots or the 'scouse' speakers of Merseyside. The same applies in the case of Anglo-Indians, Cape Coloured, and similar groups, although their visibility may accentuate their strangeness.[1] In some cases, however, notably where poorly educated West Indians or Southern Irish from a rural background are involved, local workers may find them difficult to understand, and the advantage of having English as a first language is nominal rather than real.

The Commonwealth immigrants to Britain also include a large group whose first language is not English—immigrants from India and Pakistan, South-East Asia, various African territories, and the Mediterranean islands. These are subdivided into a non-English-speaking majority and a minority who have learned English as a second language, usually at secondary schools in their home country. In Croydon the majority of such immigrants appeared to belong to the latter group, or have learned English adequately since their arrival here, and no particular problems were reported in the industrial sphere at this time.[2]

(iii) *Education, Class, and Culture*

Among non-English-speaking and English-speakers alike the language question is closely associated with educational and socio-economic class background. A Pole or a Pakistani coming from a middle-class urban background is often better equipped to break through the barrier of language than is a working-class West Indian or an Irishman with a few years of primary school and a background of rural underemployment.[3] Where the educational and training facilities and the whole socio-economic and cultural environment are more closely related to those of the receiving society, as in the

[1] See pp. 221–3, for a more detailed discussion of visibility.

[2] But see Desai, *Indian Immigrants in Britain*, London, Oxford University Press for the Institute of Race Relations, 1963, p. 9, on the initial difficulties experienced even by university-educated Indians in making the linguistic adjustment from English as a language largely written and read to English as used verbally in everyday situations.

[3] Although such a middle-class newcomer can encounter some class hostility if he is occupationally down-graded to a manual or lower white-collar job.

'old Dominions', urban Ireland, and among the small Europeanized élites of the West Indies, West Africa, and the Asian Commonwealth, absorption is likely to be faster.[1]

The greatest cultural similarity undoubtedly exists between the 'Anglo-Saxon' immigrants and the English receiving society, and these immigrants are usually absorbed most rapidly and easily in industry, as in the society as a whole, although acceptance of Anglo-Indians and other visibly distinguishable immigrants with an 'Anglo-Saxon' cultural background is slowed by such factors as the rough colour-class identification still common in Britain.

Some immigrants come from cultures which are not so directly associated with that of the host society as the 'Anglo-Saxon' cultures, but which are nevertheless compatible in a number of important elements. This applies to many European immigrants, who come from cultures and societies which have, like Britain, been influenced by the same religious, social, and political ideals and movements, which have an ancient, intertwined history, and which are more or less urbanized, industrialized, and cosmopolitan in outlook.

In the industrial sphere, the majority of European immigrants[2] are familiar at the time of their arrival with urban life, industrial routine and discipline, the function of trade unions, the concept of a 'fair day's work' (although in some cases their standards on this score may be higher than the local ones). This is probably a more important factor for their long-term absorption than the more immediately noticeable cultural and behavioural differences which provoke initial objections from local workers.

In the short term, however, considerable friction and ill-feeling can be created on both sides by such conspicuous differences in everyday behaviour and cultural patterns, involving, for example, food and eating habits, dress and hair-styles, toilet habits, drinking habits and behaviour, method of fighting, choice of language, jokes, and use of swear-words, manners, and demeanour to members of their peer-group, to the other sex, to superiors and inferiors, and even dancing style in the social club or sportsmanship in the games field. Such frictions were reported in Croydon, but to a far lesser extent than in the South London firms which I visited in 1956–7.

[1] See Berry, op. cit., p. 239, on cultural kinship and rates of assimilation.

[2] An exception must be made for some Southern Italian, Spanish, and Portuguese peasants, and for younger refugees (like some of the 1956 Hungarians) who arrive from Communist-dominated East European countries (see below, p. 259 n. 1).

This could be attributed to the difference between the small, rather traditional South London firms, mostly engaged in heavy industry or marginal and seasonal light industrial production, and the more progressive light engineering and industrial firms of the Croydon industrial area, with their modern conditions, higher labour turnover and special provisions for handling personnel problems. Moreover, Croydon industry seems to have attracted something of an élite of immigrant workers, through the processes of selection and self-selection already mentioned.

(iv) *Some Specific Values and Attitudes*

While many cultural and behavioural patterns are superficial and susceptible to rapid adaptation under the pressure of a new society, some are the outward expression of values and attitudes that are part of the very ethos of a community. These cannot so easily be changed, and in cases where they conflict with the values and attitudes of the receiving society, they must undoubtedly hinder the process of absorption.[1]

Such basic differences and conflicts are more likely to emerge and provoke friction in informal social contacts or in situations where two groups find themselves living at close quarters in the same house or street. In the industrial situation, there was a small amount of friction in Croydon over differing attitudes to women and sex, but the main difficulties seemed to arise over differing attitudes to work, often complicated by considerations of social status. Immigrant attitudes to work varied from the energetic, even 'rate-busting', attitude of some European immigrants to the seasonal rhythm and high mobility of many young Irish men and women, and the strong aversion to domestic work and anything that resembles menial work found among West Indians;[2] a similar aversion was found among technically and professionally qualified Asians and Africans, some of whom would object if they were expected to do manual bench work.[3]

Another complex of values and attitudes which is particularly common among West Indians and Anglo-Indians has also led to misunderstanding and friction in the work situation. This complex includes the 'white bias', the colour-class hierarchy and the

[1] For instance, 'strangeness' and 'unpredictability' may slow up-grading and promotion (p. 310).

[2] Cf. *Dark Strangers*, pp. 82–83. [3] See Telelux, pp. 334, 336.

strong class and colour-consciousness that are central elements in these communities. In Britain it has often led newcomers, at work as elsewhere, to interpret all situations and set-backs in terms of colour prejudice and discrimination. This hypersensitive reaction, widely reported by management informants in Croydon under the term 'chip on the shoulder', often inhibited more complete acceptance by local supervisors and workers who, while they might associate colour in general with strangeness or low status, were not colour-conscious to anything like the same degree as the newcomers, and found it irksome to have to watch their words and behaviour so closely with individuals whom they would otherwise have regarded as quite acceptable.

(v) *Motivations, Intentions, Expectations, and Preconceptions*[1]

Croydon industry has received workers from both ideologically motivated and economically motivated immigrant groups. The ideological motivation has been blurred or eroded among many Poles by time and circumstance. In the early days of settlement it was, however, manifested in organized political and other activities aimed at liberating and returning to the homeland. To the able-bodied, work was a necessity for subsistence but the goal was still the traditional ideological one and few initially sought full absorption or advancement in the British economy or British society—theirs was a state of mind expressed in the Polish phrase 'sitting on one's suit-cases'.

Among the Poles, particularly the ex-servicemen, moreover, considerable initial bitterness was felt over the hostility shown by trade unions and British labour generally in the immediate post-war years, and the British reluctance to accept the industrial skills which they had acquired in Poland. But this was interpreted less as rejection by the host society than as Communist-inspired and therefore part of the whole chain of political and military events which had brought Poland under Soviet domination and prevented the exiles from returning home. And, as with all peoples and nations whose geo-political history has conditioned them to periodic occupation, persecution, and exile, an exile tradition of resistance, endurance, and abnegation has grown up over the decades. This

[1] See S. N. Eisenstadt, *The Absorption of Immigrants*, London, Routledge and Kegan Paul, 1954, pp. 2–4, on the importance of understanding the immigrant's motives for migration and his 'image' of the new country.

tradition has often stood Poles, Hungarians, and others in good stead at work as well as in the wider society.

For most of the older Polish exiles the ideological motivation has persisted and intra-group political, cultural, and social activities continue to provide satisfaction and prestige, although the goal of liberation and return has receded far into the shadows and permanent exile has become more or less accepted. But for the middle-aged and young, particularly for those with professional and artisan training or financial acumen, the migrant has been replaced by the settler and the ideological goal has gradually yielded in priority to economic goals. These economic goals still, however, have an 'ideological' tinge, since a bigger pay-packet enables the exiles not only to achieve security by buying a home of their own but also to help their families in Poland and perhaps to contribute to ethnic voluntary and parish organizations here.

Meanwhile the earlier attitude of minimal expectancy lingers on and is reflected in cautious attitudes to the idea of promotion and the widespread willingness to accept permanent economic down-grading while working for the up-grading of the second and younger generation. Thus the ideological motivation has, almost paradoxically, furthered the economic absorption of the majority of the war-time and immediate post-war East European exiles, by causing them to enter industry with low aspirations. Moreover, most were subject to direction of labour and restrictions on job mobility for the first years of their entry into British industry and this, harsh as it often seemed, often had a compensatory stabilizing effect.[1]

By contrast with the ideologically motivated immigrants, those who came to Britain for economic reasons have naturally been concerned above all with economic goals, whether it is a question of the accumulation of a nest-egg or of the acquisition of a skill or

[1] This did not apply to the post-1956 Hungarian refugees. They differed from the earlier exiles on two further counts, both of which were likely to hinder rather than promote absorption, economic or otherwise: (1) Not all were, in fact, ideological refugees; some were very young people who left the country in an adventurous spirit and a minority were non-political criminals released when the jails were opened during the rising. (2) Before arriving they had lived for years under Nazi or Communist-dominated totalitarian régimes, in which go-slow methods, poor workmanship, industrial sabotage, theft of materials, and similar actions were widespread and indeed one of the few possible ways of registering protest. Unlike the Poles, few had experienced the discipline of army life nor were they familiar with a type of labour relations in which neither the management nor the trade unions are state-controlled.

profession. Like the ideologically motivated, the initial intention of most economic migrants other than the Anglo-Indians and Cape Coloured[1] has always been to return home as soon as the object of the migration was achieved. But this twin goal of economic achievement and return is in reality achieved only by a proportion, possibly a minority, of economically motivated immigrants in Britain. So far, most of the successful ones seem to have come from Southern Ireland, the Mediterranean Commonwealth territories or from the ranks of the Central and South European workers admitted for specific work on Ministry of Labour vouchers.

Among such migrants there is usually a close correspondence between intentions, working ability, and expectations of the receiving society. Those migrants who intend to stay only a few years, working hard and saving money or learning a skill, and who at the same time do not cherish high expectations of immediate or complete acceptance by the receiving society, can generally reach a reasonable degree of accommodation in the economic sphere.[2] If after a few years such migrants decide to settle, they have usually got through the initial teething troubles of accommodation and are ready and acceptable for further absorption.

A fairly close correspondence between intentions, working ability, and expectations is imposed on the European economic immigrants by the selective and restrictive processes of the Ministry of Labour. Immigrants from Southern Ireland and Cyprus have not been so strictly selected or controlled, but they tend to be self-selected in the sense that they have established a bridgehead in particular trades or occupations, that they are following a familiar trail, are received by established members of their own communities and in general know what to expect of Britain.[3]

[1] These and similar immigrants are usually settler-minded from the start, having made a permanent choice between two countries and two ways of life. The English way is seen as closer, more compatible, and likely to offer more economic opportunities for these migrants and their children than remaining at home under the new Nationalist régimes, as the former modest rights and privileges of the mixed groups are whittled away. Such immigrants therefore arrive with the intention of settling permanently and of seeking assimilation as individuals and family units. Their ambitions are usually modest and their working skills or abilities adequate to win them acceptance in skilled, semi-skilled, or 'white-collar' work. A number of gifted individuals have also found success and acceptance in the world of the creative arts.

[2] See article by John Barr on the absorption of Italians in Bedford, 'Napoli, Bedfordshire', *New Society*, 2 April 1964.

[3] See Jackson, op. cit., p. 18.

Such a close correspondence between intentions, working ability, or potential and expectations has less frequently been found among migrants from the coloured Commonwealth territories, at least until the immigration restrictions were imposed in mid-1962. In the earlier years of settlement the West Indians, in particular, afforded a good example of a group characterized by impermanent intentions and low working potential, allied with high expectations of high wages, industrial advancement, and immediate and complete acceptance by the receiving society.[1] This combination of characteristics, combined with complete freedom of entry, residence, and job-finding, often led to poor working performance, high labour turnover, excessive pretensions over skills and wages, and friction in relations with management and local labour. It thus operated to slow adaptation and acceptance until intentions became more permanent, expectations more modest and working potential higher. In the last half of the 1950s, however, after the recession and redundancy of 1955–6, there was a shift towards the pattern of intra-group self-selection,[2] reception, induction, and aid found among the Southern Irish, Cypriots, and Maltese, as the various West Indian settlements became more established, and earlier migrants have established modest bridgeheads as a regular source of labour in an increasing number of firms, industries and areas.[3] In Croydon, for instance, one heard much less about the unadaptability, aggressiveness, absenteeism, high turnover, and other traits which were so widely commented upon in the earlier years of West Indian settlement.

Newcomers' expectations of the receiving society are influenced not only by their motives for coming but also by any preconceptions about Britain or any 'special' cultural and other relationships with this country that may exist in their countries of origin. If the preconceptions and anticipated relationships are greatly at variance with reality, this again will be a factor impeding accommodation.

For instance, many people in former colonial territories such as the West Indies, the various African countries, and even India and Pakistan, still have an outmoded and distorted image of the

[1] See *Dark Strangers*, p. 79.

[2] By that time West Indians had been arriving in increasing numbers for several years. It was also a period of minor recession, in which some unsatisfactory workers were made redundant and new arrivals took far longer to find work.

[3] For this process among Indian immigrants, see Desai, op. cit. *passim*.

'mother country', derived from experience of an upper-middle-class colonial service, armed forces, missionaries, traders, and planters, and from exposure to British-orientated educational systems, the social exclusiveness of the local British élite, and the splendid trappings of colonial rule. The shock of exposure to the workaday, de-colonialized, drabbly affluent 'Little Britain' of today is often severe, particularly for immigrants such as the West Indians who, unlike most Asian migrants, do not wish to work and live in self-segregating communities. Later, of course, such preconceptions and expectations are modified, as earlier settlers report back to the home country and brief newcomers on what to expect.

The Irish migrants have formed an entirely different set of historical stereotypes and preconceptions about the English. In earlier years most were induced to migrate to Britain, not by any enthusiasm for the country or its people but by famine, unemployment, proximity, and the cheapness of the fare, compared with the cost of even a steerage passage to the New World. More recently the hatred and bitterness have become somewhat blunted and life in Britain has acquired considerable attraction because of its urban sophistication and amenities, good wages, and freedom from family and social controls, combined with continued proximity to home, so that a complete break does not have to be made.[1] This appeals to those migrants who do not wish to make the great and usually permanent decision to settle in the United States or Canada. Some Irish in Britain continue migrant in intention, working several spells in Britain before settling down at home; but others accommodate themselves quickly and settle in the established first- and second-generation Irish communities which have grown up in so many British cities. In some areas these communities seem to be not fully integrated in the wider society, but marginal, deprived, almost self-depriving, and at the bottom of the urban occupational ladder. This could have been the case in Croydon, but the available evidence did not point to it.

Before 1939 the preconceptions and stereotypes current about Britain and the British in Poland and other East European countries were not based on any particularly close or 'special' relationships nor on a great deal of first-hand contact. There were historical and political links, mostly of a friendly nature, and Britain was recalled, with France, as a country with free institutions which

[1] See Jackson, op. cit., p. 28.

had traditionally opened its doors to earlier waves of political exiles and refugees.[1] France was more of a cultural magnet and inspiration, for the Poles at least, but Britain was widely respected and even admired. These views were reinforced after the fall of France in 1940, when the Polish Government and its surviving armed forces moved to Britain to continue the fight. The close links forged between ordinary fighting-men and civilians during the war years survived even the bitterness and sense of betrayal engendered in Poles, Yugoslavs, and others by the series of political events that followed Soviet Russia's entry into the War and occupation of East Europe, which left most of them with little choice but to remain in exile indefinitely.

After the 1939–45 War, when intra-continental migration again became possible, a further process of self-selection took place. Those Poles and others who were adventurous or found Britain particularly uncongenial migrated overseas, leaving behind those who had come to terms with British life or were willing to do so. Several thousand, indeed, had already married British girls. In the years that have passed since then, political bitterness has tended to give place to the more traditional feelings of respect and appreciation, even among the least adaptable and assimilated members of what is increasingly a British 'Polonia'.

(d) *Working Communities and Cultures*

We have now discussed under separate heads the principal ways in which the three main interest-groups involved—management, local labour, and the immigrants themselves—can influence the processes of industrial absorption. The emphasis so far has been rather on differences of approach than on interaction; it may now be useful to consider the interaction of management and labour in different working communities and 'cultures' in relation to the absorption of immigrant workers. For although management usually calls the tune, and the local labour-core may seem too weak, indifferent, or remote from senior management to exert any direct influence on a situation, the two interest-groups are bound together in an association which has a specific 'culture' and is at least potentially a working community, albeit more or less hierarchical and at times in a state of internal conflict rather than consensus.

[1] See Zubrzycki, op. cit., pp. 31–38.

Although the range of variation is limited by the fact that all working communities and cultures are functioning within the same wider local framework, there are, as we saw in Croydon, considerable differences of working climate between industries and industrial sectors, based on such factors as the type of manufacture, the nature and status of the work done, and the sex of the majority of the labour force.[1] But although similar kinds of working community and culture are frequently found in a particular industrial sector or industry, there can also, as we have seen, be considerable differences between firms in the same sector or industrial group, and even between departments, sections, units, and occupational groups within the same firm. These are produced by the operation of other variables, mostly arising out of the three factors above that were used for the original classification into industrial sectors: these variables include the size and age of the firm or unit; formal and informal organization; general management–labour relations; the size of labour-cores and degree of job security; the presence or absence of opinion-forming individuals and groups, including trade unions and the closeness of ties with the locality.

In Croydon the range of working communities included firms in which informal organization was confined to small core-community of supervisors and long-term employees[2] and also firms with a closely integrated informal organization which embraced most of the staff and labour force. It included small, traditional 'skilled' firms, usually owner-managed, where the management–labour division was barely perceptible and labour turnover was low, and also large mass-production firms with a complex vertical stratification in which the top management was to the majority of hourly paid workers little more than a string of names on a letterhead, in which working groups were frequently formed and broken up and

[1] See p. 48, for an account of the classification of the various industries into four main sectors according to these criteria.

[2] Lupton refers to the close identification of some workers with management in a number of small garment firms as a feature common to the industry. It does not, however, necessarily involve a convergence of interests or goals between workers and management. He presents the two firms which he studied as lying at either end of a continuum in terms of clusters of factors influencing workshop behaviour—at the one end a small firm, intense competition, lack of mechanization, high labour costs, women workers, weak trade union workshop organization, lack of worker control, etc., at the other the reverse situation (op. cit., pp. 194–9). See also p. 2531, for informal ties connecting management and labour groups. D. C. Miller and W. H. Form, *Industrial Sociology*, Harper & Row, New York and London, 1964.

cliques were discouraged, and in which labour turnover could run as high as 25 per cent. In such large firms, however, the variations in the degree of culture and group cohesion between departments, sections, and shifts were often quite striking.

Also within the Croydon range were small, ruthless, highly competitive firms in seasonal or marginal industries, traditional, rather paternalistic establishments, and status-conscious, white-collar departments. Working communities ranged from the rigidly hierarchical and authoritarian to the informal and egalitarian,[1] but all were going concerns—whether the organization was based on joint consultation, informal consensus, endemic conflict, paternalism, or plain old-fashioned bossmanship. The different types of community and culture tended to be self-perpetuating, particularly in a situation of full employment which permitted those workers who did not like a particular firm or working-group to find work elsewhere. On the other hand, those who found the atmosphere congenial would stay on and bring in relatives, friends, and other likely recruits. Clearly this also applied to immigrants. A particular factory or working group tried to recruit the most suitable, while those immigrants who found the atmosphere congenial were more likely to stay and to introduce their own recruits.[2] This selective process would usually lead to 'clustering' by one or more of the different immigrant groups.

Harmonious and well-integrated working communities, and strongly individualistic working cultures are most likely to be found in establishments located in small towns or villages with a settled population. In Croydon there was still a certain element of this local stability and local association,[3] but integrated working

[1] See Miller and Form, op. cit. pp. 762–64, for a suggested hierarchy of authority relations.

[2] Cf. pp. 223–7, for 'clustering' and the 'favoured nation' principle.

[3] For instance, in some of the smaller factories, in shops and offices and in local government administration. Moreover, most of the organizations that moved into the area after the War, while they were less hampered by local ties and taboos, had also made a definite effort to build up a steady local labour nucleus, even though this was more likely to include settled immigrants who were or became local residents.

A study by Sigmund Nosow of the industrial distribution of various 'origin' groups (Negroes, foreign-born, Southern-born, locals) in a Michigan city shows a comparable variation of employment patterns. The industries were classified by type, size, and pattern of ownership (local or absentee). The relevance of non-economic norms, and the presence of selective hiring policies, were shown by

communities and cultures were usually found in established firms employing a large percentage of skilled or semi-skilled workers, of married men, and of older women. Even in large firms with a high overall labour turnover, certain departments or working units were highly integrated and had evolved their own culture almost against the overall ethos. The age of the firm obviously affected the development of a special culture and sense of community, and size seemed to have a considerable influence. When the labour force exceeded a certain number—perhaps 500 (more than the managing director or works manager could know by name)[1]—pride in the firm's name and product could remain but loyalty would be focused on to a particular division, department, or section. In smaller firms the core-community was often small and there was a greater tendency for a highly individualistic culture to be evolved, often influenced by a single individual.[2]

In Croydon the well-integrated, harmonious working communities were not usually the most ready to try out immigrant workers, whether because they did not suffer from any great labour shortage or because of a strong desire on the part of local labour as well as management to preserve the existing character of the firm.[3] Where such firms had taken on immigrants, only a minority had usually stayed the course; but these had achieved a more complete acceptance and assimilation than could be attained in less stable and close-knit communities.[4]

The kind of working community and culture to which all

the fact that local workers were most strongly represented in transportation, wholesale and retail trade, and 'other manufacturing' firms, which were usually small and locally owned. Negroes and the foreign-born were disproportionately concentrated in the large, absentee-owned plants, in the forges, foundries, automotive, and other service industries. ('Labor Distribution and the Normative Order', *Social Forces*, 1956.)

[1] See also Brown, op. cit., pp. 121–2, 300, and Taylor, op. cit., pp. 124–5.

[2] As we have seen, even Croydon's 100-plus industry contained a fair number of these small firms, which have been relatively little studied by industrial sociologists.

[3] Cf. Hughes, pp. 180–1, op. cit., for the successful connivance between foremen and older workers to keep Negroes out of a particular workshop. See also pp. 214–19, for a longer discussion of the use of informal quotas as a mechanism to protect the character and culture of a working community.

[4] See Firm A, pp. 74–9, for an instance of this process; in the single case in which this firm operated against its own 'culture' by taking on a large group of West Indian women on the 'economic man' principle the experiment was a complete failure.

newcomers to industry, from school-leavers to immigrants, are exposed undoubtedly exerts an important influence on their later absorption in industry and ultimately in the wider society. Casual labourers or seasonal workers in a firm dominated by a small exclusive core of management and long-term employees may find it less difficult to be hired, but they are less likely to be admitted to the working community or encouraged to participate fully in its culture. Instead they are usually kept in the earliest stage of accommodation, as expendable, interchangeable 'economic men'. In some 'transit-camp' industries and firms in Croydon, however, a minority of immigrants were settling and themselves becoming part of the working community, like the long-service unskilled local workers who have established themselves as personalities and institutions in a particular factory.

The kind of working community and culture was strongly influenced by the nature and status of the work done, as such descriptions as 'heavy industry' or 'white-collar and professional sector' imply. The differences emerged even more clearly when individual establishments and departments were surveyed. Very different cultures were likely to prevail in, say, a board-room, a scientific laboratory, a nurses' common room, a typists' pool, a craftsmen's closed shop, an older women's semi-skilled shift, and a gang of manual labourers.[1] The different climates found in various kinds of professional and white-collar work were particularly striking. These will be discussed again in the section dealing with the influence of the fourth interest-group—the public—on the entry and reception of immigrants in industry. Here, however, it may be noted that certain kinds of professional and white-collar work (for instance, in hospitals, welfare work, teaching, and work with an element of service) involve close, even intimate contact and *rapport* with people, while others (for example, laboratory work, engineering, accounting, etc.) are more concerned with ideas and inanimate

[1] 'Other studies carried out by my colleagues emphasized the differences in worker behaviour, from industry to industry, from factory to factory, from workshop to workshop. We began to suspect generalizations about worker behaviour. . . . It now looked as if there were fruitful lines for advance. It might be wise to look first at the social and economic environment in which a factory is "embedded" rather than to start with detailed observation of behaviour—to look at technology, size, organization, etc., and then to go on to compare the behaviour of people in the organization to see whether different combinations and weightings of these variables seem to be associated with different kinds of workshop behaviour' (Tom Lupton, *New Society*, 15 November 1962).

objects, and involve contact mainly over technical matters. Not only do these two kinds of work frequently attract psychologically different types of people—they continue to condition the climate of their particular working communities.[1] In offices, however, the climate seems to be imposed less by the requirements of the work and more by considerations of precarious security and status and by the presence of class-conscious supervisors.

So far as the entry and reception of immigrants was concerned, the climate usually appeared to be more propitious in those non-manual working communities in Croydon where the security and status of members was less precarious. This was generally the case in working groups with the highest professional or technical qualifications and opportunities (and the least fear of redundancy). Members of such groups are also more likely to have been exposed during their training and occupational lives to a more tolerant, less insular set of ideas and attitudes than the class-conscious majority of white-collar workers. It was interesting to note that such attitudes extended as far as white-collar workers in the education department in Council C, and that the tolerant climate in a co-operative firm had ensured the employment of a handful of Asian and African clerical workers.[2]

In those Croydon retail and clerical establishments where security and status were the main considerations the climate seemed to be more favourable for immigrants in the more 'select' firms. Although this may sound paradoxical, it was probably attributable to the greater sense of ease and security felt by staff in these establishments; the situation was frequently paralleled in industrial firms where there was a secure and harmonious working community.

Despite the variety of working communities and cultures found in Croydon, and the differing influences which these exert on the absorption of immigrants, it must be stressed once again that the majority shared one very important characteristic—managers and men alike thought in terms of the ultimate assimilation of individual newcomers rather than of pluralistic integration or segregation. There was a general expectation, conscious or unconscious, that newcomers should conform, adapt themselves and finally join 'our own people', at least in the industrial sphere. This expectation could be of increasing importance in furthering assimilative absorption in the wider society in the years to come.

[1] See Telelux, p. 343. [2] See pp. 152, 144–5.

(e) *Sponsors and Blackballers*

In addition to the economic, socio-cultural, and other factors already discussed, the culture of a working community is often influenced, if not determined, by the views and behaviour of an individual or a small clique. In Croydon this feature was most in evidence in the smaller firms and in certain working units within all the 100-plus firms surveyed—and we found a number of these with their own highly individualistic, if not idiosyncratic cultures, built up and maintained by a particularly forceful personality or clique in a position of formal or informal leadership. Examples of such individualistic working communities were the 'hilarious' and the 'select' firms (E and F) in light engineering (pp. 65–8), the highly paternalistic light industrial Firm A (pp. 108–11), some of the older women's shifts in Telelux (p. 303), and parts of British Rail (p. 97 f.).

Such opinion-forming individuals and cliques do not only condition the climate of the working group—they also influence the way in which immigrants are received in these groups. This influence may be exerted in the direction of 'sponsoring' the newcomers or of 'blackballing' them. Where 'clusters' of immigrants and 'favoured nation' groups were found in Croydon firms, their existence could often be traced to the activities of such sponsors (or to the presence of compatriots who had been sufficiently accepted to sponsor later comers). On the other hand, the absence of all immigrants or of certain ethnic groups, or a history of past failures and sackings, could sometimes be definitely attributed to the presence of 'anti-sponsors' or 'blackballers' in management, the personnel department, among supervisors, or in the informal organization of the working unit.[1] In Telelux, for instance, it was possible to trace a chain reaction right down the line, produced by the presence of sponsors and anti-sponsors at fairly high levels in the management hierarchy.[2]

Outside agencies such as employment exchanges, trade unions, employers' associations, co-ordinating committees, or churches can also play a sponsoring role, and there was some evidence of

[1] It might appear, and indeed it would be reasonable to expect, that there is more blackballing among workers and lower supervisors than in senior management in Croydon; but, as most of the material came from management spokesmen, this can be no more than a hypothesis for further testing.

[2] See Charts on pp. 396–7 for 'chains of sponsorship' and evidence of 'lily-white tradition'.

this in Croydon. The employment exchange, which had, in conjunction with local welfare organizations, been very successful in placing Hungarians a few years earlier, was not at this period being as active a sponsor as exchanges in areas like Brixton. This was not because of any change of attitude but for the simple reason that there was less need; most earlier immigrants were settled and did not register, while most new immigrants were finding their own jobs and not coming to the local exchange. There were reports of successful placings by agencies concerned with hotels and catering, and the brick industry's scheme for recruiting Italian labour was a successful example of industrial sponsorship. The favourable opinions expressed about Barbadians on the railways and elsewhere were a reminder of another successful arrangement, that between the Barbadian Government and various British industries, notably public transport and catering.[1] In Croydon, however, the survey provided more instances of sponsoring (and the reverse) by individuals or cliques, in particular firms and working groups, than by outside agencies.

Sponsoring is usually selective, and restricted to one or two similar immigrant groups, a feature which contributes to its success. But successful sponsorship appears to depend above all upon the position and prestige of the sponsoring individual or group within the receiving community.[2] The effectiveness of such sponsorship can, however, be countered by blackballing activities on the part of other powerful agencies, as for instance, by closed shops in the printing trade and engineering tool-rooms, or, to take an instance from outside Croydon, by British miners when the National Coal Board sought to introduce Italian and Hungarian miners into the industry.[3] Moreover, sponsoring individuals or groups that are themselves on the periphery of the receiving society (for in-

[1] For further details of this, see *Dark Strangers*, pp. 96–97.

[2] This and other aspects of sponsorship were elaborated by Sydney Collins in a paper on 'Recent Trends in Race Relations in Britain', in which he contrasted the higher prestige in British society of those who had sponsored Jews, Chinese, and the Hungarians in 1956 with the lower prestige of most sponsors of West Indians and Muslims. (*Race Relations Journal* (*S.A.*), Vol. XXVII, No. 1, January–March 1960, pp. 47–51.)

[3] Where there is a management–union disagreement over the entry of immigrants, management is more frequently found on the sponsoring side, while the unions (at least at local level) are more likely to act as blackballers. No instance was found in Croydon of a union successfully sponsoring the entry of immigrants against management, although this has been reported elsewhere.

stance, earlier arrivals or peripheral pressure groups) are unlikely to assist the entry of newcomers into the inner core-society and can even, by over-enthusiastic and injudicious lobbying, hinder the acceptance of the newcomers by the overall host society.

Sponsoring activities are variously motivated—they can arise out of cultural or temperamental predisposition towards or close association with a specific group of newcomers (through visits to their homeland, family ties, and so on); or out of a generalized attitude of philanthropy or positive tolerance; or again, out of individual psychological needs, power-drives and frustrations. Similar motivations operate, but in reverse, in the case of anti-sponsorship or blackballing activities. In both kinds of activity, those with extreme motivations seem to operate less effectively than those whose more moderate views and actions do not go against the general climate of opinion in their own community. In other words, not all would-be sponsors or blackballers become opinion-formers, but only those who operate within the culture of the group or society.[1] And the Croydon evidence suggested strongly that selective sponsoring by middle-of-the-roaders is likely to be far more effective, at least in the industrial situation, than indiscriminate benevolence. For sponsorship is a factor which can secure the newcomers' entry into an establishment, but cannot ensure their further acceptance unless their working ability or potential and their general suitability are such as to meet its requirements. It may well be, too, that sponsorship is more effective in establishments and work-groups which also contain some members who are not active sponsors but the sort of people who, in the revealing phrase used by an informant in Telelux (see p. 343), act as 'social cement' in a group.

(f) *Pioneers, Leaders, and Interpreters*

Established immigrants sometimes sponsor the entry of more recently arrived compatriots, although there are also instances of settled groups or individuals resisting or even blackballing the entry of newcomers of their own or other groups, usually either for

[1] Individuals with a 'wog complex', acquired after some first-hand experience, however superficial, are, however, in a fairly strong position in this respect, particularly as a good number occupy personnel and supervisory posts. In general, blackballing is likely to be more effective if it appears to be the product of knowledge or reason, than if the blackballer is regarded as generally immoderate unreasonable, and extreme in his views.

status reasons or to demonstrate their solidarity with the local working community.

Apart from acting as sponsors there are some other positive roles which immigrant individuals and pressure groups can perform, particularly in the phase of accommodation. These are the roles of pioneer, interpreter, and leader. In Croydon the pioneers were most in evidence—the individuals who, with initiative and perseverance had found themselves jobs and won sufficient acceptance to ensure an easier entry for later comers and protégés. In some cases the successful pioneer arrived at a particular firm by accident, but in others there could be an element of self-selection, as for instance an order of job-preference different from that of local workers; this meant that the immigrant pioneer in certain industries was likely to be of better calibre than the average local recruit. At times, of course, the pioneer could prove unsuited to the particular requirements and climate of the firm and entry for others was rendered more difficult.

As absorption proceeds, successful pioneers may become interpreters or go-betweens between newcomers and the local working community. Some may also become informal leaders. In Croydon industry, however, with its 'assimilating' ethos and its low reliance on ethnic gangs, few interpreters or leaders were found, in contrast to areas and firms which have come to rely on large contingents of non-English-speaking immigrant labour.[1] Interpreters and informal leaders were found in only a few establishments, notably the railway workshop, some building gangs, the die-casters, and some firms which employ a good deal of seasonal labour, as, for instance, the sweet manufacturers (Firm B).

* * *

The activities of opinon-formers, whether sponsors or blackballers, and pioneers and interpreters, can clearly exert a considerable influence on the processes of immigrant absorption in a particular working group or community. The presence of such individuals or cliques is not always discernible, but it may well be that they (or at least the opinion-formers) exist in most working groups and situations. Where they were in evidence in Croydon their influence was clearly one of the main reasons for the variations found

[1] See Peter Wright, research note on 'Go-Betweens in Industry', Institute of Race Relations *Newsletter*, January 1964, pp. 28–30.

between establishments and work-groups which resembled each other in most characteristics. These variations could be considerable, but they were of course limited by the fact that for effectiveness such action had to be taken in accordance within the general climate of opinion in the work-group or establishment, which in its turn operated within the larger local society, and in conformity with its major norms and values.

(g) *The Public and the Wider Society*

The fourth grouping involved in the process of industrial absorption is the receiving society at large. It is not so directly involved as the other three groups, but exerts an important influence in two capacities: firstly as the public (in this case the consumers or clients who are served in various ways by the working community) and secondly, and even more important, as the local or overall culture-bearing community which, while not in the strict sense an industrial interest-group, sets the range of climates for the industrial area and expects newcomers to adapt to its major norms and values.

(i) *Consumers, Clients, and Public*

Consumers and clients can influence the work situation either directly, by their reaction to the presence of immigrants in particular occupational roles, or indirectly, as a reference group, cited by management or employees, for a variety of motives, to oppose the entry of newcomers to a particular profession, occupation, or establishment.

The extent and course of the public's influence, both direct and indirect, actual and putative, on the entry and absorption of immigrants in the work situation seem at first sight to present a picture that is full of anomalies and aberrations. In Croydon, as we have seen the public accepted immigrants, coloured as well as white, as doctors, nurses, ticket collectors, railway porters, domestic servants, street cleaners, and professional sportsmen and entertainers.[1] On the other hand, the Croydon public did not accept, or was said to be hesitant about accepting, immigrants, particularly 'coloured',

[1] See *Dark Strangers* (pp. 128–30) for a note on 'acceptable' occupational roles in Brixton. There were at this time no coloured busmen or postmen in Croydon but this was because there was as yet no chronic shortage of local applicants, rather than being attributable to doubts about the public's willingness to accept coloured immigrants in such jobs.

as meter-readers and repair-men, refuse-collectors, waiters and waitresses, shop-assistants, and receptionists. As for accepting coloured immigrants as policemen, this was not yet even a matter for discussion (although a policewoman was appointed in 1968).

Clearly, no single criterion—such as the degree of authority or intimacy involved in the service or relationship, or the level of professional qualifications—affords an adequate explanation of these seeming inconsistencies of acceptance and non-acceptance.[1] For a doctor exerts at least as much authority (though with a different sanction) as a policeman,[2] while a nurse performs services that are far more intimate than those provided by a refuse-collector or waitress; and professionally qualified and unqualified roles appear in both the acceptable and unacceptable categories. Instead, the explanation appears to lie in the whole content, context, and scope of each role, the degree of institutionalization and delimitation, the extent to which it is regular or intermittent, and to which the relationships which it involves with the client or public are intimate or distant, lasting or sporadic, and encroach upon or are compatible with other kinds of social relationship.

We have already noted that there was, on the whole, a greater tolerance of newcomers among the more highly qualified professional workers[3] than among the less secure white-collar workers. This tolerant attitude has certainly furthered the acceptance of immigrant professionals by the public in the case of the medical services, but it has been less effective in the case of teachers. The explanation for this is possibly to be sought not only in the kind of service provided in each case but in the degree to which the different roles are formally defined and the extent to which they spill over into informal and intimate social life. Thus, most members of the public come into contact with doctors and nurses only in the circumscribed and rather abnormal circumstances imposed by illness and need, and thus only in their professional roles. At

[1] Nor does the explanation lie in the factor of chronic personnel shortage, since this applies in almost all cases in both the 'accepting' and the 'non-accepting' occupational groups.

[2] Although both are 'general' occupational roles, like those of teacher, priest, Member of Parliament (Michael Banton, *Roles*, Tavistock Publications, London, 1965, p. 40).

[3] This discussion will refer mainly to various 'coloured' immigrant groups. Tolerance was not always so evident in the case of professionally qualified refugees from Europe, particularly in the medical profession (Cf. Tannahill, op. cit., pp. 82–83).

such times, the whole *mystique* of the medical profession, of years of training, hospitals, surgeries, uniforms, and clinical paraphernalia, depersonalize the relationship and make it easy for patients to view a doctor or a nurse as a doctor or a nurse first, and a Pakistani man or a Jamaican girl second. It is significant that of the small number of objections from patients reported in Croydon most came from the hospital for old and chronic sick patients, and not from the two general hospitals.[1]

The teacher, on the other hand, is operating within the everyday neighbourhood framework; he is paid to supplement the parents' activities, to act almost *in loco parentis* in the upbringing and education of their children, by inculcating a knowledge of the society's values, norms, and culture, and by imparting the skills which will enable the pupil to take his adult place and earn his living in the society. Ideally he should be a culture-bearer who is at the heart of society, not an outsider who is unfamiliar with its traditions and patterns. Like the healer, he is performing a general role, but his success depends far more on personal knowledge of and a personal relationship with individual pupils. And unlike the role of the healer (at least since the decline of the family doctor), that of the teacher is, ideally at least, more lasting and overlaps a great deal more with both public and private social life; he has dealings not only with his pupils but with their parents, local officials, and local society in general.

Thus the public may be less willing to accept immigrants as teachers than as doctors and nurses, mainly because the teachers' role is more personalized and longer sustained and overlaps more into the informal social sphere.[2] Nevertheless, coloured and other immigrant teachers are increasingly being accepted by pupils, parents, and the public as teachers in a number of areas, and in these cases the professional aspect of the role seems to be dominant, particularly in the classroom.[3]

[1] See pp. 161–2.

[2] If these hypotheses are correct, one might expect to find the public somewhat more hesitant about accepting newcomers as family doctors than as surgeons and interns; the evidence in this study was entirely concerned with the latter.

[3] A West Indian teacher, Stuart Hall, describing his experience as a teacher of teenage boys in a local secondary-modern school at the time of the Notting Hill disturbances, reported that boys in his class displayed hostile attitudes to coloured people in the mass, but excepted him and other West Indians whom they knew (*Growing Up in Paddington*, 19 February 1963—report of conference

In Croydon the thin-end-of-the-wedge principle had been in operation in teaching for some years; local residents were reported to be increasingly accustomed to and tolerant of foreign and coloured teachers, although two dark-coloured, negroid-featured teachers caused some initial perturbation among parents, until they established themselves in the role of teachers and not of unusually dark strangers, to whom current stereotypes would still ascribe other roles.[1]

At lower status-levels, in occupations requiring less stringent technical qualifications, the various roles seem less formally defined and, with a few exceptions, less general; their content and context should also be examined to try to account for the discrepancies between the public's reactions, or assumed reactions, to immigrants in such 'acceptable' roles as railwaymen, busmen, postmen, domestic servants, entertainers, and sportsmen, and in such 'non-acceptable' roles as policemen, meter-readers and repair-men, refuse-collectors, shop assistants, receptionists, waiters and waitresses.

When we scrutinize these occupations more closely, we find that, while all involve 'categoric' relationships, some roles are in fact more circumscribed and clearly defined than others. This is not so much because of any technical qualifications as because those who perform them are visibly identifiable by means of a uniform or badge, and because the performance of the role takes place in a circumscribed area of contact, usually in public and over a limited period. All these elements are included in the roles of

organized by Paddington Council of Social Service). E. R. Braithwaite, a Guyanian writer who taught in an L.C.C. school in the East End for some time, recounts how his class came to accept him as teacher or 'Sir', and how this was extended to some parents; for instance, a woman who turned him away from the door when he was looking for a room, changed her mind under pressure from her daughter, a pupil of the writer, who was embarrassed and ashamed that her teacher should be treated in that way. (*To Sir, With Love*, London, Bodley Head, 1959, pp. 102–5; see also pp. 150–1.) From the receiving end, I was told by a 13-year-old, middle-class girl: 'Most people hate most teachers, anyway—it doesn't matter whether they're old or young, married or unmarried, black or white.'

[1] It could also be that fellow-teachers would share these stereotypes; moreover, their status and sense of security are lower than those of members of the medical profession, as a result of such factors as decades of dependence on the State, lower salaries, dilution, and so on (this refers less to public school masters and mistresses: see R. Lewis and A. Maude, *Professional People*, London, Phoenix House, 1952, p. 85, pp. 200–5). Status insecurity can, as we have seen, produce resistance to the employment of newcomers in non-professional white-collar occupations.

railwaymen, busmen,[1] postmen, and also those of sportsmen and entertainers, in each of which immigrants are accepted by the general public.

Visible identification is also present to a greater or lesser extent in all the non-acceptable roles; and the roles of shop-assistants, receptionists, waiters and waitresses are also restricted to public places of work, although they are often more protracted and involve a good deal of intimate service, whether in the serving of food or assistance to customers in trying on clothes, and so on. This duration and degree of intimacy may be partial reasons for non-acceptance by the public. But in view of the fact that when immigrants (even those of high 'visibility') who were suitable for the job were taken on for such work in Croydon, they were almost invariably accepted by the public without protest, it seemed reasonable to assume that many, if not most, of the doubts and hesitations as to public reactions voiced by local supervisors and employees reflected their own notions about various newcomers and their pre-occupations over security and status rather than any actual experience of public reactions. Ultimately, of course, client-groups and the public themselves begin to include immigrants, and as their purchasing power or influence rises objections, from whatever source, decrease and disappear.

At first sight, the roles of meter-readers and repair-men from the public utilities seem to resemble that of a postman, but there is one very significant difference—while meter-readers and repair-men wear uniforms or distinguishing badges and carry out a limited task, they, unlike the postman, actually enter the home. What is more, they come at unheralded hours, usually when the man of the house is at work and his wife is on her own. The right of entry into the Englishman's castle-home that goes with these roles constitutes a very large intrusion into the most private and intimate sphere of social relations and definitely militates against the acceptance of strangers, particularly younger male immigrants. Whether objections are actually raised by housewives or their menfolk or reflect the views of local male supervisors, the occupational roles involved are minor ones, not sufficiently general and formalized to ensure an entrée to anyone who is performing them, as would probably happen in the case of those performing such general roles as doctor,

[1] In these, as in some other occupations, the public seemed to accept immigrants rather more readily than do their fellow-workers.

nurse, teacher, or priest. Instead, the individual immigrant is seen as a strange man who, if he so wishes or is not aware of local *mores*, may endanger the security of the home.[1]

The roles of domestic servant and policeman constitute rather special though contrasting cases. In the former case, the actor performs all of his or her work inside the house; in the latter the role-bearer has the right of entry in certain circumstances. Both are distinguished by some kind of uniform and both are involved in a long-term relationship, but the nature of the relationship is completely different in the two cases. The master–servant relationship is an extension of the well-defined employer–employee relationship in the intimate familial atmosphere of the home; ideally it is based on choice and compatibility between the two parties, which eliminates the element of strangeness and makes the immigrant entirely acceptable.

The policeman's role is very different, although he is called upon to be servant as well as master. Like those of the teacher and the priest, his is a general, 'sacred', round-the-clock role in relation to society as a whole. And like the priest, he is concerned with the norms and values of the society, of which he is very much a part.[2] His particular role is to uphold social norms and, where necessary, enforce social control and public order. His relationship with the public involves the exercise of guidance, authority, and at times force over all its members, as the delegated agent of society. It is not therefore surprising that British public opinion and the established police forces have been reluctant to contemplate the appointment of immigrants as policemen, particularly in the early years of settlement when they would still be regarded as strangers to the community.[3]

The occupational roles we have been considering are all achieved roles, but they vary greatly in content and context—from general

[1] The role of the refuse-collector seems to constitute a marginal case. He does not usually go inside the house; nevertheless a hint of nervousness as to possible client-reactions was reported from Council C (p. 151).

[2] See Banton, *Roles*, pp. 32–34, 157–8, on the general role of priest.

[3] See Banton, *The Policeman in the Community*, London, Tavistock Publications, 1964, pp. 215–42 and *passim*, on the British policeman's role. He points out (p. 189) that the problem of separating public and private roles is greater for the policeman because he is lower down the social scale than other persons holding roles of comparable authority. This factor could of course be relevant here, in that status insecurity might contribute to the policeman's disinclination to contemplate the appointment of 'coloured' police.

and major roles that are enduring and achieved through the possession of certain qualifications and traits to minor, peripheral roles that can be taken up and changed almost at will by individuals who have little training, and little or no lasting identification with the role. The relationships with clients or the public involved in these roles range from the sporadic to the regular, the distant to the intimate.

(ii) *The Role of the 'Stranger'*

The question of an immigrant's acceptability (either actual or imputed) to the public in various occupational roles may be examined from another aspect. For, apart from their achieved occupational roles, immigrants are also strangers to a greater or lesser degree, depending on their social and cultural background and the preconceptions and notions held about them in the receiving society. Generally the role of the stranger is not an achieved but an ascribed one, which varies from one society to another.

In England the role of the stranger is a fluid, ill-defined one, lacking the immutable rigidity and universality of such ascribed outgroup roles as those of the Negro in the Southern United States, of Jews in Muslim countries, of particular castes and sub-castes in India, or of women in some patriarchal societies.

In this country the stranger (this includes not only foreigners but migrants from other parts of the country) *can* cease to be a stranger and achieve the status of a member of the local in-group, but only after years of probation and endeavour. Meanwhile, he can win acceptance in certain major and well-defined roles, starting with occupational roles. Not all occupational roles are achievable with equal facility, as we have seen. We may advance the hypothesis that once the stranger has proved his qualifications and suitability he is acceptable in those institutionalized and formal situations in which the achievable occupational role is, for one or more reasons, superordinate to the rather vaguely defined role of 'stranger'. On the other hand, in situations where the role of 'stranger' dominates or is regarded as incompatible with the occupational role, there is role conflict and he is not acceptable.

If we apply this hypothesis to the occupational roles which we have been considering, it appears to explain why immigrants are acceptable to the public as doctors, nurses, domestic servants, postmen, busmen, railwaymen, sportsmen, and entertainers, why they are less acceptable as teachers, shop-assistants, and waiters, and least acceptable as meter-readers, repair-men, and policemen.[1] It also explains why as absorption proceeds, the various groups of immigrants gradually become acceptable in roles, such as that of teacher, in which they were unacceptable before. For as the newcomers adapt themselves, their strangeness becomes less and less evident and dominates fewer and fewer occupational roles. Moreover, immigrants themselves gradually spread through the various client-groups and publics, thus providing an incentive to employers to employ their fellow-countrymen to serve them.

To conclude, it may be said that the existence of a direct client-relationship is undoubtedly a complicating factor and usually one that impedes absorption, either because the public really 'doesn't like it' or because management and local labour, for one reason or another, believe that this would be the case. The amount of resistance, however, varies according to the particular roles and relationships involved, and it is gradually modified as the newcomers become less 'strange' and more acceptable.

(iii) *The Wider Society—Industrial Absorption and Overall Social Absorption*

These client-groups and publics which we have just been considering are part of the overall receiving society, both national and local. It now remains to consider, first, how far this wider society influences the absorption of the immigrants in industry, and second, how far industrial absorption influences the process of their absorption in the wider society.

Clearly, the wider society exerts an indirect but important and enduring influence on relationships in work-groups and working communities, because these are part of that society, and operate in conformity with its major norms and patterns. The influence of the wider local society is, however, likely to be more strongly focused and channelled in compact, settled areas where the working community and the local society coincide closely (for instance, Warner and Lunt's 'Yankee City'[2] or the old-established mining towns of Northern England and Wales).

[1] See Institute of Race Relations *Newsletters*, 1964–5 (Indices), for references to discussions of these questions.

[2] W. L. Warner and R. Lunt, *The Social Life of a Modern Community* (Yankee City Series, Vol. VI), Yale University Press, 1941, pp. 1–3.

Croydon is not an area of this kind, although it contains sub-areas which have traditionally provided the steady labour force for particular factories. Such traditional firms have usually been slower to accept newcomers, but on the whole the prevailing industrial climate in Croydon favours their entry; as we have seen, the area has attracted a considerable number of progressive, labour-hungry firms which, while accepting the need to establish good relations with the local community and to build up a settled nucleus of local labour on which to draw, have been willing that this nucleus should contain some immigrants.

The industrial absorption of immigrants is often slowed and made more difficult in local communities confronted with grave social problems which may be exacerbated by the arrival of immigrants—problems such as a housing shortage, or poor or inadequate educational, health, and welfare facilities. Croydon was less affected by such problems than were many older London and Midland boroughs; and at the time of this survey the situation had not been noticeably worsened by the arrival of various immigrant groups, mainly because of the moderate numbers, the relatively slow build-up, and the fairly wide residential dispersal. Only in the case of the largest and most residentially concentrated group, the West Indians, were such familiar features as problems of overcrowding, different living standards and patterns, pressure on maternity beds and schools, beginning to be mentioned. As the inflow continued, certain local tensions and resentments developed, but not as sharply as in some other urban areas, perhaps because of the fact that West Indians had for several years been an accepted part of the local labour force in many firms.

This brings us to the second query: whether and to what extent the satisfactory absorption of immigrants in industry promotes their overall absorption in the receiving society. In Croydon the general picture seemed to be that of a set of working communities that were relatively self-contained, with not very much overlap of members into other compartments of social life—such as family groups (except where close kin were employed in the same factory), recreational groups, civic groups, and so on. The great majority of those working in Croydon industry would part from their fellow-workers, local as well as immigrant, at the end of the working day; at the most they might share a pint at the pub outside the gates, attend a union meeting together, or go on an annual outing. In the commonly used phrase quoted by Zweig: 'Home and work don't mix.'[1] Workmates, particularly men, were not often invited home, and links between work and private life had been still further weakened by the ascendancy of television (which keeps families at home) and the car (which allows people to live at a distance from their work and also to take the family outside the neighbourhood for outings).[2]

Where there is some overlap, as for instance in roles and relationships involving the public, there may be role conflict, and the wider social relationships and roles may dominate those of the work situation.[3] In such cases immigrant workers who are accepted in the work-situation may still be seen as strangers in the wider context.

On the other hand, as the immigrants become absorbed in the work-situation, as they adapt themselves, become accepted in a wider range of skills and professions and in positions of responsibility and authority—in short, cease to be strangers and become accepted as individuals—this process should ultimately exert an influence in the wider social sphere, less by an extension of interpersonal contacts than through increased acculturation and accep-

[1] F. Zweig, *The Worker in an Affluent Society*, London, Heinemann, 1961, pp. 84, 104–19. He notes (p. 118) that skilled men, young single men and women, were more likely to meet outside, if not at home, and this was borne out by my informants. In a small number of cases, such off-the-job social contacts between immigrants and local people, usually in these categories, were noted in Croydon; this seems an area in which further inquiry could be productive. (Cf. J. Chadwick-Jones, 'Inter-Group Attitudes', *British Journal of Sociology*, Vol. XIII, No. 1, March 1962, pp. 57–63.)

[2] A Pole, long settled in Croydon, added a note from personal experience: asking how Poles could expect the English to be sociable with them when they were not sociable with one another after working hours, he wrote: 'My chief, an engineer, has been giving or getting a lift from work with the firm's solicitor for the last thirty years. I asked the engineer if the solicitor's house was nicely furnished. "I don't know," he answered, "I've never been inside it." Yet this same man visited me twice in hospital' (*Polish Daily*, 4 May 1962).

[3] For instance, a male immigrant may be accepted as a member of a works sporting team but not welcomed in a working-men's club, where he might meet the womenfolk of members on an informal social basis. In Telelux, one informant expressed the view that the recent unpopularity and final fade-out of the 'family day', an occasion on which families had been encouraged to inspect the works, might be due to the local workers' unwillingness to let their families see them working alongside West Indians and Asians. 'They don't mind working with them but they don't want it spelled out at home.' (Cf. Hughes, op. cit., pp. 184–5, for the limitation of friendship between Whites and Negroes to the work-situation; also Banton, *Roles*, Tavistock Publications, 1965, pp. 191–2, for some general remarks on the difference between the work and leisure situations.)

tance. For the work-situation is not only the first and most important sphere of association between immigrants and local people but it is also the sphere in which the immigrants are most needed and in which the majority make their main effort to adapt to and be accepted by the receiving society.[1] This serves as a sort of apprenticeship for wider social life. As local people become accustomed to Polish charge-hands, African technicians, Asian doctors, West Indian craftsmen, and Anglo-Indian counter-staff in the work-situation, and as the newcomers come to know the local people inside the boundaries of the working community, it seems inevitable that in the increasingly mobile open-class society of contemporary Britain, they will gradually (if they so wish) become more acceptable in less defined and institutionalized spheres of association—in pubs and clubs, neighbourhood organizations, recreational groups, informal social groups, and ultimately in the home.

This overall absorption is more complex and moves much more slowly. In Croydon the process had gone a considerable distance in the case of the more settled post-war immigrant groups (Poles, Southern Irish, Anglo-Indians), and was getting under way for more recent arrivals like the West Indians and Hungarians. With younger and second-generation immigrants the absorption is likely to move faster in Croydon and Britain generally, but here again it may well be the later association at work more than the earlier association at school[2] that could cement acceptance and lead ultimately to overall absorption in the wider society. Finally, it should not be forgotten that as time goes by the receiving society itself comes to include an increasing number of old-timers and second-generation immigrants, who can act as sponsors or interpreters for the newly arrived, and so speed their acceptance.

(3) EVALUATION AND PREDICTIONS

It is not easy to evaluate the relative importance for the absorption of immigrants in industry of the various sets of factors outlined above, in view of the wide variation of situations, climates, and

[1] Richmond, op. cit. p. 64, stresses the strong correlation between occupational success and general success in life among West Indian immigrants in Britain.

[2] See Patterson (ed.), *Immigrants in London; A Study Group Report*, London, National Council of Social Service, 1963, p. 40, for a reference to the way in which local school-leavers slough off the school patterns and accept the adult norms of the factory and the neighbourhood.

relationships found even in this one fairly homogeneous industrial area. Further light may be thrown on their influence if we review them in terms of prediction or social conjecture, by attempting to indicate those factors and sets of factors which appeared likely to exert a continuing, even a decisive, influence on the processes of industrial absorption in the future.

We distinguished a major set of external, antecedent factors—economic, environmental, and demographic—of which labour shortage was the most important, pre-conditioning 'pull' factor in Croydon, as it seems to be elsewhere in Britain. Fairly soon, however, internal[1] socio-economic and cultural factors were found to come into play in most industries and firms, and the 'pull' factor of labour shortage began to lose its precedence. This could be because particular immigrant groups or individuals were found unsuitable in certain firms and occupations, or because alternative methods of meeting a labour shortage were found more satisfactory, or again, because even in the work situation social and cultural factors increasingly dominated the consideration of economic absorptive capacity.

On the other hand, it is known that, given continued economic expansion and labour shortage, economic consideration regains its importance periodically, as immigration declines and those who have entered the society achieve increasing adaptation and acceptance. The history of immigration into the United States affords examples of such cycles or phases when either economic growth or considerations of social and cultural cohesion and absorptive capacity have dominated immigration policy and practice.[2] In the present synchronic study of an area of recent immigration it was, however, difficult to trace any such succession of cycles and phases, although the material from a number of 'transit-camp' and other firms suggested that they might have occurred earlier in the post-war period.

Croydon afforded little opportunity for direct study of the consequences of removing the 'pull' factor of labour shortage. The sur-

[1] 'Internal' and 'external' factors have been defined here in a somewhat different way to the definition given by T. Lupton, *On the Shop-Floor*, London, Pergamon Press, 1963, p. 198. Some of his 'external' factors (e.g. the characteristics of an industry and the influence of the trade unions) are here classified as 'internal', in terms of the major interest-groups involved in the industrial situation. (See also p. 229, above.)

[2] See Borrie, op. cit., pp. 114–15.

vey was made in a period of general expansion, and information about the preceding period of mild recession (which did not affect all industries and sectors) was based on informants' sometimes imperfect or blurred recollections. It appeared that whereas some employers had been hesitant about taking on new arrivals during this recession, those immigrants who were already in employment had, with a few exceptions,[1] been treated on the same basis as other workers, whether the principle was 'last-in, first-out' or relative efficiency. Whether this position would be maintained given a major recession can only be conjectured: it would probably depend less on the dimensions of the recession than on the degree to which various immigrants had become absorbed in their particular working communities at such a time. Thus, with the passing of time, absorptive processes should reach a point of no return at which even a major slump should not have too adverse an effect on the employment of immigrants, although their situation would differ from locality to locality.

Another external factor of potential importance is the demographic one. Its importance would emerge more clearly if we were to compare the size, rate, and density of immigrant settlement in a roughly self-regulating area like Croydon and another area such as Southall, where the build-up has been more massive, speedy, and concentrated. It would also be useful to compare the situations resulting from (*a*) the controlled industrial placing and residential settlement of Poles and other East Europeans in the early post-war period, and (*b*) the uncontrolled settlement of Irish and Commonwealth immigrant workers; and to inquire into the effect on a group's acceptability (both industrial and overall) not only of its size and degree of dispersal but also of the extent of continued reinforcement by new arrivals. This would apply to the Irish and West Indians but not to the Poles or other refugees, nor to the Anglo-Indians. On the questions of size, rate, and density of immigration, the Croydon survey certainly suggested that a moderate inflow, a slow build-up, and fairly wide dispersal, at work as well as residentially, were likely to promote accommodation and keep immigrant–host frictions and tensions down.

The slow build-up and wide dispersal which characterize most of Croydon's industry were, like the selection and self-selection of particular groups of immigrant workers in the area, regulated at

[1] For examples, see p. 217.

least as much by internal socio-cultural factors as by the economic absorptive capacity of the area.

These internal factors were associated with the needs, objectives, values, norms, and attitudes of the main industrial interest-groups —management, workers, immigrants—operating separately or interacting in a working community; with the activities of sponsors and other individuals; and with the influence of the public and the overall society.

From among these sets of factors one can single out a few which have exerted and will continue to exert a widespread and lasting influence on the entry and absorption of immigrants in industry. First there is the pragmatic, usually positive approach of the most powerful single interest-group, management; its concern in most cases (in Croydon) certainly not only with the newcomers' working ability but with their general suitability for membership of a particular working community (that is to say, with their cultural absorbability as well as with purely economic considerations); and its frequent willingness to experiment with special methods of selection, induction, and training for integrating various groups.

This approach and this concern cannot, however, be effective if the third major interest-group, the immigrants, do not possess the working ability or potential required, and are not in general suitable for membership of a particular working community (considerations which are also taken into account, though from a different angle, by the local labour-core).

The great majority of first-generation immigrants in Croydon were, as we have seen, restricted in their choice of employment by one or more handicaps: these included lack of skills or paper qualifications; a poor command of English; inadequate schooling; conspicuous differences of class and cultural background; unfamiliarity with urban industrial life and discipline; different attitudes to work; unreal expectations and pre-conceptions about their reception; and, sometimes, the existence of derogatory notions amongst local management and workers about their working ability and general characteristics. On the other hand, Croydon industry offered such a wide range of occupations, industrial climates, and working communities that the various immigrants were able to fit themselves in without undue difficulty. Despite the relative lack of formal selection, moreover, it was often the more able, energetic, adaptable, and settler-minded immigrants that had been attracted to Croydon industry, where they were being absorbed not exclusively in the lowest unskilled jobs but at various levels of the hierarchy, and were creating 'clusters' and 'favoured nations' which in turn were attracting newcomers of similar quality.

A newcomer's working ability and general suitability are particularly important in areas where industry and the local community are closely linked; but they are also important in areas like Croydon, where the prevailing industrial climate is not only expansionist but assimilationist in ethos, and where most working communities are based not on the rabble hypothesis but on stable labour-cores and specific self-perpetuating 'cultures'. The kind of working community and culture found in a particular firm or department has an important influence on the intake and subsequent absorption of immigrants. Some working communities are closed and self-sufficient and accept no immigrants; others accept one or more groups but reject others. In some the processes of absorption are long-drawn-out and comprehensive, in other working communities, less traditional and less integrated, they are faster and less thoroughgoing.

Individual immigrants with professional or skilled qualifications can gain entrance in a wider variety of working communities, as can settled immigrants with local references. But for the bulk of semi-skilled or unskilled newcomers the most satisfactory would appear to be the large, progressive, mass-production firms, with their special techniques for selection and training, their flexible organization and their high labour turnover. In second place come the 'transit-camp' firms, with their large requirements of casual or seasonable labour. In non-manual working communities, on the other hand, the climate for immigrant workers is more propitious in higher-status, highly qualified groups than in those permeated by anxieties over status and security.

Working communities are generally based on the interaction of management and workers or, rather, of management and the long-term local labour-core (which may contain a few earlier immigrants). Management and local labour can coexist more or less in opposition or can co-operate in a smaller or larger core-community. In the former case the labour-core, if it wishes to oppose or limit the entry of immigrants, is likely to do so either overtly through joint consultation channels, or union representatives, if they exist, or covertly and subtly, by means of face-to-face pressures in work units. Such pressures are particularly effective in situations where formal and informal organization more or less coincide. In a few other situations the local labour force may be apathetic or powerless to impose its views on management and the entry and absorption of immigrants proceeds on a two-way basis between the latter and management. On the other hand, in cases where there is a core-community of supervisors and local labour, the latter's views are expressed by the supervisors, who usually share them.

In Croydon the influence of the second major interest group in industry, the labour force, has been exerted less through unions (other than skilled unions, closed shops and branches in publicly owned establishments) than through the long-service local labour cores found in most firms. At the time of this inquiry, this influence seemed to be less important for the entry and absorption of immigrants than that exerted by management. This situation could, however, change in the years to come, given greater trade-union strength or some reorganization of industry to provide more extensive consultation and a larger say for the labour force. On the other hand, labour's approach will not necessarily continue to be negative and based on old anxieties and preconceptions. A growing number of immigrants are becoming active in the unions and accepted in labour-cores and local labour is increasingly judging them as individuals, on their ability and general capacity to fit in.

The presence of opinion-forming individuals and cliques at all levels of the Croydon industrial hierarchy was noted; this helped to explain the very different situations that have developed in apparently similar working communities. Their influence, particularly as sponsors, seemed likely to grow, as their numbers were increased by established immigrants sponsoring later arrivals.

The fourth interest-group involved in some industrial relationships—the public or client-group—is popularly supposed to resent or resist the employment of immigrants in a number of services and occupations. Closer examination showed that while there was a modicum of actual public resistance to encountering immigrants in certain roles, much of the resistance was attributed by employers and management (particularly at lower levels) in status-conscious and insecure white-collar and service occupations. Where there was actual resistance, it seemed to arise out of a combination of variables, notably the content, context, scope, and duration of the relationships, and from role-conflict in occupational roles which were not thought appropriate for strangers; it was, however, being modified by increasing acceptance and by such devices as the 'thin-end-of-the-wedge' principle, so that a growing number of occupational roles involving contact with the public were becoming open to an increasing number of immigrant individuals and groups.

Public reactions are thus not so much of a deterrent factor in industrial absorption as is generally supposed and any deterrent effect is likely to decrease in importance as accommodation proceeds. Even at this time public reactions were far more positive in many occupational contacts than were those of local workers—for instance, the public was more ready to accept immigrant busmen and railwaymen than were local workers. And as the publics and client-groups come to include an increasing number of settled immigrants, this is, as we noted, likely to promote more positive attitudes among the public as a whole, as well as to induce more establishments to employ immigrants in contact-jobs.[1]

The wider local society conditions the general industrial climate of the area and thus exerts an indirect influence on the industrial absorption of immigrants. The ethos of Croydon's core community was on the whole tolerant, metropolitan, upwardly mobile, and forward-looking—and this was echoed in, and reinforced by, the expansionist, assimilationist climate found in many parts of the industrial area.

In conclusion, it should be stressed once again that while the external economic 'pull factor' was most important in securing the entry of immigrants to Croydon industry, the ensuing processes of absorption (including the informal regulation and dispersal of intake) have been mainly influenced by internal socio-economic and cultural factors arising out of the attitudes, norms and goals of the major interest-groups involved in the industrial situation, particularly higher management, the immigrants and the working community.

For the most part this influence has operated in a pragmatic and positive way; and it is encouraging to note that it has usually been exerted through first-hand contacts, relationships, and judgements rather than through the second-hand notions and irrational attitudes that are often important in less institutionalized and more

[1] See Blumer, op. cit., pp. 437–8.

intimate social situations. For instance, in Croydon industry colour started as the badge of the stranger, but its connotation was changing as absorption proceeded and the stranger-bar was increasingly set, not at the gates of industry but at supervisory levels. There was still a widespread tendency, particularly among workers, to associate colour with lack of skills and low socio-economic status, but this has been weakened by the presence of increasing numbers of students and professional trainees in local government and other establishments, by the operation of the 'thin-end-of-the-wedge' process in shops, offices, and professions, and by the up-grading and promotion of coloured 'pioneers' on the shop floor.

Employers concerned with efficiency and workers in face-to-face situations have also been among the first to realize that dark pigmentation or negroid features do not necessarily indicate any profound cultural or ethnic links and that there is no such thing as a 'coloured immigrant worker'—but various kinds of West Indians, Africans, Euro-Africans, Asians, Eurasians, Arabs, and others, often at odds with each other and usually requiring a different approach. And as absorption in primary groups proceeds and the individual is accepted as an individual, there is an increasing tendency for dark skin colour to become less socially 'visible'.

In the industrial situation, indeed, the factor of colour is usually less important, as the comparison with Irish, Poles, and other European workers in Croydon has shown, than such attributes as the possession of skills, aptitudes, adaptability, a knowledge of English, and an adequate socio-cultural and educational background to enable one to fit into a given working group and community. If the majority of 'coloured' immigrant workers are found to be deficient in these attributes, preconceptions may harden into stereotypes, thus prejudicing the prospects of the locally born, English-educated second generation, whose members, unlike their elders, will differ from their coevals mainly in pigmentation.

The danger of such an accentuation and hardening of the colour factor in Croydon seemed, however, smaller than in areas that are less tolerant and assimilationist or that have attracted a less able, adaptable, and varied selection of immigrants—and this appeared a hopeful augury for the future since Croydon, in the expanding south-east, was and is in many ways representative of the evolving industrial climate of Britain.

PART IV

DETAILED STUDIES OF THREE SELECTED FACTORIES

CHAPTER 9
TELELUX

(1) *The Overall Picture*

The Telelux company was part of a large organization with close European links.[1] The Croydon works to which this case-history refers was opened in the early 1930s when Telelux needed room to expand and moved down from South London. Expansion was rapid after 1936 and at the time of this inquiry[2] the firm was still characterized by a pattern of dynamic expansion and development, accompanied by continuous hiving-off and segmentation of working units, and mobility of personnel, processes which had a somewhat inhibiting effect on the formation of rigid, long-term working groups and cliques.

Telelux was concerned with the development, production, and quality control of a large range of valves and tubes. In 1958 it employed a total labour force of some 2,800, rising to just over 3,000 in 1959 (and including representatives of some twenty-five nationalities). Of the total, about two-thirds were hourly paid workers, the remainder weekly or monthly paid in the proportion of nearly eight weekly paid to every three monthly paid employees. 'This is not, properly speaking, a mass-production factory but a development centre,' said one personnel officer, commenting on the unusually high percentage of scientists, technicians, and other weekly and monthly paid staff.

Rather less than half the hourly paid workers were men at the later date. One-third of them were skilled, two-thirds semi-skilled; there were also a few labourers for service and cleaning. The female labour force totalled over 1,000, divided more or less equally between full- and part-time workers, the latter on morning, afternoon

[1] This cosmopolitan, European orientation was said by an informant to be rather rare among big British firms, more of which have connexions with the United States.

[2] Telelux was first visited in October 1958, during the general survey; then in early 1960 for this more detailed study. The time-lapse explains any minor discrepancies in numbers and situations. For overall numbers, see pp. 71–4.

or evening shifts. Almost all women workers were semi-skilled.

The labour force was reported to be comparatively young but there was no compulsory retirement at 65, and individual workers who were able and willing to carry on sometimes did so. There were also a number of middle-aged women with long service, who were in a position to exert a considerable influence in certain work-groups and departments.

Labour turnover was relatively small, particularly among male workers. It was higher among single than married men and, as might have been expected, considerably higher for full-time women; it was highest of all among part-time women. Despite considerable inducements in the form of benefits and pensions, the average length of service was not yet very high. This was mainly because of the large-scale expansion of the past decade or so and the recent transfer of a number of long-service men to another works. Average length of service was considerably higher on the skilled than on the semi-skilled side, one major reason for this being that mass production processes employing men had only recently been developed. It had also been found that skilled men tended to settle earlier in a job and with the firm.

Among semi-skilled full-time women workers the average length of service was longer, because the firm had started to use female labour for mass production at an earlier date. Part-time female day workers, some of whom had started with the firm as full-time workers, also had a good average length of service.

Absenteeism was reported as very low among men, much higher among women, although in the latter case it tended to drop with the length of service.

Most of the work at Telelux was not heavy, and working conditions and services were good. As a personnel officer said: 'There's still some social status to it.' In a survey carried out just before this one a very large majority was reported as regarding the atmosphere as 'pleasant and friendly', with 'good mates and helpful supervisors'. There had been instances of men meeting their future wives at work and in quite a number of cases several members of a family were working in different departments. The great majority of the labour force was locally born and bred, and lived within five miles of the works. This applied particularly to women workers, many of whom lived near enough to go home to lunch. Indeed, the bulk of the labour force was still drawn from the first- and second-generation inhabitants of a large local estate, built in the pre-war years and with an established communal atmosphere of its own, such as had not yet developed in many post-war estates.

Labour relations were smooth and there had been no strike since 1935. Both male and female labour was highly unionized, the over-all estimate being between 85 and 90 per cent. of the works labour force.[1] Six unions were represented, the A.E.U. having by far the largest membership with six out of every seven shop-stewards. The seventy or so shop-stewards were organized under an annually elected Works Convenor.

On the whole, wages were somewhat above the Federation rates. There was a large gap between skilled and semi-skilled rates, and also between average wages, as skilled workers were in short supply and tended to work longer hours. Semi-skilled production work was paid according to a complicated premium payment plan, the jobs being grouped in four classes according to the nature of the work, the difficulty and responsibility involved, and other criteria. Above the four classes came the replacement operative who could do all four kinds of job (and take over in the charge-hand's absence), and above him or her the whole many-tiered managerial and supervisory hierarchy of the senior and junior monthly and weekly paid employees, this hierarchy being underlined by the existence of separate canteens and other differential privileges.

The Telelux works contained some seven production divisions, each under a divisional manager and containing a varying number of departments concerned with development, production, and quality control. There were also a number of specialist service departments, including engineering, personnel and training, and special laboratories. The various divisions and service departments were large, autonomous, and for the most part socially remote from one another. Community feeling and loyalty tended to cluster round a division or, even more frequently, a department, rather than about the plant as a whole.

The dynamic and tolerant social climate that was found in most production and research units was the outcome not only of enlightened personnel policies but also of the fact that this was a relatively new industry, expanding, international in outlook, and with

[1] The percentage rose to 100 in the engineering department, dropped to about 80 to 85 per cent. among the weekly paid supervisors, and was said to be very low among the monthly paid.

few traditions. The large size of the firm, the high scientific 'loading' of its staff and the repeated pattern of expansion and segmentation of work-units, mobility, and upgrading of personnel were also contributory factors. Despite the fact that most hourly paid workers came from one large local housing-estate, the term 'our own people' was much less frequently used by management and supervisory informants than was the case in many smaller firms in the Croydon area. Some informants who had worked at other smaller plants in the same group commented on the fact that general working relations at Telelux seemed cooler and more impersonal. This did not, however, mean that employees were treated as 'economic men'. On the contrary, great pains were taken to transfer unsettled or difficult individuals to work which they could manage and to work-groups which they would find more congenial; moreover, dismissals were extremely rare, and on several occasions I was told: 'His [or her] job will soon disappear with increasing automation, but some other little job will be found for him—you can't sack old, long-service employees.'

(2) *Recruitment, Selection, Induction, and Training*

Like other firms, Telelux first considered the recruitment of 'coloured' workers (in practice, mainly West Indians) because of a shortage of labour: 'The West Indians first began to appear in 1952–3, when we were experiencing a chronic labour shortage. I sometimes wonder whether we would have taken them on but for that.'[1] Agreement to recruit West Indians was reached with the unions on the basis of a 4 per cent. quota, which from time to time since then had been somewhat exceeded, without any objections being raised. Up to the time of this inquiry, in fact, no precise statistics were being kept and the 'quota' was based mainly on overall impressions, and on rough self-regulating mechanisms within the various departments and work-units. The size of the quota also varied considerably from department to department: 'Some are very ready to say "no more", while others always seem happy to take them.' Even in the most welcoming departments, however, the quota never seemed to rise much above 10 or 12 per

[1] This seems to have been the reason for the earlier recruitment of Poles and ex-E.V.W.s, although informants' memories about this period were vague and scanty, these groups having been more or less absorbed by now.

cent. Limited redundancies were reported to have occurred in recent years, but no demands had been made for coloured workers to go first. Union representatives were aware that the quota had expanded. One commented: 'I think there are more than the original quota now. We wouldn't count heads. I just wouldn't want too many and I suspect the management may be taking on too many when local workers are available. But I'd disapprove of departments refusing them altogether.'

Recruitment of West Indians began with men. In the early period, this gave rise to some problems with local girls and consequent objections by mothers. This source of friction was stopped when the firm began to recruit coloured women—often wives or women friends of men already working there. Most West Indians came not from the employment exchange (Telelux was on the periphery of the Croydon industrial area) but to the gate, or, increasingly, through recommendations by fellow-countrymen already employed there. ('There's a good deal of pre-arrangement in the departments. A coloured man will go to his supervisor and ask if he can send his friend along.') This had, it was said, helped to improve the standard of applicants. All applicants were seen by the personnel department, whether or not there was a vacancy. If it was felt that the quota has been temporarily exceeded, this was explained to applicants: 'I tell them that we try to maintain a proportion that reasonably reflects the proportion of West Indians in the community outside (in fact it's far above). This goes down well and I've never had a murmur of protest.'

For the preliminary interview no special techniques were used and coloured applicants were, in the words of one informant, 'treated the same as anyone else. I deal with everyone on the basis: "Is there a job they can do here?" We used to have problems of selection at first but we're used to them now. One of the problems is difficulty of communication, another that they don't know what to expect or what they want to do.' There was a tendency to discourage West Indian men from seeking labouring jobs:

> These are low-paid and for unambitious types. The West Indians are often much keener than local people to get on and it's not fair to a manager to have a constant changeover of labour. It's best to start West Indians, particularly the urban type, off as operatives, even though a male operative's job is more monotonous and the work of a Class I operative and a labourer are more or less the same as regards job content.

Women operatives needed dexterity and good eyesight at Telelux, and many jobs required young eyes. Before the introduction of special dexterity tests some applicants (including a lot of West Indian women) used to be rejected at the interview because of obvious clumsiness, large hands, or other indications of lack of dexterity. At this time, however, applicants were first given an eyesight test (which most coloured women, being in the younger age-groups, were said to pass), then interviewed and finally given a dexterity test. If they passed this they were submitted for any available vacancy, and underwent the full medical test.[1]

Once accepted, newcomers at all levels went through a three-day induction course in which no special provisions were made for immigrant workers, other perhaps than to make an extra effort to establish communication. Thereafter male hourly paid workers would go straight on to the shop floor, while most women would undergo a training period averaging six weeks, during which the rejection rate for West Indian women was said to be relatively high. An informant in the training school commented that they seemed to fall into two categories: those who were very difficult to train, and those who were well up to the normal standard. Another said that there had been initial failures: this was because it was not at first realized that many West Indian women had a longer learning curve but that, given a little longer, they would reach the same standard, although they usually continued to *appear* slower.

Although the initial rejection rate was higher for West Indians than for local workers, the average turnover of both men and women was reputed to be somewhat lower. A very high percentage of West Indian men were on shift-work, which was well-paid but not very popular among younger local men. West Indians and other coloured Commonwealth immigrants were said to make ready use of the personnel department, bringing a large range of problems concerned with family life, house loans, income tax, and so on. Such immigrants also made considerable use of the medical department. An informant here commented on their good personal hygiene, tendency to be demonstrative over pain and illness, and the frequent difficulty of establishing communication. He added:

> Unlike the local workers, they usually come in the lunch hour instead of leaving their work. They're slow and not accustomed to factory life,

[1] The medical test had not uncovered any conspicuous incidence of diseases such as tuberculosis among coloured Commonwealth immigrants.

but soon get into it. They don't feel out of it because there's a relatively large overall number of them, and they stick together and help each other out. The lack of intensity in the life of this factory helps. They also adapt to the climate, which is a great shock, after the first month.

Of the Poles, Hungarians, and other political exiles, this informant said that he had noticed no particular differences in comparison with local workers and no higher incidence of mental illness. In his view, language was their main difficulty.

(3) *Placing, Personnel Problems, Recreation, etc.*

Telelux had a definite policy with regard to the recruitment, placing, and integration of immigrant workers, particularly West Indians. Apart from the limiting quota, there was a definite policy of dispersal and scatter through as many departments as possible.[1] Only in one case had the experiment been made of trying out an all-West Indian work-unit, composed of women with no experience of factory life. This was being discontinued; objections had been raised on grounds of segregation by other coloured workers and by the unions. A union representative said: 'We're suspicious of this arrangement. Their output is good or the management wouldn't tolerate it. Promises have been given to stop it.'

Management policy on up-grading and promotion was also gradualist but positive. There were a number of European supervisors and even a Pakistani head of department. There were also a few European charge-hands, and the promotion of carefully chosen Anglo-Indians and West Indians to charge-hands over all-male work-groups had begun. This move had been accepted by the works convenor and most shop-stewards. Among the shop-stewards themselves there were or had been a number of immigrants—Poles, Anglo-Indians, and West Indians—and it was from among them that the immigrant charge-hands had been drawn. Said the works convenor, speaking of local labour in general:

Shop-steward is not a job most people want. They tend to be the most intelligent and energetic types and they learn something during the year they serve, which may make them better chargehand material as a result. It's surprising the percentage of ex-shop-stewards who become supervisors, though they aren't always the most militant ones.

[1] It was hinted that in past years departments operating a total bar had sometimes found themselves starved of new intake until they took in a few immigrants.

Major personnel problems were as a rule referred to the personnel department. One such problem, connected with Commonwealth immigrants, was the early one already referred to—that of white girls going out with coloured men; this was dealt with by introducing coloured women workers. The employment of coloured women had initially produced some complaints of a different kind from local women workers, relating to alleged unhygienic habits in the cloakroom; these had, however, been dealt with individually, and no more complaints had been received. Of these and similar difficulties a union representative said: 'They would be localized within the units—the rest would simply gossip. For instance, during that trouble with coloured men and white girls years ago, other women simply said: "Well, it would have happened with some man anyway." '

The complaints were more than balanced by live-and-let-live or goodwill fellowship. Local workers were shocked at the Notting Hill disturbances which occurred some eighteen months before this detailed inquiry began, and many were said to have gone out of their way to show friendliness. As for the immigrants, no instances had been noted of West Indians or other groups ganging up or being organized or stirred up by informal leaders, although coloured people were generally regarded as being more colour-conscious than most of the whites among whom they worked. Personnel department informants expressed different views about the extent of immigrant workers' participation in the factory's informal organization and recreational activities. One thought that they kept together and took little part in social activities. Another reported that they seemed to mix in at the canteen, where the general tendency was for work-units to sit together.

The recreation club, with some twenty sections, had a membership of over half the total staff and labour force. A wide cross-section of hourly paid, weekly paid (very strongly represented), and even monthly paid employees belonged; the club was run democratically and status in the works hierarchy was not important ('some department heads were surprised at first to find that they were actually treated like the rest; indeed, we mix up the status groups deliberately'). The most popular sections were horticulture, swimming, cricket, football, and cinema. People from certain departments and sections tended to concentrate in particular recreational sections—largely because of existing congeniality and because a keen secretary was likely to interest fellow-workers. As with the local workers, the younger, unmarried immigrants, especially students, were most strongly represented in the recreation club.[1] A West Indian was the star cricketer, and there were several others in the team. Young Dutch men gravitated towards rugger and swimming, which also attracted most other overseas workers. Hungarians were strong in table-tennis, and an Anglo-Indian was secretary of the badminton and tennis section. Several coloured girls played netball. Fewer Poles participated than in the past, mainly because most were now married and settled. An Indonesian girl and a West Indian charge-hand were active in the dramatic section. At the dances only one incident of rowdyism, between some Teddy-boy types and a West Indian youth, had occurred within my informant's memory (three years). This was immediately smoothed over; the coloured men, unlike most of the coloured girls, generally brought their own partners, but were said to be favourites as jive partners.

The club organizer reported that most immigrants who joined seemed to persevere with club activities; he considered that participation made it easier for them to be more fully accepted at work. This seemed to be true, but it did not necessarily promote social relations outside the factory. In most cases the clear delineation between the job situation and the home seemed to have been retained. In this connexion, one personnel officer made an interesting comment:

> We used to have a regular open day for families to come and see round the works. There haven't been any for five years now. They're not wanted. I wonder whether a man's status at home suffers if his family sees him working alongside coloured workers, and also realizes that a coloured worker can do the job?

(4) *The Inquiry*

There was insufficient time to survey all divisions and departments; so, after discussion with the personnel department, three units were selected, of which two were production divisions of differing character and social climate, and the third a laboratory, differing from the production divions in that it employed

[1] Participation was predictably lower among shift-workers, part-timers, and married workers, many of whom, however, liked to go on coach outings.

mostly monthly and weekly paid staff. Sufficient general information about the other production divisions and research units was provided to indicate that those selected were not show-cases for good race relations, or conspicuously different in social climate from the remainder. It was, however, made clear that in the clerical and administrative sections, and in the virtually closed-shop engineering department,[1] immigrants were much less acceptable, as indeed had been found to be the case in most Croydon firms. One administrative section was said to refuse to take coloured people altogether; it was, however, pointed out by a personnel officer that most coloured applicants for clerical work in Telelux were in fact students, whose temporary availability and other preoccupations often made them awkward to employ. The engineering shop also had no coloured or European workers, although one Pole with acceptable qualifications had been tried out there. 'They're an élite, and the union's very left-wing. The union also made a row when we took on a few Hungarians after 1956.'

(a) *Division I*

The first of the two production divisions studied was Division I; this differed from Division II, not so much in size, age, or the nature of the work, as in the way in which labour needs had been met and the general climate of opinion, particularly in Department B. Inside Division I, there were also considerable differences of experience and working climate between its three component departments. (See chart on p. 396.)

Department A: At this time, the largest department was Department A; it was only about three years old—two years younger than Department B, which had been the nucleus of the whole division. Department A had built up fast from an initial working force of a score or so to well over 200. The same manager had been in charge throughout, and immigrants had been part of the labour force from its early days.

Despite its youth, this department contained a fair number of employees who had been with the firm for a considerably longer

[1] Of one other service department with a mainly skilled labour force it was said: 'There's constant labour trouble there, and constant trouble over coloured workers as well. Where labour relations are bad, the rest often follows. The supervisor is openly prejudiced. There's one dark-skinned man there, but he's been in England for a long time—he's not a recent immigrant.'

period. These included the majority of supervisors, who had gradually come in from other departments or divisions, and a number of operatives, mostly part-time women who lived locally.

Department A occupied one whole floor in the plant. It employed about 220 hourly paid workers, of whom 210 were women, a considerable proportion of them being part-timers. The department contained two sections which were producing slightly different types of the same basic product. Most of the women's work required excellent eyesight, and in a few units in Section 1 operation required greater manual skills than were needed in Section 2. Most of the work consisted of individual operations, although a few machines required co-operation by two or three operatives. Earnings were not as a rule affected by the speed or efficiency of other operatives, although an individual operative sometimes would establish a faster operating rate for a process. Section 1 had been further developed than Section 2: it had one technical unit and a production unit which was shortly to be divided into two separate units, and it employed 90 per cent. of the present total of hourly paid workers in the department. Section 2, on the other hand, was just being developed and at this time employed only about forty operatives. The latter workers, unlike the operators in Section 1, had all been selected by the recently established training school. One supervisor said rather plaintively about Section 1:

> It has a lot of real old dears, including some rather rough types. There's always a lot of gossip and even a bit of cat-calling down that end, and they're as likely as not to sing out 'Hey, Bill, come 'ere' right across the floor to the supervisors, or by-pass the chain of command and go straight to the Divisional Manager as they did before we built up. It makes it difficult to maintain authority.

From the Recreational Club it was learned that Section 1 contained a handful of extremely energetic long-service women, all part-time workers, who regularly organized occasional outings to a musical show or the seaside for the entire division. The small potential cliques that existed in most units in this older-established section did not, however, appear to be in a sufficiently strong position to impede the entry and acceptance of immigrant workers, even if they wished to do so; but, in fact, there was no evidence of such resistance or hostility.

West Indian and other immigrant workers had been with this

section since the start, though some individuals had left and others had come in. At this time the small total of male hourly paid workers included two West Indians, two Anglo-Indians, and one Pole. The hourly paid female labour force also contained six West Indians, two Germans, and one Hungarian, all full-timers, out of a total of about 160, including part-time workers.

The immigrants in Section 1 were scattered fairly widely through the two units and the six working sub-units. Two contained no immigrant workers at all, but one of them was a special sub-unit requiring special technical skills for which no immigrant applicants had so far been offered by the personnel department. In the other, the foreman expressed some doubts about the charge-hand's attitude: 'He is an ex-army officer with very fixed ideas on a number of subjects . . . I would hesitate to put coloured or other immigrants in there.' Several immigrants worked or had worked in the other sub-units; one had as many as five full-time West Indian female operatives out of a total of twenty full-time and thirty part-time women.

Section 2 was less developed than Section 1, employing only forty operatives (two men, thirty-eight women). There were no male immigrant workers, but among the women there were three West Indians and one Anglo-Egyptian. The latter was the only part-time immigrant worker in the division; she settled in the Croydon neighbourhood after the Suez crisis.

While the overall percentage of 'coloured' immigrants in Section 2 was about 10 per cent., that in Section 1 was less than 6 per cent.,[1] contrary to the impression passed on to me by the personnel department and Department A's own manager, that the department had up to 10 per cent. of coloured workers. Both section managers, on the other hand, were well aware of the actual position, but accepted 10 per cent. as a rough maximum. 'We have far fewer than that at present, but 10 per cent. is the figure that sticks in my mind as a desirable quota,' said one. Neither of these managers felt that they had reached a limit or were employing too many, and almost all the lower supervisors interviewed agreed that they could take more in their respective working units and groups. In fact, however, none of the managers or supervisors interviewed had troubled to work out the exact percentage, and it seemed likely that in this

[1] There were no European immigrants in the sections at this time, but this seemed to be accidental rather than by intention.

division, as so often elsewhere, the quota was less an exact stipulation than a vague notion which varied according to such elements as the performance and acceptability of 'coloured' Commonwealth workers in each situation. For instance, in Section 1 coloured workers had proved fairly satisfactory; most supervisors were therefore ready to take more and to talk in terms of a quota which was about double the existing percentage.

In Section 1 most informants regarded West Indians as satisfactory or adequate workers and as good time-keepers.[1] In two sub-units individuals were singled out for particular praise: 'Mrs. —— is absolutely outstanding. The fastest operative we've ever had. . . . Mr. —— began as a labourer but he was too good for it. Both he and the Anglo-Indian are first-class workers who move around and do several jobs.'

On the other hand, one supervisor, who had come in recently from a training unit through which passed a large number of West Indian women trainees, had certain reservations about their speed and adaptability:

> As a rule I find coloured workers quieter and more reliable than the average. Few have any chip on their shoulder. I think that as a general rule the rate of learning is slower with the West Indians. Their manual dexterity often seems lower and their eyesight poorer.[2] They're usually slow starters and more patience is needed to train them. In the early days we let some go whom we could probably have trained, given an extra week or so. But of the coloured girls I have now, I doubt if any would be adaptable enough for up-grading to replacement operative.

Only one West Indian was regarded by all informants as unsatisfactory, lazy, and unco-operative. This was a labourer whose job was to do odd jobs and cleaning for both sections. One supervisor described the following encounter with him:

> The foreman thought he wasn't pulling his weight or getting enough done, so he called him in and gave him a time-table of periods during which he was to do jobs for each charge-hand. My sub-unit wasn't here at the time so he didn't seem to realize that he also had to do work for me. I called him over but he has a bit of a chip on his shoulder and he complained bitterly about having too much work put on him because of his colour. 'We're all the same flesh and blood, even though my skin

[1] The section manager said: 'I've only had to warn one immigrant about bad time-keeping. That was an Anglo-Indian who had a lot of trouble at home.'

[2] But see p. 298 for a somewhat different opinion.

is black,' he said. Some supervisors might have made an issue of it and taken against the coloured man. I simply let it go and got the foreman to straighten him out later.

The two German women were described by informants as excellent operators with 'a good attitude to the job'. Their excellence had, however, led to some friction with other operators, for instance, on a few occasions the German girls set new rates for certain operations which the others considered to be too fast. Of the solitary Pole in Section 1, his supervisor said: 'He's elderly, speaks broken English and has heart trouble. He's really only semi-employable but I've found him an easy little job that he can do.'

Problems of communication could arise not only in the case of Europeans who spoke poor English but in the case of some West Indians. According to one supervisor: 'I have some difficulty in explaining the different pay scales to them and really making them understand why certain operatives who seem to be doing the same sort of work should be getting more than they do.'

Apart from the single case of the West Indian labourer, the supervisors in Section 1 agreed that there were no real frictions either between the immigrants and themselves or between the immigrants and their fellow-workers. This they associated with the generally good atmosphere within the group.

People seem rather to put themselves out to help newcomers than the reverse. They tend to accept them as they find them. There's good and bad in all races....

There's no horsing of any newcomers in this section. The shop stewards wouldn't stand for it and neither would we. The general practice is to introduce every newcomer to the operative next door, and to appoint an unofficial sponsor to show him or her the way around the plant. All the coloured immigrants are well accepted in the working group but most keep themselves socially aloof.

Most of these informants regarded West Indian workers as quiet and reserved. This opinion was expressed rather approvingly, as if to indicate that such conduct was likely to make the immigrants more acceptable. It seemed, however, possible that the newcomers' quiet, reserved behaviour reflected an inner uncertainty about working relationships on and off the floor. The same inference could be drawn from the fact that in the dinner and tea-breaks most West Indians, Anglo-Indians, and Germans were reported to sit with compatriots, sometimes from other working groups, rather than with their work-mates. As no operatives were interviewed, it was not possible to say whether this self-segregation arose primarily out of uncertainty or out of preference for companions of the same origin and background. In the case of West Indians, however, it could well be the latter, since most lived in the same districts of South London and were thrown together by the fact that they travelled to and from work by the same bus or train.

Two informants explained this self-segregation of West Indian workers in terms of colour-consciousness on the part of the workers themselves: 'But for one or two, the coloured workers are almost fully accepted. But they seem to have a complex inside themselves and they bunch together.' . . . 'I don't think of men as coloured, just as good or bad operatives. But they introduce their own colour bar in reverse with their chip-on-the-shoulder attitude. There is some sort of a culture bar, however, more than there is between the European immigrants and ourselves.'

Only two of the immigrant workers in Section 1, an Anglo-Indian and a West Indian, seemed to mix in socially with fellow-workers. Both were men who had been with the firm some years, and both were high-grade operatives in the same sub-unit, which was under a charge-hand of very liberal views. The latter was particularly friendly with the West Indian, who usually went to mid-day dinner in the canteen with him and a third friend, a former charge-hand in this section, who was now a foreman elsewhere in the division. The charge-hand and the West Indian also maintained social ties off the job.

I went round to his new place last Saturday. He's married to an Irish girl and they have a nice-looking child, nearly white. He was in the forces and is here to stay in this country. I noticed what a high standard of living they have, better than some of those who are on a much higher level in the factory.

In Section 2, relationships between supervisors, local workers and immigrants did not seem to differ in any significant way from those in Section 1. If anything, higher-level supervisors in Group 2 showed a more active concern with the individual well-being of their operators, although this could have been attributable to the small size of the section. One of these supervisors, who came from a lower supervisory job in another division, employing about 8 per cent. of coloured women, could indeed almost be classed as a 'sponsor':

Coloured workers are extra-cautious at first, but they do mellow after a while. I bend over backwards to put them at ease. I keep them informed of what's going on all the time to prove there's no discrimination. It's usually necessary to have several little chats with girls, but it pays off. For instance, at first they didn't go to the tea area in the break. This looked like stand-offishness to the other girls. But I had a talk to them and found they weren't sure whether they were supposed to go there. I explained it and now they mix in at the tables and don't sit by themselves. Another time a coloured girl came and said she wanted to move to another division. Only after a chat did I find out that she felt she couldn't keep up with the speed. With a little extra push she made it and now she's quite happy.

Another supervisor showed similar solicitude:

They mix in well and there are no objections from the girls. The men in Section 1 may come in for a bit of joking when the Test Matches are on but it's all very friendly. Some time ago one of the coloured chaps got very upset over Little Rock. He worried himself ill and I had to reassure him for weeks that it couldn't happen here. I must say we disapprove of the South African and American attitude to colour. It shows a very low standard of education. I couldn't stand living in that atmosphere.

A third informant was in charge of a sub-unit engaged on high-grade work. He clearly judged each case individually and had some interesting comments to make on various working relationships, including one involving local workers and an immigrant charge-hand:

I don't care if they're sky-blue-pink so long as they do the job. I've just taken on a Barbadian girl who looks excellent and seems well educated. I believe she was a teacher at home. The last coloured girl I had just couldn't keep up with the rate. Twice I actually caught her asleep on the machine. In my last division I worked under an Anglo-Indian charge-hand and always found him a gentleman. There were a couple of coloured chaps there. One had a terrific chip-on-his-shoulder, though he was a half-caste born in England and so light you wouldn't have known he was coloured at all if he wasn't always harping on it. There was a white South African who came into the sub-unit and objected to working under an Anglo-Indian, and particularly to sitting at the same table with coloured people. The Anglo-Indian and the others were *part of the group* so the men told the South African that if he didn't like it he could go and sit elsewhere. After three weeks he handed in his notice.

All the interviews in Department A indicated that the immigrants were reasonably well integrated into the hourly paid working group. On the other hand, the matter of promotion seemed less straightforward than in all-male working groups such as that described by the last informant.

In this particular department the appointment of a non-English manager or supervisor at or above the foreman level seemed unlikely at this time; discussion was, in practice, confined to the possibility of appointing male immigrant charge-hands over sub-units mainly composed of female operatives. It should be recalled here that it was policy throughout Telelux not to make women operatives up to charge-hands but to appoint men. There appeared to be general agreement among the male supervisors of female labour that women workers brought more emotion, more intensity, and more moodiness into the working situation than did men, and that the task of supervising them required great diplomacy, caution and a sympathetic ear for their troubles. As one veteran supervisor said: 'Give them a shoulder to weep on occasionally, don't let the old stagers boss the joint and be scrupulously fair or they'll be accusing you of favouritism—that's the way to handle them.'

Seen in this light, it was perhaps easier to understand the reservations expressed by most informants in this department about the promotion of immigrants to charge-hand over women operatives. One managerial informant said:

Recently we had to consider twelve applicants for a charge-hand's position, two of them being coloured. One West Indian was quite definitely the best of the lot on all counts. But none of the selectors felt able to take the final responsibility of putting a coloured man over women operatives. It isn't just that one or two of them might object on sexual grounds. It's rather that the women treat their charge-hand as a sort of father-confessor, and tell him about all sorts of family and personal problems. I can't see them doing that with a coloured man. The first coloured charge-hand here would have to be exceptionally good. And then one must also consider the general labour situation. It's hard enough to get local labour now. You don't want people to start saying: 'If you go to work at Telelux you'll have a black man bossing you.' I think that when they start appointing black policemen in London that will be the time for promoting them here.

At higher managerial level reservations about up-grading immigrants tended to be expressed in terms of working efficiency:

I would be against the promotion of a coloured man to charge-hand at present, especially over women. Europeans would be more acceptable provided they spoke good enough English. But the factor of unpredictability also enters into the decision. One likes to be able to predict how a man will react in certain situations and emergencies. If there's a mistake and the man in charge loses his head, several pounds' worth of stuff may have to be scrapped.

At lower supervisory levels, informants were in closer touch with their operatives, and their replies were usually couched in terms of working relationships. It was generally agreed that a good European charge-hand would present few difficulties. So far as coloured workers were concerned, it was interesting to note that most foremen and charge-hands (particularly the new-style, specially trained supervisors) took a less cautious view than higher management: they thought that coloured charge-hands would be acceptable in an all-male unit. Two of the charge-hands who expressed this view had in fact worked as operatives under an Anglo-Indian charge-hand in another department.

I would have reservations about putting a coloured charge-hand over women, but not over men. Some of the girls are very emotional and they can flare up in anger at the supervisor. I think a West Indian might have trouble in handling them, and some with a chip-on-their-shoulder might interpret these outbursts as directed against them and their colour, instead of realizing that they're part of the day's work.

The supervisor already quoted, who had also worked under the same Anglo-Indian charge-hand, thought that Anglo-Indians would be acceptable as charge-hands, but not West Indians as yet: 'Anglo-Indians are different—they're not the negroid type. If you put an obviously coloured charge-hand over whites, especially over women, I think you'd have a riot. One must wait some years for that to be accepted.'

Several other informants felt that the degree of colour was important in this connexion: 'The degree of colour *does* make a difference. People are getting used to them but they still associate dark colour with backwardness. The problem will be solved in the next generation by the schools.'

Three informants expressed sympathy with one Anglo-Indian

high-grade operative in the department who had recently had his application for a charge-hand's vacancy turned down:

He doesn't talk about it much, but he took it to heart and thinks it's because of his colour, although he's really only a bit sun-tanned to look at. It may have been colour that made them turn him down, although there are two or three Anglo-Indian charge-hands in the plant now. But I think it's more likely the fact that he's in his fifties and nowadays most new charge-hands are made up when they are in their early twenties.

Only one supervisor, a charge-hand of several years' standing, had no reservations about the appointment of a coloured charge-hand. This informant had not served under a coloured charge-hand but was on very friendly terms with one West Indian male operative: 'In my view the right West Indian could be made up to charge-hand now and the women would accept it, although they might crab a bit at first.'

To sum up, only one informant in this section was unreservedly in favour of promotion for coloured immigrants and only one unreservedly opposed to it; the remainder either approved with reservations or felt that it would be better postponed for a few years, until the local labour force became more used to the regular presence of coloured workers. These relatively tolerant attitudes provided a considerable contrast to the much less flexible views encountered in many smaller and more traditional industrial establishments and were undoubtedly associated with the general climate of change, expansion and experiment that pervaded Telelux.

Department B: Department B came into being two years before Department A, as the original nucleus from which the whole of Division I was built up. It differed considerably from Department A in policy and practice with regard to coloured immigrant workers. The difference was summed up by one supervisor who had been in the department from the start: 'At the beginning the production process was tricky so we decided to keep the section white.[1] Later on, as we expanded, we had to take coloured operatives, and

[1] At that time Telelux had been taking on West Indian and other coloured operators for five years. It was difficult to establish whether the original decision was inspired by any definite antipathy, or simply by caution and conservatism. It was also maintained by several informants that the work was more complicated and faster than in Department A, and that few of the immigrants submitted by the Personnel Department had been able to make the grade.

now we make no objection to them. But it's the local married women who've pulled the department through.'

The 'lily-white' tradition and the reliance on part-time local women workers as an alternative to full-time immigrant labour had been somewhat eroded by expansion, labour shortage, and changes in the supervisory staff. These two trends had not, however, entirely disappeared in the Department, and were particularly noticeable in Unit 1, only seventy of whose 240 workers were full-time even then, the rest being on morning, afternoon or evening shifts. This unit came under an old-style foreman who had been with the department from the beginning. Eighty-one per cent. of its labour force consisted of female part-timers; another 12 per cent. were full-time women workers and the remaining 7 per cent. were full-time male workers. There were only three immigrants at this time: a West Indian man, an Anglo-Indian woman, and an Irish girl.

Unit 2 was engaged on the same type of production; but it was set up more recently and employed a labour force which was only one-third the size of that in Unit 1. This section relied much less on part-time female workers, who constituted only 30 per cent. of the total. It also had several full-time West Indian and European women workers and one West Indian man (the only hourly paid worker in the section). Somewhat surprisingly, the departmental manager and both unit managers estimated that each unit currently employed about 10 per cent. of immigrant workers—a gross overestimate (even if the calculation was restricted to full-time workers) and one which probably reflected the rather negative attitudes widespread in the department.

The persistence of the 'lily-white' tradition in Unit 1, despite the later arrival of management personnel who were more ready to employ immigrant labour, could be attributed to the continued presence of one or more supervisors from the first stage, to some tacit approval at higher level and to the self-perpetuating nature of such working-group arrangements. This latter consideration is particularly important. For if most of a unit's production is organized on a part-time basis, a vacancy will usually be filled by another part-time operator. As recent immigrants rarely or never seek part-time jobs, the newcomer is likely to come from the same labour source as her predecessor, i.e. in the case of Telelux, from the local pool of married women whose children had grown up or reached school age. Sometimes, newcomers might even have heard about a vacancy from friends who were already working in the unit. In particular, the evening shift in Unit 1 tended to be self-recruiting; it was described as 'a pleasant social group—almost a club'.

One charge-hand gave a vivid picture of informal relations in this kind of unit:

I must say I was nervous about taking a supervisory job over women, as I've never worked with them before. But I like it now, and as I've been with the firm over twenty years the old hands can't put anything over on me. Every charge-hand has his own methods, but I favour calling the girls by their Christian names, and I try to keep it all on a light-hearted level. There's a nice atmosphere here. For instance, it's my birthday today and when I came in I found a whole lot of cards on my desk and also a cardigan one of them had knitted. I stood them all a cup of tea in the tea-break. That's the birthday custom here.

At this time Unit 1 probably contained a rather higher proportion of 'old hands' than most working units in the department.[1] This did not, however, necessarily mean that the atmosphere on the floor was particularly clannish or hostile to outsiders. One informant said:

There's been no friction between colonial and white women. In fact, the girls made a terrific fuss of the first one we had. Then I took another one to keep her company. There was a bit of trouble with one coloured man, but that was because the girls said that the smell of the coconut oil that he put on his hair made them feel sick.

The unit manager then described an episode which might easily have been misinterpreted by the immigrant concerned and perhaps have led to bad relationships:

When the first coloured labourer came, the women refused to sit near him in the tea-area. Some of the supervisors thought this might be due to prejudice or smell; but when I went into it, it turned out that they didn't feel free to talk their usual sort of women's talk in front of a man, whatever his colour. The coloured girls mix in all right in the canteen.

The main resistance to immigrants in this unit appeared to have

[1] Their days were, however, numbered. As one informant said: 'The work in this unit will be increasingly small-scale and tedious. The immediate future is with the young girls, as an operative's eyesight often becomes inadequate for this work in the thirties. Then will come mechanization and automation, and the trend will be away from female operatives to male machine-minders.' Another added: 'There's a diminishing nucleus of old-stagers as operatives leave or get transferred. We aren't really too cliquey and it's not policy to encourage cliques.'

come from the original supervisors and was expressed in terms of their working ability:

We've had three West Indians. One was very good and two were unsatisfactory because they were slow. They didn't like the speed of our piece-work and couldn't make the rate, although I shifted them around to various jobs. I would take new coloured applicants with a good working record, but on past experience I doubt their ability. The unit also has a Jamaican labourer who didn't seem to get through enough work. He pulled himself together after he got a warning. I gave him an exact timetable and he now keeps to it. He's difficult to understand and at first he *would* keep his hat on.

Only two working groups in Unit 1 had a majority of full-time female operators. The charge-hand of one of these groups, a fairly recent arrival in the division, was the only supervisor in the unit who seemed to have much experience of immigrant workers:

In this group we have two girls to a machine. Two jobs are involved, one more complicated than the other. The girls are expected to be able to do both jobs and to swap around. They are paid the same whichever job they're doing. I've had two West Indians working together. They were slow and not very good. Neither could master the more complicated job properly and in the end they were transferred. At present I have a Southern Irish girl and an Anglo-Indian girl. The colleen went off home for Christmas and she hasn't come back yet [this was in February —S.P.]. The Anglo-Indian is a good worker and quiet. She works with another quiet sort of girl and there's no difficulty.

Despite the lack of enthusiasm for immigrant workers found among most supervisors in Unit 1, informants agreed that there had been 'no real trouble'. Only two incidents could be recalled involving coloured workers:

One coloured man had trouble with his wife and became mentally disturbed. Finally he accused the charge-hand of visiting his wife on his day off. The charge-hand actually brought witnesses to prove he was in another part of London but the chap wouldn't believe him. In the end he went off his head and was taken off to hospital. But he's out again now, and working in another department.

A year or so ago an industrial photographer came to photograph the plant. The two coloured girls were at their machine on the edge of the picture, and he asked them to move out. They were very hurt and started talking about the colour bar. The photographer (he was a foreign gentleman too) tried to explain in his bad English that it was a question of lighting, which had to be different for different skin tones. Finally he asked an Indian girl operative to explain but I doubt if they ever really understood it. I must say I felt bad about it myself. I couldn't see why he shouldn't have left them in.

Informants in Unit 1 had no very definite views on the subject of promotion for immigrant workers, probably because it had not entered the domain of reality. One informant had clearly never considered the question at all, while another said, after reflection, that if it ever happened he felt sure that there would be some resulting friction. When asked whether they would accept more coloured operatives, these informants were somewhat evasive.

The rather more tolerant atmosphere in Unit 2 was associated with its greater reliance on full-time operators; it also seemed to date back about one year, to the entry of some new-style supervisors. One of them described the general climate of the unit:

The old hands can still make things fairly hot if they want to, from the work and personal point of view. They still try to jump straight over four supervisory levels to the Division Manager. And they're always telling me what the previous supervisor used to do. But their influence is waning now. One or two of the most energetic have been transferred to other units. A year ago it was impossible to establish a new rate here under any circumstances. One immigrant girl, an Italian married to an Englishman, got into trouble over that when she first came. She made a new rate and the older women objected. The difficulty was to make her understand their objections because her English was very bad at first. But the resentment was individual, not against her as a foreigner. She's accepted now, though a few are envious and accuse us of favouritism because she's easily the best operative we've got and so she often gets picked out for Saturday work along with a few other good workers.

In Unit 2 West Indian operatives seemed to be taken more for granted by the supervisors as a permanent component of the labour force than in Unit 1, and to be judged on their individual merits, as the following comments indicated:

West Indian women often take longer to train than local girls, but they are just as good in the long run. One of those we have now is a little discontented. She hasn't been able to make her bonus yet so she thinks she's being picked upon because she's coloured. In fact, I tried to help her by suggesting to the two girls she sits with that they should let her go on their machine in order to learn the job. I pointed out that they wouldn't lose anything financially by it, but all the same they made a terrific row. One said to me: 'It's not fair—she's come and asked for our job.' So far I've won half the battle. She's on the machine mornings only.

One coloured girl has just been taken on as a service operator. This means fetching and carrying and doing little jobs for the charge-hand. The job needs some education and initiative and I'm afraid this one won't work out. She dozes off in corners and has no sense of responsibility.

One of the jobs in this group is less skilled than the others, but it needs a sense of rhythm and might suit the coloured operatives best. One coloured girl didn't start off too well but has picked up. At present she can't understand the bonus system. She sees other operatives apparently doing less on different jobs, but getting more money. She's a prickly type and has difficulties at home. She recently accused me of picking on her, but I didn't react. In fact I don't notice colour on the job. I treat them all as individuals and generally speaking get on all right.

Apart from minor frictions over the job itself, personal relationships between immigrant and other workers seemed to be fairly good:

Usually each new girl sits on her own for a few days during the tea-break. Then one of the others asks her to join a group. The coloured girls mix in at the tea-breaks but seem to go off together when they leave the unit. One Jamaican girl has made friends with a German girl, but that's not a very good thing: the latter is a trouble-maker. The Italian woman gets on all right. She has a real Latin temper but keeps it in check.

A West Indian male operator has just come in to the unit—you can see him over there, the light-coloured chappie with the intelligent face. It seems he was a clerk in Barbados. Though he's only been here a fortnight, he's already asked one of the girls to marry him. She just laughed and showed him her engagement ring. The coloured labourer is also looking for a wife. They seem to be quick workers but there's been no trouble over it.

I can't remember any complaints about personal hygiene in relation to coloured workers. There've been four complaints about the smell of sweat, but they concerned English or Irish girls. At our other factory I could imagine some difficulties arising. There were some jobs on which we had to make a sweat analysis of the operative, as the wrong individual make-up could upset the chemical process. I can imagine some coloured people completely misunderstanding the purpose of this and taking offence over it.

On the question of a quota, one supervisor said: 'The section's capable of absorbing more and I wouldn't expect trouble unless there's redundancy. You *might* get trouble then. For instance, at the other plant we had to lay off some girls, and there were accusations from local operatives that we were favouring the Irish girls, keeping them on at local workers' expense.'

Promotion of immigrants to charge-hand, which would, as in Unit 1, involve appointing a male over female operatives, was not even an issue for serious discussion in Unit 2. Informants expressed differing views about a more modest aspect of up-grading:

We should have a dozen replacement operatives but we've only got half that number. We just can't get a good enough standard. I don't think there'd be any resentment over up-grading if a coloured girl were good enough. There's no competition for the job. Even the Italian refused it because it means too much responsibility and change. On the other hand, one or two of the older women on testing are very status-conscious. It might be difficult to put coloured girls on the same job.

Department C: Department C was a technical department; it was still a nucleus and far smaller than the other departments, with thirty-five employees in all. The proportion of weekly to hourly paid staff was far higher here than in the production departments, being approximately 1:2. The weekly staff all had some technical qualifications or were working towards them. This department was, therefore, less comparable in organization and atmosphere to Departments A and B in the same division, and closer to the Research Laboratory (pp. 339 f.)

Department C had been in existence for three or four years, and was divided into three groups. One was the original technical group, which consisted of eight weekly paid technical staff and four hourly paid technical assistants. The second was a testing group, divided into two sub-groups, each containing about ten hourly paid female testers. The third group existed at this time mainly on paper; ultimately it was to be composed mainly of male artisans.

This small department had two immigrants on the weekly paid staff (a Pole and a West African, both in their twenties) and two or three amongst the hourly paid women. It also shared the services of one of the West Indian labourers from another department.

As in Research Laboratory, the presence of immigrants on the weekly paid staff seemed to be taken more or less for granted by their English supervisors and colleagues and by the hourly paid staff who worked under them.

Informants gave the impression that on the weekly paid level relationships were primarily a matter of individual abilities and temperament:

There's not a very close social life here anyway. We don't have a Christmas get-together or anything like that. Off the job our tastes differ quite a bit and the difficulty would be to decide what to do that would please everyone. It's a question of individuals rather than national groups. I must say that I personally had never met a foreigner until I came to work here but I think they fit in well. With N. (the Pole) it's a matter of accent (but he's gradually losing that). The black chap is accepted too. He married a girl of his own race just before Christmas and his standard of living is equal to our own. He hasn't got any sort of chip on his shoulder, either. One of his colleagues, who worked with him in the other factory, often jokes and calls him a 'sun-burnt Irishman', and P. just laughs and calls him something equally complimentary in return.

There's no friction over status between the hourly paid English assistants and the weekly paid personnel they work under, foreigners or not. You do sometimes get these frictions among technicians, but in this case the hourly-paid men are elderly, unqualified and quite content with their jobs. As for further promotion of the West African, there are special circumstances that might make this a problem. When he was at another of our factories he was in authority over some girl testers and there was a lot of unpleasantness. I've never been able to get to the bottom of it but I don't want this to follow him around. Women are more likely to flare up and we're a bit uncertain about his reaction. So at present he works directly under me on a special job, where he has no contact with the production side, although he meets the visiting government inspectors. I wouldn't anticipate any promotion problems with the Pole. He's been educated in this country and he's easy to get on with. His Christian name starts with Z and is quite unpronounceable so he tells everyone to call him Sid.[1]

Among the hourly paid women workers in the second group there were an Anglo-Indian, a white South African, and a Ukrainian refugee. The two supervisors there were long-service employees who had worked in other Telelux plants before coming here. Both these informants had a sympathetic attitude to all the workers under them, although one favoured an informal 'Christian name'

[1] His name turned out to be 'Zdzislaw'.

approach to operatives, while the other did not. Both took the presence of immigrant workers for granted, judged them individually and expressed the view that more could be absorbed in the unit without difficulty. One said:

This unit has only existed for eighteen months, so we're not much of a community yet, but some of the girls have several years' service, and one part-timer has twelve. Several have relations working spread out over the factory. There's a friendly atmosphere but we don't meet outside as we used to do on the other plant. When I was there I had a small unit consisting of an Indian, a West Indian, a Hungarian refugee, and two British—all men. It was the finest working team I ever had, though there was a little feeling between them at times. In another unit, I had two West Indians, very good operatives and very willing. One did think he was being picked on because of his colour but I managed to sort that out. Altogether I had a lot of West Indians there—women and two labourers (or general duties men as I prefer to call them—we're all trying to be middle class and on our dignity these days). We spread them out and tried to integrate them. There was no differentiation. I've always been a strong union man[1] and you know the unions are very concerned with racial discrimination....

I'll take West Indians here if they can do the job but personnel haven't sent any along as yet. I've got an Anglo-Indian woman—at least I think that's what she is, I haven't inquired—she's an ex-schoolteacher and one of the best. There's no trouble between her and the white South African. The European woman who's just arrived (Russian, I think) speaks very poor English. I'm helping her out with the timesheet. I asked her as a joke whether she was going to school to learn, but she looked at me very old-fashioned.

The prevailing climate in this small department seemed to be attributable to the skilled or qualified nature of the work, to the tolerant, non-generalizing attitudes of the weekly paid staff and supervisors, and finally to the positively sympathetic young departmental manager, who said: 'I wouldn't stand for any discrimination, but in fact I haven't found any.'

(b) *Division II*

Division II had the same basic structure as most other production divisions at Telelux: it was composed of three departments concerned with development, production, and testing. Until lately

[1] This informant now belonged to A.S.S.E.T., the 'foreman's union', but had previously been a very active A.E.U. shop-steward.

it had a fourth small department but this was in process of dissolution at the time of my interviews and its personnel (thirty male operatives, including two West Indians, two Anglo-Indians, and a Pole) were being dispersed to other departments and divisions. The young departmental head had already gone to take over the much larger production department (in Division I) with a 'lily-white' staffing tradition. As we have seen, that tradition was slowly being undermined and it seemed likely that his transfer would further the process.

Division II had been going for some five years and it manufactured a product which was in increasing popular demand. As the divisional manager said: 'We're now in the limelight. The product's impressive and we have the biggest turnover.'

The division had therefore expanded fast and at this time employed some 450 workers, 350 of whom were engaged on production proper. The divisional manager had been with it from the start, having originally been manager of the development department which was its nucleus. As a result of its rapid expansion the division was still geographically dispersed, not only on different floors but in different buildings. This separation had accentuated the tendency usually found in large firms for workers' feelings of loyalty and community to be focused less on the firm as a whole than on a smaller and more 'tangible' unit. In this case, according to the manager, the department, rather than the division, was the largest segment which attracted such feelings to any appreciable extent. Departmental exclusiveness was also enhanced by the existence of considerable differences in education, skills, and job status between the personnel of the two smaller technical departments and the main production department, with its large proportion of hourly paid, semi-skilled operatives.

The Production Department: This department came under a departmental manager and was divided into four sections. Two of them were engaged on production, one on assembly, and the fourth on test dispatch. The two production sections employed men only and worked a three-shift day (6.30 to 2.30; 2.30 to 10.30; 10.30 to 6.30). Assembly was done by women on day work and test dispatch by three all-male shifts and one small day-team of five men. There was also a developing unit which was set up four months before this inquiry and was temporarily attached to Section A; this had one male day shift but was to be built up into a third three-shift, all-male production section.

Section A: Each production section came under a section leader, who was a monthly paid junior executive. Both leaders were about thirty years old and each had been with the firm for four or five years. Section A's leader himself came from an unnoticed and virtually assimilated immigrant group, having arrived in Britain as a young refugee from Hitler's Germany in the 1930s. Each of the section's three production shifts came under a foreman and consisted of two charge-hands, four leading hands, twenty male operatives of various grades, and one or two labourers. The work was broken up into jobs for teams of two or three but there was no group bonus and consequently no possibility of friction over lowered earnings in the event of one member not pulling his weight. The section leader described the working units as 'small, friendly groups, many of them youngsters who may live fairly close to each other and the factory and often go out together'.

Contrary to the more general practice this section leader did the initial interviewing of men sent up by the personnel department and then passed them on to one of his three foremen for final selection. These three men differed greatly in character, degree of authoritarianism, and views about non-local labour and this had exerted a considerable effect on the composition and social climate of their particular shift. The section leader said: 'It's the foreman's attitude to an applicant that counts, not that of the men, though most foremen would take that into account as well.' He gave his own approach to selection as follows:

I'm interested in getting promotable labour as expansion is ahead for us. Most of our shift workers are in their early thirties. Generally speaking the most suitable labour consists of married men in the age-group 28 to 40 with families. Unmarried men have tax problems with overtime and also they don't like shift-work.

At this time, Section A had no European workers, with the exception of a Maltese, but had until recently had one Hungarian and a Yugoslav. The Hungarian was a radio mechanic who left the firm for a better job. He was said to have had language problems, but there had been no friction with other workers on political or other grounds. The Yugoslav was still with the firm but left the section when he was up-graded to weekly paid technical work.

The main group of immigrants here consisted of West Indians, of whom there were a dozen or so. One of them was a charge-hand and most of the others were in the higher operative classes. This West Indian group constituted about 12 per cent. of the sectional labour force, but the percentage had in the past been as high as 20 per cent., with considerable variations from shift to shift.

Most in sympathy with the section leader's positively unprejudiced views was the foreman of Shift 2, in which the West Indian charge-hand was working. Of this promotion the section leader said:

It was my idea and I tried it out with the foreman who has no prejudice and whose shop is generally speaking the happiest one. It's the foreman's attitude that counts, rather than that of the men. At the beginning —nine months ago—two or three of the other foremen in the department were dead against it but they've got used to it now. This particular West Indian is a very good worker. He's been here for eight years (longer than most workers) and was a senior operative and an active shop-steward for some time. He's not very dark or negroid looking, either, which may help. There were three charge-hand vacancies at that time and another West Indian put in for one. I told him that I couldn't appoint two at once and he accepted that. The only real trouble the first man's had has been with another West Indian; it may be because they're from different territories but the other man's very militant and I have a suspicion that he feels that the charge-hand is letting down the side by 'collaborating' with management.

The foreman of Shift 2 described the situation in more detail. He had been with the firm for nine years and took over the shift nearly four years ago:

About 50 per cent. of the operatives are long-service—five to ten years. Some see each other off the job, but not many live on the Tresco Estate, unlike the female labour force. There's a nice atmosphere and good working conditions on this floor, and relations with the union are good. There are four coloured men in one unit but only one in the unit with the West Indian charge-hand. He's the only one, white or coloured, who's caused any trouble over the appointment. His home life is bad and he's a general troublemaker. A charge-hand's job is mainly checking but he also gives orders to the leading hands. This particular one is with people who know him as an individual and there's been no difficulty. He's entered into our way of life and then he's a keen sportsman and used to play cricket for the firm — that helps a good deal.

I was hesitant about interviewing the West Indian charge-hand himself but he showed interest in the inquiry, perhaps because he wished to stress a certain sense of achievement. He proved to be from Guyana, and was a personable, intelligent, athletic young man who came to the interview room not in the customary white overalls but in an elegant tie and well-cut tropical-weight suit. Asked about his relations with his unit and others in the shift and section, he said:

I've many friends here and it's not the first time I've been a pioneer. I was a shop-steward and convenor before and I'm proud of it.[1] Some outside the unit and some of the foremen objected but I take a philosophic view and put it down to ignorance. The only one I've ever had trouble from is the West Indian in my unit. He says I'm trying to be a white man. Of course it's a matter of upbringing. My mother and father are of mixed blood and we're more class- and colour-conscious in B. G than they are in Jamaica. In fact I wouldn't associate with many of the West Indians who are here, just as I wouldn't associate with a lot of the English workers. That's why many of us don't join the clubs. We don't like being patronized or forced into them to mix with just anyone.

This informant seemed well enough adjusted to his work situation although he was, perhaps inevitably, rather self-conscious about it and his superficial nonchalance seemed to cover a certain submerged prickliness over colour and class. He was unmarried and had not yet made a final decision whether to stay permanently in Britain or to return home: 'I find England a bit stiff. The best time I had since I left home was in Paris. I met an English friend there and we had a marvellous international party with some American girls and others who tagged on. Class and colour didn't seem to matter there.'

Shift 1 had six West Indians in its total strength of twenty: one was a Guyanese, the others Jamaican. This was a far higher percentage than in most working groups in Telelux and most of the West Indians were concentrated on one of the two units. One of them was a leading hand, one an inspector (Grade 4), three were Grade 3 operatives, while the remaining one was a labourer. The foreman here was one of the younger, new-style foremen, which the firm had been training, away from the 'sergeant' tradition and

[1] It was interesting to learn from this informant that he had, in fact, been six years with Telelux, not eight as the section leader had said. The discrepancy may have been due to forgetfulness, but the attribution of longer service to a particular employee could also imply a high degree of acceptance of him in the working community.

towards the technical supervisor model. His views were fairly objective but a good deal less favourable than those of Shift 2's foreman:

Almost all the white workers have been here four or five years—the longest has eight years' service. The West Indians have about two years' service each. They brought one another in and they're fairly stable. There is a feeling of shift community but the coloured men tend to keep apart and don't talk much. In the canteen they sit in groups or join with coloureds in other sections. They join the union but they don't join the clubs much.

As for their working ability, they look slow but they get the work done. They tend to be colour-conscious and abrupt in their manner, which puts some people against them. We had a white South African on the staff but he didn't object to their colour. There were some complaints about the up-grading to leading hand but nothing came of them in the end. That up-grading means another weekly pound in the pay-packet so we always have to be careful who we appoint.

This informant was one of the foremen who were said to have objected to the appointment of a coloured charge-hand. When asked about this, he said: 'Yes, I was against it because I thought it was too early. My own men said they wouldn't work under him. It will be the second generation that will be brought up in English ways. They've got a different background now.'

Asked about other workers from different ethnic backgrounds, this informant said he had personal experience only of the Yugoslav, who had formerly worked in this section. He commented: 'He was too good for the job—he's got a staff job now.'

The foreman of Shift 3, a man with thirteen years' service with the firm, was older and more closely patterned on the traditional, authoritarian model of an industrial foreman. He clearly stood no nonsense from anyone, but had a pleasant, downright manner, and gave the impression of being fair-minded. He served in the army in India ('when white men were in the ascendancy') but displayed no obvious 'wog complex'.[1] In the past this shift had some East European workers, but according to him had more experience of West Indians:

At present there's only one West Indian, who started five years ago

[1] He did say, towards the end of the interview: 'I don't think I'm really prejudiced, though I don't like to see mixed marriages. But it's the girl's business, not mine.'

as a labourer and is now a Grade 4 operative. But usually we have about five on a shift of twenty to twenty-five. That's the best workable proportion. The coloured intake some years ago seemed better educated than the new ones, but although some are slower than the average at learning the work they are usually as good in the long run. They usually work in mixed teams and mix in fairly well with the other men. The one we have now takes his meal breaks with the white men on this shift and doesn't sit with coloured men from other sections.

The labour turnover in this shift had settled down in recent months and the labour-core in each working unit consisted of men with five to six years' service with the firm. This informant was concerned to keep things that way:

My real prejudice is against single men because they don't stick. The ideal shift-worker is between thirty and forty-five years old and married. Most Irish don't fit the bill though we had one who stayed and became a charge-hand. The coloured chaps stick once they get here because it's a good job. All other things being equal service counts so they get in line for up-grading to leading hand. As for promotion to charge-hand, there was a bit of dissension when S. [the Guyanese charge-hand on Shift 2] was made up to charge-hand, but it was well handled because he was kept on the shift where they knew him. I think the feeling against it was probably due to jealousy and then darkness and negroid looks make it more complicated. Yet there's quite a tendency to vote coloured men in as shop-stewards—nobody else much wants the job. There's not been so much trouble over the promotion of white Europeans.

The developing unit already mentioned, which was attached to Section A, came under a graduate engineer with two charge-hands under him (the foreman's place was still vacant); they were in charge of the two existing day-shift sub-units, each of which had eight to ten male workers. Most of the selection of the unit's personnel had been carried on by Section B's present leader, and it had not yet crystallized into a cohesive entity. It was, therefore, difficult as yet to see it as a stable working community and the views expressed by informants were in part based on earlier experiences in other sections. Its labour force included a West Indian, a Maltese, and an Irishman, all in the same sub-unit.

Most of the work in this developing unit was done by men working in teams of two or three. One of the singleton jobs was done by the West Indian, about whom the graduate head of the unit and the charge-hand held rather differing opinions. The graduate engineer said: 'He works alone because he likes to tease the other chaps. I shall be pulling him up about it soon.' On the other hand, the recently promoted charge-hand, a rather genial character with nine years' service with Telelux, commented:

He's been here three years but only one week with me. He used to be on shift till they took him off because of stomach trouble. He seems O.K.—he's the quiet type and mixes in all right at the canteen. I eat there with the men myself, like most charge-hands and foremen, so I'd notice any friction. But in my nine years here on the floor I only remember one bit of colour trouble—when the men ribbed a coloured chap about the Homburg hat he wore. He didn't have any sense of humour and took it badly. As for the others, the Maltese seems more like an Italian, accent and all. The Irishman doesn't like the heat here. Most Irishmen don't usually like a job that keeps them still for eight hours anyway. They like to move about, do different jobs and so on. I thought the coloured chap would like the heat but he tells me it's a different sort of heat where he comes from.

Section B: Like Section A this section had three shifts, each with a foreman, two charge-hands, and thirty-five men. Community feeling in this section seemed to be less strong than in Section A. The section leader also contrasted his men's attitudes with those prevailing in Section C (where the operatives were all women):

The leading lights among the women there have twenty years' service or more. Most of them come from the Tresco estate and quite a number are related or friends off the job as well. Here there's not much community spirit and no feeling for the factory. There are one or two old-timers but nothing like a nucleus. Only five out of 100-odd come from the Tresco estate. Shift work may prevent the development of any close community feeling.

According to the section leader, there were six West Indians, one Pole, and some Southern Irish (all men) in this section.[1] The latter was not so much of a 'sponsor' as the leader in Section A but his approach was objective and tolerant:

We've had coloured operatives for at least five years and the department as a whole had more than most. Their turnover seems about aver-

[1] In fact, detailed inquiries in each shift showed that there were rather more. Such minor inaccuracies reinforced the impression that quotas in Telelux were rarely precisely or rigidly applied.

age. I leave it to the foremen to see the men sent over by the Personnel Department. We're still extremely short of labour and the alternative is often a coloured man or nobody at all. . . . Some shop stewards are a bit 'anti' so they're not used on trouble involving colour. But in this section we don't have much of that—there was no demand for coloured men to go first when we had some redundancy during the credit squeeze. The main spot of bother I remember was with a West Indian hot-gospelling type who tried to convert the others during the tea-breaks. But the same sort of thing happens with whites. I've one now who's a Jehovah's Witness and there's also a Rosicrucian.

Shift 1 was found to contain thirty-seven men, of whom five were West Indians and two Poles (not one, as the section leader had said). There were also some Southern Irish; in past years there had also been a Malayan and a Pakistani. This foreman was also cast in the traditional foreman mould, a bluff, downright ex-regular serviceman in his forties. On labour relations in general he said:

One of the men has nearly twenty years' service, another over ten, but the rest have about two to three. Some know each other off the job. I try to make a pleasant atmosphere for the men—you get better work that way. The shop stewards don't have much to do here, unlike most factories. They come to me first before running to the convenor—there are so many trivial complaints I can dispose of at once.

This informant accepted West Indian workers, though with certain reservations over numbers and promotion.

The five West Indians we have now all have two or three years' service. There are two in one sub-section and three in the other. Two are doing a class 2 job and one of them is the best worker of all the men. He's completely accepted by the other men and I personally never notice his colour. He's just an individual to me now. At the other extreme we used to have a Bible puncher who was training to be a missionary. He annoyed everyone by pestering them in the canteen—in the end he went. Most of them won't take a reprimand easily, which makes for difficulties. We've some migrant Irish—they come in for the winter when the building goes off. This lot are fairly stable but I'd want a quota for them like the West Indians. As for promotion, I think an all-coloured unit would do best under a coloured charge-hand but I was against the appointment in Section A. It's too early yet and there might be difficulty in the event of redundancy. Being elected as a shop-steward doesn't mean one will be accepted as a charge-hand—no one wants the job of shop-steward. Promotion of Europeans is different and I don't think the men would object so much. They're not so noticeably different and they're more like us in behaviour. I'd a French-Canadian chap who would have been made up to charge-hand but for his bad English and there's a Pole who does the charge-hand's job in one of the sub-units now. He's an ex-R.A.F. officer and speaks good English—he's got an English wife too.

While accepting coloured workers, with certain reservations, this informant displayed a fair degree of 'wog complex', apparently stimulated by his experiences in the armed forces overseas:

I don't like to see coloured men with white women—though I must admit that here it's the white women who are after them, and the coloured men don't reciprocate. Some are educated but a lot are not far from savages. Their behaviour is so different it often sets up trouble even in the canteen. For instance, we had an Indian untouchable. He was so used to being avoided in India that he would always move away or stop eating when someone came near. Understandable if you know India but difficult to explain to the men, who only wanted to be friendly.

The Polish acting charge-hand in one sub-unit of this shift proved to be a fairly representative example of the more adaptable, middle-aged, ex-professional officer. He had accommodated himself satisfactorily to life in Britain and was partly assimilated in economic, civic, and even private life (thanks to his English wife, who came from a similar professional background) without having basically rejected his Polish cultural, emotional, and patriotic affiliations. For the work-situation he had simplified his real name, Franciszek Gabkiewicz, to Mr. Frank Gee, but had not anglicized it formally. He spoke excellent English, but became a good deal more forthcoming about his present and past life and his relationships at work as soon as the discussion switched to Polish.[1]

At this time Mr. Gee was in his late forties. When the War broke out he had just embarked on a legal career. During the War, after a spell of flying duty, he became a liaison officer between the Polish Air Force and the Royal Air Force. Like many Polish airmen, he married an English girl. After the War his father-in-law gave him a position in his business, but Mr. Gee, who was of an independent and philosophical frame of mind, preferred to strike out on his own, even in a more modest capacity. He came to Telelux on the recom-

[1] See p. 365 for the way in which the use of the mother-tongue can influence the nature of the information and the whole emotional intensity of the interview.

mendation of one of the senior executives, who was a colleague of his in the Royal Air Force. He earned a good wage, had twice been a shop-steward, but had refused formal promotion to a charge-hand's job because this would mean a considerable drop in his weekly earnings. His wife had a good office job and they lived in their own house in one of Croydon's better suburbs. Mr. Gee was not greatly perturbed by his lowered occupational status, since his standard of living was higher than that of many British white-collar or even lower professional workers; it was also higher than that of most exile members of the pre-war Polish intelligentsia. He said:

> One has to accept one's fate. There are compensations. And here in the factory we Poles stick together and meet quite a lot, though we don't advertise it. There are several like me. One is a shop-steward in another division. He didn't want to apply, because of being a foreigner, but his foreman put him in for it. There are two others, one on this shift, of whom I see a lot. We get on all right with the English workers.

Shift 2 had two sub-units, each containing ten men. It had a small nucleus of three or four men, but the others were said to 'come and go'. There was reported to be little mixing on or off the job, except for three men who played football or snooker.[1] The shift had no foreman at this time and was under the senior charge-hand, who was less objective and more unguarded in his statements than the majority of informants at foreman level. The shift contained several Irishmen, mostly related to one another, and three West Indians, two in one sub-unit, one in another. There was also an apprentice, of whom the charge-hand said: 'I think he's Anglo-Indian. You can tell he's got a bit of India in him.' All three West Indians were in the second lowest grade:

> One is the best worker in his unit, the other the worst. He's surly, with a chip on his shoulder, and I hate having to give him instructions.[2] The first chap you can't help liking, though he doesn't look clean and smells a bit. When he's on night-shift he comes to work with his pyjamas on under his suit. Earlier we had some trouble on the night-shift when the others thought a coloured man wasn't pulling his weight. When one

[1] The charge-hand said: 'I suggested getting together for a Christmas drink last December but only a handful picked up the idea, so I dropped it.'

[2] This informant seemed to be under the impression that West Indians do not speak English at home. He said: 'It's difficult to give instructions to a chap who's only recently learned the language.'

man spoke up the coloured man hit him on the face and I had to hold them apart. It was a chance to get rid of the coloured chap, who was a trouble-maker, but I don't like getting rid of anyone so I had him transferred.

The charge-hand clearly regarded most West Indians as strange and different:

> They don't behave like you or me. On the buses they sit separately but talk loudly across other people. They've all got a chip on the shoulder. One of the old hands said he was never against coloured people until he had to work next to them. But they've got a lot of go. Look how they buy houses and cars on the H.P. If I had that much energy I'd own two houses by now. But I think it would have been best to build up industry in Jamaica and let them stay there.

Despite his repetition of a number of unfavourable clichés about West Indians and his avowed disapproval of mixed marriages, this informant was careful not to generalize and it was interesting to learn that he had been on friendly terms both on and off the job with the West Indian charge-hand (see p. 322–3) when they were in the same unit: 'We were good friends then and I had him along to my house several times. He has a concealed chip on his shoulder too and makes up by being rather overbearing socially. On the job he's very rigid—first as a shop-steward and then on the other side as a charge-hand.'

The third shift had thirty-six male operatives in three sub-units, and there was also a labourer. It had been in existence for only a few years and as a result of recent large-scale reorganization was said to be 'in a state of flux' and to have had a large labour turnover. Most of the men lived locally, but only about eight had as much as three or four years' service. There were four West Indians and one Egyptian, only one of whom had more than a year's service. One West Indian was in the lowest grade, the others in the next lowest one.

The foreman here was young, taciturn, and rather suspicious about the purpose of the inquiry. Of the West Indians he said:

> They're slow on the whole and curiously enough they can't stand up to the humid heat, especially in the annexe, where it's worst. They tend to complain of tummy upsets when they're on night-shift. A lot leave because of the shift-work, especially the young and unmarried. Some have a chip but mostly get on all right with the others. They sit with

them in the canteen and went off for a Christmas drink with some of the chaps last year. The ones we have aren't interested in sport. I don't know about their social life off the job—so long as they work all right here that's all we want.

This informant refused to be drawn on the subject of promotion of West Indians, even in the case of the charge-hand; he pointed out that in his own shift the matter was still academic since the West Indians were only in the lower grades. The leader in Section B had already commented that as a general rule a newly promoted foreman would have been with the firm between five and ten years and a charge-hand would have at least two years' service.

Section B provided a considerable contrast with Section A as regards general stability and community feeling and also in the extent to which various immigrant individuals and groups had been absorbed and become part of the regular labour force. The difference could be attributed primarily to the fact that Section B had in recent years suffered redundancy followed by a rapid build-up. The human factor had, however, been extremely important. Those in positions of authority at all levels of a hierarchy tend both to select and to attract like-minded subordinates. In the case of Section A this had produced a friendly and tolerant working atmosphere, and in one case what might be called a hierarchy or chain of sponsorship or tolerance running down from the section leader through the foreman of Shift 2 ('the happiest shop') to the West Indian 'pioneer' charge-hand and the unit of local workers that accepted him in this position (see chart on p. 397).

Section C: This section presented a considerable contrast to both the production sections just described. The work was entirely day work and the labour force consisted of ninety women, mostly part-time, divided into two production units, and of some higher-grade operatives in a third, rather smaller inspection unit. The three charge-hands[1] were all men (there was no promotion for women beyond leading hand on the shop floor at Telelux). These three men differed somewhat from the charge-hands already interviewed in Department A, being older men of long service (fifteen to twenty-five years) with a conspicuously fatherly demeanour. As we saw in Division I, this seemed to be the preferred type of charge-hand for women operatives, accepted both by the women themselves and by

[1] The foreman's position was temporarily vacant at the interview period.

management. The section leader in this department commented: 'Women need more tact in handling than men and there's much more cliqueyness among them. They're O.K. as long as you let them cry on your shoulder every now and then.'[1]

Of the ninety-odd women in this section, a large number had been with Telelux for many years as part-timers or full-time workers, some having as much as twenty years' service. Many had worked in this section since it was set up several years ago. They had two shop-stewards, and were highly unionized, a relatively rare situation with female labour. A considerable number lived on the neighbouring Tresco estate and were acquainted with one another off the job. Any cliqueyness was positively displayed in such sectional enterprises as the orphanage committee, which collected dues of 6*d*. a week from the majority of employees in the section and organized periodic outings for the children. There were said to be three unofficial leaders among the women, all older women from the Tresco estate; they ran the orphanage committee and one of them was also a shop-steward.

This was the kind of situation into which outsiders and immigrant workers often have considerable difficulty in fitting. In this particular case the position would seem to have been eased by the fact that the charge-hands were tolerant and easygoing and that the units contained no particularly biased or prejudiced individuals. The section leader said:

> We've tried up to ten West Indians since the section was set up. Most of them were lazy and useless but the three we've got now are all right and have been here a fair time. There's been no trouble except in one case, eighteen months ago, when a coloured girl was sent to Coventry for doing the rate when the shop-steward was fighting it. That blew over and they seem to fit in all right though they are a little aloof.

The elderly charge-hand who was acting as foreman gave more details about working relations:

> The girls here are quite a tight community. But the three coloured girls we have now have adapted themselves, share a good joke with the rest and mix in all right in the canteen, though they tend to go on their own to the cloakroom. They're all married to coloured men who are working on shift here. There's also a white girl who's married a coloured worker. I've noticed that she sometimes goes to the canteen with the

[1] See pp. 309–11, 313.

coloured girls and sometimes with the whites. There's very little friction and that mostly over work. We've been lucky. When they first came we saw how they roll a bit as they walk and we thought their work might be like that—slapdash and uneven. But they're good workers and can keep up on speed and efficiency with the others. We haven't had much experience with other immigrants—a few years ago there was a Polish first hand who was very good, but there aren't many Polish women working nowadays.

Asked about promotion this informant said: 'When they asked for my views on the appointment of S. as a charge-hand in Section A I said I had nothing against it provided he was good enough and got on with the men, as is the case.'

Section D: This section was concerned with test dispatch and had three shifts, each employing fifteen to sixteen men under a charge-hand, plus a small day-team of four men. Each shift had a nucleus of men with ten or more years' service with the firm and labour turnover was very low. There had never been any European workers here, although no clear reason for this could be ascertained. Coloured men had been working in the section for three or four years only. At this time there were seven West Indian men in the section, evenly spread over the shifts. The section leader, a graduate engineer with a pleasant, unassuming manner who had worked his way up from the shop floor, mirrored the rather clannish, conservative atmosphere of the section:

I'm not in love with them but I take them. But one must consider our own permanent people. West Indian workers seem to be either the highly intelligent type who want to go to night school so take day jobs or else the labouring type. Only one of those we have now is of high grade. It's really an embarrassment to offer him a low-paid job—he'd be better off in the lab. The others are slow, whereas the job needs quickness and dexterity. It's also hot and there have been complaints about sweat and smell from the other men. I put two together on testing in a closed booth and I must say I myself didn't like going in there. The other difficulty is that they're clique-ish and always attributing a ticking-off to their colour, so that special caution is needed.

Of the three charge-hand posts, one was vacant and one of the two existing charge-hands was on temporary loan from another section and knew little about working relations on his shift. The other charge-hand, however, knew a good deal about the whole section. He had been with the firm for seven years and had recently been promoted from the floor in the same shift. He was also in charge of the small day-team, which consisted of old-timers with no West Indian workers.

Although this informant was not particularly enthusiastic about West Indian workers he discussed the matter in a fair-minded way, displaying considerable knowledge of their circumstances and relationships with the other men.

I've three in my shift, one very good, another very slow. I worked side by side with them before I was made up to charge-hand. They don't mix in in the canteen but sit together. They're all saving up to go home. One has to be careful how one speaks to them. I think they're more colour-conscious than the English. They've got some good reasons for it—Notting Hill and so on—but it makes it difficult on the job. I've got some trouble with two who are on a job that one man could do, whereas the rest of the shift are working full out on other jobs. These two don't show willing when I send them up for spares and so on. I try to send whites when I can, to show I'm not picking on them specially. Actually none have ever accused me of picking on them because of their colour. Speaking frankly from my short experience, I'd rather have white workers.

At the time of the interviews the atmosphere in this section was being disturbed by a 'storm in a milk-cup' dispute which had been in progress for some weeks; the major issue, involving a free issue of milk which had been withdrawn, was being thrashed out with the unions at departmental level. A threatened stoppage had been averted, but there had been a quarrel between a militant Irishman and a West Indian man who had obeyed the convenor and gone back to work. In this the local labour force supported the West Indian.

The Irishman lost his temper and called him a blackleg. Words passed and now they're not on speaking terms. I heard that the coloured chap was upset and trying to move to another section so I took him to the section leader, who told him he wouldn't stand for the Irishman badgering him and to come to him again if it went on. I hope the whole thing will die down. The other men took the coloured man's side and made a point of telling him so. They're a fair-minded lot.

The Development Department: This department was, as the youngsh, lively manager said, more of a laboratory than a production unit. Most of its forty-five members (the great majority men) had technical and scientific qualifications and there were few hourly paid workers.

The hierarchy was shallow by comparison with that of the ordinary production departments. Under the departmental manager came six graduate engineers, one in charge of a service section, the other five running separate projects with the aid of a small, specialized staff of technical assistants (weekly paid, with 'O' level education and some higher training), laboratory assistants (weekly paid, promoted from hourly paid labour force), and a handful of hourly paid assistants with some skills. There was considerable cross-linking, each section providing information and services for the others.

The department was due to expand by taking on another fifteen or so staff members over the next year. It had existed more or less in its present form for six years; before that its manager had been the man who was now the head of the division.

According to my informant these 'laboratory' departments on the production side attracted a number of hourly paid misfits and mavericks from the engineering department:

> By that I don't mean the bad workers but the ones who can't fit in to the organized union set-up and who like to work on their own. Engineering is less routine and more interesting here because they do the whole job. That lures them up despite the fact that the hourly paid workers are comparatively badly paid. They're on the top time-rate but they're still underpaid. There's a certain prestige apart from the interest of the job—for instance, very few people are on Christian name terms here. In the production departments foremen and charge-hands complain that some of the old girls shout their Christian names right across the floor. As for the technicians, very few come out of the research labs to the production side here but I'm trying to winkle some out. The work's interesting at all levels. There's some cross-linking with production departments but more outside this plant with the research lab. near Redhill and even with the main European factory.

The departmental manager then enlarged on the atmosphere and relationships within the department:

> I warn everyone at the start that in a small department with small working groups they must fit in. If there's any trouble I won't keep the people involved. But despite the absence of Christian names there's a very cordial atmosphere here. But people shouldn't be too familiar off the job—they need to get right away from it, even if they live near by

(and there are a fair number of local types here). As for attitudes to immigrants, there's no xenophobia in this department. Any feelings would be on a personal basis.

In this department there were, at the time of the interview, six weekly paid immigrants: a Pole, a Southern Irishman, an Indian, and an Anglo-Indian, all men, and two Anglo-Indian sisters. The hourly paid workers included a Pole and two West Indians. In addition, one of the six section leaders was an Austrian Jewish refugee who originally came to Britain in the 1930s. Of him my informant said:

He came up from the engineering department some years ago. Like some of our hourly-paid workers he had difficulty there—in his case because he's a quiet, studious, retiring type and he was the only graduate (the Vienna Technical University); there they have a rather rough and ready approach to work.

The departmental manager had himself worked on refugee resettlement in Germany after the 1939–45 War and had a German wife. After enumerating the immigrants, he made an illuminating comment: 'I'd no idea we had so many. I don't think of them in those terms, but as individuals. As far as foreigners go, we've also got a Yorkshireman and he's quite different from the local types—blunt and obstinate.'

The manager was knowledgeable and sympathetic about the various immigrants, who were fairly well spread over the six sections.

The two Poles were not in the same section and were also separated by a difference of job status and probably also of social class and educational background:

The T.A. is about forty and came to the Division about five years ago as an hourly paid worker on the production side. He reached the equivalent of School Certificate level before the War and we gave him part-day release to go to night school. He got his O.N.C.[1] but has failed the H.N.C. once, perhaps because of his English, which isn't too good or fluent. He was in Sweden during the War and I think speaks Swedish at home with his Swedish wife. He has quite an accent and tends to be a bit opinionated. He's been here over a year but hasn't entirely shaken down yet. Like most Poles he's violently anti-Communist and this sometimes leads him to adopt a rather anti-labour attitude, particularly

[1] Ordinary National Certificate.

because the engineering union is so militant here. . . . The other Pole is more than ten years older. He's a short, powerfully built chap with a poor vocabulary and he's difficult to understand. But he's a very good tool-maker with a pre-war training. He seems to have worked all over Central Europe and after 1939 went through the Polish Air Force into war industry. We got him up here because he was at odds with all the militant A.E.U. types in the engineering shop—on political grounds as well as personality differences. He's anti-union and finally resigned from it. Even here he gets on pretty badly with the others in the small engineering section and is more or less permanently in Coventry, but that doesn't seem to worry him.[1]

My informant said of the Anglo-Indians:

The man isn't obviously coloured but he's the diffident, reserved type and he had a man over him for a while who'd been out east and showed a bit of wog complex. Now he's on a weekly basis and has a responsible job but nobody directly under him. He hasn't any technical qualifications and can't go further. Others are beginning to overtake him and he's not too happy about it, though he accepts it. Then there are two Anglo-Indian sisters who have been here a long time and look and are completely English.

The lone Irishman was highly regarded by the departmental manager, who said of him:

He came up from the hourly paid group. He's very good at the practical work and one of our best men, the kind who can be the backbone of a department like this. He's young but quite settled—he went back home for Christmas for the first time in five years but reported back here on time . . . In the same section is one of the West Indians—black as your hat but has a nice little face, not very negroid in features. In personality he's nice and well-spoken. He's not married but seems quite settled. He's been with us two years and with the firm for eight. The only spot of bother came when he was in another section under a woman technical assistant who's been here a long time. She has an

[1] This informant admitted that his work in D.P. camps in Germany had left him with a not over-favourable opinion of Poles, Russians and other East Europeans. Such views are sometimes found among British and American officials who had to deal over a long period with the desperate, hate-filled, often demoralized, starving, verminous human flotsam left alive in the Nazi labour and concentration camps, who contrasted so sharply with the clean, meek, well-disciplined German civilians outside the D.P. camps. This informant, who may also have taken over some of the attitudes of his German wife, also disliked the authoritarianism and rigid protocol which he had found characteristic of the liberated Polish P.O.W.s from the 1939 campaign, who also came under his administration in Germany.

awkward manner and there was a conflict of personalities. I know it was nothing to do with colour because I asked her beforehand if she would mind having him—the section's secluded and they work a lot in dark rooms. But he may have thought colour came into it and also resented having a white woman over him. I don't know but anyway I thought it best to move him. The other West Indian is also well-spoken and a steady worker. He's been with the company about five years. Unlike the other he's got a sallow complexion and is even less negroid in type.

A number of Indian technicians had been tried in this department, but only one was working there at this time. The manager had very definite views on the working ability of this group:

The one we have now is the only competent one I've ever found. Many apply for weekly and senior jobs but their qualifications are no good. It's a waste of time to ask them for interviews and I never take them now. Manual dexterity isn't essential at that level (they're lacking in that) but we need common sense and ideas and they've done too much superficial memory work.

The issue of promotion was clearly different in this kind of department, as it depended mainly on individual ability, qualifications and personality. Some immigrants were hampered by language difficulties, others by age ('By the time a man gets to 50 he's reckoned to have reached his final grade'). My informant doubted whether most of the individual immigrants in his department would go much further but said that there had been no objections from colleagues or subordinates to them holding their present posts. 'It's the person that counts. As I said before, it's a small department.'

The Testing Department: Like the development department, this department was a laboratory with a mainly technical staff. It was, however, even smaller, with a total strength of twenty-five members, including two women clerical workers. It was divided into two sections, each under a monthly paid section leader. Unlike the development department, however, the testing department had no non-English staff at all, with one partial exception: 'There's one chap with a slight foreign accent—he's an Austrian Jew who came to Britain before the war, but he's no different from anyone else.' The main reasons for this seemed to be the fact that there was no particular shortage of staff, and also the rather insular and conservative attitude of the manager, who had been in charge since the department was set up six years before, and had been working with the company for much longer. Asked if he would take on European or coloured immigrants as weekly staff, he said:

Maybe I'm old-fashioned but if I'm presented with two equally good candidates I'd choose the Englishman. But if the non-Englishman were obviously more brilliant I'd take him. With the Poles and other Middle Europeans I feel there's a different attitude to the job. They need more supervision and while I wouldn't call them sly I've had experience of some who change their figures to suit the theory. The Asian way of thinking is most remote of all; the Germans, Scandinavians and Dutch are the nearest to the Englishman, who'll give you a straightforward yes or no on the problem. Coloured men I find slow to learn but as good afterwards on operatives' jobs. I've had Europeans on the exchange scheme and they get on well enough. I don't think the rest of the staff would object to having them on a permanent basis.

(c) *The Research Laboratory*

At Telelux most production divisions had their own specialized development departments and laboratories, but there were also two larger laboratories with more general functions. The laboratory chosen for study was mainly concerned with assistance to development groups and advice to customers on the best use of the company's products. As one of the section leaders said, 'We're half-way between a research lab and outdoor contact—not real back-room boys.'

This laboratory afforded a considerable contrast to the production departments, with their high proportion of hourly paid workers. It had a staff of nearly seventy, of whom only six were hourly paid (all were skilled craftsmen). The remainder were divided about equally between weekly and monthly paid staff; they were mostly men, with a handful of weekly paid women laboratory and clerical workers. The average 'working life' of qualified women was said to be about four years, and for this reason men were preferred for laboratory work.

The work of this laboratory required specialists in physics, electronics, and electrical engineering. Graduates were rarely local but were drawn from all over the country; they entered at the lowest monthly paid grade, except for most of those with Indian qualifications, which were regarded as the equivalent of the Higher

National Certificate (H.N.C.).[1] Like all weekly paid staff who had passed their H.N.C., Indian qualified graduates were, however, annually considered for promotion to the monthly staff. Monthly paid staff were also allowed generous time off for postgraduate studies under a two-year scheme; those who secured a Ph.D. or D.Sc. degree received a higher salary rate. Most weekly paid staff were recruited from selected grammar-school leavers (mainly local) with an Advanced Level (G.C.E.) pass in mathematics or physics; they worked in the department while taking their H.N.C. in two stages under a special five-year training scheme. There was a considerable status gap between weekly and monthly paid staff, underlined for the latter group by such indices as access to the 'monthly' canteen (dining-room), the privilege of not clocking in, and so on. Promotion through the various weekly and monthly grades was not automatic, and it was the practice to warn individual staff members when they seemed to be approaching their highest potential grade. As one section-leader explained: 'This sometimes has a stimulating and salutary effect, but if weekly paid men don't make the monthly grade they tend to leave. Apart from the blow to prestige as others pass them, the salary is too low as they get older and have to keep a family. But some just aren't up to it. I expect responsibility and a professional attitude from the monthly staff.'

For this reason, staff turnover was lower in the monthly than in the weekly grades; it was lower still in the higher monthly grades. For instance, all six section leaders had between ten and fourteen years' service with the company. There was, however, a fair amount of internal turnover as new departments, sections, and groups were set up and developed.

In this laboratory the ethnic composition of the staff changed frequently because it contained so many students and trainees; numbers and distribution of non-staff at the time of my visit were not, however, regarded as particularly unusual. The six hourly paid, skilled workers were all English, as were the small clerical staff (with one possible exception—a typist who looked as if she might be an Anglo-Indian). On the other hand, eleven of the twenty-nine monthly paid laboratory staff were of non-English birth (two Netherlanders, one Pole, one Hungarian, one Turk, two Austrian Jewish refugees, four Indians); this total included the

[1] Qualifications from a small number of Asian universities were classed as 'English-valued' and acceptable.

laboratory manager and three of the six section leaders. Again, of the twenty-seven weekly paid technical staff, six were not English-born (two Dutch, two Poles, one Israeli, one Indian). In both groups some were more or less permanent staff, while others were on short-term training schemes but might, it was thought, stay on with the firm.

The laboratory's manager listed a number of reasons for the high proportion of non-English in these grades: the general shortage of skilled and qualified men; the international character of the company; the impersonal approach and the lack of insularity found among most scientists and technicians; the advantage to the department of having staff with a knowledge of languages and a cosmopolitan approach in such matters as reading technical journals in other languages, attending the necessary conferences and making professional contacts with colleagues and firms in other countries. Another favourable point advanced was that in this company there were no security restrictions prohibiting the employment of alien nationals or those who were not British-born. An additional and extremely important factor was that the laboratory's Dutch manager, although long settled in Britain and considerably anglicized, had consistently followed a non-insular pattern in his staff appointments and promotions. As one of his section-leaders commented with approval and admiration: 'It's he who sets a liberal pattern and holds us all together. Without him there might be some trouble on racial or ethnic grounds.'

The laboratory was divided into six sections, each working on a specialized set of problems and projects. The hierarchy was shallow and not autocratic, the prevailing pattern being one of responsibility and co-operation rather than authority and delegation. Nevertheless, the working atmosphere varied considerably from section to section; mainly it would seem, according to the personality and attitudes of each section leader.

All six section leaders were graduates in their thirties. The senior section leader had been with the department for fourteen years, three years longer than any of his five colleagues. He knew the general purpose of this inquiry and started by saying: 'We're all 100 per cent. English here.' His five monthly paid male staff had anything from two to seven years' service and his weekly paid staff consisted of two men and four girls (the largest concentration of female staff anywhere in the laboratory).

This informant gave a first impression of insularity and even intolerance but further discussion showed that his approach was primarily dictated by conservatism, class-consciousness, and professional exclusiveness. For instance, when asked about the degree of association between the various section leaders, he said: 'Very little. You've only got to look at their names. There's closer association within the section, even between monthly and weekly paid, than between section leaders.' Later, however, he elaborated on this:

I don't mean that different nationalities can't get on—it's rather that the approach to problems is often different. This could in theory be a help but here it rather hinders. You can't talk things out. Of course it may be due to the individual personalities involved and not to the national background. But I think that Commonwealth people, coloured or not, are closer to us in their ways of thinking than most Europeans, even the Dutch.

Colour isn't an important factor. I'd take them in the section if necessary, and if they are good enough but I've one or more senior men whom I couldn't put them with as they wouldn't accept them, or *vice versa*. There's one in particular, a blunt Northerner, whom a coloured man certainly wouldn't get on with or understand. We do and we like him. I also doubt whether most of the non-English would get on with these coloured chaps.

During the interview the informant revealed a certain professional class-consciousness emerged in relation to his colleagues as a whole:

There are only a handful of Oxbridge men with the company, including myself. We're not getting the type of men we want because the research lab over at . . . draws them off. The people in the department come from all sorts of backgrounds. You'd be surprised if you saw the way some of them live. But we come here to work, not to mix socially, though I think the work would improve if there were more association.

Section 2 provided a considerable contrast to Section 1. It was a fairly new and developing section under a lively, liberal, widely read leader who was, as he pointed out, a stranger in Croydon under two counts: 'I came from Austria in the 1930s as a child refugee and was brought up in the North of England. When I came South I had to start assimilating all over again—I felt very strange down here.'

This section contained two groups; until a year ago Section 6 was also a group within the section and its leader was still reporting progress to this informant.[1] One of the two remaining groups was led by a Ceylonese graduate with an 'English valued' degree and four years' service. With him worked one monthly paid Londoner ('the sort of person who acts as social cement in any group'), a weekly paid woman and three weekly paid local men. Of the Ceylonese it was said that he had rejected his country and family links but sought no close contacts here and appeared to be immersed in work. The other group was led by a Londoner with an Italian name ('but third-generation at least and completely English') and contained three weekly paid students, a local man, an Israeli, and a Dutchman working for six months under an agreement with a Dutch technical college. The section leader had some interesting comments on the atmosphere and working relations within his group and the laboratory as a whole:

> There's a tolerant climate but I wonder whether this Southern English tolerance is the tolerance of indifference or the tolerance of acceptance. Some coexist at such a low level of tolerance that I wonder how they can stand it. Apart from anything specifically English, there's the scientific personality as well. There's considerable pre-selection—scientists are usually those who prefer to work with material things rather than with people. Then there's rather a rarefied atmosphere here—the scientists who go into the production side tend to be more career-minded. They have greater material rewards, more stress and some insecurity, which makes for more friction in relations with colleagues then we have here. The main tensions are between monthly and weekly paid staff, and the foremen also feel nervous on intellectual grounds when they come in contact with scientists. In the self-service canteen, where everyone can go, you see the status and interest groups coming together, not just the working groups. In the lab itself the atmosphere has got much less stuffy since the women came in.

Section 3 was rather more 'British' than Section 2 in atmosphere. It was led by a Welshman with eleven years' service in the company and had five monthly paid workers, one from the North of England, a pre-1939 European Jewish refugee, two recently promoted local men, and an Indian with an Indian degree who was

[1] Yet another instance of the constant development, expansion and hiving-off of units so typical of Telelux. This whole department had only about ten staff ten years ago.

working for his M.Sc.[1] There were also three English weekly paid staff, all school-leavers doing their H.N.C., and a Dutchman who had come for six months as a student some years earlier and later returned on a permanent basis.

This section leader had worked in one of the firm's other research laboratories and commented on the closer social ties there:

The people at S. were much more intimately linked. It may be because many of them there have been there since before the war and are not formally qualified. Here we're mainly ex-servicemen and post-graduates working hard to extend our qualifications. There hasn't been a social outing for five years, so far as I remember. Social contacts are increasing now but they're still not very close. Of course most people live quite a distance away and from each other. But quite a few came to see me at home (eight miles away) when I was away ill for some months and I've seen more of them since. Christian names are used between section members and between myself and the section. Between sections it's mainly 'Mr.' or surnames, and surnames between the various section leaders, though I'm nearly on Christian-name terms with M. and R. now [the two English section leaders].

On the subject of non-English colleagues this informant held rather mixed views:

At the other lab. I had some trouble with two darkies[2] earlier but they had quite a few Indians and I took a chance on the one we have now. He got ribbed a lot but settled in well—he's easygoing, light-coloured, and has a good sense of humour. He's also strong on the theoretical side. The darkies were more prickly. One was well-liked and a good cricketer but there was trouble over a girl. She was the daughter of a Colonial Office official and interested in how he was getting on. He immediately thought she was interested in him and proposed marriage. She ran out of the room aghast; he hung around, wrote her letters threatening suicide and finally he had to go. Another was a West African with a good degree but he didn't like working at the bench—thought it lowered his status—so finally he had to go too, though he got more consideration because of his colour than he would have done otherwise.

[1] Some of the ways in which individuals could achieve monthly or weekly paid status were illustrated in this group. Apart from the graduates or graduands one of the two local men had come up from a skilled job on the shop floor, taking the H.N.C. in his thirties.

[2] This was the only time I heard this term used (apparently to denote a coloured person of negroid origins) by an informant in this laboratory, although some other monthly paid staff in other departments used it, especially during general conversation after the formal interview was ended.

This section leader reported no difficulties with the Dutch weekly paid worker other than a 'small problem of language'. He added: 'To be of European extraction is sometimes an advantage in such things as a knowledge of languages and wider international contacts. But there are very different technical outlooks and approaches.'

Section 4 was led by a post-war Polish exile who has been eleven years with the firm. A boy of seventeen when the 1939–45 War broke out, he was deported to and imprisoned in the Soviet Union, came out with the Anders Army and got himself transferred to Britain to continue his interrupted education. He got a B.Sc. soon after the War but had difficulty in getting a professional job until he came to Telelux, because of government security regulations affecting foreign nationals.

Despite his long years of training and settlement in Britain and the fact that he spoke English at home with his British wife and British-born children, this informant admitted that he still encountered language difficulties (we were talking in Polish):

> Learning languages isn't one of my talents and English is particularly difficult to learn well. Then I haven't got much ear so I still have quite a heavy Polish accent. At first I wanted the children to speak Polish but I changed my views on that. Why bother? It only stimulates national feelings and they're going to live here as Englishmen.

This informant had accommodated himself more or less completely to life in England, had become a British subject and maintained no links with the organized exile community ('Exile life is so futile—though it's all right for the old') other than personal ones. The fact that he had not changed his rather difficult name, continued to read Polish publications and was willing to talk Polish even in the work situation did, however, suggest that he was not seeking full assimilation and was unlikely to achieve it. At work, however, he was more or less assimilated, in the sense of having adjusted himself to the job's demands and achieved fairly complete acceptance by his superiors, colleagues, and subordinates.

The rest of Section 4's staff consisted of three monthly paid men (an Englishman with four years' service, a Welshman, and a Dutchman) and four weekly paid men—three English and one Pole. Working relations were good, according to the section leader.

Section 5 had recently hived off from a unit of Section 1 and its working atmosphere still reflected the easygoing, friendly climate prevailing in that section. The youngish section leader, a graduate Englishman, had two groups under him, each led by English monthly paid staff with six years' service. In one group were an Indian and a Hungarian (monthly paid); the other had a monthly paid Indian who was there on a two-year training course.

This section formed quite a team, since all but two of its members had been together before they came into this department or hived off from Section 1. Working relations were fairly close and in some cases even extended off the job:

The two senior English chaps are very easy to get on with and that helps. The Hungarian got his degree here and speaks extremely good English—he's very intense but nice. He rather keeps away from other Hungarians and doesn't seem very interested in politics. Nor does he get together with the Poles more than with anyone else. He's the assimilating type and has a lot of outside English friends. I know, because I asked him if he had people to go to at Christmas in case he might be left on his own.

About the Indians and other Afro-Asians this informant said:

They all have a lot of degrees but are shy in their relations with whites. I think it's some sort of hangover from colonial times. These two usually lunch together with other Indians. The Ceylonese from Section 2 doesn't mix with them and is more accepted among the white people—he's a personal friend of mine. Some of us have tried having the Indians along to our houses but they still remain rather shy—one in particular—and he always will walk three feet behind one—I can't think why. I don't think it's anything to do with caste as they seem to drop all their religious and caste practices here.

We also had a Malagasi but it didn't work out. All graduates show what they can do at the bench but he was full of intellectual arrogance and superiority, and he disliked and was unable to do routine work with his hands, saying that was for uneducated people. He moved from section to section but it didn't work out.

This informant admitted that his approach was not particularly cosmopolitan ('At the university the ex-servicemen wave made the atmosphere more insular than usual'). He was understanding and kindly, but clearly the assimilating type of foreigner, such as the Hungarian, was more likely to fit into and be accepted in this particular section. Of an Israeli student who had recently left he said approvingly: 'He was very English in his attitude and way of thinking.'

In this interview the question of different ways of thinking and approaches to scientific problems was also raised but the instance given suggested that the real issue might, as the informant himself suggested, be one of 'comprehensibility' rather than an actual difference of approach:

The only real friction was between one of our senior English staff and a Dutch student. The Englishman's as easy as can be but he used to get really upset with the Dutch chap when they were discussing work. One example is the word 'control', which apparently has a rather different meaning in the two languages.

Section 6 was led by a Turk who had been with Telelux for ten years and with the same section for nine. Like the other non-English section leaders he displayed wider intellectual interests and more social curiosity than most of his English colleagues. He was a self-exiled liberal, settled and married in England, accommodated to life here but far from assimilated, except in the work-situation. Of life outside he said philosophically: 'One just has to get used to English reserve. Over ten years I've never had more than an exchange about the weather. Anywhere else you would get together, have a fight, do *something* together.'

This section was small, with one other monthy paid worker, an Oxford graduate whom the leader found, professionally and socially congenial, and four weekly paid staff: an Indian with a Madras degree, two English (one a woman) and a Pole.

He is in his late forties and came over from the shop floor. He had a secondary-school education in Poland and was an N.C.O. in the army. He's trying to get his O.N.C. but it's hard at his age. In past years I've had another Polish student, a French Canadian, an Irishman, and some English.

Relations within this section were said to be close: 'We're all on Christian-name terms. I used to be strict as a supervisor but I changed when I found that leniency works better here.'

* * *

Section 4's leader probably summed up the general climate of the Research Laboratory best:

Everyone here is used to the presence of foreigners, first of all because of the Dutch at the top. The English are intelligent types and most of them have been abroad. Then we work individually on international problems—every man's specialized and his own master. There's no feeling here like you get in artisan jobs, with the trade unions resenting foreigners. Off the job social life's limited, but that's understandable, considering how far apart they live and how many different places they come from.

CHAPTER 10

CHOCOLAC

(1) *The Overall Picture*

The second detailed study was made in one of two factories belonging to Chocolac Ltd., a family firm that had recently become a limited company. The other, earlier-established factory was some miles to the north-east, in metropolitan London, and was run as a separate unit. The two establishments did, however, share the technical services of chemists and confectioners, who worked at the older factory. One of these, at executive level, was an elderly Central European Jewish refugee who came to Britain in the 1930s. Supervisory informants saw nothing unusual in the fact that a non-British-born individual should hold a high position. One commented: 'The confectionery trade is a pretty cosmopolitan one as regards personnel and terminology; most of our technical terms are in French, such as *couverture* and *conche*.'

Chocolac specialized in chocolate-making, but also manufactured other types of sweets. This kind of work involved dexterity and personal cleanliness but no formal skills. The labour force here consisted of a fair-sized nucleus of 'old faithfuls', as the personnel officer called them; this nucleus was augmented by other whole-time and part-time workers, mainly women, students, and other seasonal workers, particularly in the pre-Christmas peak production season from August to October. Labour turnover was low among the old-timers, both part-time and full-time workers; some of the seasonal workers were, in fact, either former full-time workers, relatives of existing employees, or local residents who came in year after year to earn extra money in the peak production period. For the rest, however, the seasonal fluctuation and the comparatively low wage-levels (compared with local light engineering rates) had led to a fairly high labour turnover and an annually recurring labour shortage, particularly among male workers. After the War this was the main reason for the firm's willingness to try out immigrants of various ethnic origins.

Working conditions in Chocolac were generally agreeable. The firm was located in an attractive, mainly modern building set in its own green and airy grounds, amid flower-beds, trees, and playing-fields which were used by the firm's football and cricket teams. Inside, most work-rooms were large, clean, and painted in light colours. Inevitably some of the work was hot and rather heavy; but conditions in work-rooms, canteens, and cloakrooms had to and did, like the workers themselves, conform to the hygienic regulations enforced in food-production. All workers wore white overalls and caps; male supervisors wore overalls but no caps, while women supervisors wore overalls and a distinctive headgear rather reminiscent of a nurse's cap.

Wages at Chocolac were those set by the relevant industrial agreement, and augmented by fixed bonuses of up to one-third of the basic wage. The bonuses varied according to the department; so that work in some departments was better paid and more sought after. Hours were normal and there was no shift or night work. There was a pension scheme, while 'fringe' benefits included a good canteen, health and welfare services administered by a trained nurse and a personnel officer, and a social club with recreational and sports facilities.

The Chocolac factory was first visited during a peak period; but the second, more intensive survey was carried out some fifteen months later, in the post-Christmas trough. This was at the request of the management, as Chocolac carried no spare supervisory staff who could have been deputed to assist in the inquiry during the seasonal rush. This timing, however, proved advantageous: firstly, because it was possible to compare the labour force at peak and off-peak periods; secondly, because most informants were not unduly harassed or pressed for time; and thirdly, because the basic structure and composition of the stable labour-core was more easily visible.

This report is based on three long interviews with the personnel officer, one with the firm's nurse, and further interviews with the assistant staff engineer and with seven out of the firm's fifteen supervisors or working foremen. These interviews enabled me to get a first-hand picture of working relationships in the engineers' department and all but three of the production departments (in four cases supervisors were in charge of two departments). Of the eight supervisory staff not interviewed personally, three were in the largest department, which had four supervisors, one was on sick leave and three were in charge of extremely small departments which they could not easily leave, and about which the personnel officer and other informants were able to supply adequate information. There was an additional reason for not interviewing one of these three, the working foreman over a group of three men. To quote the personnel officer: 'He's a South African by origin and pretty dark, though he never says anything about his background and nobody here bothers. But he's had a bit of trouble outside getting lodgings—has to pay £4 10*s*. for two rooms—and I think this inquiry might upset him.'[1]

It may be considered a defect that more rank-and-file workers were not interviewed. Such interviews would, however, have been very difficult to arrange in this relatively small and sparely staffed firm. Moreover, the small size of most departments and the fact that almost all supervisors not only worked alongside their groups but were old-timers who had themselves been promoted from the floor, some very recently, meant that they were fully aware of views and behaviour in their own working groups and often with those in others. In general, too, the shallow supervisory hierarchy in this establishment, with only two or at the most three tiers from production manager to chargehand, made for informal and close relations between the various levels, as I was able to see for myself during my interviews or in the canteen. The personnel officer expressed a view which was reiterated by several supervisory informants:

This firm is very much of a unit. Everyone knows everyone else and most people seem very happy. Most of the supervisors are known by their Christian names. Most of them are local people and have been with us for decades. For instance, in the main chocolate department the three senior supervisors have 44, 37, and 35 years' service respectively, while the fourth, the baby of them all, has been with us since he left school ten years ago, with just a break for call-up. I myself have interviewed everyone who has come here in the last four years and know their background and personal circumstances. The executives and supervisors usually eat in two smaller rooms off the canteen but all levels

[1] It seemed probable that this foreman was one of the hundreds, if not thousands, of better-off, middle-class Cape Coloured people who have come to Britain since South Africa's Nationalist Government began to enforce its *apartheid* policy. Even more than the Anglo-Indians this group seeks anonymity and assimilation, and forms few or no minority group links or associations.

mix freely in the social club. My chief partner at table tennis is a West Indian in the Cocoa Department.

It was often possible to get a picture of organized labour's views by interviews with trade-union officials (as in Telelux). In Chocolac, however, there was no recognized union, although some workers in the engineers' department were believed to belong to the A.E.U.; nor was there any formal consultative machinery. Most of those active in sporting and social activities were also supervisors and were interviewed in both roles. The picture given here is therefore from the supervisory angle, and some allowance should, as in the general survey, be made for the natural tendency for such informants, however close to or recently promoted from the shop floor, to present working situations and relationships in a rose-tinted light and to gloss over the tensions and frictions that exist in even the best-run and happiest working communities.

(2) *The Working Community*

Chocolac employed nearly 300 full-time workers, of whom rather over half were men.[1] Of this total some thirty-five, most of them women, were employed on the office side or in sales. There were also about 140 part-time women workers in the factory, half on morning work and half on afternoons. There were no immigrants among these part-time workers nor on the executive or clerical staff, with the exception of one coloured male costing clerk (nationality unspecified) of whom a supervisor said: 'There was a bit of talk at first but they soon got used to it.'

With the exception of the engineers' department, which was under the separate authority of a staff engineer, the works labour force came under the control of the works manager, assisted by a production manager. There were fifteen production departments and a canteen staff. Each department was theoretically in the charge of a supervisor but, in practice, according to the personnel officer: 'If a supervisor leaves there's a tendency to put the department under an existing supervisor and pay them more. Or it may be put in charge of a working foreman.' Some of the larger departments had charge-hands, but in most the supervisor or working foreman also acted as a charge-hand.

[1] This was at the post-Christmas trough period, when the detailed survey was made.

When Chocolac was first visited all three components of the labour force (male and female full-time workers and female part-time workers) were appreciably larger. Much of the drop was attributable to the seasonal swing, but there had also been some redundancy due to increased mechanization and to a temporary falling off in sales in the intervening period. Redundancy in practice was based on efficiency and such considerations as length of service or suitability, and there was never any demand from local workers for immigrants to go first. Some immigrants were, however, made redundant and the main groups to suffer from this seemed to have been transient Irish workers and West Indians. The number of Irish had fallen from twelve to three, although some of this drop could also be attributable to the high mobility of this group; of the score or so of West Indian men and four or five women employed earlier only nine men and one woman remained. There were various reasons for this, which emerged in the survey of individual departments. The overall number of immigrants had not, however, declined appreciably and in fact was rather higher than at the time of the first visit in proportion to the overall labour force. Only two immigrant women remained (a German and a West Indian); but there were thirty-one male immigrant workers, nine from Europe (five Poles, one Hungarian, two Lithuanians, and one Greek) and twenty-two from the Commonwealth (nine West Indians, ten Indians or Anglo-Indians,[1] one coloured South African, one Cypriot, and one Canadian). From some interviews it emerged that West Indian women had not proved so acceptable as the men, although it was not entirely clear whether this should be attributed to poor working ability and low adaptability on their part or to the clannishness and self-perpetuating character of long-term local women's working groups; it seemed possible that a combination of the two factors had been at work.

(3) *Departmental Survey*

The immigrant workers were fairly well dispersed through the various departments; so far as coloured Commonwealth workers

[1] Most informants were uncertain about the precise background of workers from India, but from their names and the fact that they were described as very light in colour it seemed likely that most were Anglo-Indians. As there were more than on the earlier visit, it seemed that 'clustering' had occurred.

were concerned this appeared to be deliberate policy. One supervisor said: 'If there are too many coloured together they're a menace from the work angle—they all slow down. For that reason the firm also keeps the numbers down. If one goes we may take another in his place but not indiscriminately.'

In Department 1, which was concerned with chocolate-making, fifteen men out of the total of thirty-eight men and three women were immigrants: there were seven West Indians, six Indians or Anglo-Indians, one Cypriot, and one Pole.

There were several different kinds of job in this department. The three women, one a part-timer, worked as a team on the heavy, sticky job of wrapping the *couverture*. All three were local, long-service workers, one having been with the firm for twenty-eight years. In the same basement department were four men working in groups of two. A Welshman with thirty-five years' service and the inevitable nickname of 'Taffy' was teamed with an Anglo-Indian who came to the firm three years before this. The other team consisted of two West Indians, a Jamaican who had been there only six months and a Windward Islander with four years' service.[1] This team was described as 'slow, but conscientious, once trained'.

Next came the *conche* team, with seven members. This team, whose job was punching out the moisture, consisted of four Englishmen, three with nearly ten years of service, an Irishman, also with ten years' service, who took over the team when one supervisor was away, a Barbadian who had been there for four years, and a Pole. Of the latter it was said: 'He's one of our best workers. He's been here a long time and is a hangover from the days when we had a lot of Poles. He speaks good English but stutters and isn't very talkative so nobody's sure what he was before the War.'

The *conche* team was on bonus, so that one slow or inefficient worker could hold back the others. Nevertheless the team was said to be well-integrated and there was no friction between members over earnings.

A third section with three male workers produced small cake decorations. Two of this team were English, one with six years'

[1] The latter was described as 'almost white—can pass if he wants to'. It will be observed that informants in this firm were unusually well-informed as to the exact provenance of West Indians. The personnel officer explained this by saying: 'It was the Barbadians who first taught us to do this and not to call all West Indians Jamaicans.'

service, the other a newcomer. The third was an elderly Anglo-Indian of whom the supervisor said: 'He used to have a good engineering post on the Indian Railways. He's a conscientious worker and used to be a great sportsman in earlier years. He's quite a character and a real gentleman but he doesn't really fit in with the kind of work he has to do here.'

The fourth and last section in Department 1 was a large one engaged on refining. The team leader had been with the firm for nearly forty years and was described as a 'real Bermondsey type'. The other English members ranged from a handful of reliable old-timers to a painter who worked to supplement his professional income, a former mental patient who had 'settled down very well', and an illiterate. There were a couple of recent arrivals from Wales and the overseas immigrants consisted of two Anglo-Indians, five West Indians (one also illiterate), and a Cypriot. One of the Anglo-Indians was considered likely to move on to a more suitable job ('He's a clerical type and we use him for tally-keeping and so on'). Two of the West Indians, a Barbadian and a Jamaican, had been in the factory for four years and were engaged on the most difficult and responsible work. The principle of 'clustering' had been at work here since each had recommended and brought in a friend or relative to work in the department. The Cypriot was said to be 'a bit of a sprucer[1]—you have to keep on at him. He's been with us since 1956 but he's been in and out two or three times since then.' Other West Indians and some Nigerian students had also worked in the department in the past.

The work and working climate in this section were characterized by one of the departmental supervisors in the following terms:

It's a funny team. The work's not the best and though they're on bonus they're usually disgruntled over the pay they get compared with other departments on bonus. The West Indians are disgruntled like the rest but no more. We've got rid of all the real trouble-makers, English and West Indian. There's no objection amongst the old-stagers to the two West Indians doing the most important job. It's difficult to get anyone to do it and since the war we've had so many different types in and out that they're glad to have someone who does it properly. They all mix in together at the tea-breaks and nobody sits apart in segregated groups. Of course the West Indians have often been the nucleus of the

[1] 'Sprucer' could not be located in a dictionary, but informants in Surrey gave the following definitions: 'a good-tempered rogue', 'tries it on', 'smooth and slick'.

cricket and even football teams and that's helped. Those who have been here a few years have completely settled down.

This informant was a youngish man with a open, friendly manner; his positive approach to his work and working team had clearly helped the absorption of all outsiders in this department. He spoke of 'fitting people in' and said of immigrant workers: 'I try to give them the sort of job they can do, and there's usually something. You have to make allowances for slowness at first but once they're trained they're usually good. One chap started having fits and had to come off the machinery but we found him a manual job.'

Departments 2 and 3 at Chocolac came under a single male supervisor and were much smaller than Department 1. Department 2 contained six men and two women; another four women being borrowed from other departments each day for certain jobs. The regular workers included a Pole and a West Indian, both men.

Department 2's job was to process the cocoa beans in various ways. This was done by the men while the women packed the finished products. Speed was not essential except on packing. The men worked in groups of three, the West Indian being in one group, the Pole in the other. The Pole was over 60; he was a former non-commissioned officer who spoke little English, although he had been with the firm for over ten years. The West Indian had been with the firm for four years, but had only just moved in from another department. He was said to be youngish, light-coloured, well educated, and to have 'some legal training'.[1] Of the four English workers here, one was a long-service employee who left after thirty-five years with the firm but had returned, while a second had ten years' service. The others were said to be 'new boys' with only one and two years' service respectively. The supervisor himself (a lively man with an off-beat humour) was only 32 but had been with the firm for sixteen years, since he left school.

Department 3 had a strength of nine men (one a Pole) and one woman. The men worked as a single team on a fairly heavy, highly specialized, spraying job. All had been with the firm for three or four years and one for as many as fifteen years, although not always in the same department. The Pole was in his mid-forties; his English was poor, but he had a particular friend among his English team-mates who spoke German and acted as interpreter when neces-

[1] See p. 360, note 1.

sary. The Pole's son, who went to school in England, started work at Chocolac, but had moved on to a better-paid, more skilled job in Telelux. Other Poles had worked in the department in past years, but they left to work in Polplastics. There were also two West Africans in this department some years ago. 'But they had a fight with knives and were sacked. This episode is vaguely remembered but I don't think people generalize about it.'[1]

Departments 4 and 5 were also engaged in sweet production; they were under a single supervisor (a woman) who had been with the firm for about twenty-five years. Both departments were small, Department 4 having five men and Department 5 one man and three women. Department 4 was, according to the supervisor, 'jokingly called the Foreign Legion'. Of the five men, only one was English, an old-timer with twelve years' service who did the most responsible job. The other two skilled jobs were done by a Polish ex-ranker who had been with the firm ten years (and was sufficiently settled locally to have got a council house) and a Greek. A Jamaican with four years' service and a Hungarian who came in after the Rising were also being trained to do this skilled work. In Department 5 the three women were long-service local workers ('We seem to keep the same women more than the men'). They worked not as a team but individually and on bonus. The work here was said to be hard; it required a training period of three months.

West Indian women had worked here in the past and the supervisor said of them: 'On the whole they were very good. One was particularly nice. She was a primary school-teacher at home and left here when she got an office job. We once had a trouble-maker but there's no friction at present. I've never had any bad feeling over colour as such and in fact they all seem to get on remarkably well in both departments.'

Department 6 was engaged on a cake-making process, and came under a working foreman with eight years' service. It was one of the few departments with no immigrant workers at all, its six women workers all being long-term local residents. Such working units can be more clannish and resistant to outsiders, but they also tend to be self-perpetuating since members are usually able to introduce relatives and local friends to fill any vacancies.

Department 7 was a small department consisting of three male

[1] Two other supervisors did in fact mention this incident, but only *en passant* and without undue emphasis.

workers under the South African working foreman already mentioned. According to other informants there had been no friction over this promotion and working relationships were smooth.

Department 8 was larger than most, with twenty women workers under a woman supervisor. The latter who, unlike most other supervisors, had been with the firm for only five years, was ill at the time and so could not be interviewed personally. From other informants it was learned that the work in this department was not generally regarded as agreeable and that the working climate there was rather tense. A contributory factor here was the redundancy that had occurred in the department in recent years, leaving a sense of insecurity. This redundancy in fact mainly affected some West Indian women, who were said to have proved unsatisfactory workers. One informant said: 'I doubt if they would be taken on again here. The only immigrant now is a German woman—a very good worker who slogs along but is rather excitable. She sometimes has rows with the local girls.'

Production Departments 9 and 10 both came under one foreman; there were five men and twelve women (mainly part-timers) in the former department, six men and six women in the latter. There was only one immigrant, a Pole, in Department 9; he was a long-service worker and did one of the most responsible jobs. There was no definite evidence of insularity here; the men were fairly stable, and the use of part-time women was a pattern that, as elsewhere, tended to perpetuate the employment of local people.

Departments 11 and 12 were packing units, both under a recently appointed woman supervisor. One had been more highly mechanized since my original visit and the working teams had been cut in consequence. Between them the two departments employed two men and thirty-five women working in teams. The full-time local workers were described as 'very stable' and there was only one immigrant here at present, a West Indian who was the wife of a former employee. She was described by several informants as a 'nice, quiet type, very popular and mixes in well'. There had been other West Indian workers in the hand-packing department, but they were not generally regarded as 'suitable' or fast enough for the machine-packing. There had also been some Anglo-Indians, but they had moved on to better-paid work elsewhere: 'We had three sisters, Roman Catholics, all very popular and well-educated. They were one of our top packing teams but left when the bonus was cut.

Working relations are generally good here. Everyone's on Christian name terms and they all mix in and sit together in the canteen.'

Department 13 dealt with dispatch; it also included a stock-room in which a week or more's stock was kept to enable customers' orders to be filled quickly. Twenty-eight men and seven women were employed here on stacking and unstacking (the parcels were light, weighing only 3 lb. each). At this time all the women were English, but West Indian and Indian women had worked there in past years. They seem to have regarded the job as a 'transit camp'; the male supervisor described them as 'nice types, who soon went on to nursing or office jobs'.

The total of twenty-eight men included five European or Commonwealth immigrants (two Lithuanians, two Anglo-Indians, and one Canadian) and an Irishman. Like the other male workers, all of them had been there at least four years, and some a good deal longer. The senior old-timer was a local man with twenty-five years' service. Others came in from a nearby factory after it was taken over and later closed down. The Lithuanians came to Chocolac eight years ago. Both spoke good English and were on the most responsible work, as was one of the Anglo-Indians, who was described as 'one of our best workers'.

This department seemed to be one of the most smoothly running and best-integrated working units in the entire factory. The main reason for this was probably to be found in the personality of the supervisor, a firm and amiable man with thirty-eight years of service with the firm, who said:

I set the tone here and it goes all the way through. There's never any labour trouble up at our end. I treat all of them, regardless of origin, with dignity and respect. As for a colour-bar there's absolutely none and there's never been anything like that here—or indeed in the rest of the firm.

Department 14 was a very small one concerned with packing materials; it contained two men and one woman under a male supervisor. All were local and here again there had never been any immigrant workers, probably because the working unit was a local one of long standing rather than by deliberate intent.

Department 15 was rather a unit on its own. It was concerned with raw materials and employed nine men under a male supervisor. Of the total, five were local, one was described as an 'immigrant' from Scotland, and another came from Southern Ireland.

The other two were a Cypriot loader with seven years' service and an Indian (or Anglo-Indian) sugar-miller with six years' service. The youngish supervisor said that there had been more Cypriots and Poles in earlier years but that they have 'moved on'. He was well satisfied with the working ability of everyone in his department, describing them as 'very good, clean, and tidy workers'. The men in the department had worked together for at least four years (some had up to ten years' service) and had evolved a good working relationship unconcerned with origins, although the Indian, as one of the youngest, was said to come in for 'a certain amount of ragging, but only within bounds; he takes it in his stride, without any chip'.

Department 16 was completely independent of the production side. It was concerned mainly with engine maintenance and was headed by two executive-grade engineers, with a foreman under them, in direct charge of twenty-one men. Of this labour force four were semi-skilled and the remainder skilled (one of them was an Anglo-Indian). This was not a union shop but a minority of the men were thought to belong to the A.E.U. The men were reported to be satisfied with pay and conditions, and most have been there for a decade or more. Nor did there appear to have been much resistance to the entrance of outsiders. One of the two engineers, a cheerful elderly Scotsman of fatherly mien, said:

> The atmosphere's good and there's certainly no race prejudice here. I've never had a European immigrant apply for a job and no West Indians except for a Jamaican medical student who's just moved to another department.[1] He was a damn good worker. The only group I've had are Anglo-Indians—quite a lot apply and I've had about three so far. The one we've got now is fair with a white skin and blue eyes. You wouldn't think he was one if he didn't say so himself.

(4) *General Working Relations*

Various informants, including the personnel officer and the nurse, gave a picture of working relations off as well as on the shop floor, and it was also possible to get first-hand impression of these during the fortnight during which I was visiting the factory. In the

[1] This was the same West Indian 'with some legal training' referred to as having recently moved to Department 2 (see p. 356). It could not be ascertained whether the disparity between the alleged nature of his professional studies was due to vagueness on the part of informants or to some line-shooting by the West Indian himself.

canteen there was no evidence of any segregation of immigrants, whether voluntary or imposed. Rank-and-file workers usually sat together by departments with their charge-hands or foremen and kept to the same tables. This was not only because they knew each other better but because there was some staggering of lunch and tea-breaks. The only obvious segregation was the customary and voluntary one between the sexes. As one informant said: 'The women in particular like to gossip and talk woman-talk together and some of the old-timers know each other off the job.'

Remarkably little friction was reported between immigrants and other workers, whether on the floor or off it. This was also one of the minority of firms where no complaints were recorded from supervisory informants or other workers about immigrants' personal habits, cleanliness, or general behaviour. If any such incidents had occurred they were sufficiently far in the past to have been forgotten, only one example of violent behaviour being recalled by any of the informants.

Not only did immigrant workers mingle freely and without incident in the canteen and cloakrooms but the majority 'mixed in' at the social club and in sports. In fact, the active participation of half a dozen West Indians in Chocolac's football and cricket teams had indeed furthered their acceptance by fellow-workers on the shop floor. Such participation was important, since the lack of formal consultative machinery or unionization in this firm meant that immigrants could not show their solidarity with and win acceptance from local workers by active participation in such organizations.

The prevailing attitudes among supervisors at Chocolac to immigrants, and indeed to all workers, combined expediency and a desire for efficiency with a friendly informality. Several of those interviewed came near to being 'sponsors' and no definite 'anti-sponsors' were encountered. No significant difference of viewpoint as between supervisors proper and working foremen was noticed. In this firm, with its shallow managerial–supervisory hierarchy, the views and attitudes of supervisors seemed to differ less from those of the long-service local labour-core than they sometimes did in larger and more formally organized working communities.[1] All

[1] It was a good example of the type of core-community found in some smaller factories, in which the management–employee division was blurred (see pp. 244, 264–5).

felt a considerable degree of identification with the firm's interests and in the absence of suitable local entrants were willing to accept outsiders who could do the work adequately and fit into the informal, close-knit working community. Male supervisors and workers appeared rather more willing to accept immigrants, particularly coloured, than did the women, but this may have been due more to the working capacity of the particular immigrants involved than to other factors.

(5) *Summing Up*

From the interview material it appeared that most of the immigrants now working at Chocolac had settled in their jobs and were more or less fully accepted as part of the permanent labour force by both supervisors and their working groups. The most recent arrivals, the West Indians, were rather less accepted than other immigrants; their numbers were restricted by an informal quota, mainly because of supervisors' reservations over their working speed, but perhaps also to avoid creating an impression of a 'coloured shop' in any particular department. A few of the West Indians were, however, regarded as 'old-stagers', as were many of the earlier immigrants from Europe and India, and they were in the process of creating suitable and acceptable 'clusters' by recommending and bringing in their relations and friends. Some better-qualified immigrant newcomers continued to use the firm as a 'transit camp', as some Poles, Balts, and Anglo-Indians had done in earlier years, but this was also done by local workers and was a sufficiently frequent phenomenon not to arouse any resentment on the management side.

Most of the immigrants with Chocolac at this time had moved into the second phase of absorption, and indeed some were more or less assimilated. They were settled with the firm and doing more responsible jobs; and one able, light-coloured South African had already become a foreman in charge of a small group of local men. It would be unreasonable to expect to find many post-war immigrants in supervisory positions in this firm, in view of the small and shallow supervisory hierarchy and the long service record of almost all the present supervisors; but the fact that no informants excluded the possibility of such promotion, given the requisite ability and length of service, indicated a considerable measure of acceptance. In this context, however, it should perhaps be added that, according to several informants, the most likely candidates for promotion among the immigrants usually moved on quickly to better-paid or more professional work. Of the earliest immigrant group, the Poles, one supervisor said: 'Those we have now don't seem very ambitious or anxious for promotion. The son of one was a bright boy but he went on the staff at Telelux after a few months here.'

The main factor that induced Chocolac to try and persist with immigrant labour was, as elsewhere, the chronic labour shortage. The nature of the work favoured the newcomers. No formal skills were involved and most jobs could be learned with relative ease. The age of the firm, its local affiliations, and the existence of a fair-sized local labour-core had not in this case told against the newcomers and there had been little or no overt or covert resistance by the 'old faithfuls' to their entry and employment. The relatively small size of the firm and working groups and the close, informal relations between supervisors and workers had furthered the absorption of the newcomers as individuals. An additional contributory factor may have been the firm's policy of dispersal and of informal limitation of numbers in the case of coloured workers.

Immigrant absorption had also been furthered by the informal and friendly working climate prevailing in the firm, by the positive 'sponsoring' efforts of some supervisors, by increasingly good selection and, last but not least, by the endeavours of the immigrants themselves. From the interviews it appeared that most of those who had been there for several years had not only mastered their jobs but had made very definite efforts to participate actively in the life of the working community and to accept its conventions, language, and jokes.

CHAPTER 11

POLPLASTICS

(1) *The Overall Picture*

Polplastics (Firm H in the light industrial group) was something of an industrial curiosity, in that the managing director, a considerable proportion of the senior technical staff and works supervisors, and the bulk of the male labour force were of Polish origin. The organization was built up on the expectation that Poles would form the basis of its labour force, with other nationals being taken on only in posts where it seemed more expedient or where suitable Polish applicants with the necessary knowledge of English could not be found. In consequence, the customary roles and status levels of Poles and English in Croydon industry were approximately reversed.

Polplastics was a light industrial plant manufacturing a wide variety of plastic goods. The plastics industry is a young one. It was in its infancy in the 1930s and has boomed only since the end of the Second World War. Such an industry, with its lack of traditional organization and rules, its mass-production methods, and the relatively low level of capital investment required, offers considerable opportunities for enterprising newcomers.

The firm, which had existed in a small way in Brixton for some years, began to develop in 1947, when a demobilized Polish warrant officer (the present managing director), came in with ideas and contacts supplied by himself and a few Polish Air Force colleagues. At that time almost all employees were Polish, with the exception of the small clerical staff. A number of the technical and supervisory staff had been with the firm since that time. Polplastics prospered and outgrew its premises in Brixton. In 1954 it moved to larger premises in Croydon; a few years later it moved once more to its attractive modern premises on Purley Way.

Polplastics was first visited during the first stage of this study and during the annual period of peak seasonal production. The second, more detailed inquiry was carried out in a series of some twenty interviews nearly a year and a half later, during the annual slack period. No significant changes in personnel,[1] policy, or organization were noted over that period.

Before describing the organization of the firm, a few words should perhaps be said about the conduct of the interviews. These took place in the only free room, a small, comfortable waiting-room with a glass wall in the entrance hall to the office block. The English assistant manager, who was throughout the inquiry outstandingly helpful, interested, and patient, or his English woman assistant, would call the employee who was to be interviewed off his job, brief him roughly as to the nature of the inquiry, introduce him (or her), and leave the room. No time limit was set on interviews with office staff, but in the case of certain supervisors on the production side I was asked to keep these down to ten to fifteen minutes. In one case, a mechanical breakdown made the interview even shorter.

The interviews were with departmental supervisors or their assistants, the majority of them Polish. At the beginning of each interview I offered the person interviewed the choice of Polish or English and in all but two cases, both involving younger executives, Polish was chosen. In my view, the fact that interviews were conducted in Polish, sometimes flavoured with English technical borrowings, such as 'foreman', 'charge-hand', and 'boss', made not only for greater ease of verbal expression but also for a closer *rapport* and confidence between the interviewer and those interviewed. So few non-Poles speak fluent Polish that Poles tend to treat those who do as part of the in-group, honorary Poles. I anticipated that, as a result of war-time experiences, and political and minority group attitudes, some of those interviewed might be suspicious or apprehensive; it might be assumed that I spoke Polish either because I was connected with a British security organization or possibly even because I was collecting information for the Communist régime in Poland. Fortunately no such situation arose, except to a small extent in one case. All other Polish employees talked about working conditions and relationships with

[1] Some minor differences emerged in numbers and ethnic breakdown as a result of labour turnover and seasonal fluctuations in the interval and even during the later interviews; consequently the breakdown given here may be slightly different from that given in the diagram on p. 395.

a frankness that seemed to indicate a congenial working climate at least among the staff and long-term labour-core.[1]

(2) *Formal Organization and Working Conditions*

Towards the end of 1959 Polplastics employed about 300 employees: an office and technical staff of about forty and approximately 260 employees on the works side. Of the latter total, there were about 194 men and sixty-six women. The firm's total labour force varied slightly on a seasonal basis, being lower in the winter slack period after the Christmas production was finished.[2] There was a pension scheme, but only for the staff.

Apart from the jobs found in every factory, such as tool-making, maintenance, warehousing, and dispatch, the bulk of the labour force was engaged on two stages of production, machine-operating, and finishing. In the first stage, the machines varied in size and complexity according to the product. All were operated by men, the work being said to be too heavy for women: 'It would be heavy and dangerous, and the girls might get dreamy and mess it up,' said one of the Polish charge-hands. For men, however, it was fairly light; it was also repetitive and was therefore said to be better suited to older men ('younger men get bored quickly'). The work was classified as unskilled to semi-skilled. It was individual, in that each machine was designed for a single operator. There were no teams or gangs in the moulding room, and the noise, speed of work, and distance between the machines limited social contacts on the shop floor to a minimum.

All other employees worked a regular five-day week but the moulding room was organized on a three-shift basis, from 7.30 a.m. to 3.0 p.m., 3.0 p.m. to 10.30 p.m., and 10.30 p.m. to 7.30 a.m. The shifts changed round every week, but a few of the older and slower operatives were lent temporarily to other shifts when their turn came for night duty. Operators worked thirty-seven and a half hours a week on day shift but get paid for forty-four hours. On night shift they were paid for fifty-two and a half hours' work. The basic time rate was about 4*s.* per hour for the male machine operators.

[1] But see pp. 386–9 for a rather different viewpoint.

[2] In mid-1958, for example, the overall figure was 350. In the slack periods some casuals would go and not be replaced, but the labour-core would remain untouched.

There was overtime (time and a half on Saturdays, double rate on occasional Sundays) in the busy season.

After the first trial month, those who were found satisfactory got a rise of 1*d.* per hour, and learned to operate more complicated machines. After a further two months the rate went up another penny, and thereafter the operative became eligible for the 'efficiency bonus' of five hours' pay per week, depending on good attendance, good time-keeping, and efficient work. If an operative did not watch the machine carefully, it could turn out scrap mouldings. He was also responsible for cutting or drilling away the 'sprue' or twig on which the moulding sits. These were the operatives main responsibilities, as each machine was set by the foreman or chargehand at its optimum rate per hour, which differed from machine to machine.

There were several short breaks during the shift, but these were staggered so that the machines continued working. The works canteen served soup and snacks, but not lunches. Because of the shift times the moulding room workers preferred to take their main meal at home before or after work. This again restricted social intercourse between workers to a minimum. Except for the married couples, men and women employees also took their breaks at different times to reduce pressure on the rather small canteen.[1] There was no social club because of the shift system and the fact that employees lived scattered all over South London. Despite this semi-segregation, there was a considerable amount of off-job mixing, particularly between Polish men and English girls, whether from the works or the office. There was also another factor promoting off-the-floor social relations. Many Polish families in Croydon and South London own one or more houses, in which they take lodgers. In Polplastics one of the Polish supervisors acted as an unofficial billeting officer for any newcomer who had no local contacts. For instance, during the mild recession of 1956–8, he helped Polish applicants who came in from the harder-stricken North and Midlands.

Most of Polplastics' women factory hands worked on the second

[1] Staff did not use the canteen but placed their orders and ate in their offices or on the roof if it was fine and warm. This was said to be due not to snobbery ('especially here') but to lack of space and to avoid friction with the works personnel, 'which always tends to be jealous of the staff'. The canteen managers were English and so was the cuisine. Some Poles were said to bring their own food ('continental sausage, herring, and rye-bread, which they prefer to our version').

stage of production—that of finishing. They worked a full day from 8 a.m. to 5 p.m., at a starting rate of 2*s.* 7*d.* per hour. The women who worked on the special evening shift, from 6 p.m. to 10 p.m., received 2*s.* 6*d.* per hour.

Polplastics was not unionized, although most skilled men in the tool-room were believed to belong individually to the A.E.U. The management was not favourably inclined to the unions, for reasons which could be partly industrial, partly political. Many Polish employees shared this political suspicion and dislike of the unions, remembering the hostility expressed and shown by many unions in the immediate post-war years to their entry into British industry. The skilled workers were paid at a rate above the union minimum, which made them less insistent upon a closed shop. One informant, however, commented, half jocularly; 'Without a closed shop the union can't do anything for us. We're in the boss's hands.'

(3) *Ethnic Composition of the Labour Force*

Before starting on a more detailed study of Polplastics, I had several interviews with the English assistant manager, who was mainly responsible for personnel management. Mr. Brown had been with the firm for only five years, and had therefore had to adapt himself to its rather special organization and orientation. Before coming to the firm he had no previous contact with Poles, 'except from a distance in the Western Desert during the War'. In these interviews Mr. Brown gave a general outline of the labour force and labour relationships as seen from management level, and from an English viewpoint.

In principle, Polplastics would take on all who seemed likely to be good workers. The firm had been steadily expanding and there had been no large-scale redundancy. Individual redundancy occurred only in cases of inefficient work. In practice, however, most applicants were Polish. They came because they had heard of the factory through friends, or in answer to the regular vacancies advertisements placed by the firm in the Polish-language *Polish Daily* or notified to the employment section of the Polish Ex-Combatants' Association in South Kensington.[1] A small private em-

[1] At management level, it was said that there were few if any war-time links between Polish employees in the firm. During the detailed interviews with Polish supervisors, however, it emerged that in a fair number of cases friends or former service colleagues had been brought in by those already working there.

ployment agency run by a Pole would also send along applicants, most of them Polish, but from time to time Ukrainians, Italians, and Indians. The 'Polish' character of the works side had thus been perpetuated over the years, and in late 1959 half of the overall staff and labour force were Poles.

Polish workers at Polplastics represented a fair cross-section of the older Polish exile group in the London area. As the years went by, however, there were fewer former senior professional officers and more of what was described as 'the N.C.O. type'; the majority had a better educational background than the average local unskilled worker. The group as a whole was relatively old—the firm accepted workers up to the age of 55 or so. Younger Poles usually speak better English, have British technical or professional qualifications, and rarely enter British industry at the unskilled or even semi-skilled level. Most Polish workers at Polplastics stayed for a long period, but a minority would drift off soon after their arrival, either to hotel work or to better-paid industrial jobs. There were also a certain number of middle-aged professional men who would come to work for a month or so between jobs or to make some money to augment their low or irregular earnings as freelance journalists, broadcasters, or officials of voluntary agencies within the Polish community.[1]

From time to time work-seekers of other nationalities came from the employment exchange:[2] some were brought in by compatriots, others simply applied at the door. A fair number of local English and migrant Irish male workers applied for work, but the majority showed a very high turnover. Various reasons were advanced for this. Some applicants belonged to the work-shy, drifting fringe of near-unemployables who are known to every employment exchange. Others were able and ambitious, and would leave because they found the work tedious and relatively poorly paid. This applied in particular to those migrant Southern Irish, whose aim

[1] One of these expressed his feelings in the following words: 'I am the master of my typewriter. I dictate its tempo, norm, type of product. In the factory my machine dictates to me—tempo, type of product, and norm. And this is the difference between free labour and slave labour. And on this, *inter alia*, rests the shame of slavery—a dependence on inanimate matter.' Janusz Kowalewski, 'Slavery Once More' ('I Znowu Niewola', *Kultura*, No. 9/155, September 1960, p. 74).

[2] If an unskilled Polish work-seeker applied at the employment exchange, it was likely that he would be directed to Polplastics. In recent years, however, only a handful of Poles had registered at the exchange.

was to work for a year or so at a high rate with plenty of overtime before returning home. Another reason for the high turnover among English unskilled workers was suggested by two Polish supervisors—that most of them did not feel at ease in this 'foreign shop', particularly as they had to take orders from Polish supervisors.

These considerations applied far less, if at all, in the case of the English women workers: their turnover was no higher than in other Croydon firms, and they were said to appreciate the rather formal good manners of most Polish male employees.

The Hungarian contingent had a lower turnover than was reported from other Croydon firms. This was probably due to the long-standing, neighbourly sympathy which links Poles and Hungarians, a sympathy that was increased by the Hungarian reception of Polish refugees in September 1939 and the circumstances of the Budapest Rising of 1956. There also seems to have been a considerable degree of selection. The Hungarians were originally sponsored by a local Englishwoman with Hungarian connexions, but the Polish management and supervisors were sufficiently informed of the detailed course of the Rising not to accept all escaped Hungarians without further inquiry. As the English personnel manager said:

> I learned to distinguish between the genuine revolutionaries, who usually turn out to be the good workers, and the spivs, escapees and freed prisoners, some of them ex-Nazis, who came out earlier. I have a rough and ready test. I just ask them the date of their arrival in Britain. If it was the autumn of 1956 the presumption is that they're no good; if the winter, they're usually all right.

A handful of Ukrainians and Italians were employed in this firm. These are members of minority groups with whom Poles are likely to feel one or another kind of affinity. With the Ukrainians, the shared Slav origin, similar language, war-time experiences, and anti-Communist ideology usually outweigh old political resentments. With the Italians, it is a matter of shared religion and the affection for Italy and her people felt by many Poles who fought in the Italian campaign and subsequently spent two post-war years there in the Anders Army, before being brought to Britain for demobilization.

Another small minority group consisted of Indians and Anglo-Indians, who were said to get along well with the Polish majority;

the latter brought little or no colour-consciousness in their cultural luggage and judged the Asians according to cultural criteria. With regard to West Indians and Africans, the position was different. Polplastics had tried a few but no longer employed any; they were reported to have proved lazy and incompetent and were no longer considered. In any case, there was said to be an adequate labour supply of Poles and others. Another reason for the unwillingness to employ West Indians seemed to be that in London at least Poles have taken over local attitudes towards West Indians for the sake of conformity and to assert their own superior socio-cultural status; this would extend to the work situation, where the loss of status by former professionals and 'white-collar' exiles is most conspicuous.

Clearly, selective processes, clustering, and the 'favoured nation' principle were at work in Polplastics, as everywhere else. It seemed fairly clear that the large, long-term Polish 'core community' of supervisors and old-timers set the general climate of the works, and that employees, Polish or other, who did not find this climate congenial or who were not themselves congenial to the Polish core did not stay long in the firm.

(4) *Polish Labour Force*

During his five years with Polplastics, Mr. Brown had evolved his own image of Polish workers. His picture corresponded to that given by most English informants on the management side:

> At first I had a job to understand them, linguistically or otherwise. Now I understand them fairly well and can also make myself understood. I like them now and think they're the best of all the foreigners in this country—they work hard and are adaptable, stable, and thrifty. They like security so they buy houses the moment they're in a job. They always help each other. On the job I find them courteous and respectful. (Of course, if they *were* rude, they'd go at once.) Only a very few bad types come in and have to be turned away. In the earlier years they used to give a small bow when they spoke but that's dying away now. There used to be some trouble over rank. In earlier years apparently it was bad. The older ones couldn't forget they had been senior officers. There's not much of it left now. A lot of Poles come from other English factories. They can unfold their roots and branches here.
>
> I don't find them so very different from the English now except for

their suspiciousness, and the fact that some are inclined to tell tales on the others. I don't know whether this is racial [*sic*] or due to their war experiences. Some have had very harrowing experiences and tell me about them. If anyone tells tales I just don't listen and they soon stop.

I think the factory is a good unit. Unlike Firm —— (a large South London food-processing firm) we don't try to keep Poles and English on separate shifts or think of them by nationality. It's a good factory for Poles because they can move up, and can make use of any technical qualifications they've got while speaking their own language. For example, an assistant electrician has just been taken on. He is the son of an employee, and has just arrived from Poland. Here he can work and learn his trade in Polish until he acquires enough English. They can all rise up, especially the younger ones.

Mr. Brown was generally popular among the Polish employees, and frequently acted as a 'sponsor' in the literal as well as the sociological sense:

Most of them have delayed their applications for British citizenship, but there's been a sudden spurt in the last few months. I know because most of them come to me to ask me to act as a sponsor. The Home Office must be getting quite sick of my name. I think the reasons are first of all that they are settling down in their adopted country, and second that they want to visit their families in Poland.[1] Many are also bringing their families over from Poland for visits and I help them to fill in the forms, and also their income-tax returns and such things. They always ask me to their ex-servicemen's dances but I don't normally go. Drinking vodka and dancing till four in the morning isn't up my street. But some of the girls in the office are courting Poles and they go, and appear the next morning rather under the weather. There isn't much chance for social life on the job, but we do have a Christmas Party here and most of the Poles, staff and works, turn up for that.

(5) *The Office*

The office side of the organization employed some forty people in managerial, technical, and clerical capacities: it comprised several technical departments as well as the usual administrative and sales departments. Broadly speaking, the latter were staffed by English employees, the former by Poles. The junior clerical staff was entirely English, as one might expect in a firm which had to

[1] Non-naturalized Poles travel on refugee papers which are not valid in their country of birth.

compete on the British market for British customers. But there was such a shortage of Polish women with adequate clerical qualifications and fluency in English that even the Polish managerial staff, who might have preferred bilingual Polish secretaries, were compelled to use English secretaries and typists.

The managing director was Polish by birth. He was, however, a naturalized British subject, had adopted an English name, married a British wife, consorted socially with English people, and spoke excellent English, which he used on most occasions, sometimes even when talking to his Polish employees. During the War he had been a pilot and warrant officer in a Polish squadron of the R.A.F. The 'Polish' character of the firm was not officially stressed, although, as we shall see, Polish sentiments and undertones were strong, especially on the works side, and were not discouraged by management.

The assistant manager, who was in charge of personnel management, was English, as were his staff. They were comparatively recent arrivals. In no case did any of them seem to have had any previous contacts with Poles or Poland, as a result of travel, war service, family links, or anything else, and their appointments were made on purely pragmatic considerations of efficiency and suitability.

In the buying, sales, export, and industrial sales departments all staff were English, with the exception of the manager in the industrial sales department. Mr. A. was Polish, but his two assistants were English. He was about 40, had an attractive, brisk, and efficient presence, served with the Polish forces in Scotland during the War, and spoke excellent English, though with a fairly heavy accent. He preferred to speak English during the interview. He had not changed his name, but for simplicity's sake used his Christian name as a surname in the firm and for all business purposes.[1] Mr. A. had only recently taken steps to acquire British nationality, his main reason for this move being that he wished to visit his family in Poland. He retained loose social links with the

[1] This is a fairly common practice among Poles who retain their social membership of the Polish exile community, and who do not therefore wish to change or anglicize their surnames formally. Such a change as the latter is regarded by the exile community as going rather too far in the direction of assimilation. The use of such convenience names as Mr. Stanley (for Stanislaw), Roman, Paul (for Pawel), and Antony is, however, frequent. The best-known example is, of course, that of Joseph Conrad, whose real surname was Korzeniowski.

Polish community, and was accommodated to rather than assimilated in British social life.

Personnel in the accounts department was, as might have been expected, also entirely English.[1] A costing department had, however, recently been set up, and this was under the direction of a Pole, Mr. B., who started with the firm as a book-keeper in the accounts department, and took an L.C.C. evening course and correspondence courses with the Institute of Costs and Works Accountants. To use his own words, he had 'made his own job': cost accounting was, he said, a fairly recent specialization, not yet universally adopted in British industry.

At this time Mr. B. had another Polish cost accountant and an English typist in his department. Like Mr. A., he preferred to conduct the interview in English, which he spoke very well. He appeared superficially anglicized, lived away from other Poles in a new suburb, and found Polplastics almost 'too Polish'. He worked previously in a British firm where there were no Poles other than a machine operative, had not experienced any difficulties or discrimination because of his nationality, and seemed confident of his ability to make his way on merit anywhere in British industry.

Mr. B. was about 40 years old; he retained his Polish name in a shortened version, and had only just applied for British citizenship. This suggested that he might not be so anglicized as he wished to appear in the interview, in which the Polish aspect of his personality was submerged by his 'English business *persona*', heightened by the use of the English-language medium.

The technical departments were, as has been said, more or less Polish preserves. The drawing office had a Polish manager and a staff of four Polish draughtsmen, while the design and development department had a Polish manager and an English assistant artist.

The manager of the latter, Mr. C., was in the same age-group as Mr. A. and Mr. B. The Second World War interrupted his studies, but he was able to take a full post-war course in industrial design.

[1] Adult exiles used to the beautiful simplicity of the decimal system have had to make an immense effort in Britain and other sterling area and Commonwealth countries of settlement to adjust even their everyday reckoning to the idiosyncratic complications of shillings, furlongs, pints, and stones. Small wonder that Polish pocket-diaries published in Britain carry a page of 'weights and measures' with the British and continental equivalents.

After experience with a large English firm (where he experienced no difficulties or discrimination), he came to Polplastics in about 1951; he said that he found the Polish flavour of the firm congenial, although he called it 'Anglo-Polish' rather than undiluted Polish. He had retained his obviously foreign though not too complicated surname, but explained the changes or simplifications made by his colleagues on the grounds that English customers prefer to do business with executives who do not seem or sound too foreign.

This interview was at first conducted in English, but towards the end Mr. C. switched to Polish, saying: 'Please don't think that I have forgotten my Polish. It's just that I am used to discussing technical matters in English.'

Mr. C. had a Polish wife, and was endeavouring to bring up his children to speak Polish as well as English. He was *au courant* with exile affairs, but spoke with impatience of internal political disputes, although his first loyalty was still to Poland and things Polish. He was conscious of belonging to an exile technical élite which could hold its own in an alien society and although he reads the monthlies published in London by the younger exile intellectuals, commented somewhat slightingly on their humanistic, non-technical bias. 'There's really nothing for them to do here. They ought to go back to Poland but they prefer to be dilettantes here.' Mr. C. spoke of a possible return to Poland for himself and his family 'if something changes there. I might be better off there than here then.'

Mr. D., Polish manager of the drawing office, was at least ten years older and a great deal less anglicized than the managing director or any of the other Polish staff members so far mentioned. He admitted to speaking poor English and was relieved to be able to discuss his work in Polish.

Mr. D. was trained and worked as an aircraft engineer and designer before the War in Poland. He escaped to the West, served with the Polish Carpathian Brigade in North Africa, and received injuries from wounds which permanently impaired his health. He had been through a series of painful operations and was forced to spend most of his leisure time resting at home. The permanent discomfort and pain which he endured might well, he thought, have inclined him to take a somewhat jaundiced and bitter view of his environment.

After demobilization, Mr. D. tried to find a post in the British aircraft industry. He attributed his failure to do so to xenophobia and religious (anti-Roman Catholic) discrimination on the part of the two firms he approached (it could also have been due to post-war cut-backs in the aircraft industry). He then decided to change his field, and went to work for Polplastics in its early Brixton days, learning the techniques from the bottom.

At this time Mr. D. had worked with Polplastics for twelve years. He found British industrial hours too long, but he liked the work, firstly because 'only the boss is over me and I'm otherwise independent. In addition the work here is high tempo and varied and that helps me to keep going despite the pain.' Mr. D. also had a Polish staff under him, which made for easier communication and a pleasanter atmosphere.[1] He seemed to realize that his poor English would handicap him in competition for a position of equal status in a British firm.

Mr. D. felt a certain resentment towards the English which he expressed in cultural terms:

> I've had English assistants but they were not much good, their training is narrow and over-specialized. The Poles are all-rounders. Mine are mainly younger men, and some weren't even in the army at all. They were trained in various Polish technical colleges here or at Battersea, and are studying nights for the Higher National Certificate. In my opinion, Poles are usually more able and imaginative in the engineering and designing fields and have a wider training than the English. And the British firms know it. They're quite ready to take on Poles but pay them lower salaries. It doesn't make any difference whether they change their names or not. 'You're a bloody foreigner till you die in this country.' That's what one of my wife's cousins, who's in the Foreign Office, said to her when I thought of changing my name.

Some former officer colleagues of Mr. D. and a non-commissioned officer who served under him were employed in Polplastics on the works side. It was not stated in so many words, but it appeared that in some cases he had suggested that they applied for work here. As for his staff colleagues, Mr. D. regarded only one, a Pole, as a congenial companion; the other Poles he regarded as uninterested in 'cultural matters'. He considered his English colleagues to be on a lower cultural level, their conversation being, he claimed, limited to the weather and kindred topics. He was particu-

[1] In 1958 Mr. D. still had one English assistant and three Poles. By 1959 the Englishman had gone.

larly shocked by the English girls' habit of 'discussing intimate personal subjects in front of all and sundry'.

Mr. D. lived some way from the factory, in the Kensington area. His wife was English. He had a small circle of Polish friends unconnected with the office, with whom he talked engineering shop, visited the Polish theatre, and attended concerts or interesting lectures in the various London Polish clubs. He belonged to the active exile Association of Polish Engineers and Technicians. Despite his rather bitter attitude, Mr. D. had accommodated himself adequately to exile life in Britain. He had no wish to follow the example of so many Polish engineers by migrating to Canada, giving as his main reason his permanent ill-health and the absence of a national health scheme in Canada.

(6) *The Works*

In direct authority over the works side of the factory were the works manager and the production manager, both Englishmen. One of the two assistants to the production manager was, however, Polish and his story was of some interest.

Mr. E. was in his mid-thirties and came from that part of north-east Poland which is now incorporated in the Soviet Union. He was in the Polish Second Corps, where he received secondary and some technical education. In the Polish Resettlement Corps he was trained as a wireless operator, but found no opportunity of using this training in civilian life. After a couple of years in British industry, Mr. E. came to Polplastics as a storeman in 1949. Despite his lack of higher education, he soon proved to be exceptionally able, and after several promotions to more responsible positions he graduated to a managerial position.

Mr. E. was friendly, unassuming, and highly intelligent, with a good grasp of the entire organization of the firm, and a detailed knowledge of all its personnel. He spoke good and unpretentious English, but preferred to talk to me in Polish. Of all the Polish employees so far interviewed, he seemed the nearest to his English equivalents in the industrial scene. At the same time, he stood closest to the organized local Polish community, in whose life he played an active part. He had an English wife but had made no effort to change his name, although it was a really difficult four-syllable one. In practice, he was known throughout the factory as

'Tony', the diminutive of his Christian name Antoni, without the prefix 'Mr.'.

The lower supervisory levels in the works were entirely Polish, as was some 75 per cent. of the male labour force. In general, the pre-war and war-time Polish social hierarchy had been reversed. The supervisors were drawn from the younger men, the former junior officers, N.C.O.s and other ranks, and those with pre-war or war-time artisan training, while the machine operatives included the older generation, former officers of field rank, and individuals with a non-technical academic background. The English assistant manager said rather proudly: 'Some of the older colonels have retired now but we've still got a couple of M.B.E.s among the operatives.'

(7) *The Moulding Room*

The bulk of the male labour force worked in the moulding room, operating the machines that produced the firm's manifold products. The moulding room functioned on a three-shift basis, with the shifts changing round every week. Each shift was under a charge-hand (Polish) with two assistants (also Polish); and all three shifts came under a foreman (again Polish). The latter worked a long day, covering the morning and half the afternoon shift, but the night shift was left in charge of the charge-hand only.

Each shift had developed its own individual 'culture', influenced by the personality of the charge-hand, and the process of natural selection which had gone to form its stable nucleus. The long-term core of each shift was Polish, numbering up to 80 per cent. of the total shift-membership of thirty-five to forty. Said the assistant manager:

> With newcomers, we try to put them in the same shift with a friend or colleague. The shifts stay approximately the same for years on end. One Pole came back to work after five years and went back on to the same shift. Operators can change shifts but most stay put. Of course this makes for better work.

Although the official language of the firm was English, the working language of the moulding room was Polish. The three charge-hands spoke enough English to supervise their minority of non-Polish operatives, but the foreman, Mr. F., was a shy and uncommunicative ex-officer from north-east Poland whose English was generally agreed to be poor. His directives were usually channelled through the charge-hands, who would translate them where necessary.[1]

All three charge-hands were in their forties. Two (Mr. G., Mr. H.) were former N.C.O.s in the Polish Second Corps, the third (Mr. I.) was a former qualified engineer who had been seconded from the Polish forces and served as a staff officer in the British Army during and after the War.

The first two charge-hands differed considerably in character. Mr. G. was said to be something of a martinet,[2] while Mr. H. was calm and easygoing, with a great deal of personal charm. The latter came to Polplastics from a London rubber factory, which employed a large number of Poles. The pay was good and he had no difficulty in getting on with the English around him, but he found the work was heavy and unpleasant. Mr. H. heard about Polplastics from friends employed there, and started five years ago as a machinist. His pre-war background was urban middle class and he had a commercial training. Some years ago he took over the dispatch manager's work while the latter was on holiday. He did well, was promoted to charge-hand, and was in line for further promotion.

Outside the factory, Mr. H. was an active member of the Polish exile community. His wife was Polish, his children went to Polish Saturday schools, and the family were members of the Polish parish in Croydon, although they continued to live in Streatham.

Over three-quarters of the operatives on Mr. H.'s shift were Poles. There were also three Englishmen, one Indian, and five Hungarians. Of the Englishmen, Mr. H. said: 'These three have been on the shift for four years and they seem to like it. There have been more English in the past, but most of them don't feel at ease with so many foreigners, nor do they like being bossed by foreigners, so they move on fast.'

The Indian and the Hungarians were said to fit in well with their shift-mates, despite the difference of language. Mr. H. had experienced no difficulties with the minority of older professional officers

[1] Mr. F. preferred not to come for a personal interview, giving as a reason the need for him to be on the floor all the time, and saying that the charge-hands could give as much information as he.

[2] He was first on night shift and then away on sick leave, so that he could not be interviewed; his shift had an ethnic pattern similar to those of the other two, with thirty Poles, four Hungarians, and two Italians.

on his shift. 'On the job they adapt themselves. Off it, they live their former social lives with their own friends.'[1]

Mr. I., the former staff officer, spoke better English than his two colleagues, and although friendly and unassuming, was rather more sophisticated in his manner and viewpoint. He preferred to speak Polish at the interview and it soon emerged that away from work he was active in exile community life and organization. Despite his close war-time links with the British he seemed to have rejected the possibilities of assimilation which lay open to him after the War.

Mr. I. came to Polplastics about ten years ago, after working in a canning factory started by a Polish friend and then for a few weeks in a South London food-processing firm which habitually employed a large number of Poles. He did not like the atmosphere or conditions at this firm and left after six weeks. 'One could form a general staff out of all the ex-colonels and generals working there.'

Mr. L.'s shift numbered thirty-four, of whom four were Indian and thirty Polish. Until recently there were three Hungarians, but they went to join friends on other shifts. There were no English on Mr. I.'s shift: 'I had a few but they've moved to other shifts or gone. I'm sorry to say it about your countrymen but they had a "couldn't care less" attitude to work. Also they thought of us as foreigners, which didn't make for good relations on the job.'

The four Indians were well established in this shift (the informant did not know whether they were from Pakistan or India). One was old enough to qualify for a pension but liked to go on working. Another owned a rooming-house in Croydon and brought his countrymen along for jobs.

About one-quarter of the Poles on this shift had been with the firm for over ten years or more. One or two were war-time colleagues of Mr. I., but he was not responsible for introducing them to the firm: 'Some are old regular army officer types, but there's no trouble. They do their work and they go off home. All the same, I really admire the boss for taking on some of them. I suppose he

[1] As was mentioned earlier, the individualistic organization of the work in the moulding shop, whereby each operator stood by a noisy machine in an area some yards away from other workers, precluded much conversation or social contact between shift-mates and could perhaps help to reduce any class or status tensions that existed. In addition, the canteen breaks were short and staggered so that there was little opportunity for contact there.

does it for sentimental reasons. Several couldn't hope to get work elsewhere.'

A middle-aged writer, who worked for some months at the firm was, like most intellectuals, much more critical of the managing director's attitude to his Polish workers, which he described as abrupt and unpleasant, but agreed that it would be hard to find another factory which would have accepted one of his friends, an old man who had lost his leg, but who was working at Polplastics.

(8) *The Tool-room*

The tool-room in Polplastics, as in most English factories, was an enclave of skilled men who regarded themselves as distinct from and superior to the general run of unskilled and semi-skilled workers. This department had a Polish supervisor and some twenty men, of whom ten were skilled and ten semi-skilled. About half of the tool-makers were Polish, the other half English; there was also one young Hungarian tool-maker. The two apprentices were both English ('no young Poles have come forward as yet'). The Poles were all of the artisan—N.C.O. class. This tool-room was not a closed shop, but most of its members were said to belong to the A.E.U.

The supervisor, Mr. J., was about 50 years old, and one of the few Poles in this firm who had been able to go on working in his pre-war occupation. A skilled artisan, he served through the War as an N.C.O. in the ground staff of the Polish Air Force in Scotland. In 1944 he volunteered for work in the British war industry, and went to work in a small Polish firm in North London. Like many of the small mushroom firms that sprang up towards the end of the War, this did not long survive the peace. Mr. J. moved to Polplastics when it started up in 1947, and had been there ever since. Some years ago he considered emigrating to Canada, like so many of his Air Force colleagues, but in the end decided against it. He had only recently applied for British nationality.

Mr. J. spoke rather poor English, possibly because he had never worked outside a Polish establishment. The working languages of the tool-room were Polish and English. Mr. J. commented that his English workers showed a much higher turnover than the Poles, probably, he thought, because of the political and overall climate of this Polish-dominated shop.

(9) *Other Departments*

The plastic products went from the moulding room to be finished by women workers in the finishing shop. Here again the foreman and three charge-hands were Polish, but, with the exception of two Polish and four Italian women, the rest of the women operatives were English with some Irish. Eight of them were, however, married to Poles working in the firm. The English women did not show the same high turnover as their male compatriots and working relations were reported to be most cordial. Unlike Telelux, where the idea of appointing West Indian men as supervisors in departments with a female labour force was viewed with apprehension, on the grounds that such supervisors should be the fatherly English type, there seemed to be no objections among women workers in Polplastics to their Polish male supervisors, although the recently appointed foreman was only in his early thirties.

In the regrinding room, the remnants and rejects were reground for further use. This was a heavy, dusty job, carried out by three Polish men under the supervision of a Polish charge-hand. The latter, Mr. L., was a former frontier guard from East Poland, a cheerful, well-read, philosophical bachelor in his early fifties. Unlike most government officials in East Poland, he escaped deportation to Russia. After reaching France in 1940, he served with the Polish Grenadiers in the Maginot Line defence and was interned in Switzerland. Towards the end of the War he escaped, joined the French *maquis*, and came to Britain with the Polish forces in the West.

After demobilization, Mr. L. worked on British Railways with an all-British gang. He experienced no difficulty in getting on with them: 'Everyone can make the odd remark when they get excited, but it's not worth taking it to heart.' He found the work heavy and hazardous and left it after a year or so. After working for a year in a London garage he moved to Polplastics. His English was adequate but not outstanding. Rather surprisingly, he lived and has lived for the past twelve years with an English family in Streatham. He was of a solitary disposition, and did not participate very actively in exile organizational life.

Of the work of his department, Mr. L. said:

> The work is heavy and dusty. I had Englishmen but they went else-

where for more money. Other men are allocated temporarily if they're not needed elsewhere. This job suits me and my three. One of them was in the *maquis* like me, the others were in D.P. camps. I'm quite happy and content to stay as I am. It's no good worrying over the past and perhaps being taken off to a mental home. I just take life as it comes.

After the plastic goods were finished, they would proceed to the finished goods store. This was in charge of Mr. M. Under him were a Polish charge-hand, one Polish woman employee (Mr. M.'s wife), three Hungarian men, and an Englishman. The working language in this department was English.

The M.s had been with Polplastics since 1952. Like the majority of Poles in the firm, Mr. M. had served in the Polish Second Corps; after his demobilization they lived for some years in a Polish hostel in Sussex. Lack of work forced them to move, and they went to Brixton. Here the Employment Exchange sent them to Polplastics. Previously they owned a house in Brixton, but they later moved to Croydon.

The dispatch department employed twenty-six people. Its manager was Polish, and under him were two English clerical workers, one Polish foreman, and twenty-two labourers. Of the latter, thirteen were Polish, six Hungarian, and three English.

The manager, Mr. N., had been with Polplastics since 1948 when he was demobilized from the P.R.C. He began as an operator and worked his way up. He got his present job about a year before this; he was promoted, after being foreman in the packing section. He was about 40, and gave an impression of easygoing efficiency. He spoke excellent English, but like all the other supervisors on the works side chose to speak Polish during the interview. He was said to be very active in exile organizational life, and was a member of a Polish parish some miles to the north of Croydon. He was an unofficial room-finder for all Polish newcomers to the firm as he was in touch with so many Polish house-owners and landlords in Croydon and South London. The present Polish foreman in this department was a newcomer, brought straight into the job just under a year ago. 'He was a station-master at home in Poland,' explained Mr. N., 'so he feels quite at home dealing with British Railways.'

The Hungarians were all taken on after early 1957. Mr. N. said they were good, steady workers; he thought they probably felt better in a Polish than an English working atmosphere. He also had three Englishmen, including two lorry-drivers, in his department; they had been there for a long time, and according to Mr. N., they liked the firm and felt quite at home in it.

Most of the Polish labourers in the dispatch department were former members of the Anders Second Corps, brought in by Mr. N. himself. As the work was fairly heavy manual labour, involving lifting, the majority were not very old. Despite the preponderance of Poles, the working language in this department was English, possibly because the work involved dealing with goods destined for the English-speaking outside world. Some Hungarians were more fluent in German, but the Poles would usually answer them in English.

On the works side, Polplastics had some five other smaller departments, in which there were about a dozen Polish men and some women, all English. When the supervisor of one of these departments, Mr. O., was called for an interview, it proceeded on different lines from the others for the first ten minutes, during which Mr. O. interrogated me in detail about my background, the reason for my speaking Polish, and the purpose and sponsorship of the study. Fortunately I was to some extent prepared for this interrogation, having been forewarned that this employee had been an Air Force security officer for some years.

After satisfying himself more or less as to my *bona fides*, Mr. O. proved very ready to talk about himself and his past life. He was, however, full of meaningful refusals and silences when questioned about factory life and relationships. On the whole, it seemed best to regard these omissions as evidence of a *deformation professionel* in Mr. O. rather than as particularly significant. Unlike most other Poles interviewed at Polplastics, this informant displayed a distinct chip-on-the-shoulder about his present occupational and economic downgrading, although it would be fair to add that of all those interviewed he had probably suffered the most considerable setback in his career. And at the age of 45 he was not old enough, like most of the elderly ex-regular officers working on the factory floor, to renounce personal ambition and resign himself to a humble old age in exile.

This informant had been with Polplastics for nearly four years and was now Chief Storeman with a Polish assistant (a former D.P.) and one or two other Poles under him. When speaking of his work, Mr. O. referred to himself as stores manager, but also stressed that he had never worked as a storeman before. He was a regular Air

Force officer, who had served with some distinction in a bomber squadron of the Polish Air Force in the early years of the War, receiving the D.F.C., the highest Polish order (Virtute Militare), the Polish Cross of Valour (four times), and the Croix de Guerre. Towards the end of the War Mr. O. was transferred to the staff and subsequently to the Air Ministry, where he remained until 1949. He then went to work in a small factory run by an English R.A.F. colleague. He worked his way up to production manager, but unfortunately his friend then decided to retire and closed down the factory.

Mr. O.'s sense of frustration and resentment appeared to date from this period. He was offered a good job in Rhodesia, but his English wife refused to go on the grounds that their son's education would suffer. He then came to Polplastics, where, as he said, 'I do my job and forget about it at home.' The O. family lived outside Croydon, in the country, and Mr. O. did not participate very actively in Polish organizational life. He belonged to the Polish Air Force Association, but this had no Croydon branch. He said that there were few former airmen in Firm C:

> Some come along but they usually go off after a few weeks when they see the relatively low rewards and hard work involved. Most airmen have some technical training and speak good English so they find it quite easy to get jobs in British factories. This place is useful for the old ones who couldn't get work elsewhere.

Mr. O. did not find the factory particularly 'Polish' in atmosphere. 'Most of the management side is English.' He referred to the labour force as a 'porridge' of nationalities, including Hungarians, Czechs, Ukrainians, and Indians. 'Only Germans and Negroes are missing,' he said. Asked about relations between former professional officers and others, Mr. O. was at his most sibylline, implying only that he had a great deal of interesting information which he could not impart.

(10) *Polplastics as Seen by a Casual Employee*

Shortly after this fieldwork was concluded, a Polish exile journalist went to work in the Polplastics moulding room for several months. After he left he wrote an account of his experiences showing the firm from a very different angle to that from which it was described to me.[1] While it is one man's view, it probably reflects, if in a somewhat exaggerated form, the situation and attitudes of the older professional-class exiles who are compelled to take a manual job to keep themselves and their families, and indeed, the surprise and consternation felt by most professional workers when they confront the realities of factory life. It also suggests the tensions that are likely to arise between various groups and classes of Poles in such reversed hierarchies.

The writer describes the 'slavery' of uncreative, mechanical, hated work, imposed by the whip of hunger, tying one to the machine by the chain of the norm. The process, he goes on, takes between ten and sixty seconds, according to the size of the product, and the speed is sometimes set so high that even blowing one's nose must be divided into three operations in between movements. Meanwhile one is oppressed by the lack of laughter or song, the silence of the workers, and the chatter of the machines, and above all by the boredom of making four or five automatic and identical movements 1,300 times every day.

Of working relationships he writes that the main antagonism is that between the workers, even including the supervisors, and the 'boss'. This is chiefly because he *is* 'boss' but also because, apart from his regular 'good-morning' greeting, the 'boss' keeps himself completely remote from his men, 'although both he and the great majority of us are Poles, wandering exiles linked by many things, divided by only one, but that is predominant'.

Thus, this antagonism does not, in the writer's views, derive mainly from differences and difficulties but from the very nature of the factory situation, in which the 'boss' is the only free man and all the rest are slaves. In this case, the hostility has found classic early-capitalistic forms of expression: on the one side the boss is strongly opposed to trade unions and all forms of industrial protest; on the other, he notes a lack of effort, a certain 'go-slow' philosophy, a tendency to say: 'Don't take too much trouble. The boss won't go bankrupt anyway.'

Later this writer returns to the subject of the 'boss' and his attitude, asking why he feels unable to treat his Polish workers in a friendly manner, or to show interest in their private lives and families. He contrasts this (and the similar but gruffer and more

[1] Janus Kowalewski, op. cit.

abrupt manner of his own direct supervisors) with the very different approach of English employers in old-established firms. Such firms have personnel officers, clubs, social events, recreational facilities, vacations and old-age pensions; managers talk to the men when they are seen to be discontented, unhappy, or worried. The feeling of servitude is almost lost, attachment to the firm grows, slavery passes into patriarchy or even into free union of employers and employees—'Exploitation is less in older firms . . .' Polish firms in England, he continues, being more recently established by new and inexperienced owners, have a greater tendency to exploit their workers, particularly when they are compatriots who speak poor English, are elderly, unskilled, and physically unfit for or unused to manual labour, and are therefore afraid to seek work in the wider English labour market. Pol-plastics, he maintains, also holds workers because of the good possibilities of week-end overtime work (in any case needed to bring the low basic wage to a living wage). Despite the cool relationships, there is a certain feeling of 'being among one's own people'.

Within the labour force other hostilities emerge, notes the writer: for instance between the old-timers and new workers; between young and old; between the down-graded intelligentsia and the 'true' workers; between the supervisors and the rest. On the other hand, no ethnic antagonisms can be felt: 'On my first day at work my neighbour, a young Hungarian from the Rising, working at the machine opposite me, would run over from his machine to mine, and with quick movements correct some blockage in my machine or teach me the work—without words, by his example.'

He comments on the failure of the charge-hands and their assistants to teach the new workers their job, and quotes a Polish worker as saying: 'Only we can help one another and learn from one another. The charge-hand will teach you damn-all, he's afraid you may take his place.' This the writer doubts, since the charge-hands have been there for years, but he cites it as an instance of the hostile relations between charge-hands and workers. He also mentions the widespread view that the charge-hands favour the old-timers by giving them better machines and easier work, so that they can make a higher bonus (although, as he notes, the maximum extra bonus that can be earned is only 19*s*. per week.)

At about this time I was also able to talk to two other members of the exile intelligentsia who worked for a couple of months at Polplastics between other jobs. They both confirmed, in more moderate terms, the general view of factory relations conveyed in this article. One, a pre-war left-wing politician, stressed the surprising indifference and unfriendliness shown by the entire long-term Polish labour-core to Polish newcomers; the only attempts at friendliness noted were from former fellow-townsmen (in his case it was Warsaw). He added that there was no chance of up-grading or promotion for newcomers, all such jobs being firmly held by a few old-timers.

My other informant, a youngish journalist, was more tolerant, perhaps because he was sure of moving on to a good job after a few weeks. He was full of admiration for the managing director's initiative, energy, and success, as evidence of what a Pole could do in an alien and highly industrialized environment. He also felt that there was a considerable element of envy in the hostility felt by the Polish workers, and particularly the pre-war intelligentsia, to the managing director.

(11) *Conclusion*

In Polplastics, unlike most other firms, it was possible to get the views of some of the Polish transient workers. There was a considerable discrepancy between their views of the firm and those expressed by long-term staff and supervisory informants which needs some explanation.

On the whole, it seems likely that there was a reasonably congenial working climate among the staff and the long-term labour-core, which extended to all but the 'new boys' and the older and least adaptable ex-professional men. Professional civilians, notably writers and lawyers, seem to find adjustment far more difficult than former regular officers, who are more fully resigned to their loss of professional and occupational status and more disciplined to accept adverse circumstances. They tended to stay on at Polplastics and it was also reported that quite a number of professional-class 'transients' would come back again and again to work for a few months, usually asking to be put on the same shift.

Basically, however, the labour-core of Polplastics consisted of people drawn from an upper-working or lower-middle-class background in Poland, such as might be found in similar positions in their own country.[1] It was they who maintained some off-the-job social life in ex-servicemen's clubs and parishes in Croydon and Clapham, including national days and dances attended by some English girls from the office and works. It was they who had the best chance of up-grading and promotion. There were only a few younger officers in supervisory positions and there was probably more inverted class feeling against former senior officers and professional men than emerged from the interviews.

It seemed that, as in most British firms where they worked, such individuals simply did their jobs, remaining aloof from fellow-workers, and returned to resume their former statuses at home and in Polish clubs and institutions. This pattern of behaviour was facilitated at Polplastics by the nature of the work (noise, distance between machines, shift-work and staggered breaks). It was noticeable that the industrial situation imposed its own rules and relationships on those who might have met on equal terms outside. For instance, no contacts at all were reported between the professional staff in the office and the ex-professionals doing manual work in the factory, although several individuals could in theory have established congenial relationships in private social life. And ex-professional manual workers fell easily into the 'true' worker's habit of criticizing and suspecting the management. Even the journalist cited above writes at one point in his lament that he does not wish to be accused of telling tales about his fellow-workers.

Informants differed as to how far Polplastics was a 'Polish' firm or an 'Anglo-Polish' firm, or how far it was simply a local factory conforming to the pattern of the transit-camp firm, with a 'favoured nation' policy giving priority to Poles. Undoubtedly most English and other non-Polish transients would regard Polplastics as an entirely Polish firm, but in comparison with other entirely Polish establishments elsewhere in London it should probably be regarded rather as an Anglo-Polish half-way house. It was a part of the British industrial system, producing for the British market, and yet offering shielded employment which, while it is a convenience to the management, was not entirely devoid of national sentiment. In time it seemed likely that the firm's Anglo-Polish character

[1] This was a relatively large one, since 25 per cent. of employees had been with Polplastics for more than ten years; it included works supervisors as well as long-term workers. All three shifts in the moulding room had a fair-sized nucleus of such workers. The same was true of the qualified engineers, accountants, and designers found on the office side.

would be somewhat diminished, with the staff and supervisors speaking more English and recruitment of elderly exiles fading away. It seemed probable, however, that Poles and children of Poles would remain a favoured nation for recruitment at all levels of the hierarchy, in the same way as happens in establishments dominated by Scots, Jews, or Irish.

MAPS AND CHARTS

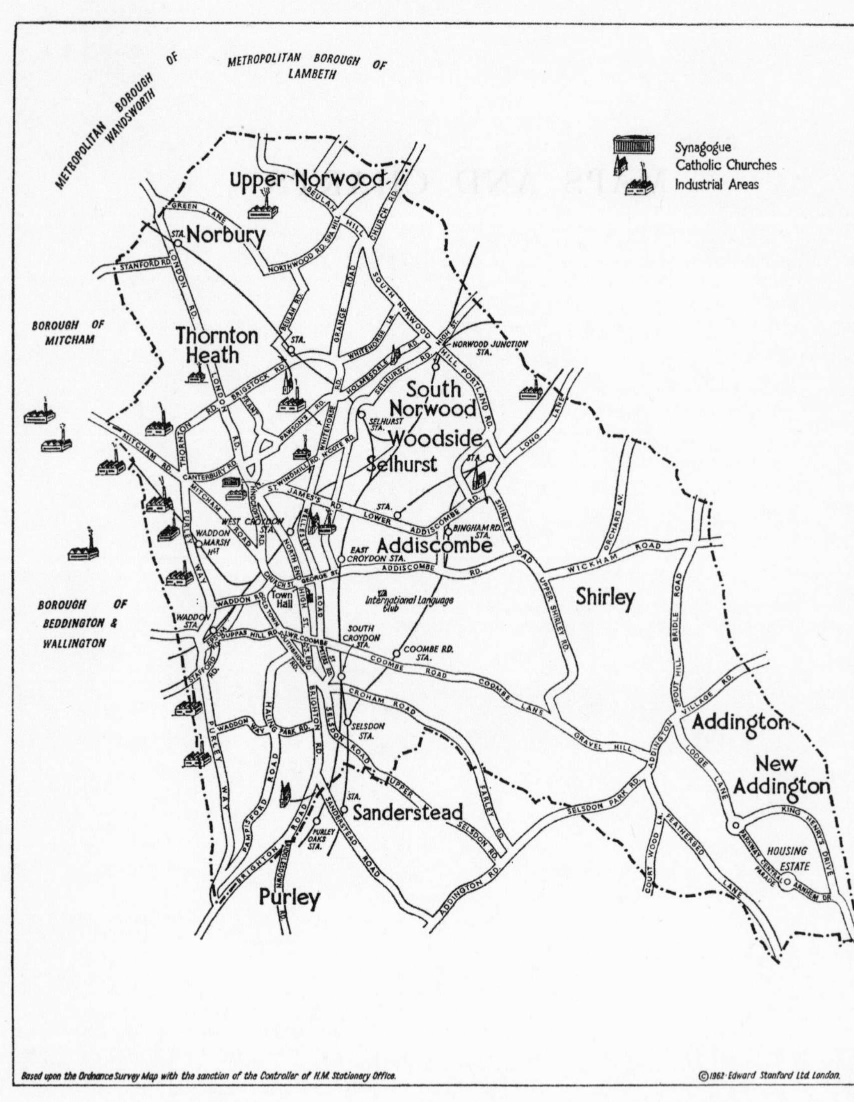

Croydon: major roads, landmarks, and public buildings.

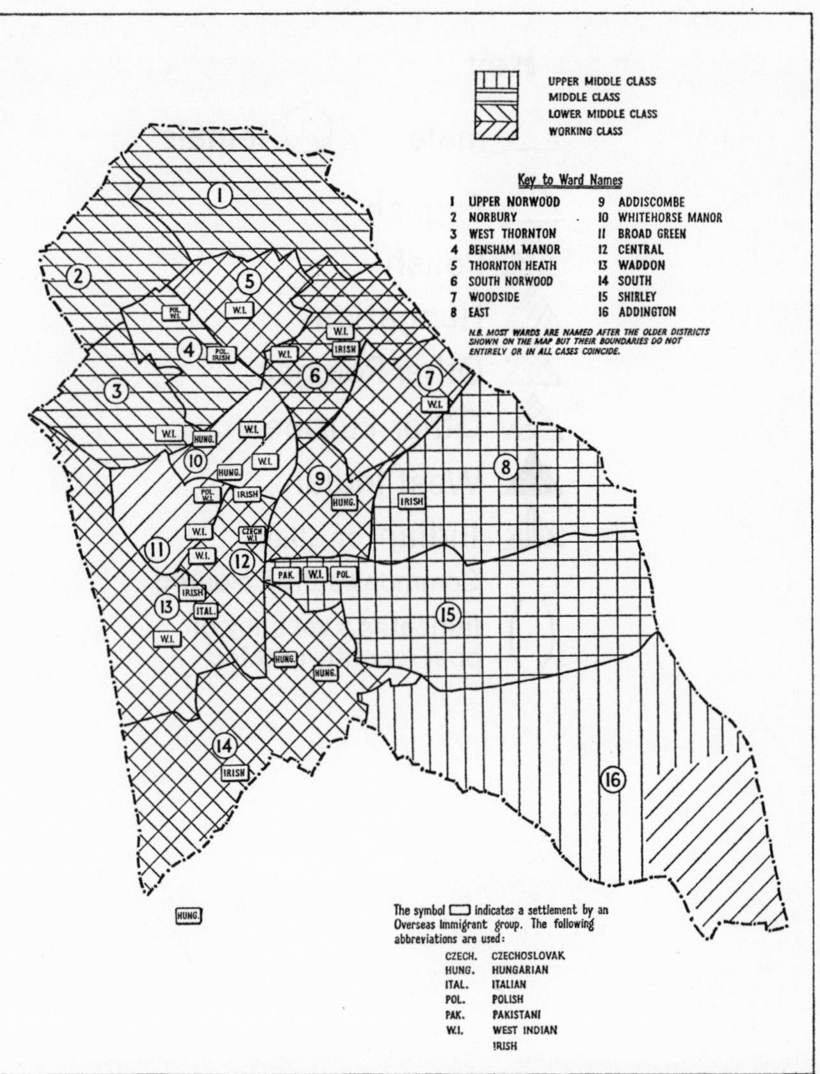

Croydon: social-economic divisions by wards, and settlement patterns of major immigrant groups.

Key

English

Polish

Hungarian

Other Refugee

Other European

West Indian

Indian or other Commonwealth Coloured

( ) Indicates a vacancy or post recently created

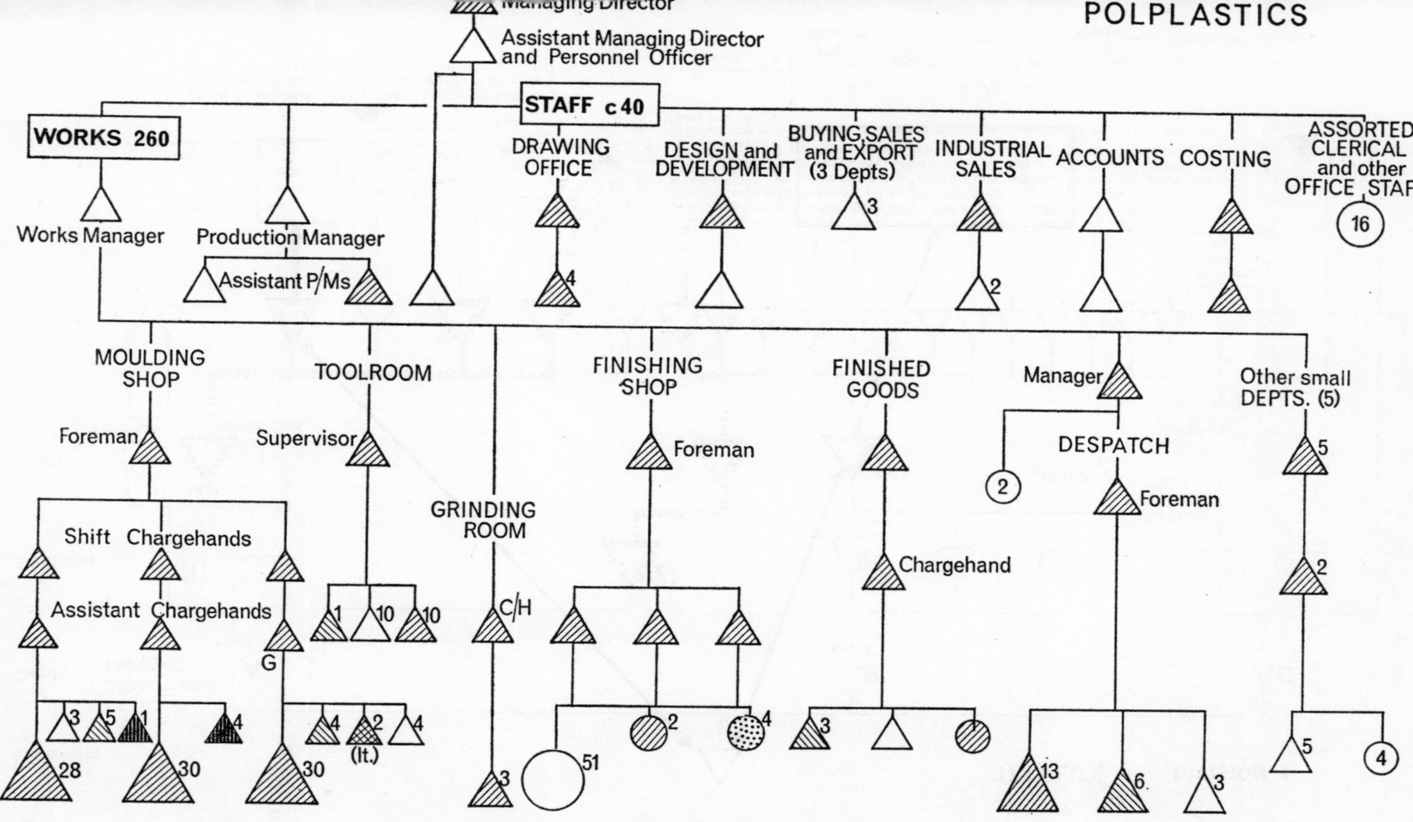
POLPLASTICS
Managing Director
Assistant Managing Director and Personnel Officer
STAFF c 40
WORKS 260
Works Manager
Production Manager
Assistant P/Ms
DRAWING OFFICE
4
DESIGN and DEVELOPMENT
BUYING,SALES and EXPORT (3 Depts)
3
INDUSTRIAL SALES
2
ACCOUNTS
COSTING
ASSORTED CLERICAL and other OFFICE STAFF
16
MOULDING SHOP
Foreman
Shift Chargehands
Assistant Chargehands
G
3
5
1
4
28
30
30
4
2
(lt.)
4
TOOLROOM
Supervisor
1
10
10
GRINDING ROOM
C/H
3
FINISHING SHOP
Foreman
51
2
4
FINISHED GOODS
Chargehand
3
Manager
DESPATCH
Foreman
2
13
6.
3
Other small DEPTS. (5)
5
2
5
4
REGMARAD

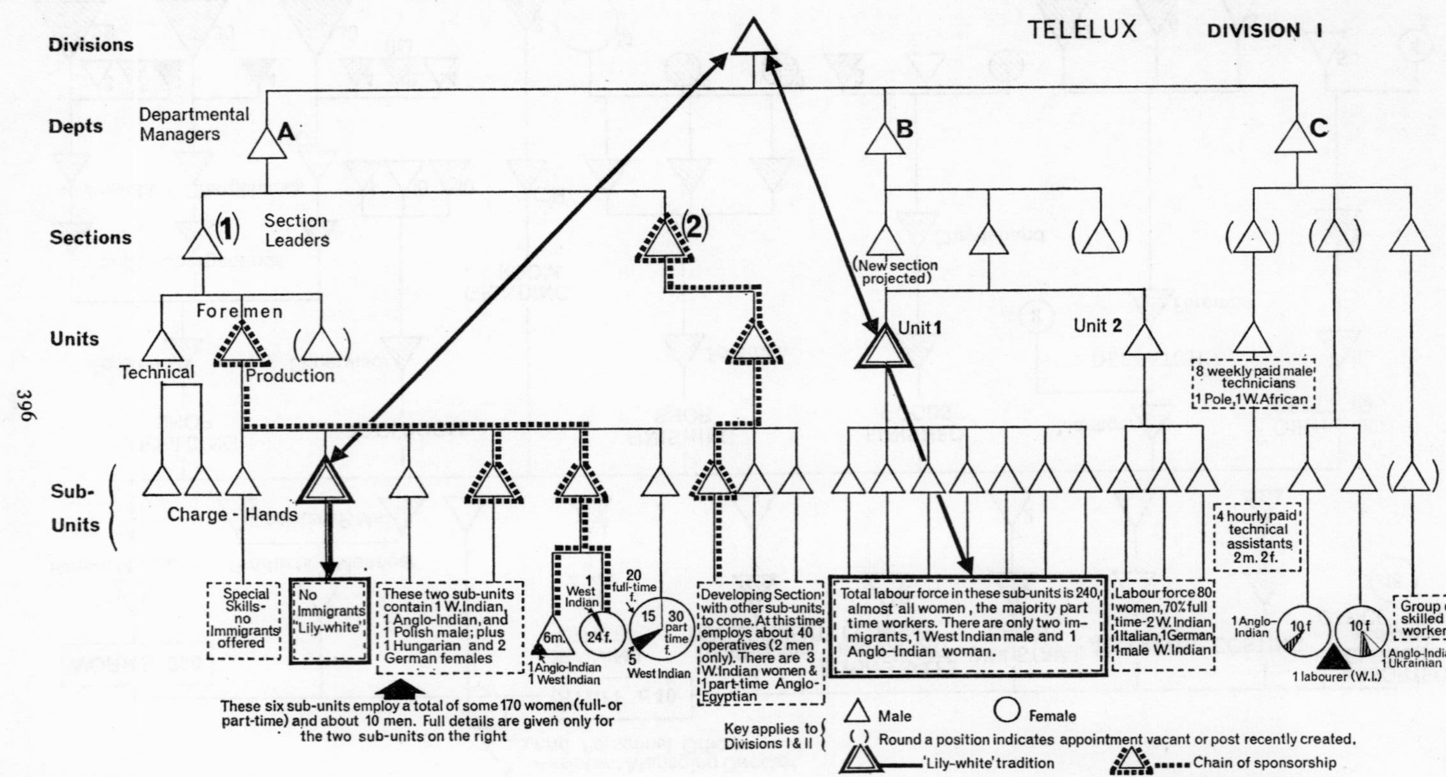
TELELUX
DIVISION I
Divisions
Depts
Departmental Managers
A
B
C
Sections
(1)
Section Leaders
(2)
(New section projected)
Units
Foremen
Technical
Production
Unit 1
Unit 2
8 weekly paid male technicians 1 Pole, 1 W. African
Sub-Units
Charge - Hands
4 hourly paid technical assistants 2m. 2f.
Special Skills-no Immigrants offered
No Immigrants 'Lily-white'
These two sub-units contain 1 W. Indian, 1 Anglo-Indian, and 1 Polish male; plus 1 Hungarian and 2 German females
1 West Indian
6m.
24f.
1 Anglo-Indian
1 West Indian
20 full-time f.
15
30 part time f.
5
West Indian
Developing Section with other sub-units to come. At this time employs about 40 operatives (2 men only). There are 3 W. Indian women & 1 part-time Anglo-Egyptian
Total labour force in these sub-units is 240, almost all women, the majority part time workers. There are only two immigrants, 1 West Indian male and 1 Anglo-Indian woman.
Labour force 80 women, 70% full time-2 W. Indian 1 Italian, 1 German, 1 male W. Indian
1 Anglo-Indian
10 f
10 f
1 labourer (W.I.)
1 Anglo-Indian
1 Ukrainian
Group of skilled workers
These six sub-units employ a total of some 170 women (full- or part-time) and about 10 men. Full details are given only for the two sub-units on the right
Key applies to Divisions I & II
Male
Female
( ) Round a position indicates appointment vacant or post recently created.
'Lily-white' tradition
Chain of sponsorship
REGMARAD

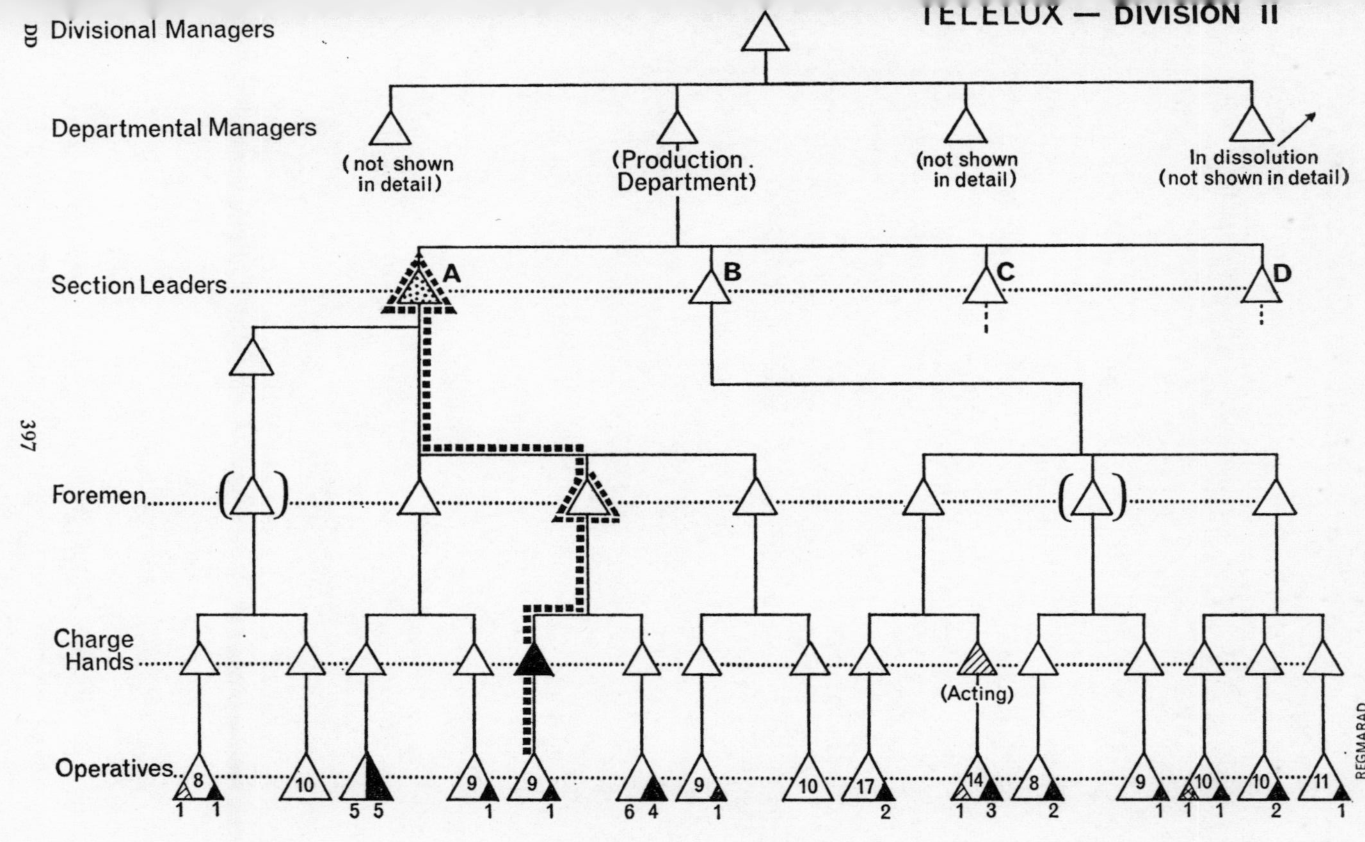
TELELUX — DIVISION II
Divisional Managers
Departmental Managers
(not shown in detail)
(Production Department)
(not shown in detail)
In dissolution (not shown in detail)
Section Leaders
A
B
C
D
Foremen
Charge Hands
(Acting)
Operatives
8
1 1
10
5 5
9
1
9
1
6 4
9
1
10
17
2
14
1 3
8
2
9
1
10
1 1
10
2
11
1
REGMARAD

DD

APPENDIX I

QUESTIONNAIRE FOR FIRMS

(1) Nature of production, skills involved.

(2) Age and background of firm.

(3) (*a*) Total labour force (office staff separately), breakdown into male and female and by skills, also numbers of apprentices and juveniles.

(*b*) Number of immigrants in each category, breakdown into 'coloured' West Indian, West African, Pakistani, Indian, Adenese, Anglo-Indian, and others, and European (Polish, Baltic, Hungarian, German, Italian, Cypriot, Maltese, Southern Irish, and others). How many now, and at peak periods in earlier years. Breakdown by sex.

(*c*) Where do immigrants live? In what age groups do they fall?

(4) Various groups of immigrants employed since when? Why originally taken on? Any old-timers (i.e. from pre-war or early post-war period)?

(5) General labour situation at various periods since the War, and now.

(6) Who suggested employing various immigrant groups? How was recruitment handled, i.e. by consultation with other workers or not? Any redundancy or other clauses (e.g. quota)?

(7) Are immigrants still being taken on? Are there many immigrant applicants, coloured or otherwise? How do they apply (e.g. to the gate, sent by labour exchange, by private recommendation)?

(8) Is any quota actually observed? Reasons for this?

(9) Turnover: (*a*) General; (*b*) Immigrant. Any changes in turnover in recent years?

(10) General redundancy policy? Any actual redundancy? What procedure actually applied if so? Are any groups of immigrants regarded as part of the permanent labour force?

(11) Selection and induction policy?

(12) Promotion policy and practice?

(13) Conditions of work and pay:

(i) Hours (overtime, shifts, part-time, etc.)

(ii) Wages (men, women) bonuses, pensions, etc.

(14) Method of work, e.g. production line; individual group; piece work or time work?

(15) General status of industry and various jobs now and formerly.

(16) Management comments on:

(i) Working ability of general labour force and immigrants, as regards previous training, speed, time-keeping, responsibility, etc. Any policy adopted for better employment of immigrants, e.g. grouping together, dispersal, allotting sponsors, etc.?

(ii) Personal aspects: food, dress, hygiene (cleanliness, odour, etc.), unintelligibility, bad language, political differences, 'chip-on-shoulder', aggressiveness, sex, babies, sociability or cliqueyness, mingling on and off job (canteen, recreational clubs)? Relations between various immigrant and minority groups.

(17) Attitudes of fellow workers, supervisors. Any actively prejudiced persons or sponsors? Any departments where no immigrants are accepted?

(18) Character of local labour force? Where from? Size of old-established nucleus? Who forms public opinion? How does it make itself felt?

(19) Works representatives (joint consultation committees or councils)?

(20) Union set up? Any political angles? Immigrants participation? Office-holding? Strikes?

(21) Miscellaneous observations; and notes; including personal views and background of the informant.

APPENDIX 2

Number of Insured Workers in Croydon Area at June 1955–65

The figures are estimates based partly on the number of N.H.I. Cards exchanged and partly on returns rendered by employers of five or more workpeople, showing the number of N.H.I. Cards held by them.

INDUSTRY†	1955			1958			1959			1960			1965		
	Males	Females	Total	Males	Females	Total	Males	Females	Total	Males	Females	Total	Males	Females	Total
1. *Engineering*															
Engineering, shipbuilding and electrical goods	13,965	7,373	21,338	14,952	8,385	23,337	17,998	9,927	27,925	18,333	10,745	29,078	15,956	8,915	24,871
Precision Instruments, jewellery, etc.	2,336	2,057	4,393	2,882	1,490	4,372	Transferred to Engineering and electrical								
Vehicles	3,661	841	4,502	3,629	810	4,439	1,824	381	2,205	2,076	539	2,615	666	212	878
2. *'Heavy' Industries*															
Building and Contracting	10,297	548	10,845	8,522	514	9,036	9,910	542	10,452	10,330	662	10,992	10,551	862	11,413
Gas, Electricity and Water	2,248	297	2,545	3,114	356	3,470	2,979	381	3,360	2,898	429	3,327	1,131	55	1,186
Transport and Communication	5,173	324	5,497	5,048	418	5,466	4,931	300	5,231	4,460	387	4,847	5,438	1,171	6,609
Metal Manufacture	725	96	821	660	77	737	686	93	779	732	116	848	900	128	1,028
Metal Goods not elsewhere specified	1,126	387	1,513	1,301	458	1,759	1,214	628	1,842	1,748	584	2,332	1,991	632	2,623
Bricks, Pottery, Glass, Cement, etc.	—	—	—	—	—	—	—	—	—	—	—	—	451	119	570
3. *'Light' and 'Consumer' Industries*															
Chemicals, etc. and allied trades	825	745	1,570	1,086	722	1,808	1,115	752	1,867	1,439	843	2,282	1,484	1,033	2,517
Textiles	313	129	442	356	140	496	60	139	199	97	188	285	206	320	526
Leather goods and fur	141	262	403	91	118	209	112	180	292	128	172	300	36	17	53
Clothing (including footwear)	344	780	1,124	331	713	1,044	87	640	727	86	666	752	75	415	490
Food, Drink and Tobacco	1,674	2,233	3,907	1,574	1,989	3,563	1,402	1,222	2,624	1,457	1,369	2,826	2,853	2,372	5,225
Wood/Cork, etc.	1,762	785	2,547	1,756	783	2,539	1,655	759	2,414	1,827	724	2,551	1,494	656	2,150
Paper, Printing, etc.	1,860	1,256	3,116	2,123	1,317	3,440	2,302	1,285	3,587	2,441	1,434	3,875	3,297	1,741	5,038
Other Manufacturing Industries	1,452	1,780	3,232	1,608	1,828	3,436	1,524	1,753	3,277	1,613	1,889	3,502	1,537	1,300	2,837
4. *Professional and 'white collar'*															
Distributive trades	7,886	8,060	15,946	8,400	8,304	16,704	11,912	9,302	21,214	10,776	9,427	20,203	8,469	10,359	18,828
Insurance, Banking and Finance	1,045	876	1,921	1,071	1,082	2,153	1,486	1,678	3,164	2,176	2,114	4,290	2,403	2,370	4,773
National and Local Government*	3,751	1,534	5,285	3,722	1,394	5,116	3,738	1,502	5,240	3,598	1,526	5,124	2,836	1,397	4,233
Professional Services	2,968	6,753	9,721	3,410	7,881	11,291	3,701	8,405	12,106	3,644	8,122	11,766	5,134	9,361	14,495
5. *Other*															
Agriculture	518	108	626	405	69	474	419	55	474	451	55	506	267	74	341
Mining, etc. and quarrying	—	—	—	—	—	—	—	—	—	—	—	—	—	—	—
Non-metalliferous Mining Products other than coal	859	155	1,014	807	193	1,000	726	141	867	649	176	825	—	—	—
Miscellaneous Services	2,121	7,611	9,732	1,880	7,262	9,142	4,234	8,508	12,742	4,407	9,116	13,523	6,897	11,527	18,424
Industry not stated	—	—	—	—	—	—	—	—	—	76	104	180	—	—	—
Grand Total	67,056	44,990	112,040	68,728	46,303	115,031	74,015	48,573	122,588	75,442	51,387	126,829	74,072	55,036	129,108

* Most Civil Servants have their Contributions paid without the use of cards and are, therefore, excluded from the above figures.

† The Ministry of Labour classification has itself undergone some minor rearrangement over the period. On this table, however, the order has been rearranged … industries and firms are grouped in this study.

APPENDIX 3

KEY TO TABLE—SECTORS I–IV

I. LIGHT ENGINEERING

LE I = Skilled (12)
LE II = Semi-skilled (6)
LE III = Mass Production (2)
Total = 20 firms

II. 'HEAVY' INDUSTRIES

HE = Heavy Engineering (2)
HI = Heavy Industry (4)
BC = Building and Contracting (12)
TPU = Transport and Public Utilities (4)
Total = 22 firms

III. 'CONSUMER' INDUSTRIES

LI = Light Industry (9)
LDC = Laundry and Dry Cleaning (3)
G = Garment Trades (4)
FD = Food and Drink (9)
Total = 25 firms

IV. WHITE COLLAR AND PROFESSIONAL

RDT = Retail and Distributive Trades (4)
A = Automobile Sales and Service (3)
C = Clerical (3)
LG = Local Government (3)
PB = Printing and Bookbinding (5)
H = Hospitals
Total = 21 firms

Total 100-plus firms surveyed = 88

Number of Immigrant Workers, and Percentages of Estimated Overall Totals of Workers in Croydon Firms Employing more than 100 people in 1958–9 —by Industrial Sector and Sub-Sector, Type of Occupation (Staff or Works), and Sex.

INDUSTRIAL SECTORS AND SUB-SECTORS	TOTAL IMMIGRANT EMPLOYEES								
	WORKS			STAFF			TOTAL		
	Male	Female	Total	Male	Female	Total	Male	Female	Total
LE I	121 (3·3)	21 (1·7)	142 (3·0)	9 (1·0)	1 (0·2)	10 (0·8)	130 (3·0)	22 (1·3)	152 (2·5)
LE II	48 (2·5)	9 (1·0)	57 (2·0)	2 (0·2)	1 (1·0)	3 (0·3)	50 (1·7)	10 (1·0)	60 (1·5)
LE III	219 (7·7)	250 (8·3)	468 (8·0)	135 (6·8)	10 (2·0)	145 (5·8)	354 (7·3)	260 (7·4)	614 (7·4)
TOTAL I	388 (4·7)	280 (5·4)	668 (5·0)	146 (3·8)	12 (0·1)	158 (3·2)	534 (4·4)	292 (4·7)	826 (4·5)
HE	14 (1·4)	1 (0·4)	15 (1·2)	2 (1·9)	1 (2·8)	3 (2·1)	16 (1·5)	2 (0·6)	18 (1·3)
HI	59 (8·0)	12 (14·1)	71 (8·6)	2 (1·5)	— (0·0)	2 (1·1)	61 (7·0)	12 (8·9)	73 (7·2)
BC	102 (2·6)	— (0·0)	102 (2·6)	3 (0·7)	— (0·0)	3 (0·5)	105 (2·4)	— (0·0)	105 (2·3)
TPU*	138 (4·5)	— (0·0)	138 (4·5)	3 (0·6)	— (0·0)	3 (0·4)	141 (4·0)	— (0·0)	141 (3·7)
TOTAL II	313 (3·6)	13 (3·7)	326 (3·6)	10 (0·9)	1 (0·2)	11 (0·7)	323 (3·3)	14 (1·6)	337 (3·1)
LI	222 (12·6)	48 (5·2)	270 (10·1)	13 (4·6)	— (0·0)	13 (3·3)	235 (11·5)	48 (4·6)	283 (9·2)
LDC	12 (6·2)	33 (6·9)	45 (6·7)	— (0·0)	— (0·0)	— (0·0)	12 (4·4)	33 (6·5)	45 (5·8)
G	— (0·0)	12 (3·5)	12 (3·0)	— (0·0)	— (0·0)	— (0·0)	— (0·0)	12 (3·2)	12 (2·6)
FD	48 (4·6)	200 (14·3)	248 (10·2)	— (0·0)	— (0·0)	— (0·0)	48 (3·6)	200 (13·2)	248 (8·7)
TOTAL III	282 (9·2)	293 (9·4)	575 (9·3)	13 (1·9)	— (0·0)	13 (1·3)	295 (7·9)	293 (8·5)	588 (8·2)
RDT	— (0·0)	— (0·0)	— (0·0)	12 (1·7)	16 (0·9)	28 (1·2)	12 (1·7)	16 (0·9)	28 (1·2)
A	2 (0·8)	— (0·0)	2 (0·8)	— (0·0)	— (0·0)	— (0·0)	2 (0·6)	— (0·0)	2 (0·6)
C	— (0·0)	— (0·0)	— (0·0)	2 (0·7)	24 (1·8)	26 (1·6)	2 (0·7)	24 (1·8)	26 (1·6)
LG†	25 (1·0)	36 (3·2)	61 (1·6)	8 (0·8)	10 (1·8)	18 (1·1)	33 (0·9)	46 (2·7)	79 (1·5)
PB	2 (0·6)	3 (4·3)	5 (1·3)	— (0·0)	— (0·0)	— (0·0)	2 (0·5)	3 (3·2)	5 (1·0)
H	19 (9·6)	68 (24·6)	87 (18·4)	14 (7·3)	123 (17·5)	137 (15·3)	33 (8·5)	191 (19·5)	224 (16·3)
TOTAL IV	48 (1·4)	107 (7·2)	155 (3·2)	36 (1·5)	173 (4·0)	209 (3·1)	84 (1·5)	280 (4·8)	364 (3·1)
Grand Total	1031 [illegible]	693 [illegible]	1724 [illegible]	205 [illegible]	186 [illegible]	391 [illegible]	1236 [illegible]	879 [illegible]	2115 [illegible]

General Note

The estimated overall totals for the 88 Croydon firms employing more than 100 workers in 1958–9, on which the percentages are based, are omitted here for the sake of simplification. They were worked out as carefully as possible, but were of necessity more approximate than the immigrant totals, since they could include casual and seasonal workers and rough estimates given by the minority of smaller firms which were not visited. There is also a certain ambiguity about the definition of 'staff' and 'works', some firms distinguishing between salaried staff and daily paid employees, while others differentiated in terms of place and type of work, so that works managers and supervisors would be counted on the 'works' side. Moreover, in the retail and distributive trades and the clerical group all employees were classed as staff, although a minority were in fact manual workers.

Where neither immigrants nor others were employed in a particular section (e.g. females on the works side of 'building and construction') no percentage is given. Where there were local employees but no immigrants (e.g. 'light industry' female staff), the position is indicated by the numerals 0·0 per cent.

* This heading covers the Electricity and Gas Boards, the local London Transport bus garages and the local British Railways stations, depots and workshop.

† This estimate excludes some 1,922 teachers employed by local authorities.

APPENDIX 4

Numbers of Immigrant Workers in each industrial sector, by ethnic group and sex, and percentage relationship to total numbers in each ethnic group.

	I Males	I Females	I Total	II Males	II Females	II Total	III Males	III Females	III Total	IV Males	IV Females	IV Total	TOTAL Males	TOTAL Females	TOTAL Total
Poles	121 (32·7)	1 (5·9)	122 (31·5)	65 (17·6)	1 (5·9)	66 (17·1)	178 (48·1)	11 (64·7)	189 (48·8)	6 (1·6)	4 (23·5)	10 (2·6)	370 (100)	17 (100)	387 (100)
Hungarians	18 (58·1)	10 (100)	28 (68·3)	3 (9·7)	0 (0·0)	3 (7·3)	10 (32·3)	0 (0·0)	10 (24·4)	0 (0·0)	0 (0·0)	0 (0·0)	31 (100)	10 (100)	41 (100)
Other Refugees	34 (85·0)	5 (41·7)	39 (75·0)	0 (0·0)	0 (0·0)	0 (0·0)	3 (7·5)	0 (0·0)	3 (5·8)	3 (7·5)	7 (58·3)	10 (19·2)	40 (100)	12 (100)	52 (100)
Germans and Austrians	6 (75·0)	17 (32·1)	23 (37·7)	0 (0·0)	0 (0·0)	0 (0·0)	1 (12·5)	11 (20·8)	12 (19·7)	1 (12·5)	25 (47·2)	26 (42·6)	8 (100)	53 (100)	61 (100)
Italians	1 (5·3)	7 (20·6)	8 (15·1)	12 (63·2)	0 (0·0)	12 (22·6)	6 (31·6)	10 (29·4)	16 (30·2)	0 (0·0)	17 (50·0)	17 (32·1)	19 (100)	34 (100)	53 (100)
Other Europeans	47 (85·5)	2 (2·4)	49 (35·0)	1 (1·8)	0 (0·0)	1 (0·7)	0 (0·0)	4 (4·7)	4 (2·9)	7 (12·7)	79 (92·9)	86 (61·4)	55 (100)	85 (100)	140 (100)
Total Europeans	227 (43·4)	42 (19·9)	269 (36·6)	81 (15·5)	1 (0·5)	82 (11·2)	198 (37·9)	36 (17·1)	234 (31·9)	17 (3·3)	132 (62·6)	149 (20·3)	523 (100)	211 (100)	734 (100)
West Indians	148 (33·8)	240 (41·0)	388 (37·9)	181 (41·3)	12 (2·1)	193 (18·9)	66 (15·1)	239 (40·9)	305 (29·8)	43 (9·8)	94 (16·1)	137 (13·4)	438 (100)	585 (100)	1,023 (100)
West Africans	29 (45·3)	0 (0·0)	29 (39·2)	23 (35·9)	0 (0·0)	23 (31·1)	6 (9·4)	0 (0·0)	6 (8·1)	6 (9·4)	10 (100)	16 (21·6)	64 (100)	10 (100)	74 (100)
Indians and Pakistanis	54 (62·8)	0 (0·0)	54 (54·5)	11 (12·8)	0 (0·0)	11 (11·1)	6 (7·0)	4 (30·8)	10 (10·1)	15 (17·4)	9 (69·2)	24 (24·2)	86 (100)	13 (100)	99 (100)
Anglo-Indians	47 (59·5)	9 (23·1)	56 (47·5)	20 (25·3)	1 (2·6)	21 (17·8)	9 (11·4)	12 (30·8)	21 (17·8)	3 (3·8)	17 (43·6)	20 (16·9)	79 (100)	39 (100)	118 (100)
Other Coloured*	27 (79·4)	0 (0·0)	27 (62·8)	3 (8·8)	0 (0·0)	3 (7·0)	4 (11·8)	2 (22·2)	6 (13·9)	0 (0·0)	7 (77·8)	7 (16·3)	34 (100)	9 (100)	43 (100)
Others†	2 (16·7)	1 (8·5)	3 (12·5)	4 (33·3)	0 (0·0)	4 (16·7)	6 (50·0)	0 (0·0)	6 (25·0)	0 (0·0)	11 (91·5)	11 (45·8)	12 (100)	12 (100)	24 (100)
Total Commonwealth	307 (43·1)	250 (37·4)	557 (40·3)	242 (33·9)	13 (1·9)	255 (18·5)	97 (13·6)	257 (38·5)	354 (25·6)	67 (9·4)	148 (22·2)	215 (15·6)	713 (100)	668 (100)	1,381 (100)
Total Immigrants	534 (43·1)	292 (33·2)	826 (39·1)	323 (26·1)	14 (1·6)	337 (15·9)	295 (23·9)	293 (33·3)	588 (27·8)	84 (6·8)	280 (31·9)	364 (17·2)	1,236 (100)	879 (100)	2,115 (100)

* These included Asians from Malaysia, Burma, Ceylon and Hong Kong, Cape Coloured, Anglo-Coloured, American Negroes *et al.* The term 'coloured' is not used strictly but as local informants applied it.

† These included Maltese, Cypriots, and Australians (the two former sometimes being described as 'coloured' by informants). The number of 'old Commonwealth' employees is certainly a considerable underestimate, as many informants did not mention them nor regard them as 'immigrants'.

BIBLIOGRAPHY

CROYDON

Anderson, J. Corbett, *A Descriptive and Historical Guide to Croydon*, *1887*

The Croydon Official Guide (eighth edition), 1959

Croydon 1000, Croydon, *Croydon Advertiser*, 1960

Delderfield, R. F., *The Avenue Goes to War*, London, Hodder & Stoughton, 1958

——, *Dreaming Suburb*, London, Hodder & Stoughton, 1958

Gaitskell, J., *Employment in Croydon*, London, Institute of Race Relations (Special Series), forthcoming, 1968

Sternman, G., *A History of Croydon*, *1883*

Youth Employment Service Report, 1955–63

Youth Employment Service Report, 1955–60, County Borough of Croydon Education Committee, Appendix II

IMMIGRANTS IN INDUSTRY

Banton, M., *The Coloured Quarter: Negro Immigrants in an English City*, London, Cape, 1955

Banton, M., *White and Coloured*, London, Cape, 1959

Barr, J., 'Napoli, Bedfordshire', *New Society*, 2 April 1964

Berry, B., *Race and Ethnic Relations*, Boston, Houghton Mifflin Co., 1965

Blumer, H., 'Recent Research on Race Relations in the United States', *International Social Science Bulletin*, vol. X, no. 3, 1958

Borrie, W. D., *The Cultural Integration of Immigrants*, Paris, U.N.E.S.C.O., Population and Culture Series, 1959

Braithwaite, E. R., *To Sir, With Love*, London, Bodley Head, 1959

Butterworth, E., Lapping, A., Patterson, S., and Warren Evans, R., 'A Hardening Colour Bar', *New Society*, 3 March 1967

Chadwick-Jones, J. K., 'The Acceptance and Socialisation of Immigrant Workers in the Steel Industry', *Sociological Review*, vol. 12, no. 2, New Series, July 1964

——, 'Inter-Group Attitudes', *British Journal of Sociology*, vol. XIII, no. 1, March 1962

Collins, O., 'Ethnic Behaviour in Industry', *American Journal of Sociology*, vol. LI, January 1946

Davison, R. B., 'Immigration and Unemployment in the United Kingdom, 1955–1962', *British Journal of Industrial Relations*, vol. I, no. 1, February 1963

Desai, R., *Indian Immigrants in Britain*, London, Oxford University Press, for Institute of Race Relations, 1963

Egginton, J., *They Seek a Living*, London, Hutchinson, 1957

Eisenstadt, S. N., *The Absorption of Immigrants*, London, Routledge & Kegan Paul, 1954

Ellsworth, J., *Factory Folkways*, Newhaven, Yale University Press, 1952

Feldman, H., *Racial Factors in American Industry*, New York, Harper & Bros., 1931

Freedman, M. (ed.), *A Minority in Britain*, London, Valentine Mitchell, 1955

Gartner, L. P., *The Jewish Immigrant in England, 1870–1914*, London, Allen & Unwin, 1960

Glass, D. V. (ed.), *Cultural Assimilation of Immigrants*, London, Routledge & Kegan Paul, 1950

Glass, R., and Westergaard, J. (ed.), *London, Aspects of Change*, London, Centre for Urban Studies, Report no. 3, MacGibbon & Kee

Growing Up in Paddington: the young immigrant citizen of tomorrow, report of a conference, 19 February 1963, London, Paddington Council of Social Service, 1963

Hiestand, D. L., *Economic Growth and Employment Opportunities for Minorities*, London, Columbia University Press, 1964

Hooper, R. (ed.), *Colour in Britain*, London, B.B.C. Publications, 1965

Hughes, E. C., and H. McG., *Where People Meet*, Illinois, Free Press, Glencoe

Isaac, J., *British Post-War Migration*, National Institute of Economic and Social Research, Occasional Papers XVII, London, Cambridge University Press, 1954

Jackson, J. A., *The Irish in Britain*, London, Routledge & Kegan Paul, 1963

——, *The Irish in London*, M.A. thesis, University of London, 1958

Kowalewski, J., 'I Znowa Niewola' ('Slavery Once More'), *Kultura*, no. 9/155, September–October 1960

Landes, R., 'A Preliminary Statement of a Survey of Negro–White Relations in Britain', unpublished communication, Royal Anthropological Institute, 6 May 1952

Little, K. L., *Negroes in Britain*, London, Kegan Paul, 1947

Lupton, T., 'Behaviour in Workshops', *New Society*, no. 7, 15 November 1962

Patterson, S., *Colour and Culture in South Africa*, London, Routledge & Kegan Paul, 1953

——, *Dark Strangers*, Tavistock Publications, 1963, and Penguin (abridged), 1965

——, (ed.), *Immigrants in London: a study group report*, London, National Council of Social Service, 1963

——, 'The Polish Exile Community in Britain', paper read to the Annual Meeting of the British Association for the Advancement of Science (Section N), (September 1961

Reid, J., 'The Employment of Negroes in Manchester', *Sociological Review*, vol. 4, no. 2, New Studies, December 1956

Richmond, A., *Colour Prejudice in Britain*, Routledge & Kegan Paul, 1954

Scott, W. H., *Industrial Democracy*, University of Liverpool, Department of Social Science, Occasional Papers no. 2, Liverpool University Press, 1955

Smith, J. H., 'Managers and Married Women Workers', *British Journal of Sociology*, vol. XII, no. 1, March 1961

Sofer, C., and Ross, R., *Jinja Transformed*, East African Institute of Social Research, 1955

Stephens, L., *Employment of Coloured Workers in the Birmingham Area*, London, Institute of Personnel Management, 1956

Tannahill, J. A., *European Volunteer Workers in Britain*, Manchester, Manchester University Press, 1958

Thomas, W. F., and Znaniecki, F., *Polish Peasant in Europe and America*, vol. I, London, Constable (1st edition), 1920

Vernant, J., *The Refugee in the Post-War World*, London, Allen & Unwin, 1953

Warner, W. L., and Low, J. O., *The Social System of the Modern Factory*, Newhaven, Yale University Press, 1947

Warner, W. L., and Lunt, R., *The Social Life of a Modern Community*, Yankee City Series, vol. VI, Newhaven, Yale University Press, 1941

Wright, P., *The Coloured Worker in British Industry*, London, Oxford University Press, for Institute of Race Relations, 1968

——, 'Go-Betweens in Industry', Institute of Race Relations *Newsletter*, January 1964

Zubrzycki, J., *Polish Immigrants in Britain*, The Hague, Nijhoff, 1956

GENERAL

Argyris, C., *Integrating the Individual and the Organisation*, Chichester, John Wylie, 1964

Banks, J. A., 'The Sociology of Work', *Listener*, 2 May 1963

Banton, M., *The Policeman in the Community*, London, Tavistock Publications, 1964

——, *Roles*, London, Tavistock Publications, 1965

Cole, G. D. H., and Postgate, R., *The Common People, 1746–1946*, London, Methuen, University Paperbacks, 22, 1961

Glass, D. V. (ed.), *Social Mobility in Britain*, London, Routledge & Kegan Paul, 1954

Gorer, G., *Exploring English Character*, London, Cresset Press, 1955

Hammond, J. L., and B., *The Age of the Chartists, 1832–54*, London, Archon, 1967

Hoffman, P. D., *They Also Serve*, London, Porcupine Press, 1949

Hoggart, R., *The Uses of Literacy*, London, Penguin, 1958

Hopper, E., 'Some Effects of Supervisory Style: a sociological analysis', *British Journal of Sociology*, vol. XVI, no. 3, September 1965

Jacque, E., *The Changing Outline of the Factory*, London, Tavistock Publications, 1951

Lewis, R., and Maude, A., *The English Middle Classes*, London, Penguin, 1953

——, *Professional People*, London, Phoenix House, 1952

Lipset, S. M., and Bendix, R., *Social Mobility in Industrial Society*, London, Heinemann, 1959

Lockwood, D., *The Black-Coated Worker*, London, Allen & Unwin, 1958

Lupton, T., *On the Shop Floor*, Oxford, Pergamon Press, 1963

Mayo, E., *The Social Problems of an Industrial Civilisation*, Boston, 1945

Miller, D. C., and Form, W. H., *Industrial Sociology*, London, Harper & Row, 1964

Morris, T., 'The Concept of Social Ecology in Criminological Research', doctoral thesis, University of London, 1955, chapter VIII

——, *The Criminal Area*, London, Routledge & Kegan Paul, 1957

Parker, S. R., 'Relations at Work', *Human Relations*, vol. 17, no. 3, 1964

Roethlisberger, F. J., and Dickson, W. J., *Management and the Worker*, Chichester, John Wylie, 1964

Simmel, G., *The Sociology of George Simmel*, Illinois, Free Press, Glencoe, 1950

Smith, B. Abel, *A History of the Nursing Profession*, London, Heinemann, 1960

Sofer, C., *The Organisation from Within*, London, Tavistock Publications, 1961

——, 'Reactions to Administrative Change: a study of staff relations in three British hospitals', *Human Relations*, vol. 8, no. 3, 1955

——, 'Working Groups in a Plural Society', *Industrial and Labour Relations Review*, vol. 8, no. 1, October 1954

——, and Trist, E. L., *Exploration in Group Relations*, University of Leicester Press, 1959

Taylor, G. Rattray, *Are Workers Human?*, London, Falcon Press, 1965

Willmott, P., and Young, M., *Family and Class in a London Suburb*, London, Routledge & Kegan Paul, for Institute of Community Studies, 1960

Woodward, J., *Industrial Organisation: theory and practice*, London, Oxford University Press, 1965

Zweig, S., *The British Worker*, London, Penguin, 1952

——, *Life, Labour, and Poverty*, London, Gollancz, 1948

——, *The Worker in an Affluent Society*, London, Heinemann, 1961

REPORTS, ETC.

Annual Abstract of Statistics, 1958

1961 Census

1951 Census of England and Wales, Occupational Tables Commonwealth Immigrants Act, 1 July 1962

Commonwealth Immigration: no. 8, Supplement, August 1964

1851 Directory

Economist Intelligence Unit report on Commonwealth immigration to Britain

Ministry of Labour *Gazette*, May 1958

Newsletter, Institute of Race Relations (Indices)

INDEX